SH[redacted]A EDITION

NARUTO

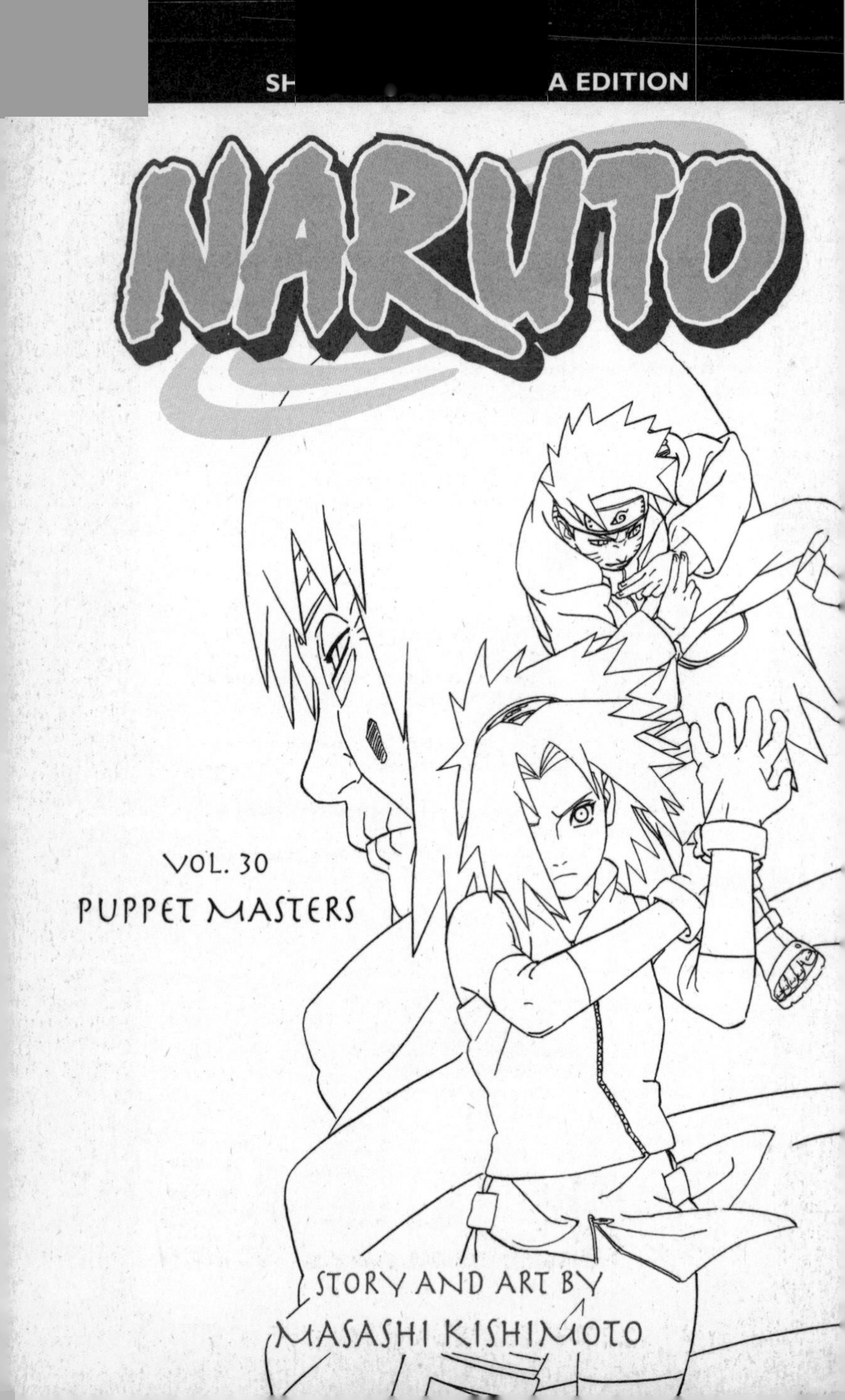

VOL. 30

PUPPET MASTERS

STORY AND ART BY

MASASHI KISHIMOTO

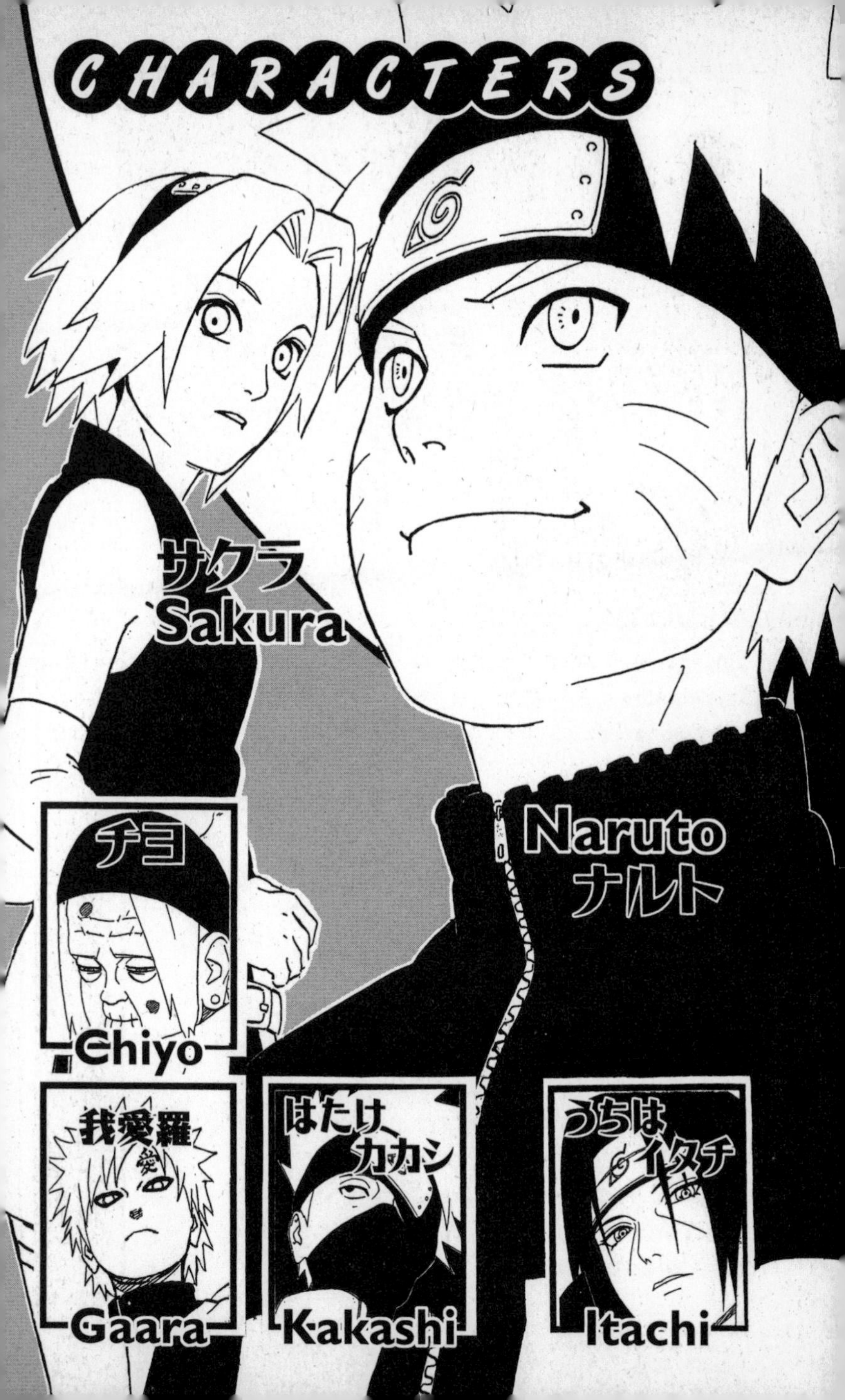
CHARACTERS
Naruto
ナルト
サクラ
Sakura
チヨ
Chiyo
うちは
イタチ
Itachi
はたけ
カカシ
Kakashi
我愛羅
Gaara

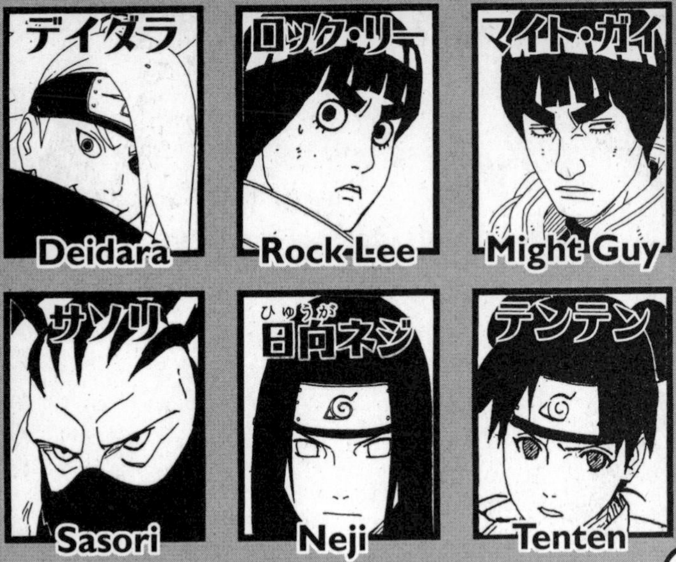
デイダラ
Deidara
ロック・リー
Rock Lee
マイト・ガイ
Might Guy
サソリ
Sasori
ひゅうが
日向ネジ
Neji
テンテン
Tenten

The Story So Far...

Naruto was once the bane of the Konohagakure Ninja Academy. Despite the rough start, he successfully joins the ranks of ninja along with Sasuke and Sakura. During the Chûnin Exam, Orochimaru launches *Operation Destroy Konoha,* an attack thwarted by the Third Hokage's sacrifice of his own life. After the battle, Tsunade steps up to become the Fifth Hokage. Lured by Orochimaru's power, Sasuke leaves Konoha in the company of the Sound Ninja Four. Naruto confronts Sasuke, but no matter how hard he fights, he can't stop his friend.

More than two years pass. Naruto and his friends mature, each undergoing rigorous training. Gaara, who has become Kazekage, is suddenly kidnapped by the dark Akatsuki organization. Naruto and the gang set out for the Akatsuki hideaway on their way to rescue Gaara.

NARUTO

VOL. 30
PUPPET MASTERS

CONTENTS

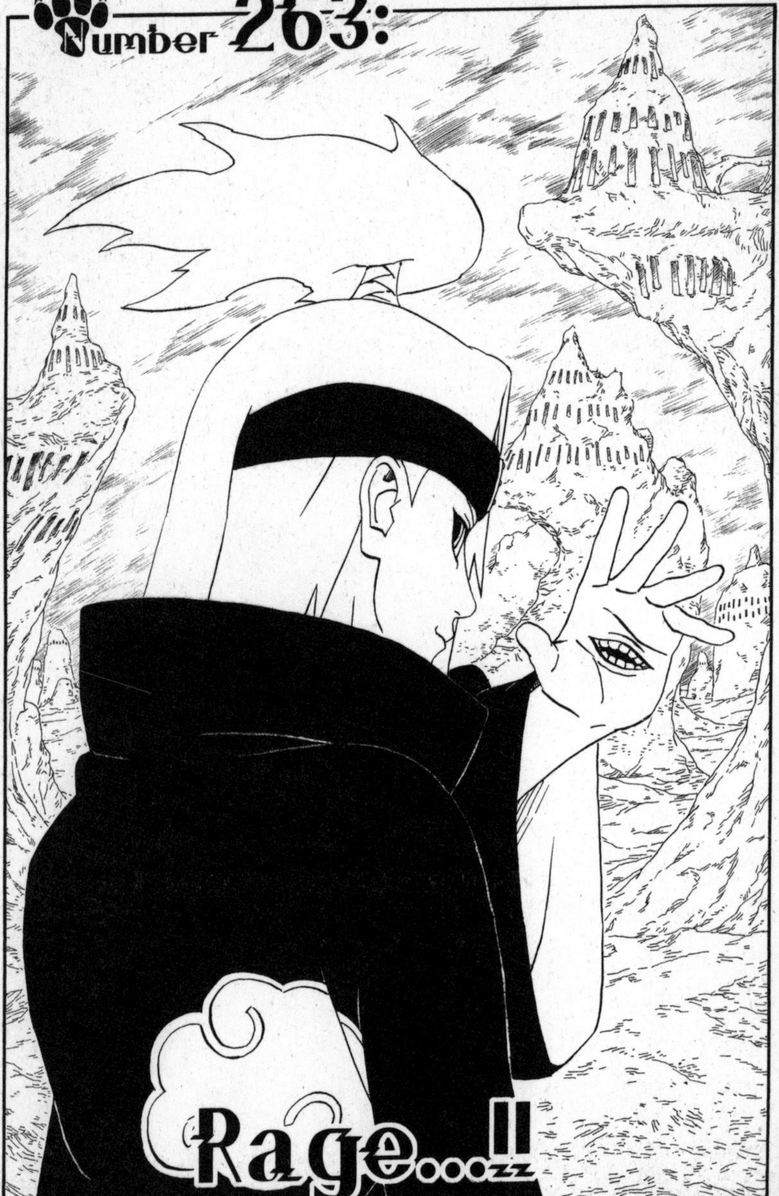
Number 263:
Rage...!!

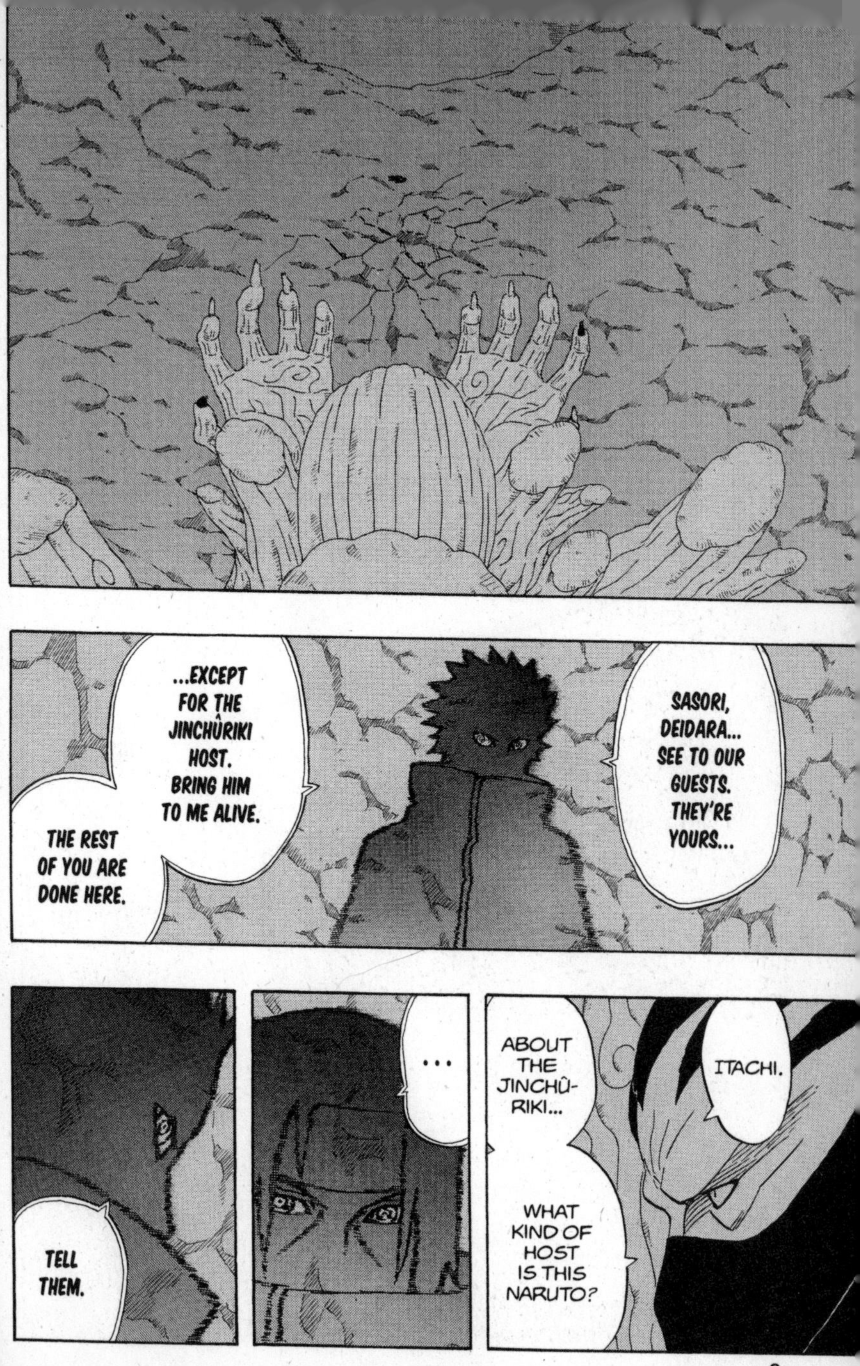
SASORI, DEIDARA... SEE TO OUR GUESTS. THEY'RE YOURS...
...EXCEPT FOR THE JINCHÛRIKI HOST. BRING HIM TO ME ALIVE.
THE REST OF YOU ARE DONE HERE.
ITACHI.
ABOUT THE JINCHÛ-RIKI...
WHAT KIND OF HOST IS THIS NARUTO?
...
TELL THEM.

READ THIS WAY

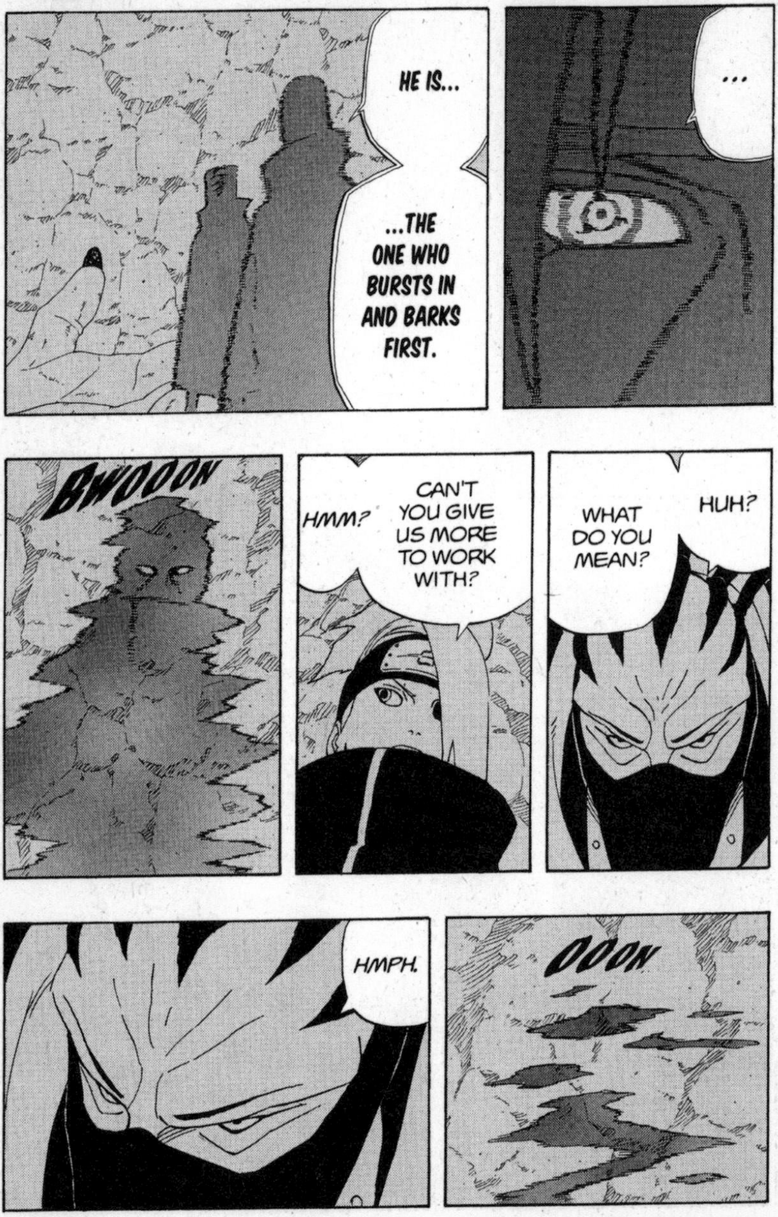
...
HE IS...
...THE ONE WHO BURSTS IN AND BARKS FIRST.
HUH?
WHAT DO YOU MEAN?
CAN'T YOU GIVE US MORE TO WORK WITH?
HMM?
BWOOOON
OOON
HMPH.

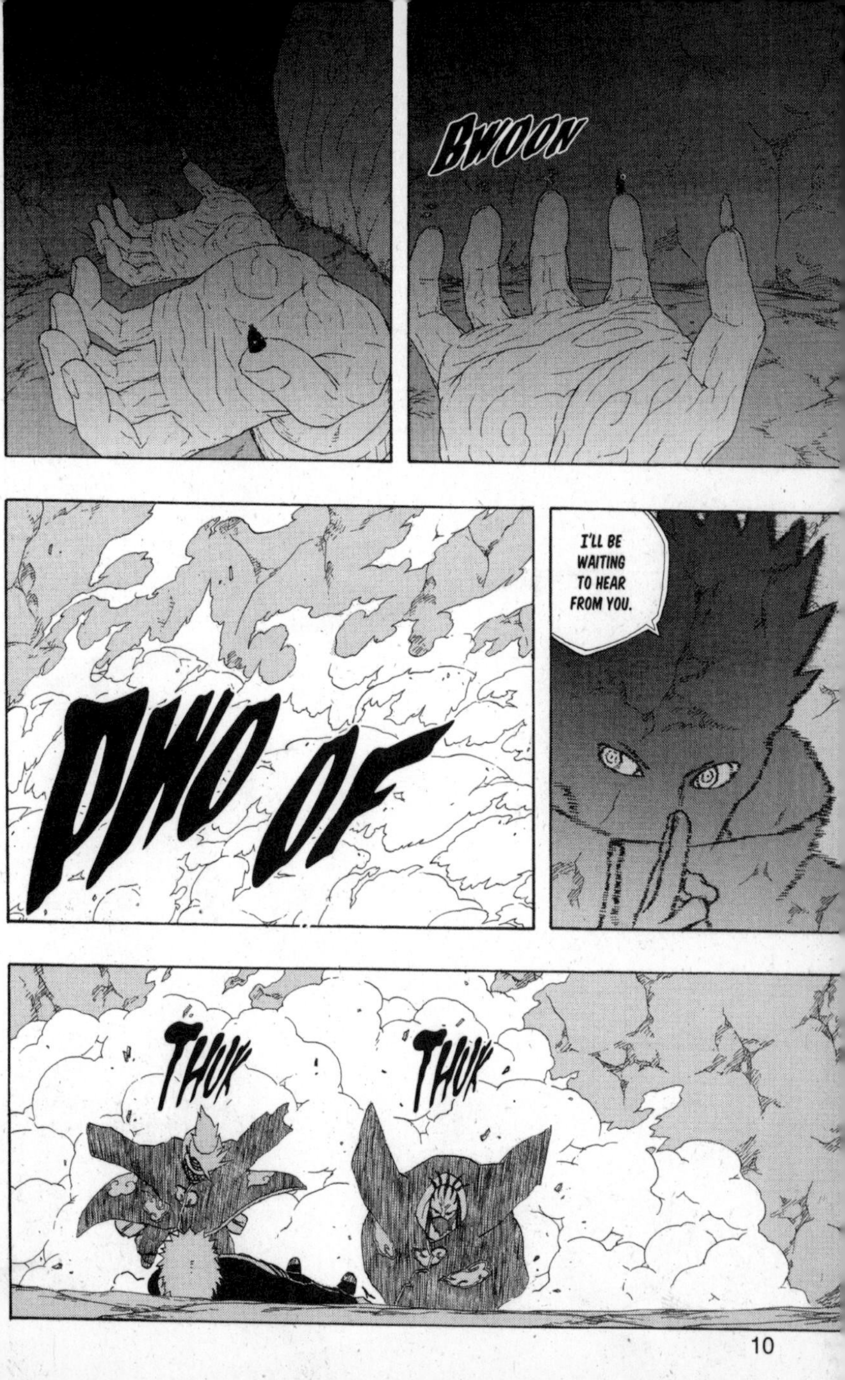
BWOON
I'LL BE WAITING TO HEAR FROM YOU.
DWOOF
THUK
THUK

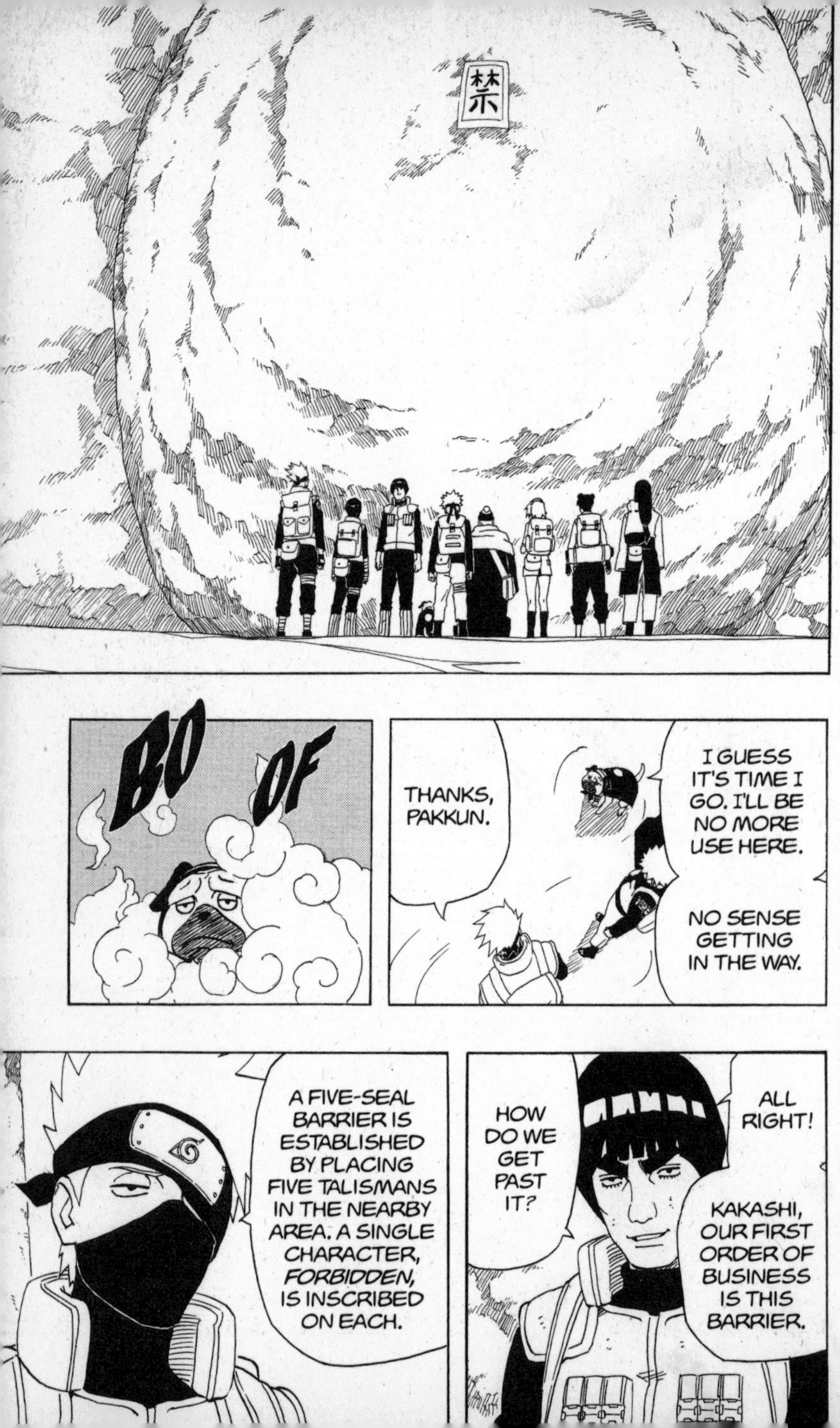
禁
I GUESS IT'S TIME I GO. I'LL BE NO MORE USE HERE.
NO SENSE GETTING IN THE WAY.
THANKS, PAKKUN.
BOOF
ALL RIGHT!
KAKASHI, OUR FIRST ORDER OF BUSINESS IS THIS BARRIER.
HOW DO WE GET PAST IT?
A FIVE-SEAL BARRIER IS ESTABLISHED BY PLACING FIVE TALISMANS IN THE NEARBY AREA. A SINGLE CHARACTER, *FORBIDDEN*, IS INSCRIBED ON EACH.

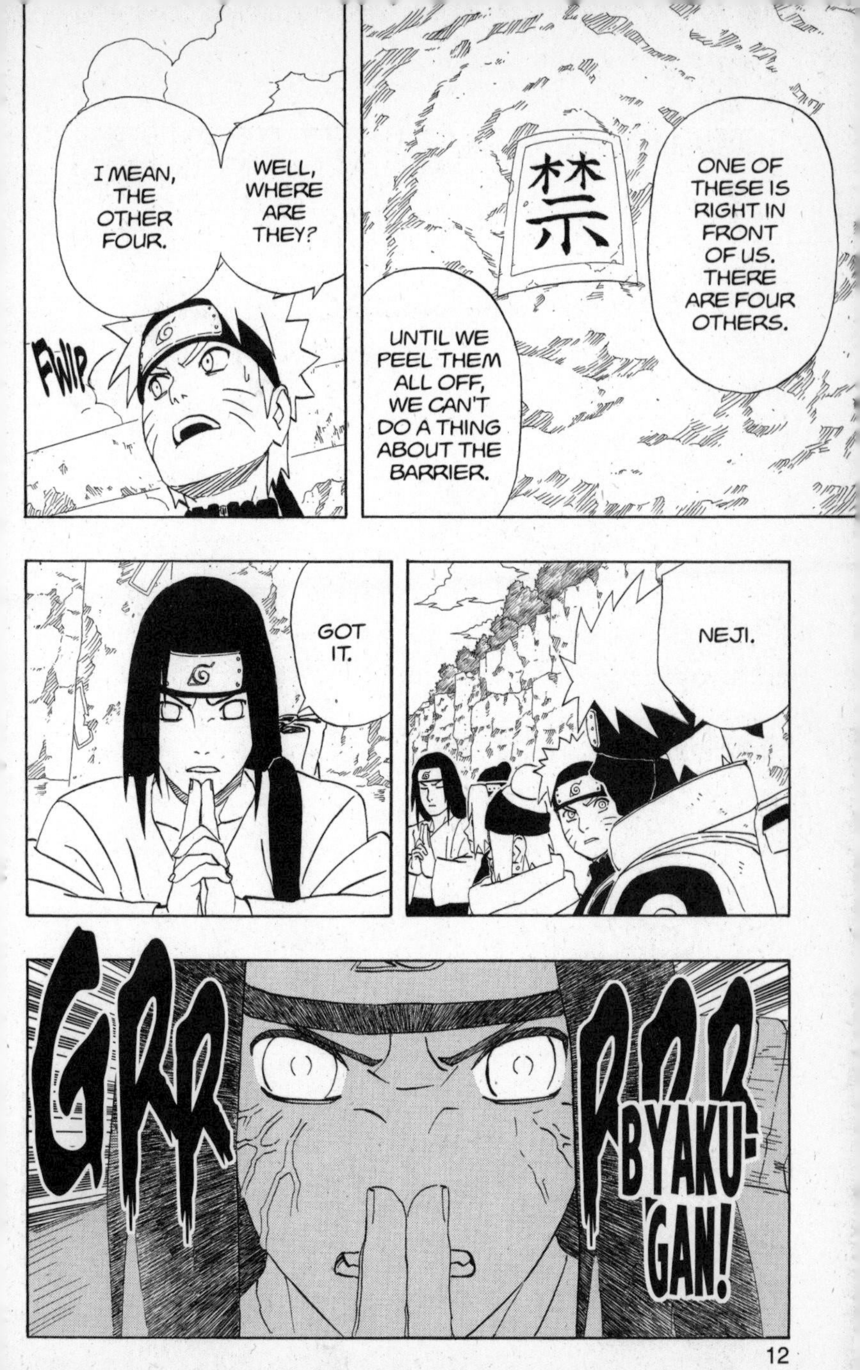
禁
ONE OF THESE IS RIGHT IN FRONT OF US. THERE ARE FOUR OTHERS.
UNTIL WE PEEL THEM ALL OFF, WE CAN'T DO A THING ABOUT THE BARRIER.
WELL, WHERE ARE THEY?
I MEAN, THE OTHER FOUR.
FWIP
NEJI.
GOT IT.
GRRRRR
BYAKU-GAN!

READ THIS WAY

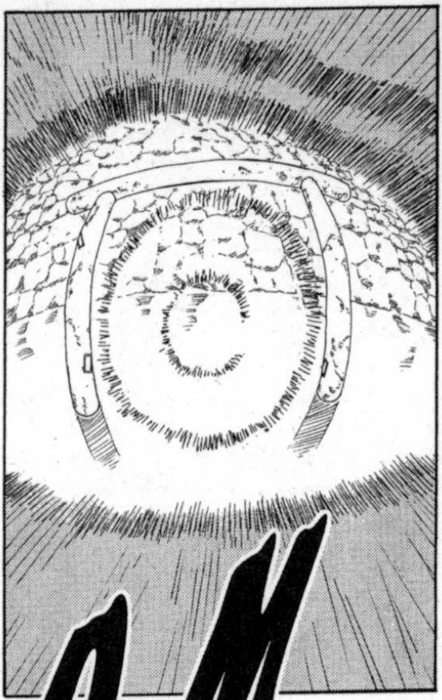

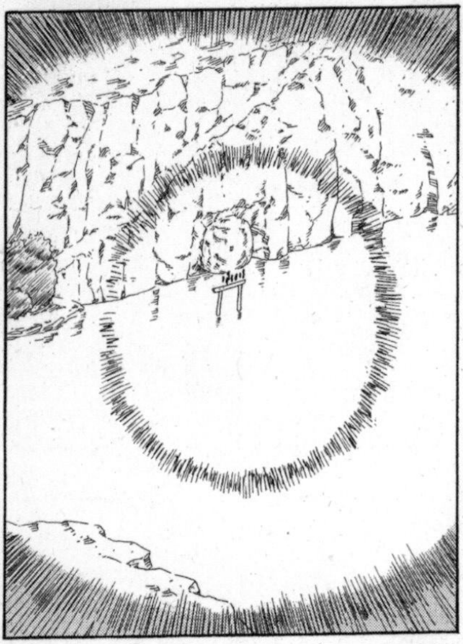

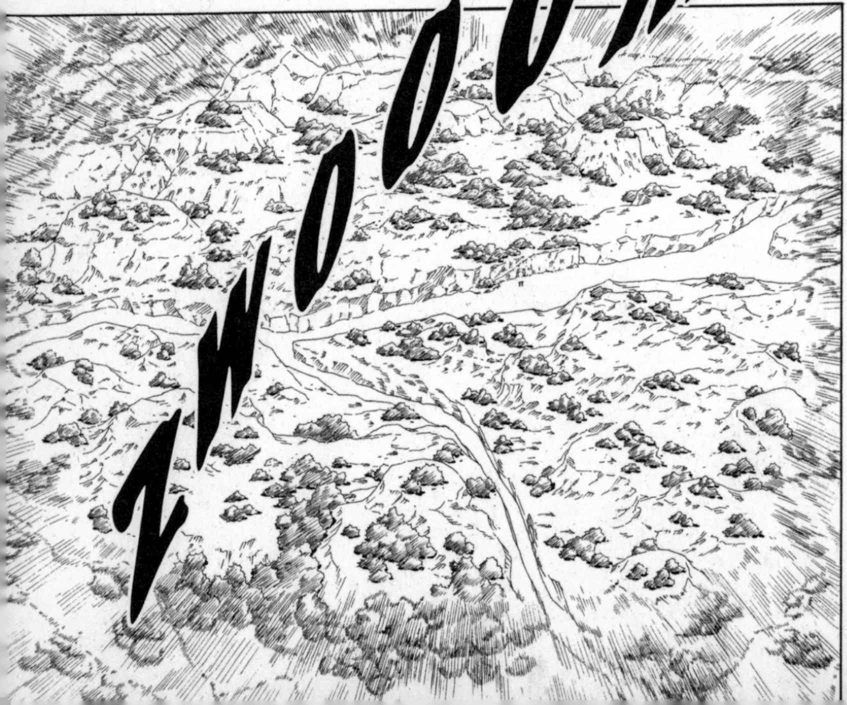
ZWOOOOM

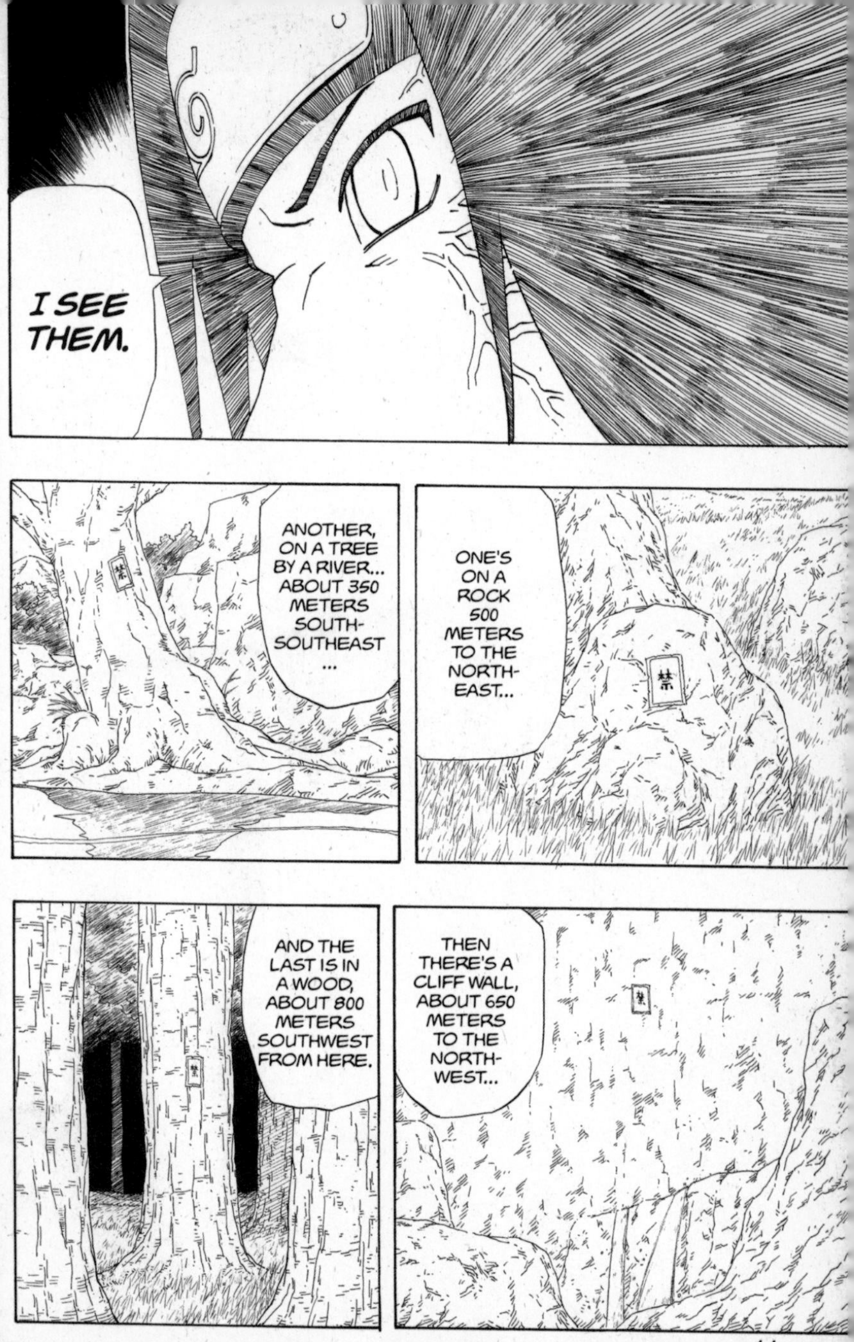
I SEE THEM.
ONE'S ON A ROCK 500 METERS TO THE NORTH-EAST...
ANOTHER, ON A TREE BY A RIVER... ABOUT 350 METERS SOUTH-SOUTHEAST ...
THEN THERE'S A CLIFF WALL, ABOUT 650 METERS TO THE NORTH-WEST...
AND THE LAST IS IN A WOOD, ABOUT 800 METERS SOUTHWEST FROM HERE.

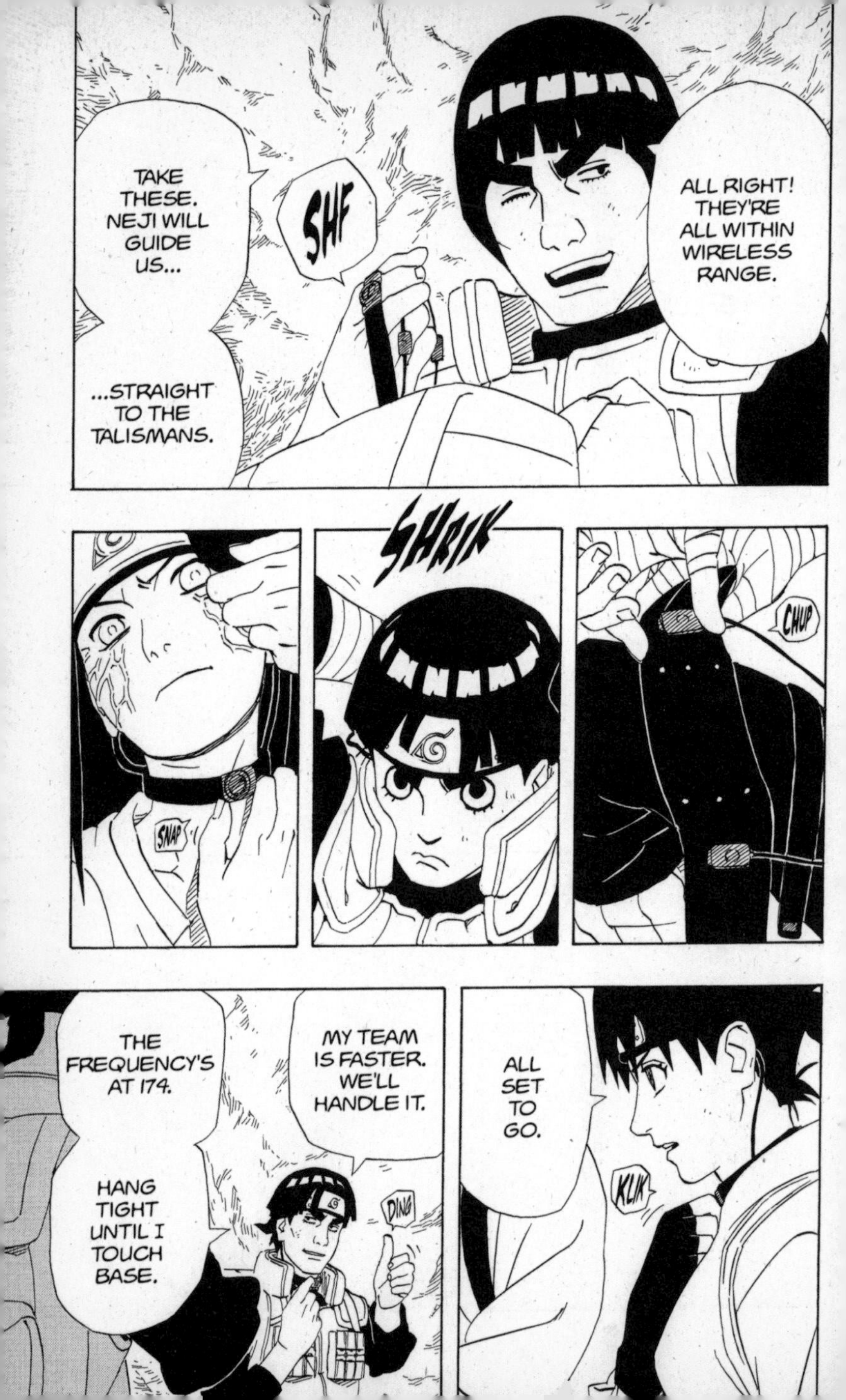
ALL RIGHT! THEY'RE ALL WITHIN WIRELESS RANGE.
SHF
TAKE THESE. NEJI WILL GUIDE US...
...STRAIGHT TO THE TALISMANS.
CHUP
SHRIK
SNAP
ALL SET TO GO.
KLIK
MY TEAM IS FASTER. WE'LL HANDLE IT.
THE FREQUENCY'S AT 174.
DING
HANG TIGHT UNTIL I TOUCH BASE.

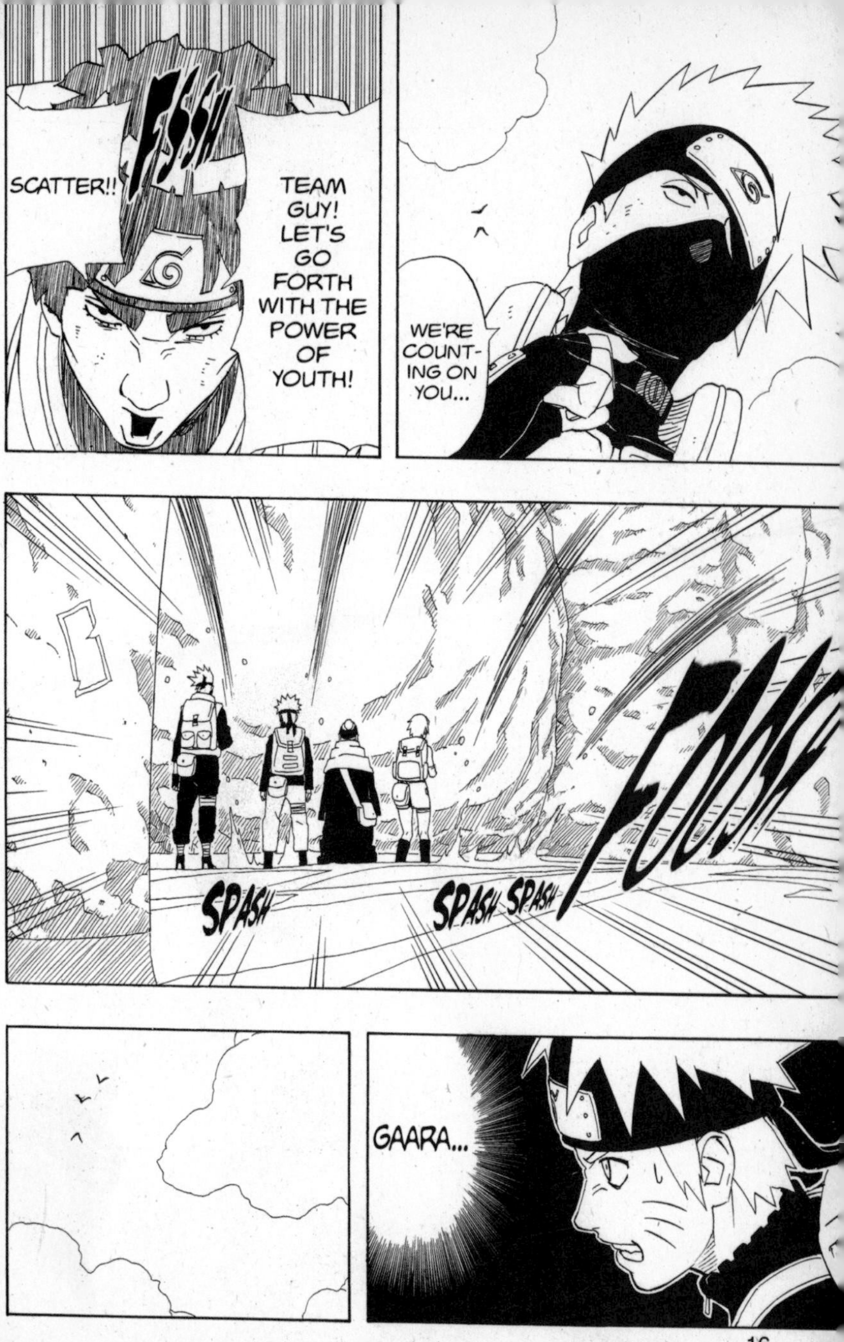
WE'RE COUNTING ON YOU...
FSSH
TEAM GUY! LET'S GO FORTH WITH THE POWER OF YOUTH!
SCATTER!!
FOOSH
SPASH SPASH
SPASH
GAARA...

READ THIS WAY

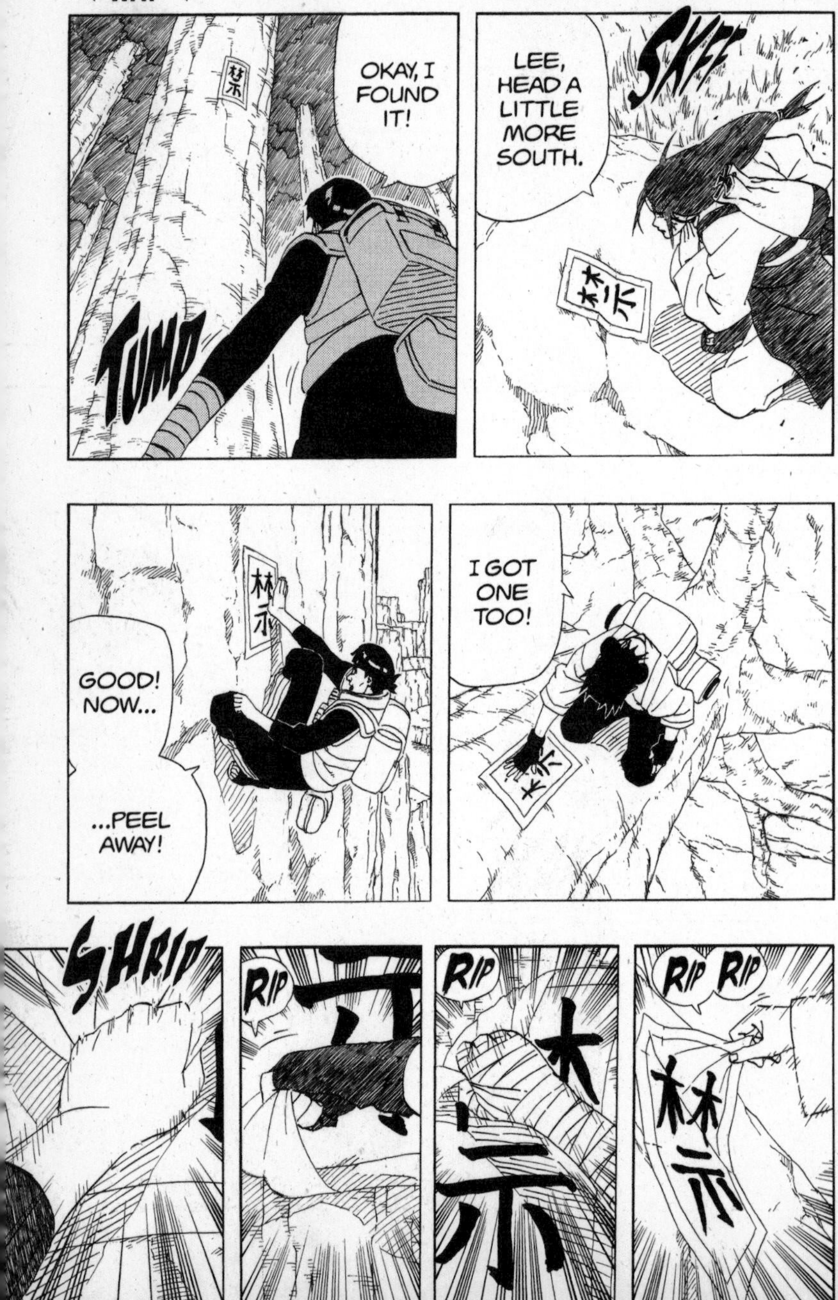
SKFF
LEE, HEAD A LITTLE MORE SOUTH.
OKAY, I FOUND IT!
TUMP
I GOT ONE TOO!
GOOD! NOW...
...PEEL AWAY!
RIP RIP
RIP
RIP
SHRIP

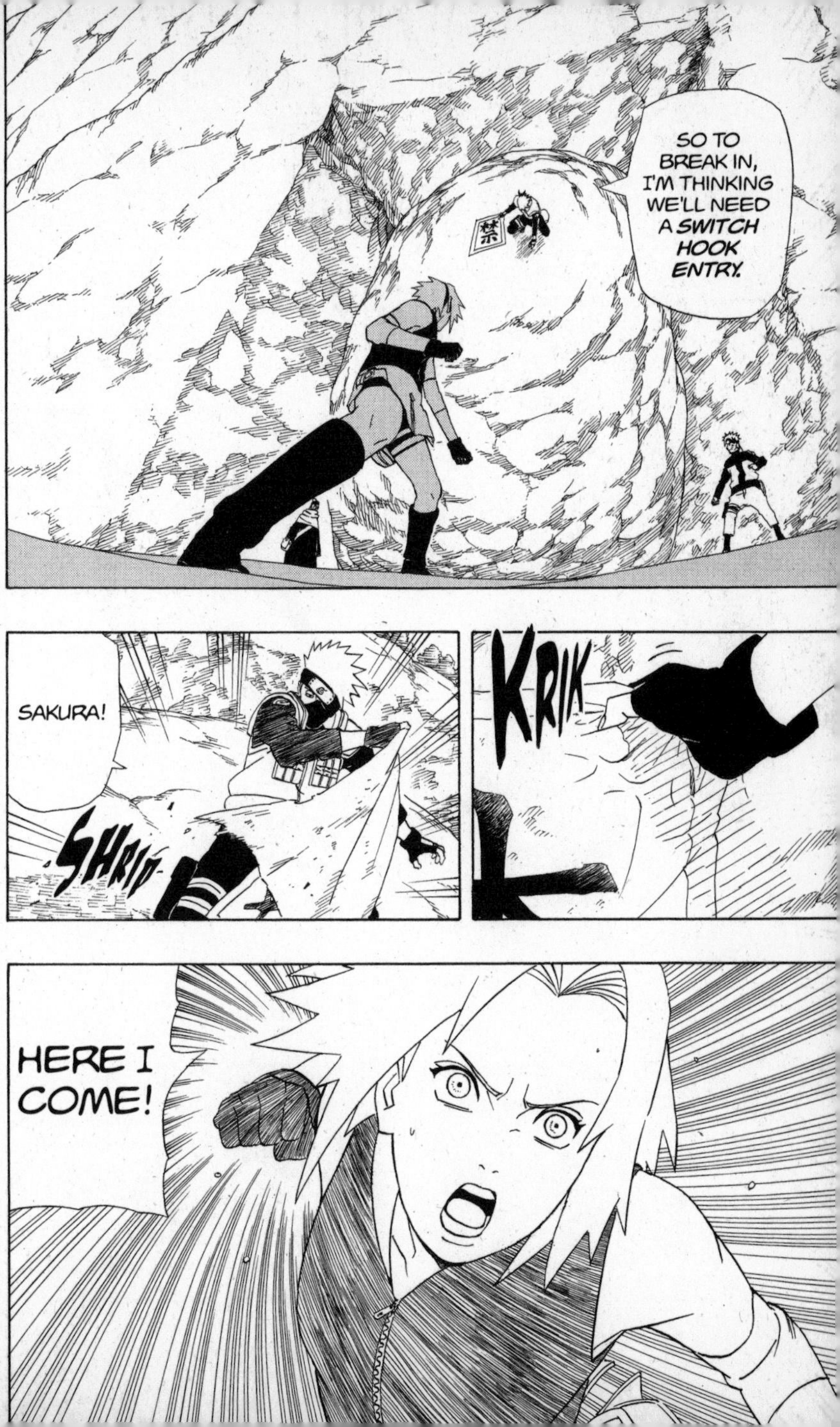
禁
SO TO BREAK IN, I'M THINKING WE'LL NEED A *SWITCH HOOK ENTRY.*
KRIK
SAKURA!
SHRIP
HERE I COME!

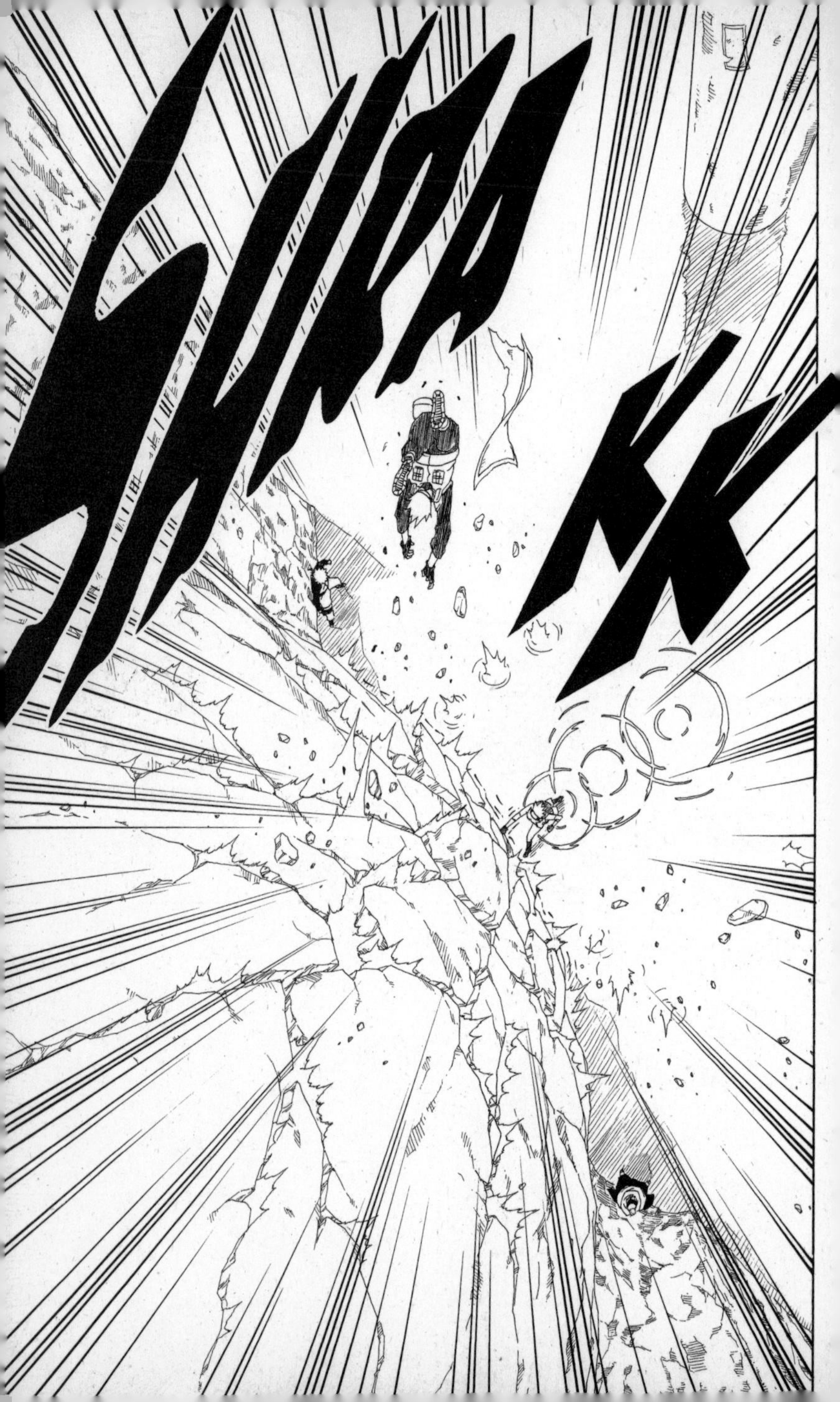
SHUPAKK

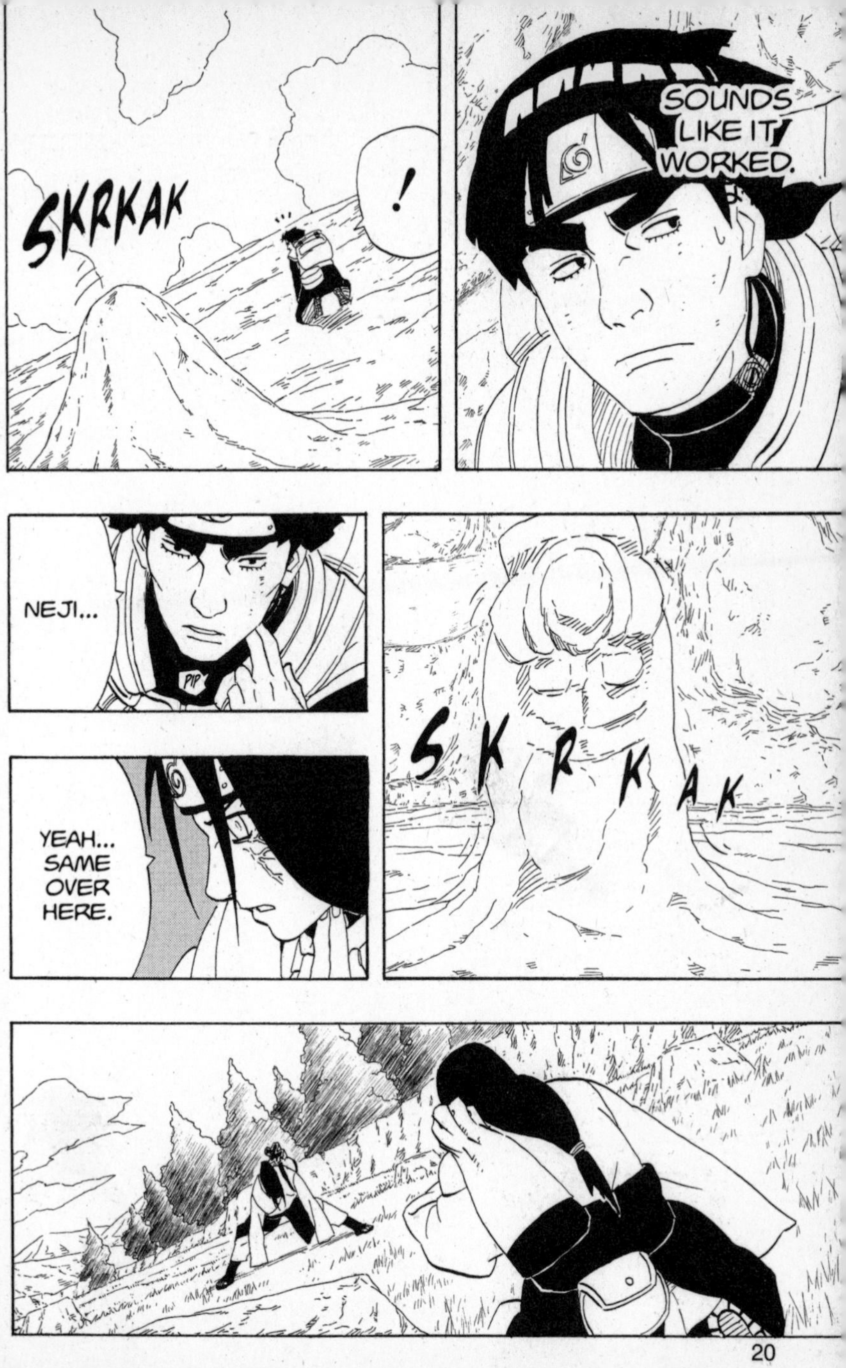
SOUNDS LIKE IT WORKED.
SKRKAK
!
SKRKAK
NEJI...
PIP
YEAH... SAME OVER HERE.

READ THIS WAY

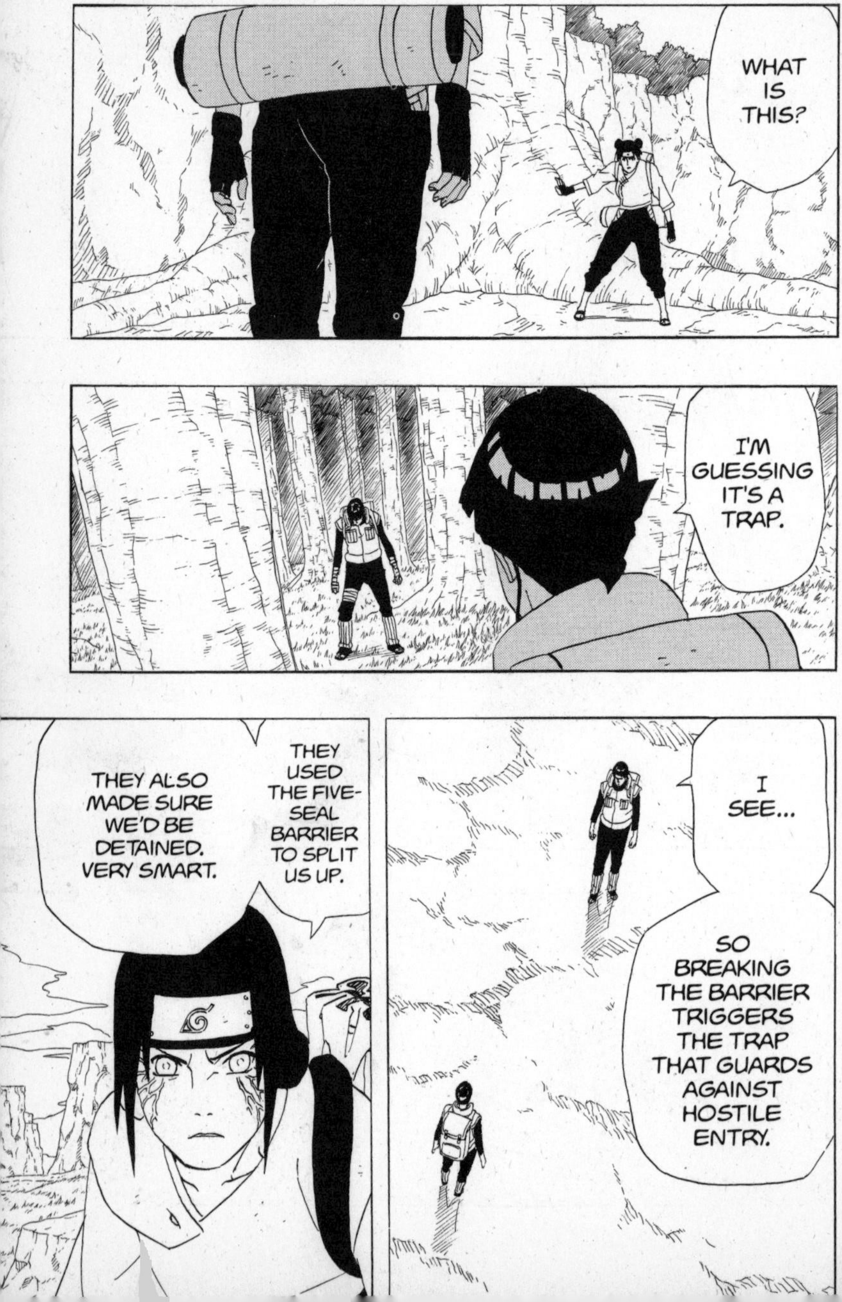
WHAT IS THIS?
I'M GUESSING IT'S A TRAP.
I SEE...
SO BREAKING THE BARRIER TRIGGERS THE TRAP THAT GUARDS AGAINST HOSTILE ENTRY.
THEY USED THE FIVE-SEAL BARRIER TO SPLIT US UP.
THEY ALSO MADE SURE WE'D BE DETAINED. VERY SMART.

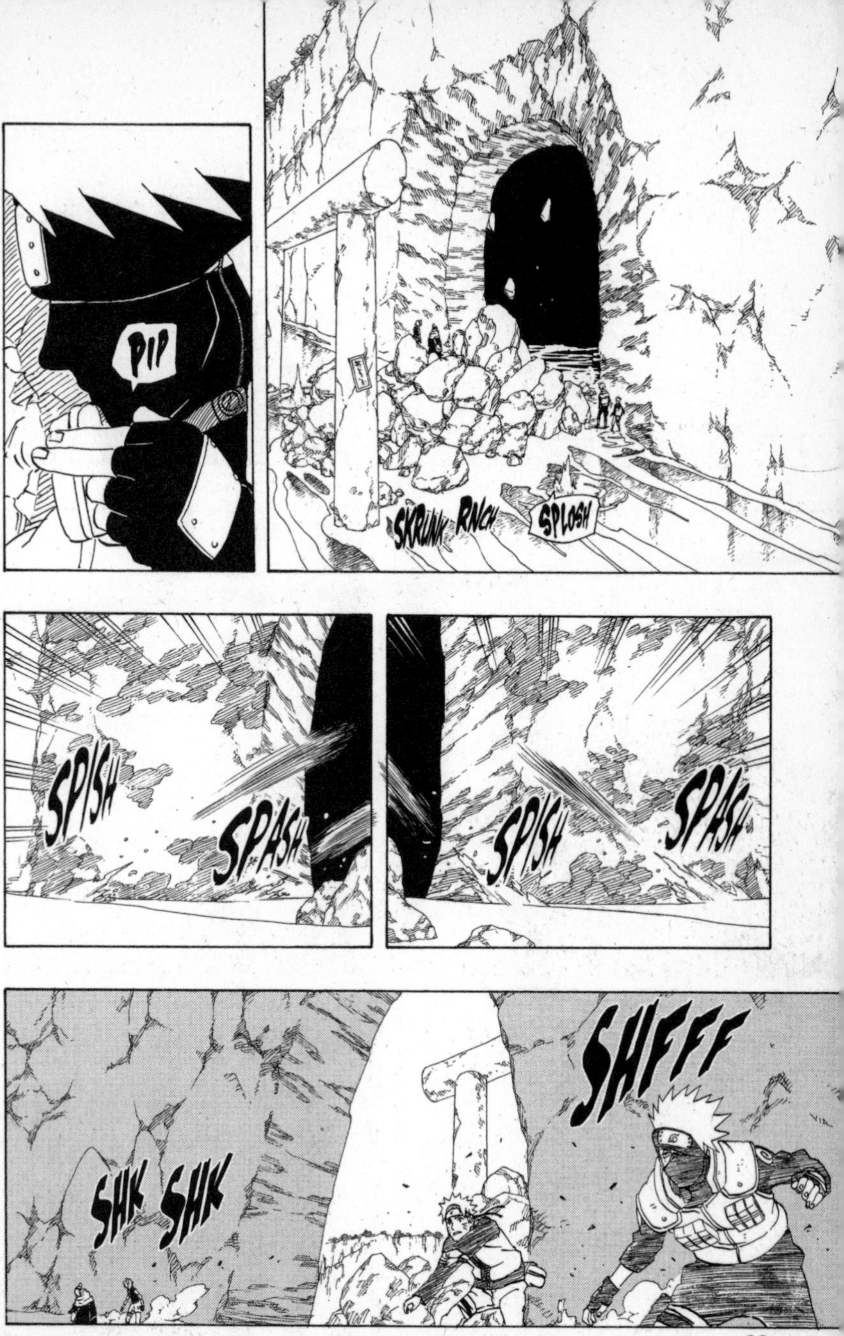
SKRUNK
RNCH
SPLOSH
PIP
SPISH
SPASH
SPISH
SPASH
SHFFF
SHK SHK

READ THIS WAY

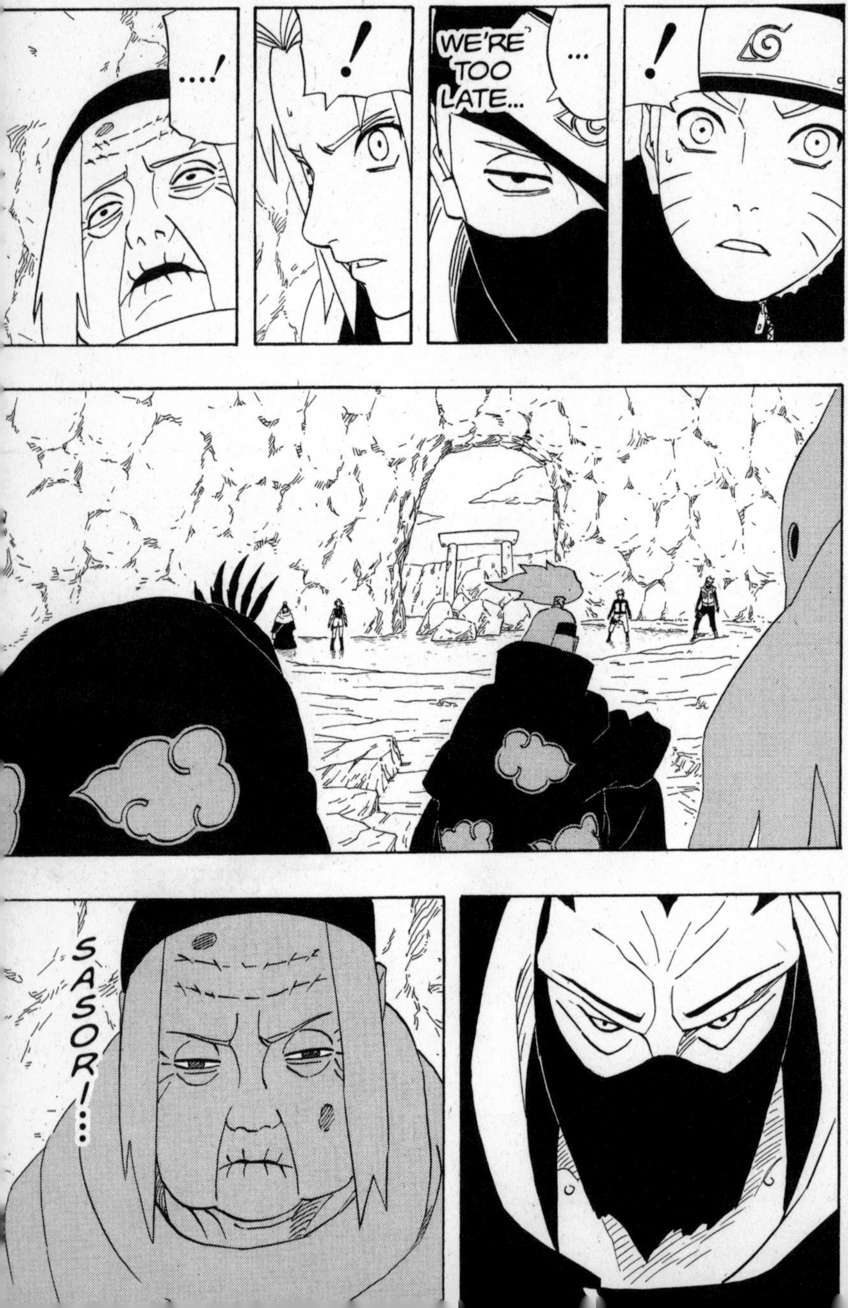
!
...
WE'RE TOO LATE...
!
....!
SASORI...

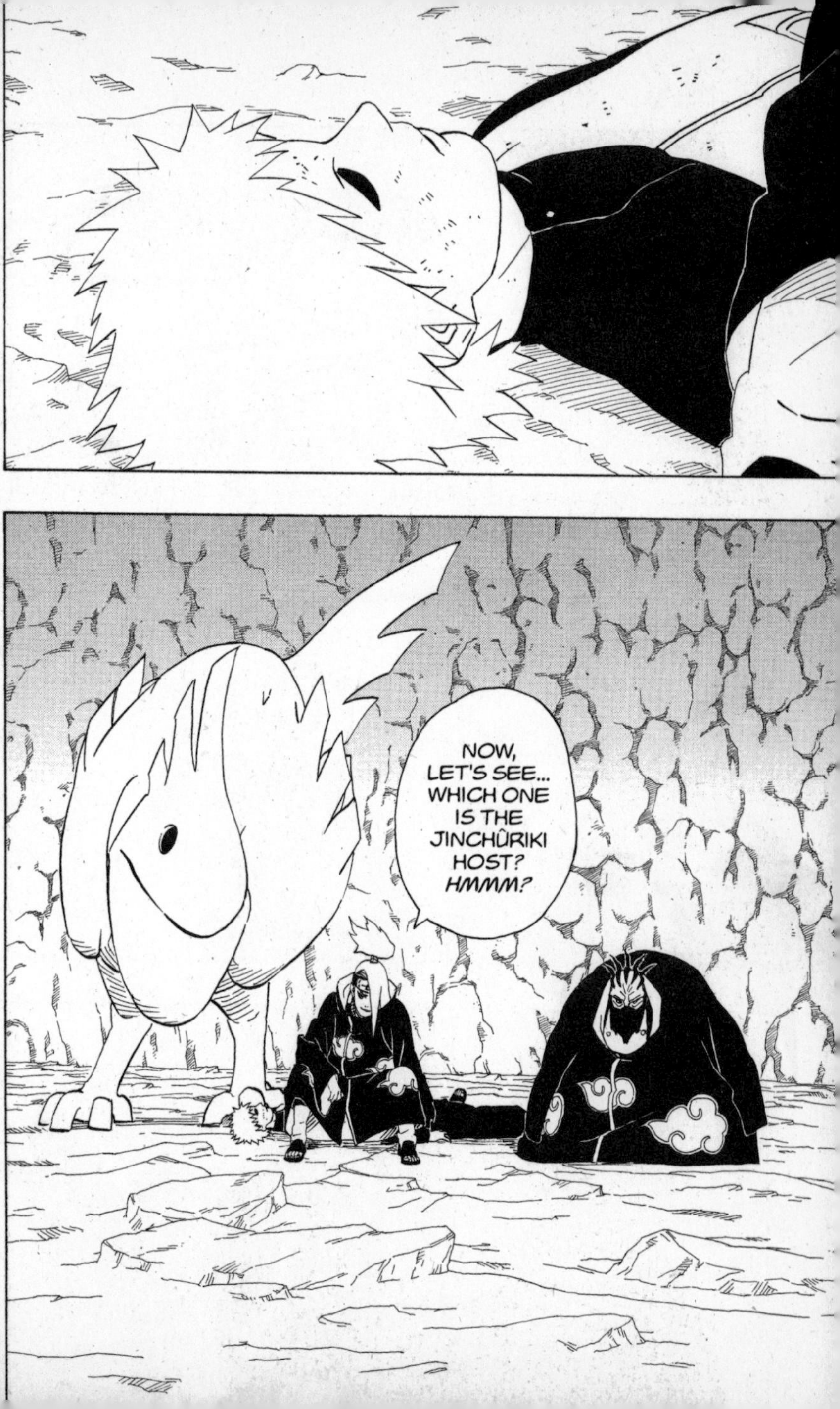
NOW, LET'S SEE... WHICH ONE IS THE JINCHÛRIKI HOST? *HMMM?*

READ THIS WAY

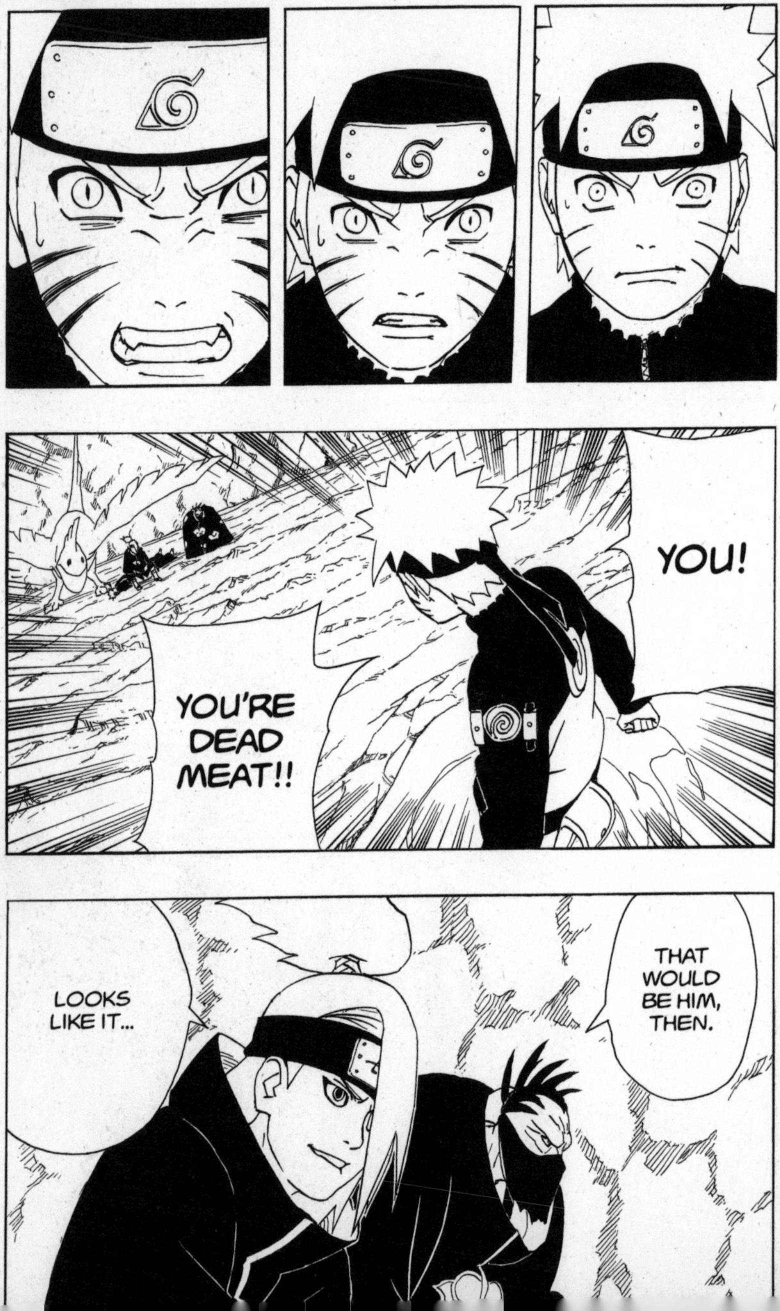
YOU!
YOU'RE DEAD MEAT!!
THAT WOULD BE HIM, THEN.
LOOKS LIKE IT...

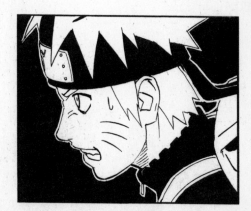

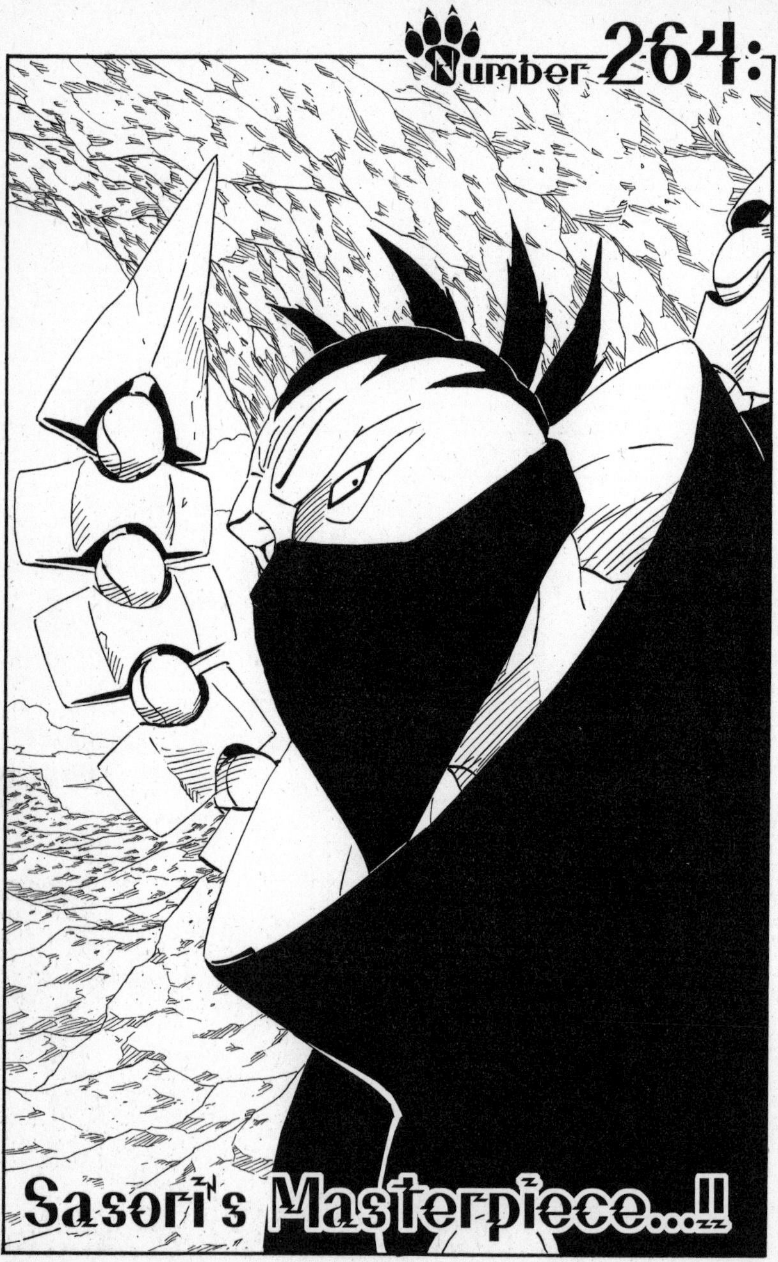
Number 264:
Sasori's Masterpiece...!!

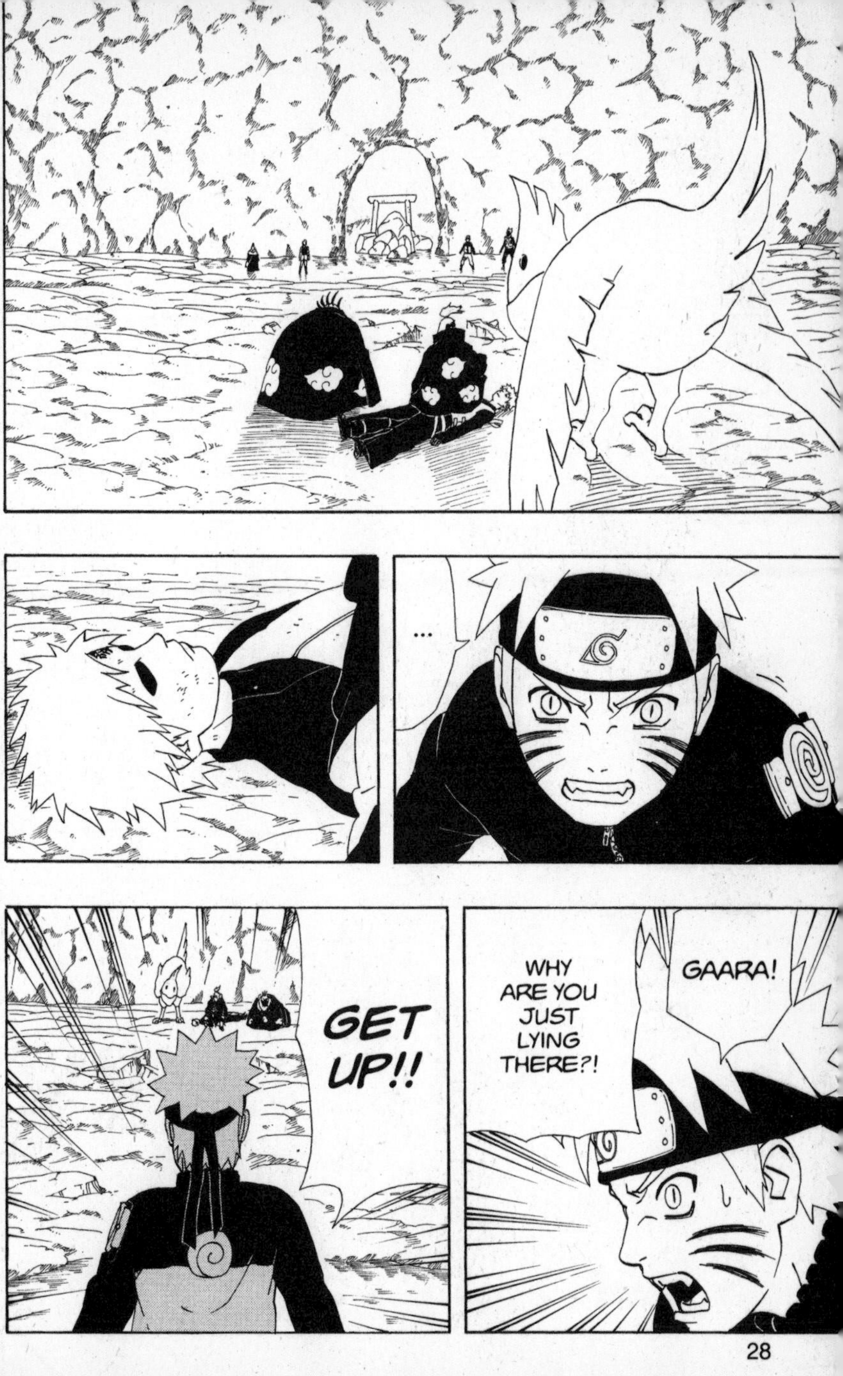
...
GAARA!
WHY ARE YOU JUST LYING THERE?!
GET UP!!

READ THIS WAY

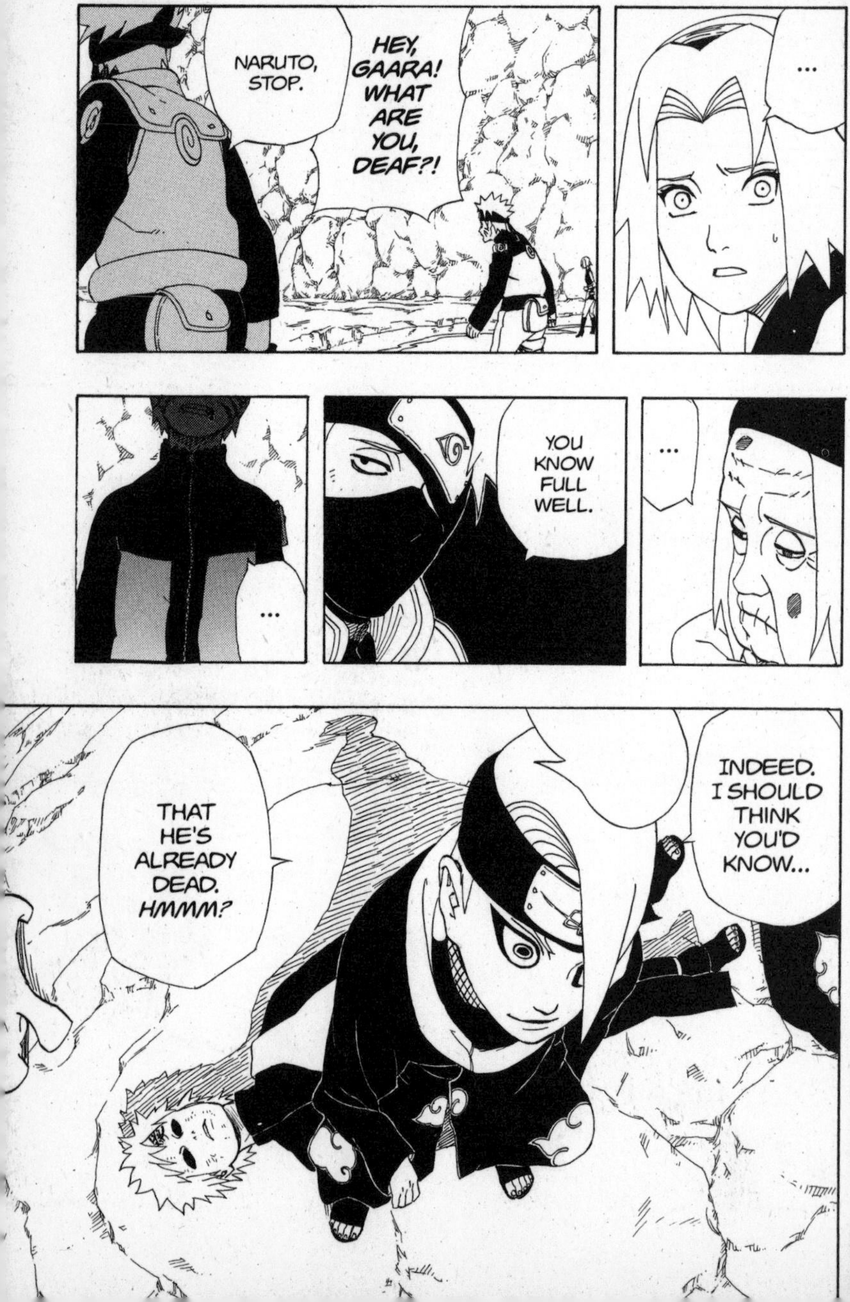
...
HEY, GAARA! WHAT ARE YOU, DEAF?!
NARUTO, STOP.
...
YOU KNOW FULL WELL.
...
INDEED. I SHOULD THINK YOU'D KNOW...
THAT HE'S ALREADY DEAD. HMMM?

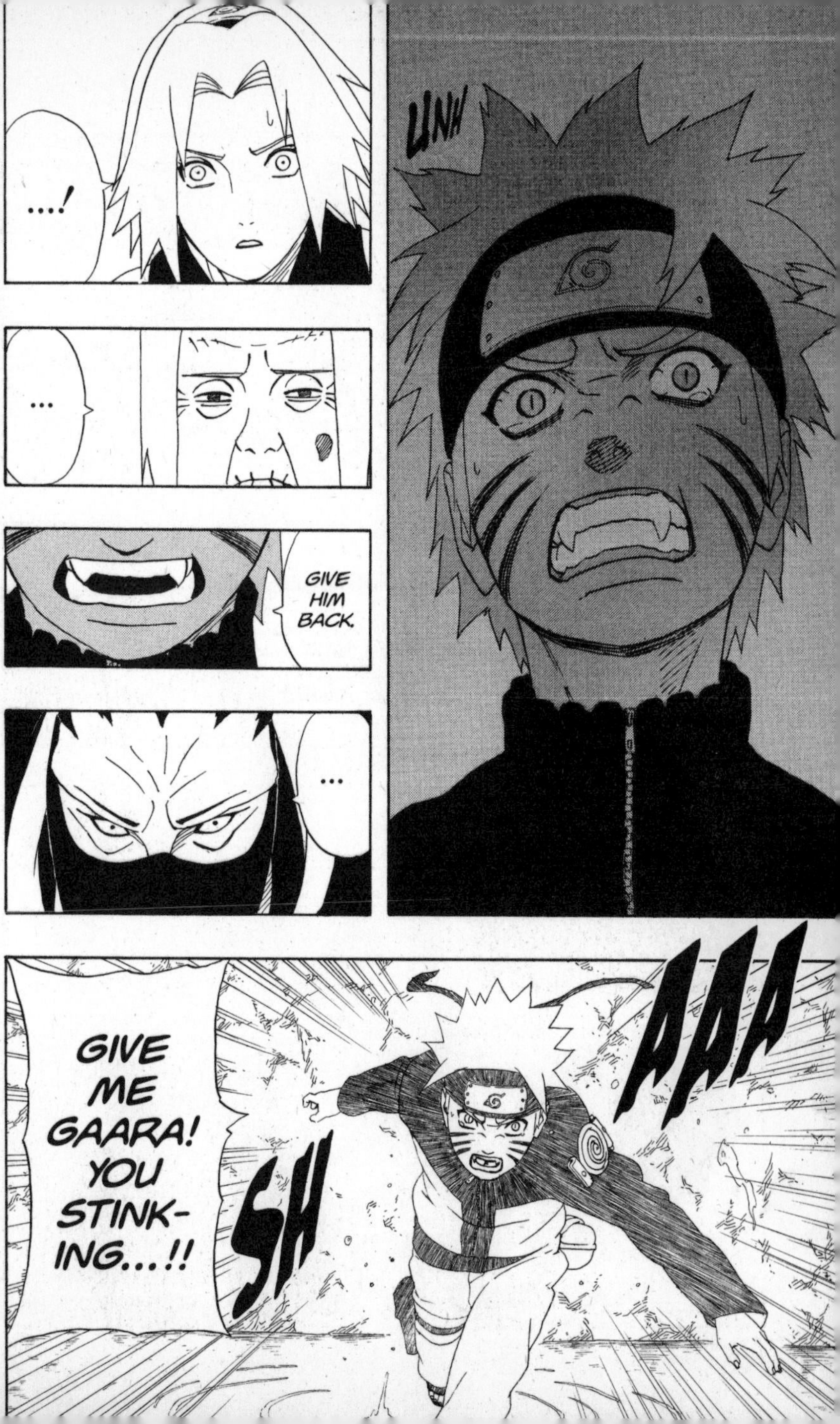
UNH
...!
...
GIVE HIM BACK.
...
AAA
SH
GIVE ME GAARA! YOU STINKING...!!

READ THIS WAY

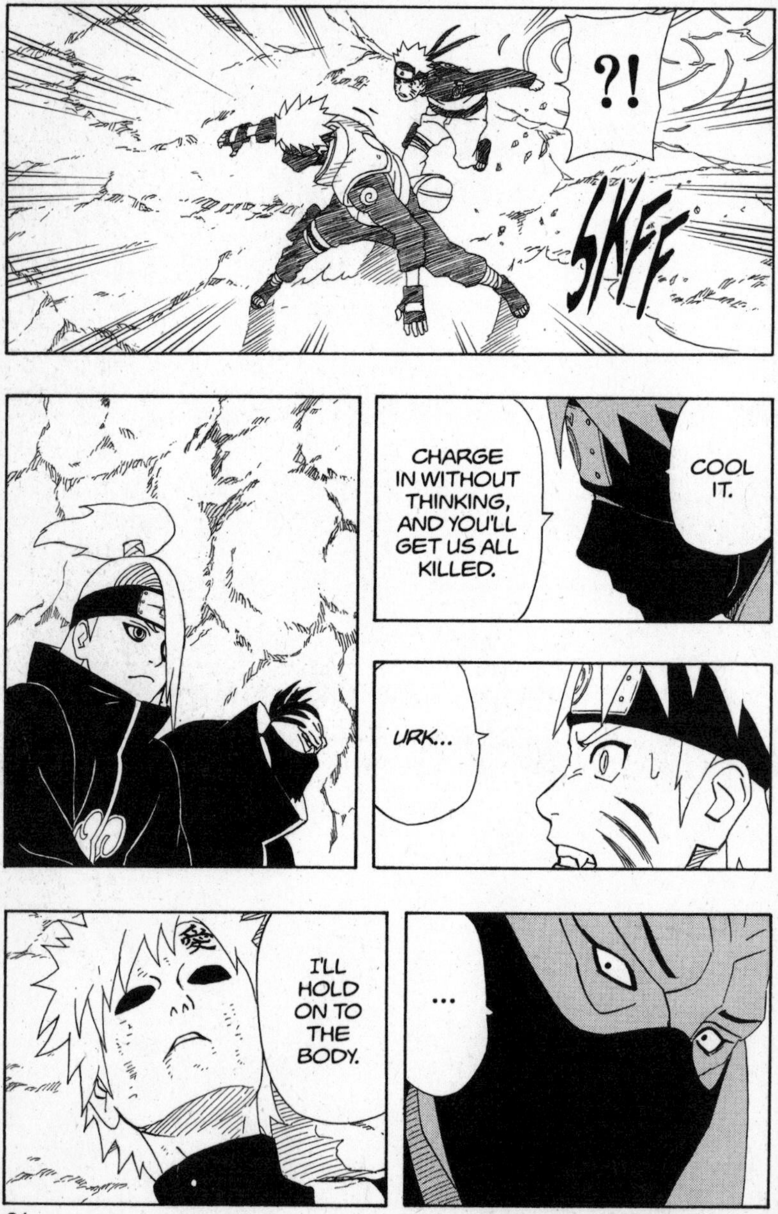

?!
SKFF
COOL IT.
CHARGE IN WITHOUT THINKING, AND YOU'LL GET US ALL KILLED.
URK...
...
I'LL HOLD ON TO THE BODY.

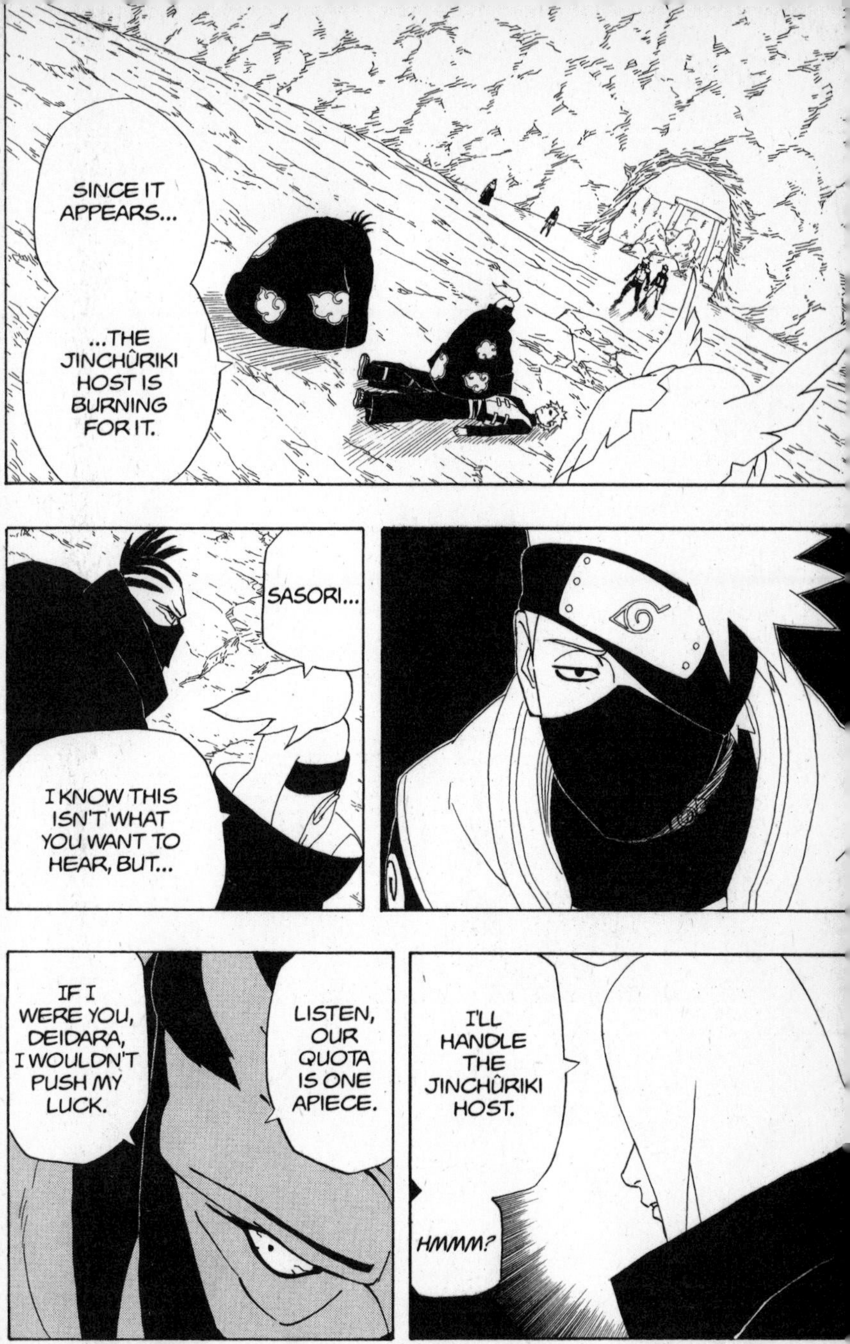
SINCE IT APPEARS...
...THE JINCHÛRIKI HOST IS BURNING FOR IT.
SASORI...
I KNOW THIS ISN'T WHAT YOU WANT TO HEAR, BUT...
I'LL HANDLE THE JINCHÛRIKI HOST.
HMMM?
LISTEN, OUR QUOTA IS ONE APIECE.
IF I WERE YOU, DEIDARA, I WOULDN'T PUSH MY LUCK.

READ THIS WAY

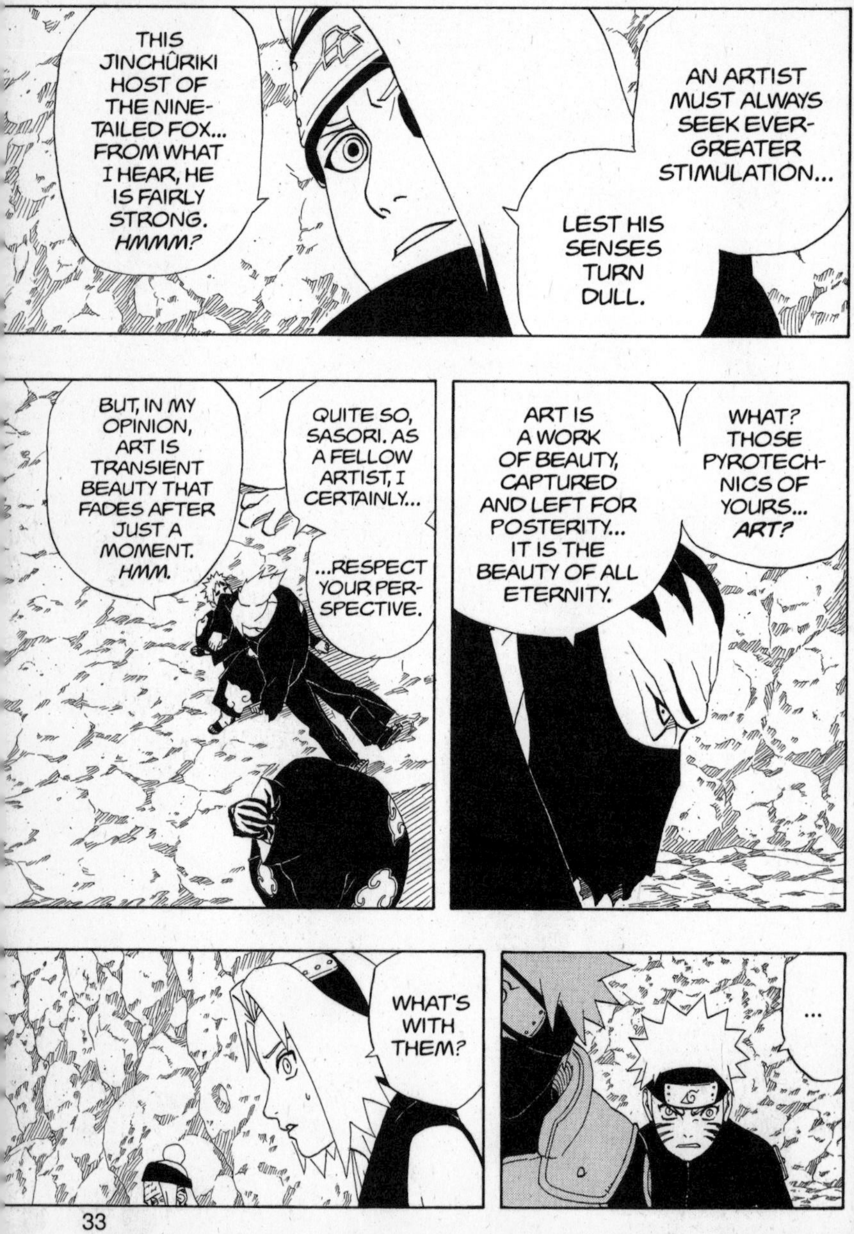

AN ARTIST MUST ALWAYS SEEK EVER-GREATER STIMULATION...
LEST HIS SENSES TURN DULL.
THIS JINCHÛRIKI HOST OF THE NINE-TAILED FOX... FROM WHAT I HEAR, HE IS FAIRLY STRONG. *HMMM?*
WHAT? THOSE PYROTECHNICS OF YOURS... *ART?*
ART IS A WORK OF BEAUTY, CAPTURED AND LEFT FOR POSTERITY... IT IS THE BEAUTY OF ALL ETERNITY.
QUITE SO, SASORI. AS A FELLOW ARTIST, I CERTAINLY...
...RESPECT YOUR PERSPECTIVE.
BUT, IN MY OPINION, ART IS TRANSIENT BEAUTY THAT FADES AFTER JUST A MOMENT. *HMM.*
...
WHAT'S WITH THEM?

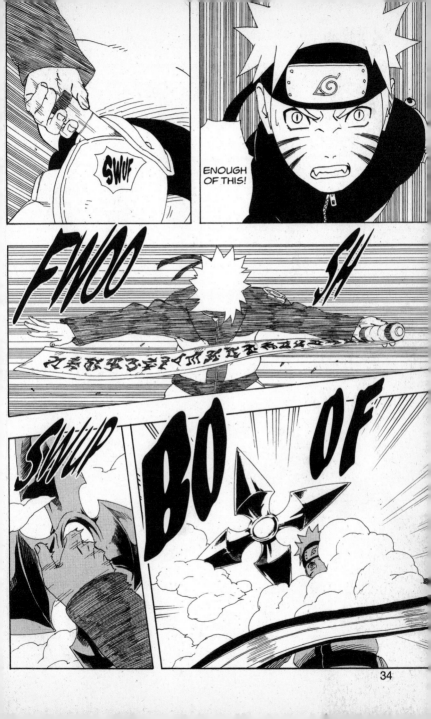

ENOUGH
OF THIS!

SWUF

FWOO   SH

SWUP   BO   OF

READ THIS WAY

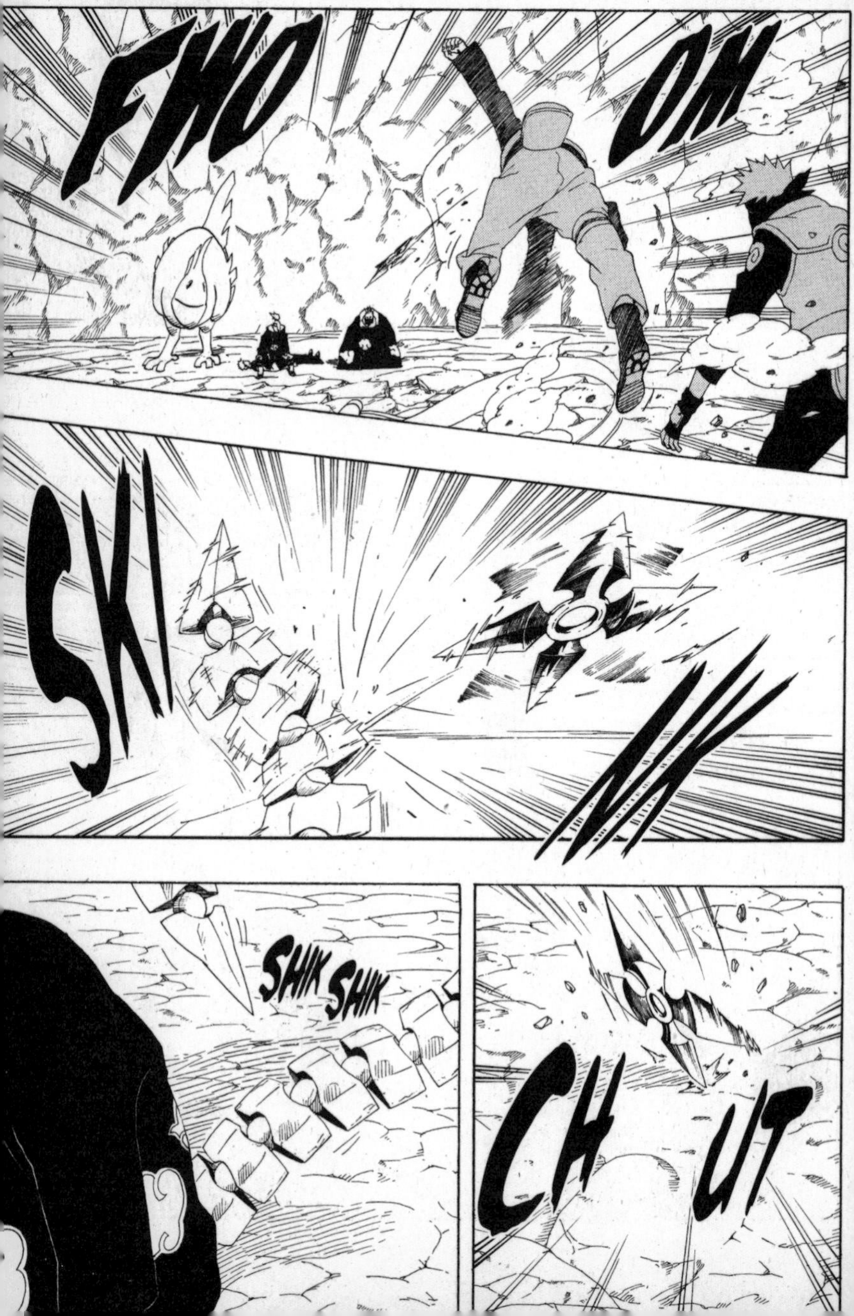
FWO
OM
SKI
NK
CH
UT
SHIK SHIK

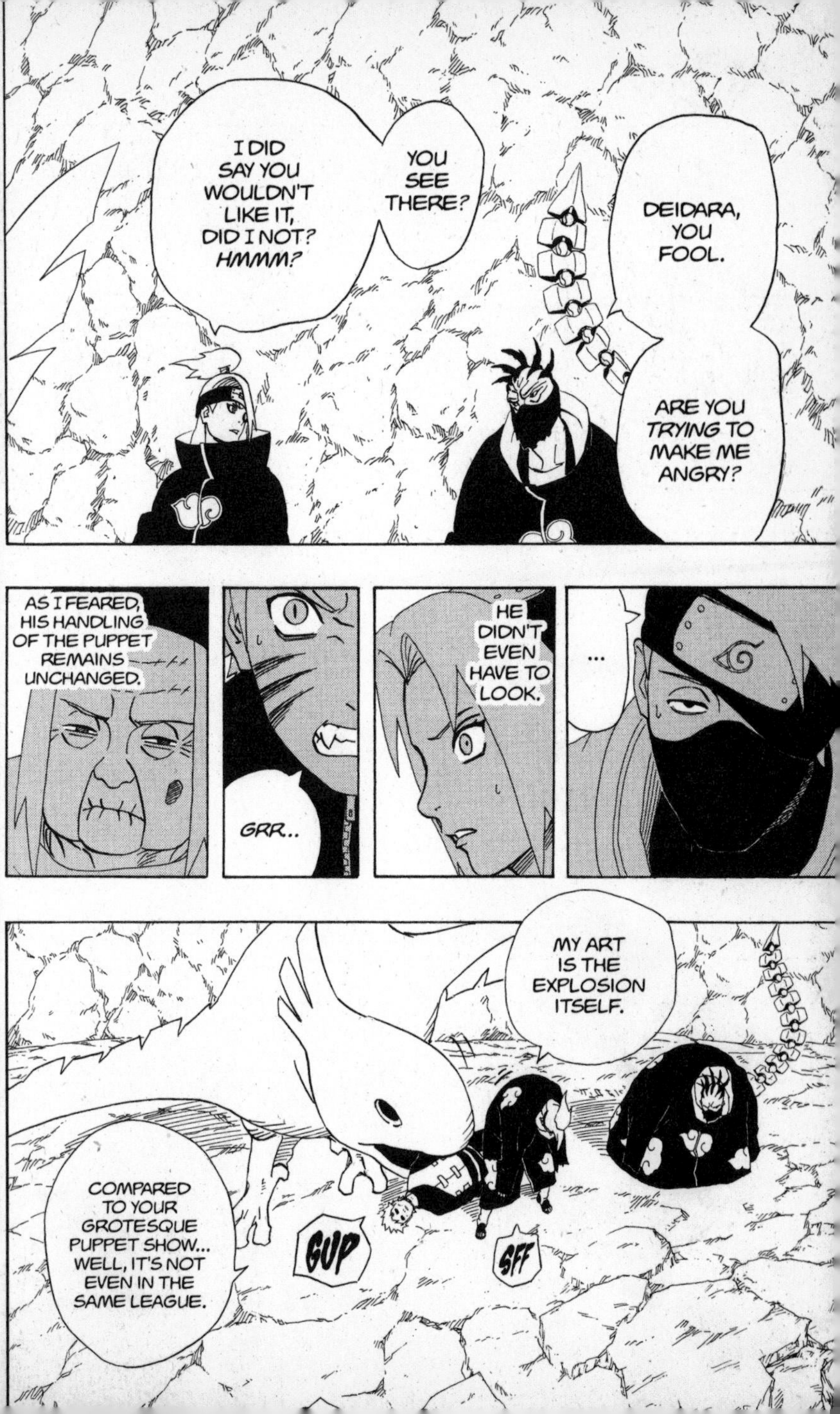
DEIDARA, YOU FOOL.
ARE YOU *TRYING* TO MAKE ME ANGRY?
YOU SEE THERE?
I DID SAY YOU WOULDN'T LIKE IT, DID I NOT? *HMMM?*
...
HE DIDN'T EVEN HAVE TO LOOK.
GRR...
AS I FEARED, HIS HANDLING OF THE PUPPET REMAINS UNCHANGED.
MY ART IS THE EXPLOSION ITSELF.
SFF
GUP
COMPARED TO YOUR GROTESQUE PUPPET SHOW... WELL, IT'S NOT EVEN IN THE SAME LEAGUE.

READ THIS WAY

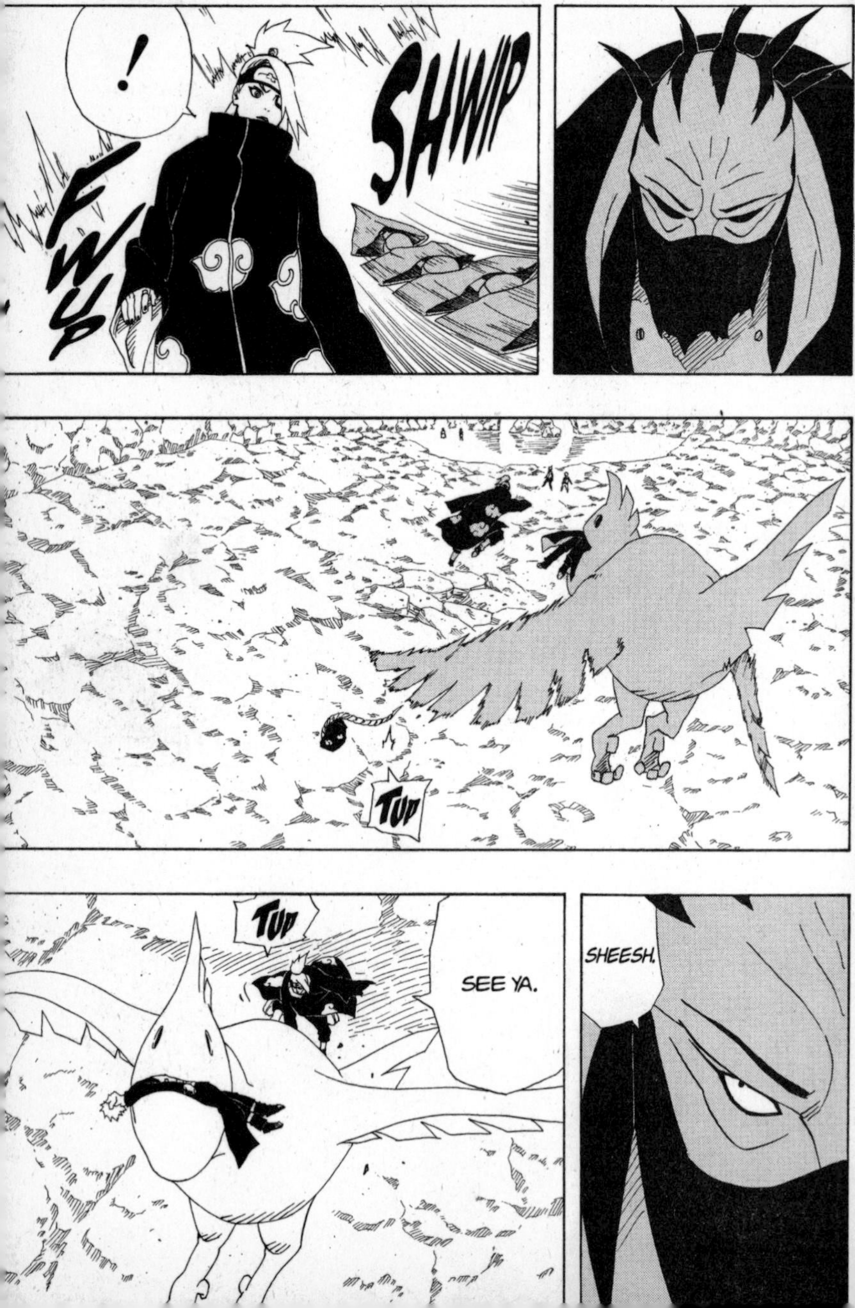
SHWIP
!
FWUP
TUP
SHEESH.
SEE YA.
TUP

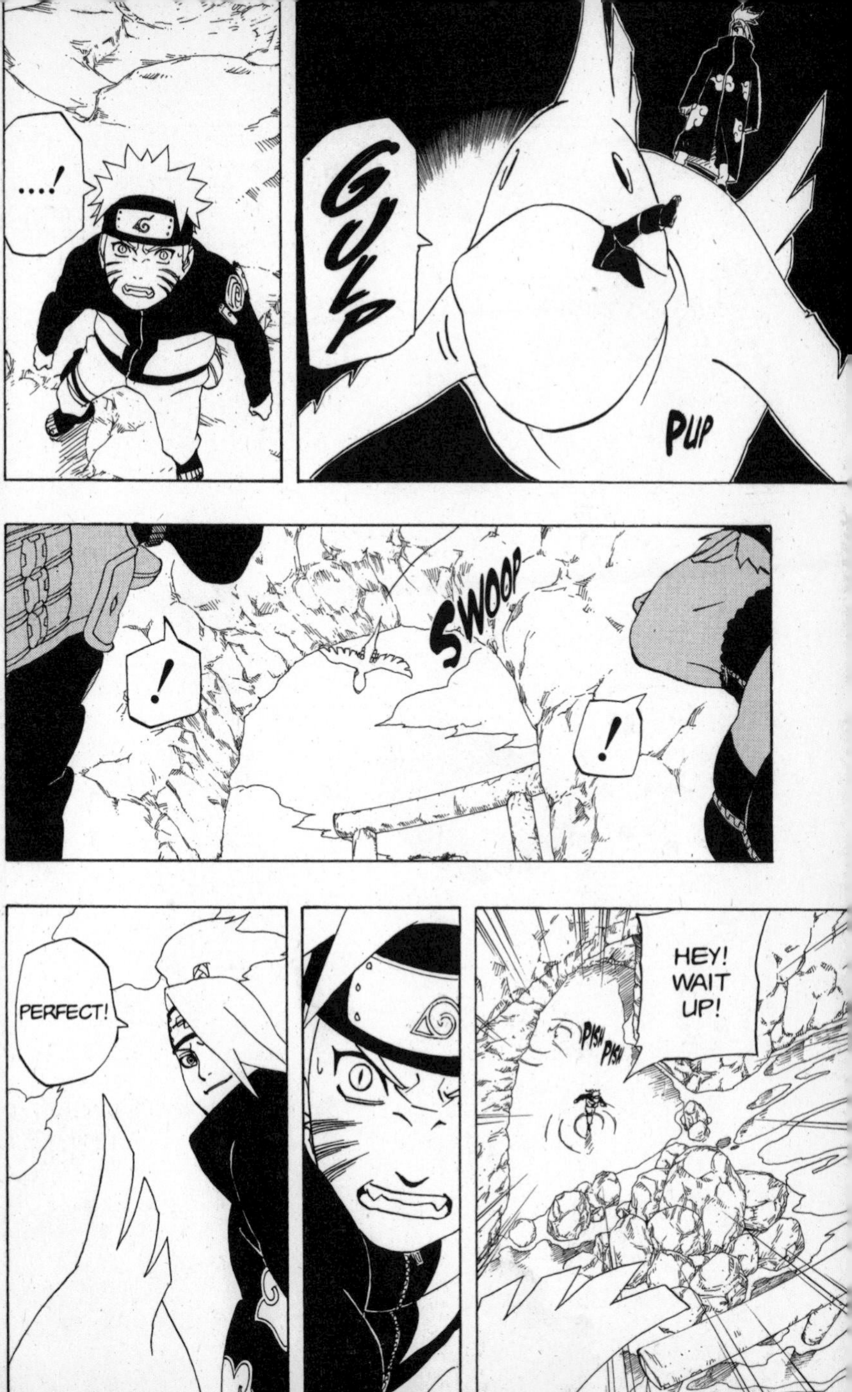
GULP
PUP
....!
!
SWOOP
!
HEY! WAIT UP!
PISH PISH
PERFECT!

READ THIS WAY

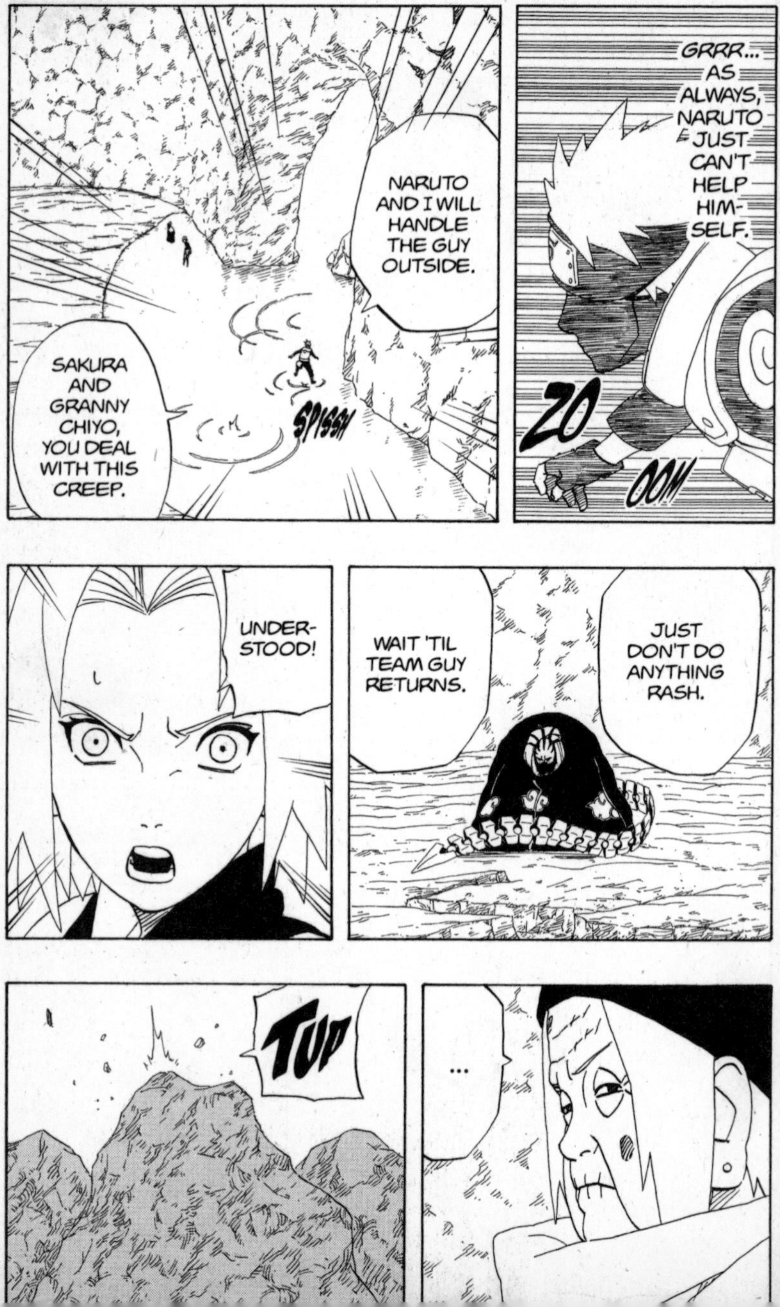
GRRR... AS ALWAYS, NARUTO JUST CAN'T HELP HIMSELF.
ZOOOM
NARUTO AND I WILL HANDLE THE GUY OUTSIDE.
SAKURA AND GRANNY CHIYO, YOU DEAL WITH THIS CREEP.
SPISSH
JUST DON'T DO ANYTHING RASH.
WAIT 'TIL TEAM GUY RETURNS.
UNDER-STOOD!
...
TUP

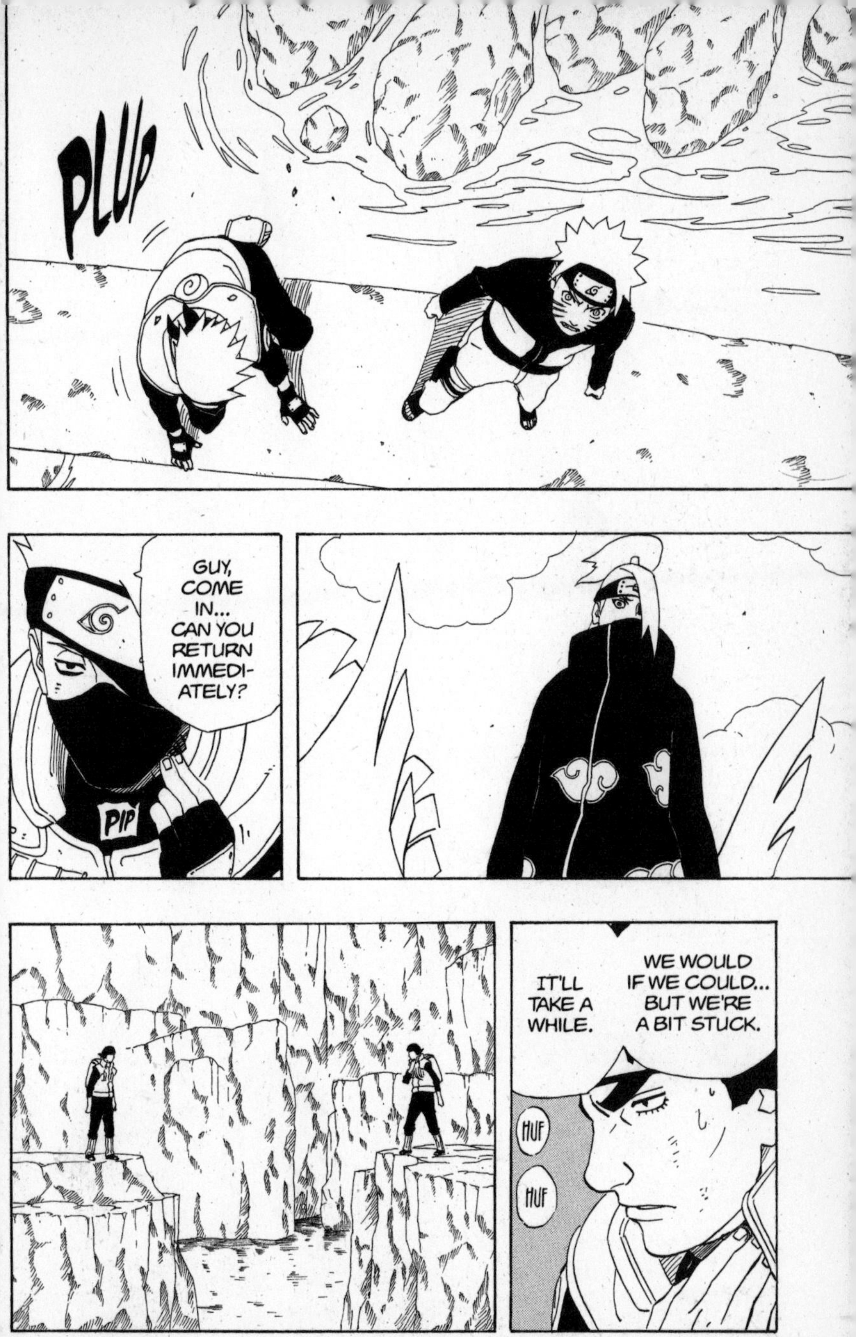
PLUP
GUY, COME IN... CAN YOU RETURN IMMEDIATELY?
PIP
WE WOULD IF WE COULD... BUT WE'RE A BIT STUCK.
IT'LL TAKE A WHILE.
HUF
HUF

READ THIS WAY

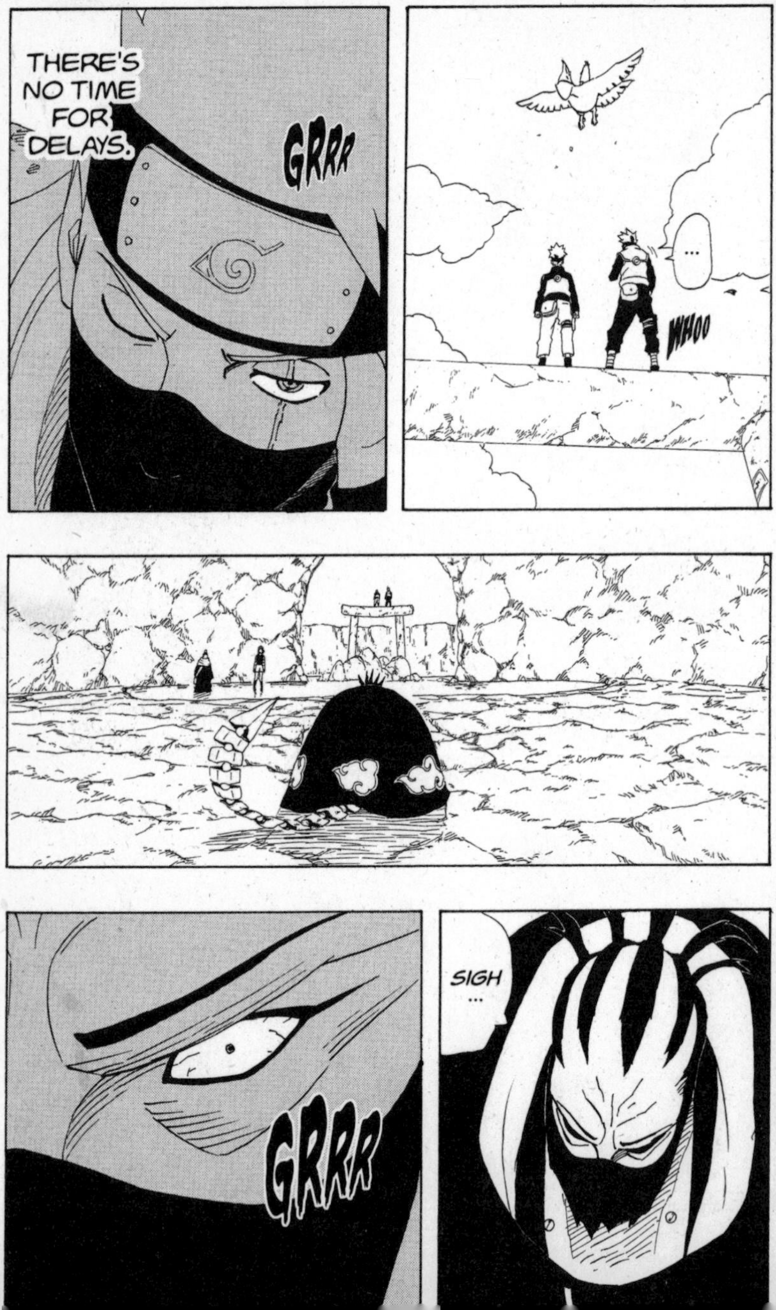
...
WHOO
THERE'S NO TIME FOR DELAYS.
GRRR
SIGH...
GRRR

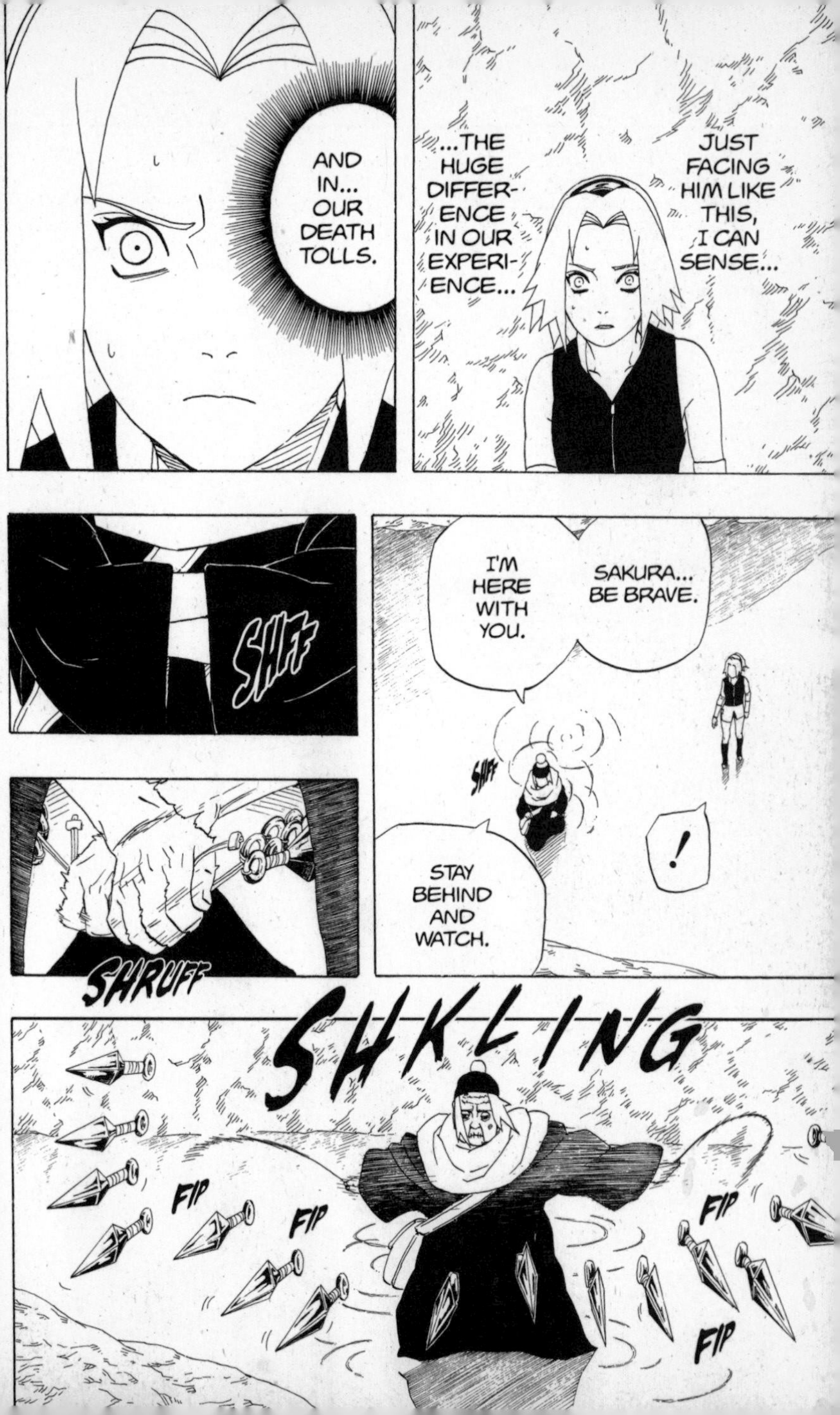
JUST FACING HIM LIKE THIS, I CAN SENSE...
...THE HUGE DIFFERENCE IN OUR EXPERIENCE...
AND IN... OUR DEATH TOLLS.
SAKURA... BE BRAVE.
I'M HERE WITH YOU.
SHFF
!
STAY BEHIND AND WATCH.
SHFF
SHRUFF
SHKLING
FIP
FIP
FIP
FIP

READ THIS WAY

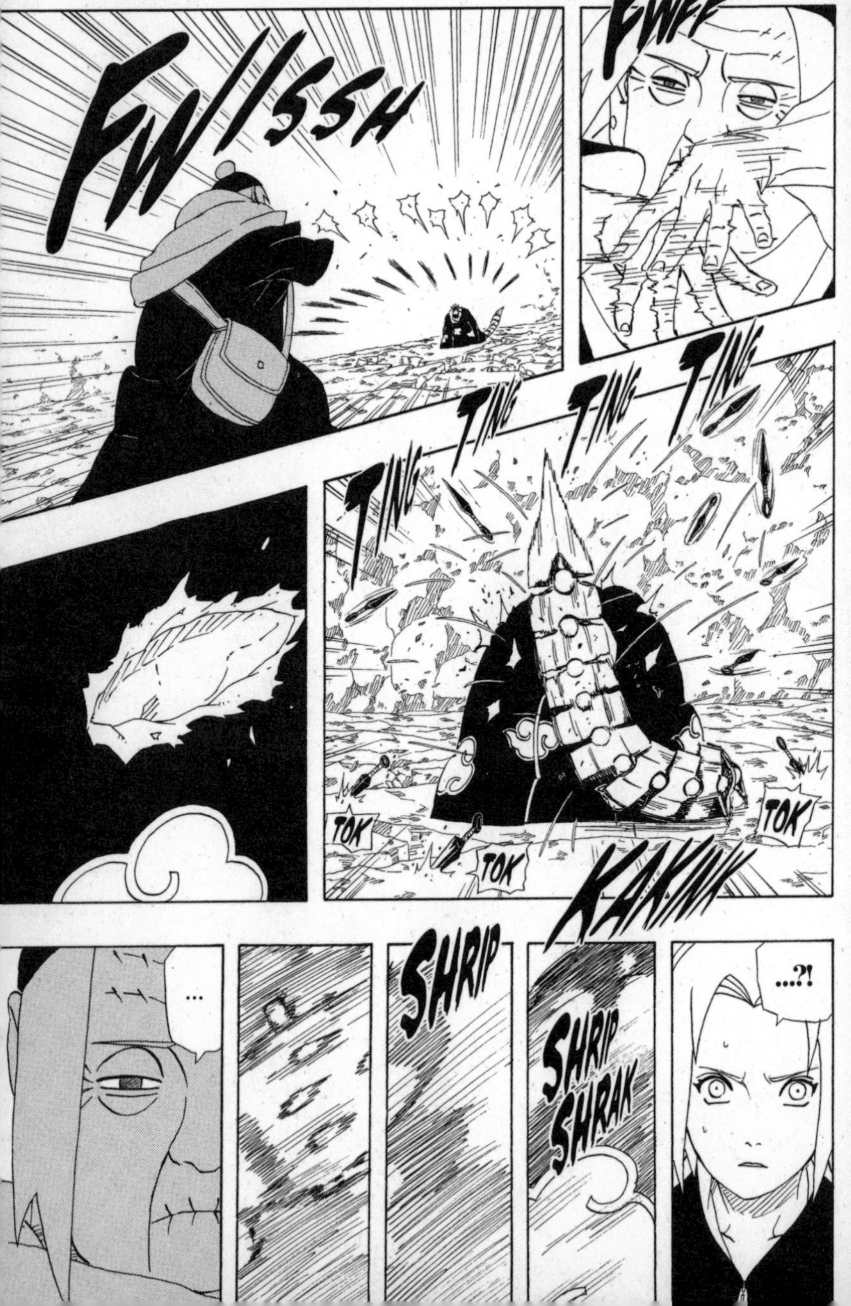
FWFF
FWISSH
TING
TING
TING
TING
TOK
TOK
TOK
KAKINK
...?!
SHRIP
SHRAK
SHRIP
...

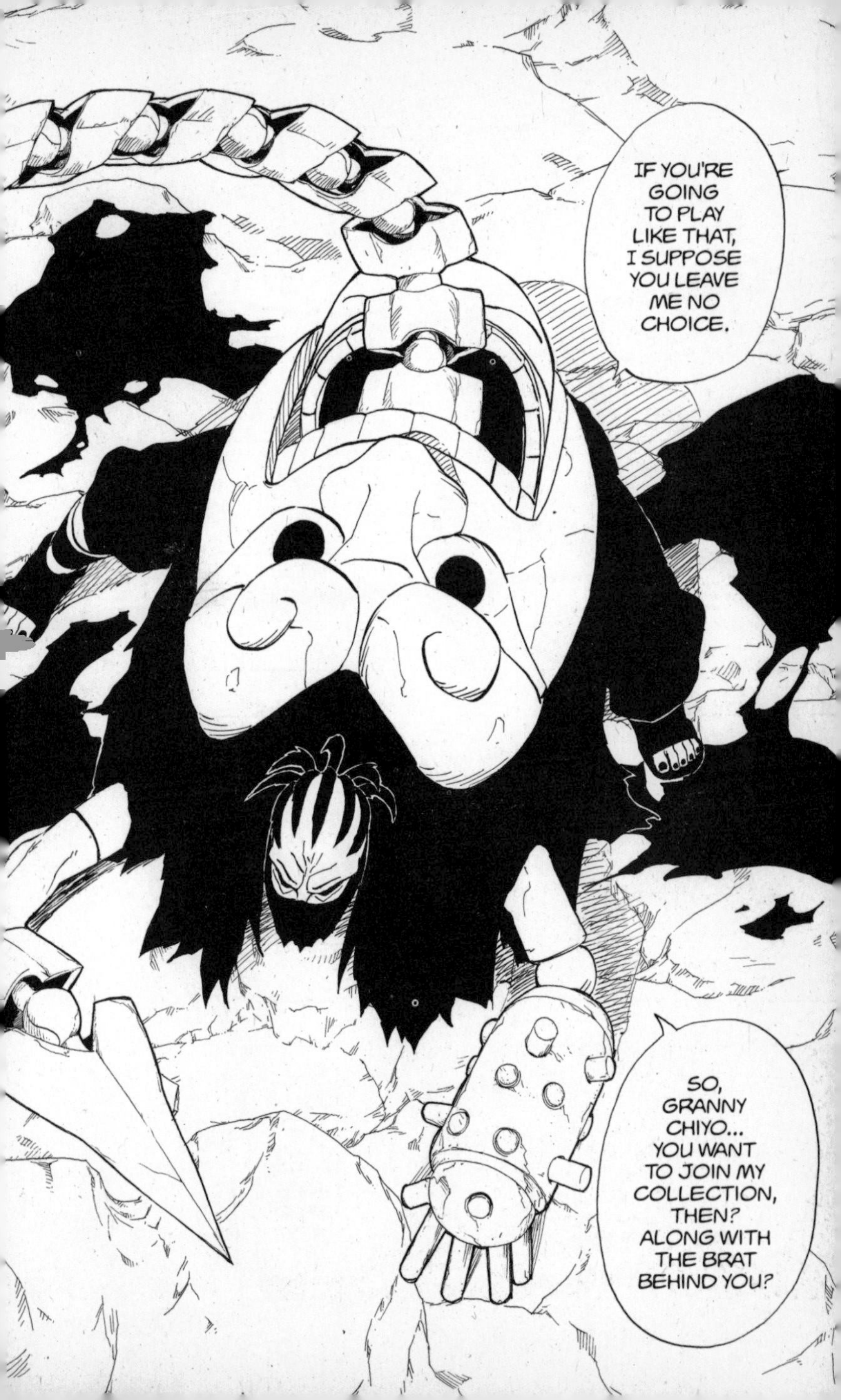
IF YOU'RE GOING TO PLAY LIKE THAT, I SUPPOSE YOU LEAVE ME NO CHOICE.
SO, GRANNY CHIYO... YOU WANT TO JOIN MY COLLECTION, THEN? ALONG WITH THE BRAT BEHIND YOU?

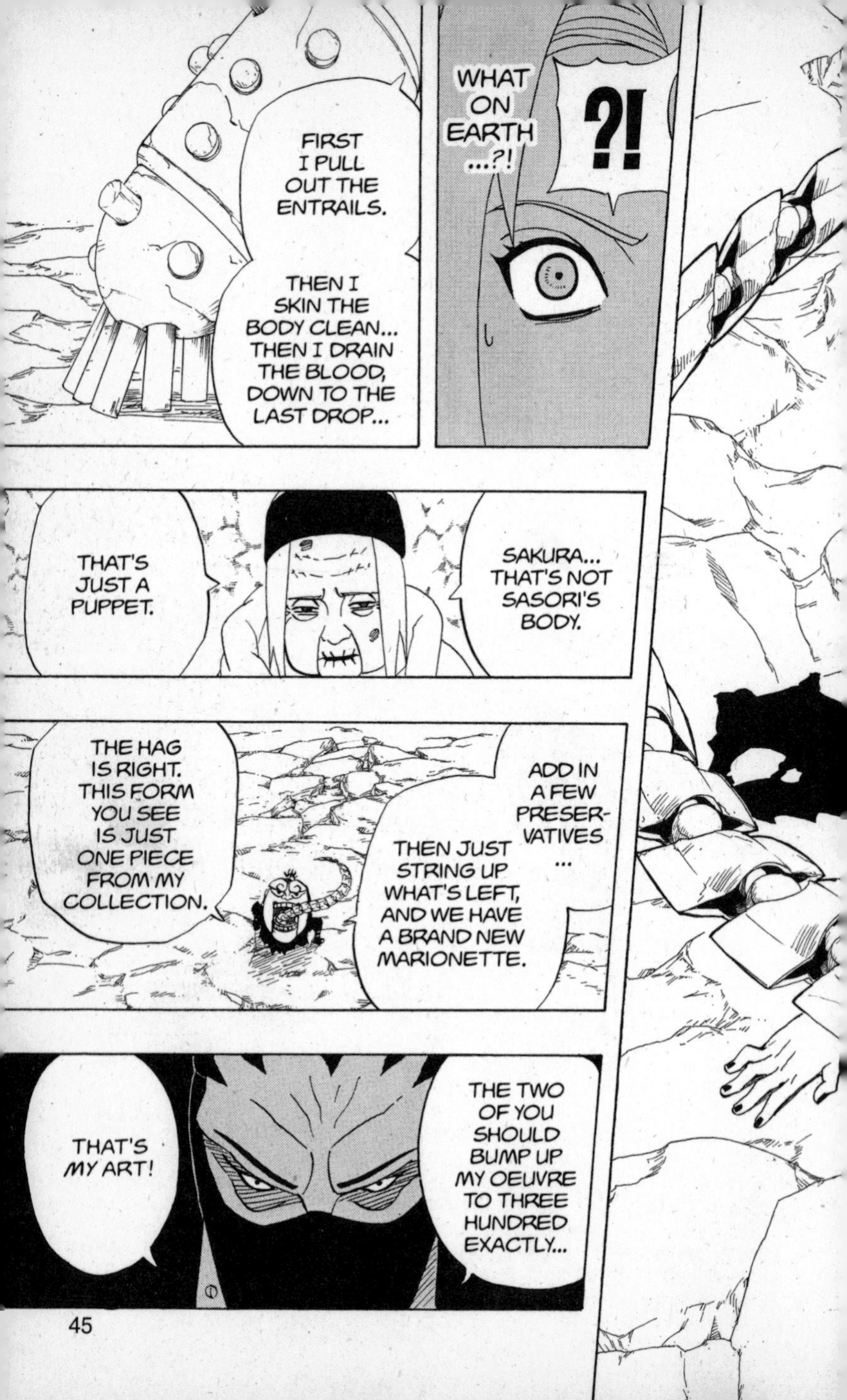
WHAT ON EARTH ...?!
?!
FIRST I PULL OUT THE ENTRAILS.
THEN I SKIN THE BODY CLEAN... THEN I DRAIN THE BLOOD, DOWN TO THE LAST DROP...
SAKURA... THAT'S NOT SASORI'S BODY.
THAT'S JUST A PUPPET.
ADD IN A FEW PRESER-VATIVES ...
THEN JUST STRING UP WHAT'S LEFT, AND WE HAVE A BRAND NEW MARIONETTE.
THE HAG IS RIGHT. THIS FORM YOU SEE IS JUST ONE PIECE FROM MY COLLECTION.
THE TWO OF YOU SHOULD BUMP UP MY OEUVRE TO THREE HUNDRED EXACTLY...
THAT'S MY ART!

THE WORLD OF KISHIMOTO MASASHI
PERSONAL HISTORY: A TRIP ABROAD

ALTHOUGH THE COLLEGE I ATTENDED WASN'T THAT AMAZING, IT DID OFFER AN OPPORTUNITY TO VISIT OVER-SEAS ART MUSEUMS. THE TRIP WASN'T MANDATORY OR ANY-THING, SO I WASN'T PLANNING TO SIGN UP. THERE SEEMED LITTLE POINT IN TRAVELING ABROAD JUST TO VISIT ART MUSEUMS. BESIDES, IT WAS SUPER EXPENSIVE. THERE WAS NO WAY I COULD SWING IT ON A PART-TIME JOB. STILL, MY FATHER INSISTED THAT I SHOULD GO, RATTLING ON ABOUT COLLEGE AND TREASURED MEMORIES. HE'D EVEN PAY FOR IT HIMSELF, HE SAID. IF I HADN'T ACCEPTED, I MIGHT'VE GIVEN HIM A CONNIPTION. (AS A FATHER HE JUST HAD TO BITE THE BULLET. THERE'S NO WAY HE COULD TELL HIS SON IT WAS TOO EXPENSIVE TO GO.)

THE TOUR BROUGHT US TO SPAIN AND FRANCE. IN SPAIN, THERE WAS ONE MUSEUM I WAS PARTICULARLY LOOKING FORWARD TO SEEING. WHEN WE GOT THERE, THOUGH, THEY WOULDN'T LET US IN. THEY TOLD US THEY'D JUST FOUND A BAG CONTAINING EXPLOSIVES. SO ALL WE WOUND UP SEEING WAS A BOMB SQUAD.

WHEN WE GOT TO FRANCE, I MADE A BEELINE FOR THE MONA LISA. I FIGURED, HEY, AFTER SPENDING SO MUCH MONEY ON THE TRIP, I SHOULD AT LEAST GET A GLIMPSE OF THE REAL MCCOY. THE PAINTING WAS SO POPULAR THAT IT HAD AMASSED A HUGE WALL OF PEOPLE, BLOCKING ANY VIEW. UNDAUNTED IN MY QUEST, I WAITED FOR AN OPENING. THE MOMENT A PERSON SHUFFLED AWAY, I DASHED FOR HIS PLACE. "AH, SO THIS IS THE MONA LISA!" NOT THAT I KNEW ANYTHING ABOUT THE PAINTING, REALLY, BUT I STILL ACTED LIKE IT TOUCHED ME.

AFTER A MOMENT OF GAWKING UP AT IT, I FELT THIS INTENSE PAIN ON MY CHEEK. "*YOWCH!*" FALLING TO THE GROUND, I REFLEXIVELY LOOKED BACK, ONLY TO SEE... AN OLD WOMAN. THIS WELL-BUILT, ELDERLY FOREIGN LADY, HER FIST STILL RETRACTING. A FIST! WELL, TWO GUESSES WHAT HAD STRUCK ME. I GUESS SHE NEEDED THIS GUY'S HEAD OUT OF THE WAY TO GET A BETTER VIEW.

SO, WELL, IF I SUM UP MY TREASURED MEMORY OF THIS TRIP ABROAD, IT GOES LIKE THIS: BEING PUNCHED DOWN BY A LITTLE OLD FOREIGN LADY RIGHT IN FRONT OF THE MONA LISA AFTER SPENDING A LOT OF MONEY TO SEE IT. THE OLD BIRD JUST STOOD THERE, TAKING SNAPSHOT AFTER SNAP-SHOT OF THE PAINTING, EVEN THOUGH CAMERAS WERE PROHIBITED. NO MATTER WHAT COUNTRY THEY'RE FROM, IT SEEMS OLD WOMEN ARE ALWAYS FRIGHTENING.

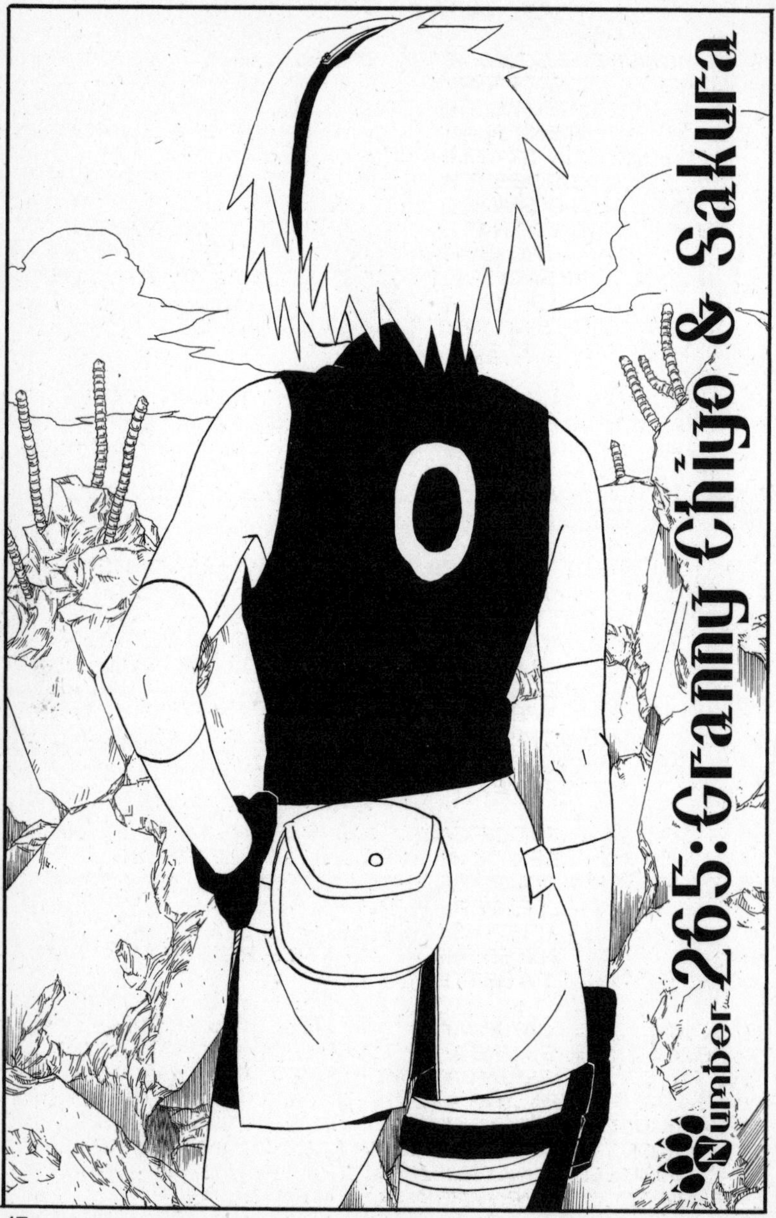

Number 265: Granny Chiyo & Sakura

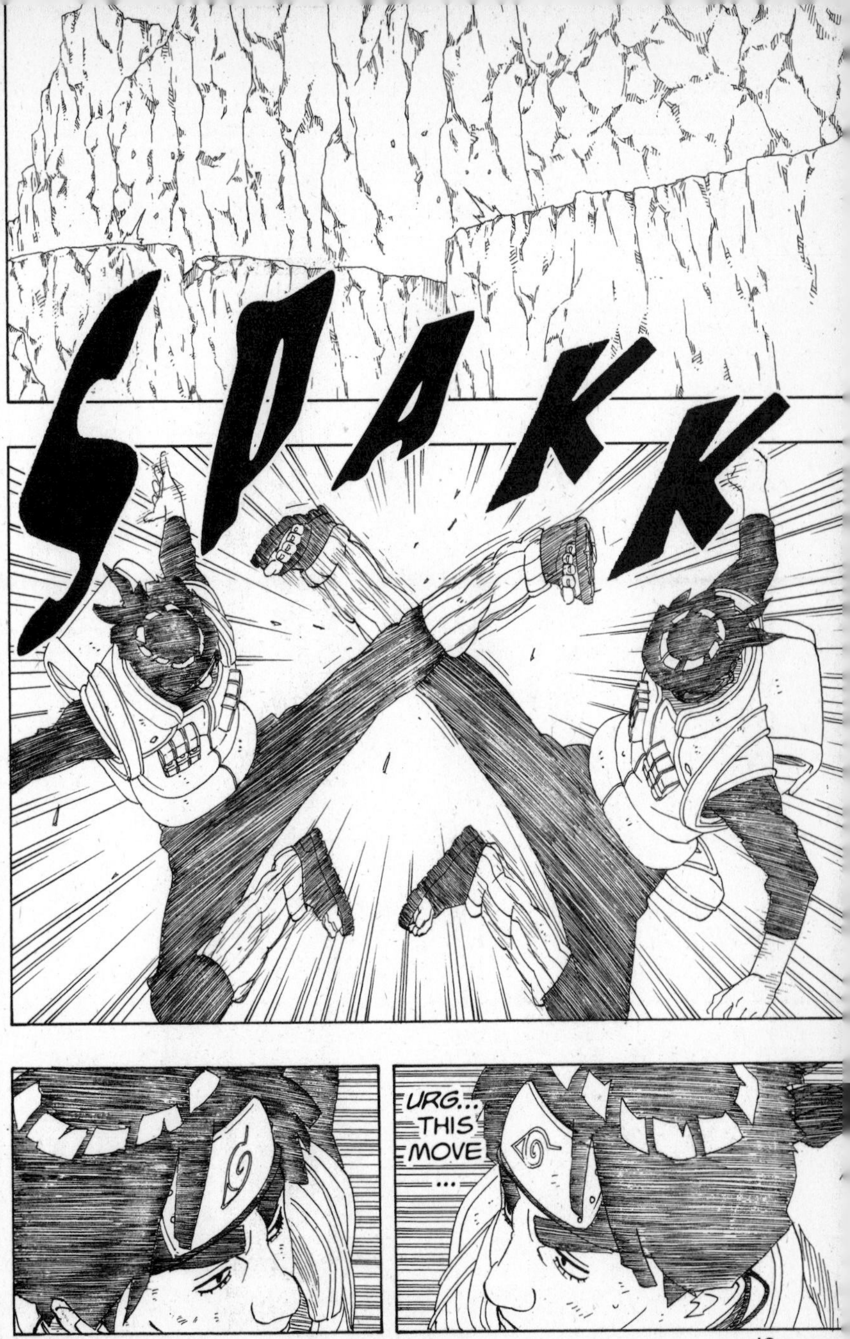
SPAKK
URG... THIS MOVE ...

READ THIS WAY

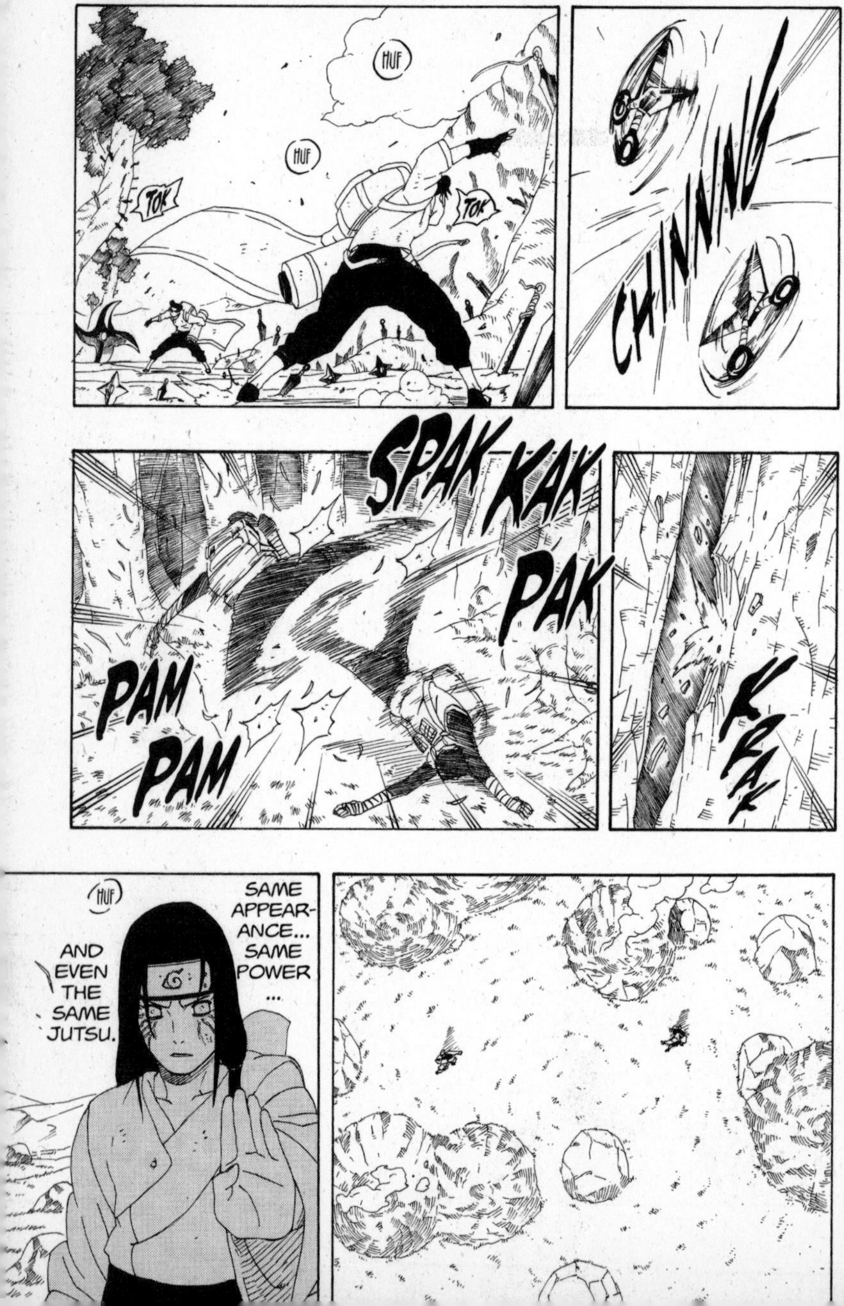
CHINNNG
HUF
HUF
TOK
TOK
KRAK
SPAK KAK
PAK
PAM PAM
HUF
SAME APPEARANCE... SAME POWER...
AND EVEN THE SAME JUTSU.

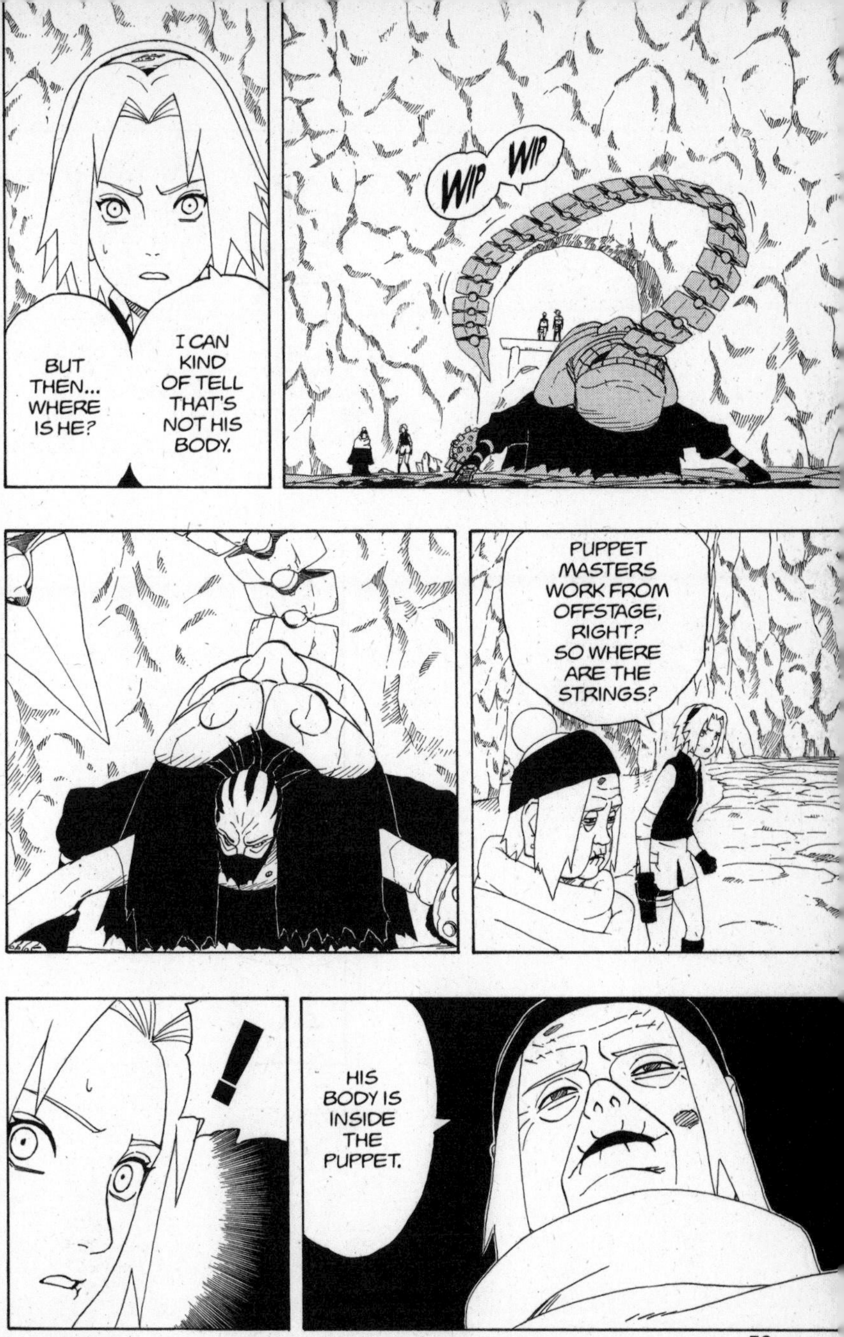
WIP WIP
I CAN KIND OF TELL THAT'S NOT HIS BODY.
BUT THEN... WHERE IS HE?
PUPPET MASTERS WORK FROM OFFSTAGE, RIGHT? SO WHERE ARE THE STRINGS?
HIS BODY IS INSIDE THE PUPPET.
!

READ THIS WAY

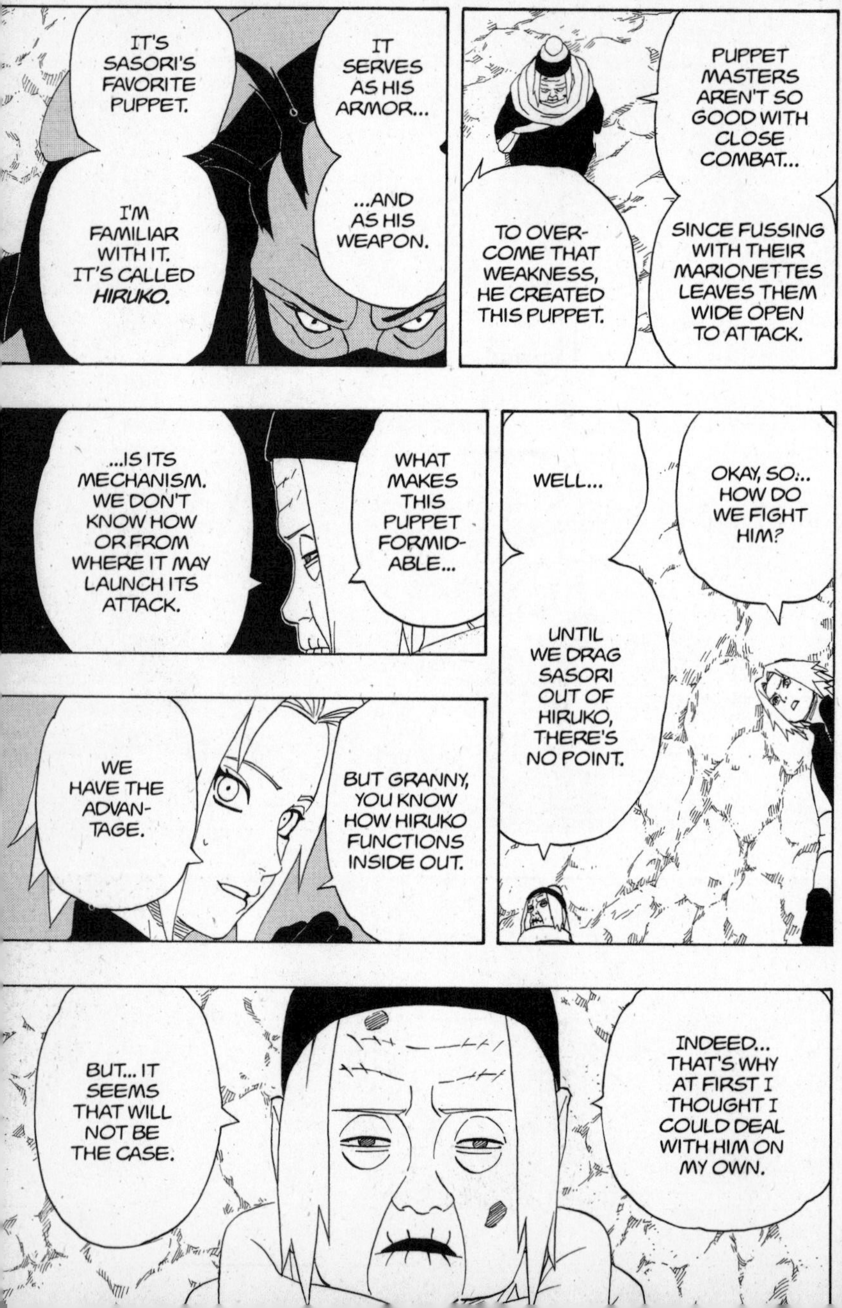
PUPPET MASTERS AREN'T SO GOOD WITH CLOSE COMBAT...
SINCE FUSSING WITH THEIR MARIONETTES LEAVES THEM WIDE OPEN TO ATTACK.
TO OVER-COME THAT WEAKNESS, HE CREATED THIS PUPPET.
IT SERVES AS HIS ARMOR...
...AND AS HIS WEAPON.
IT'S SASORI'S FAVORITE PUPPET.
I'M FAMILIAR WITH IT. IT'S CALLED *HIRUKO.*
OKAY, SO... HOW DO WE FIGHT HIM?
WELL...
UNTIL WE DRAG SASORI OUT OF HIRUKO, THERE'S NO POINT.
WHAT MAKES THIS PUPPET FORMID-ABLE...
...IS ITS MECHANISM. WE DON'T KNOW HOW OR FROM WHERE IT MAY LAUNCH ITS ATTACK.
BUT GRANNY, YOU KNOW HOW HIRUKO FUNCTIONS INSIDE OUT.
WE HAVE THE ADVAN-TAGE.
INDEED... THAT'S WHY AT FIRST I THOUGHT I COULD DEAL WITH HIM ON MY OWN.
BUT... IT SEEMS THAT WILL NOT BE THE CASE.

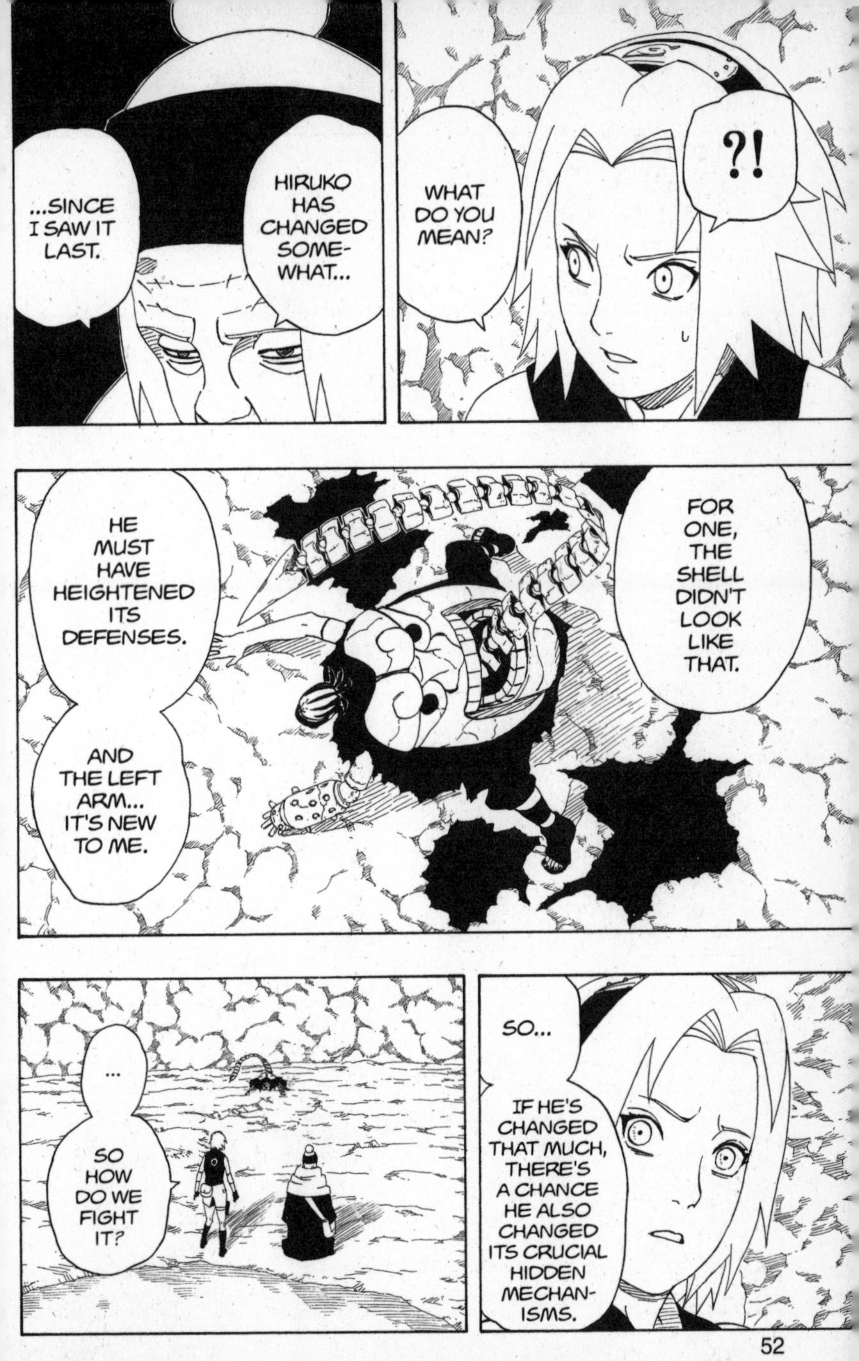
?!
WHAT DO YOU MEAN?
HIRUKO HAS CHANGED SOME-WHAT...
...SINCE I SAW IT LAST.
FOR ONE, THE SHELL DIDN'T LOOK LIKE THAT.
HE MUST HAVE HEIGHTENED ITS DEFENSES.
AND THE LEFT ARM... IT'S NEW TO ME.
SO...
IF HE'S CHANGED THAT MUCH, THERE'S A CHANCE HE ALSO CHANGED ITS CRUCIAL HIDDEN MECHAN-ISMS.
...
SO HOW DO WE FIGHT IT?

READ THIS WAY

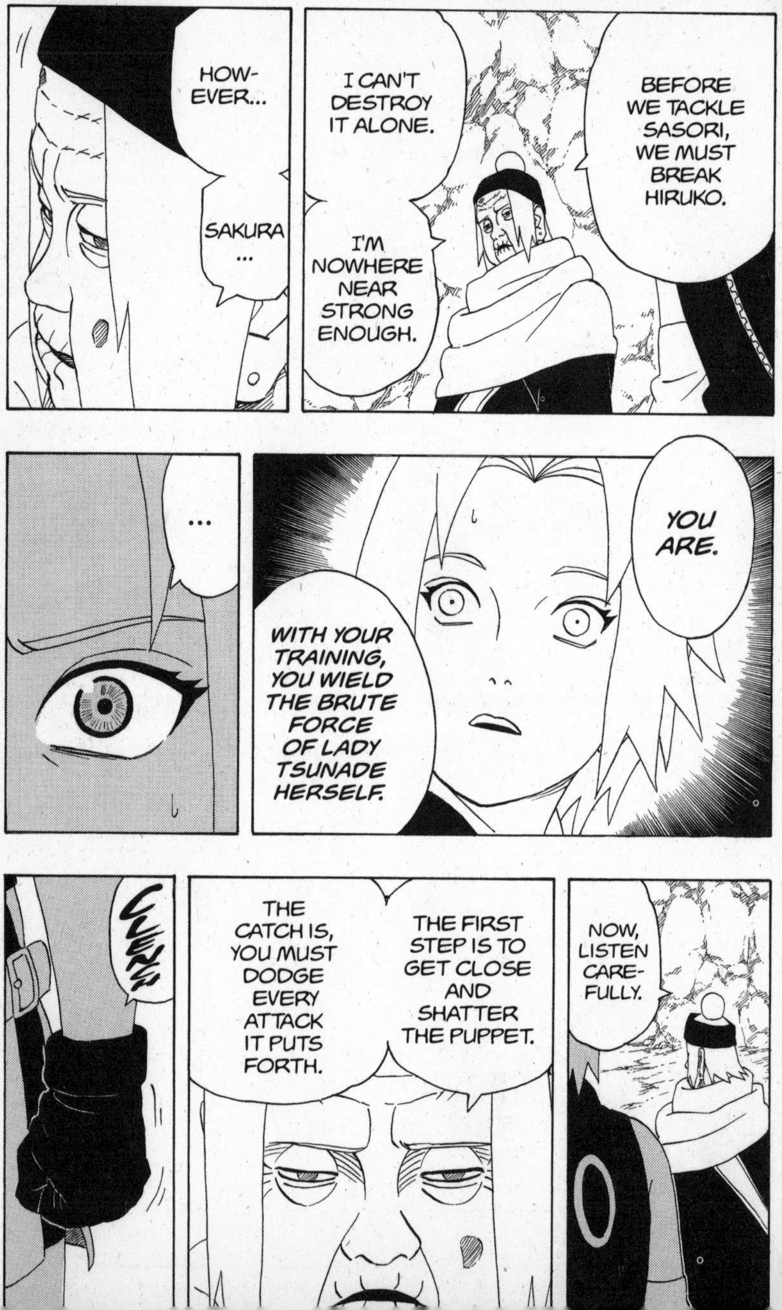
BEFORE WE TACKLE SASORI, WE MUST BREAK HIRUKO.
I CAN'T DESTROY IT ALONE.
I'M NOWHERE NEAR STRONG ENOUGH.
HOW-EVER...
SAKURA ...
YOU ARE.
WITH YOUR TRAINING, YOU WIELD THE BRUTE FORCE OF LADY TSUNADE HERSELF.
...
NOW, LISTEN CARE-FULLY.
THE FIRST STEP IS TO GET CLOSE AND SHATTER THE PUPPET.
THE CATCH IS, YOU MUST DODGE EVERY ATTACK IT PUTS FORTH.
CLENCH

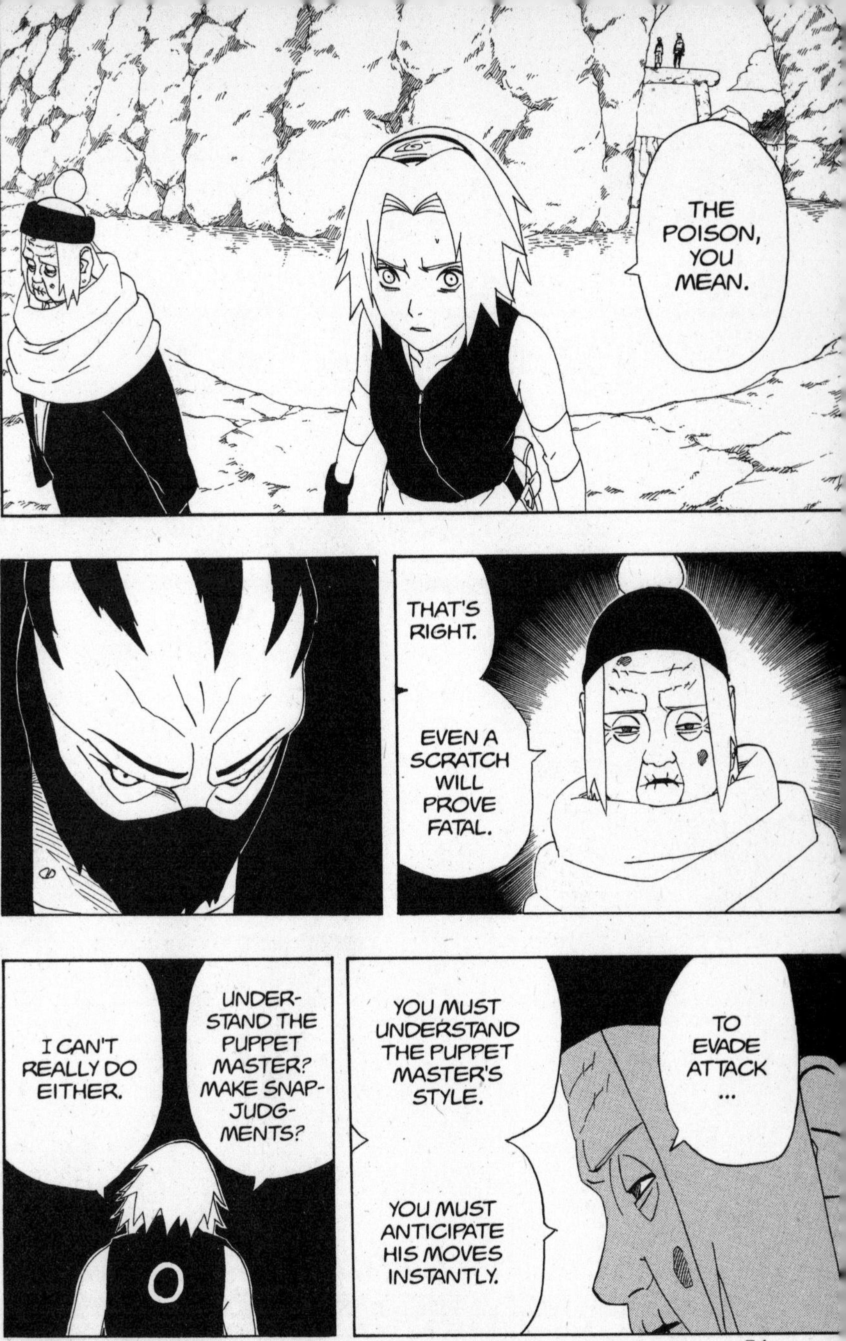
THE POISON, YOU MEAN.
THAT'S RIGHT.
EVEN A SCRATCH WILL PROVE FATAL.
TO EVADE ATTACK ...
YOU MUST UNDERSTAND THE PUPPET MASTER'S STYLE.
YOU MUST ANTICIPATE HIS MOVES INSTANTLY.
UNDER-STAND THE PUPPET MASTER? MAKE SNAP-JUDG-MENTS?
I CAN'T REALLY DO EITHER.

READ THIS WAY

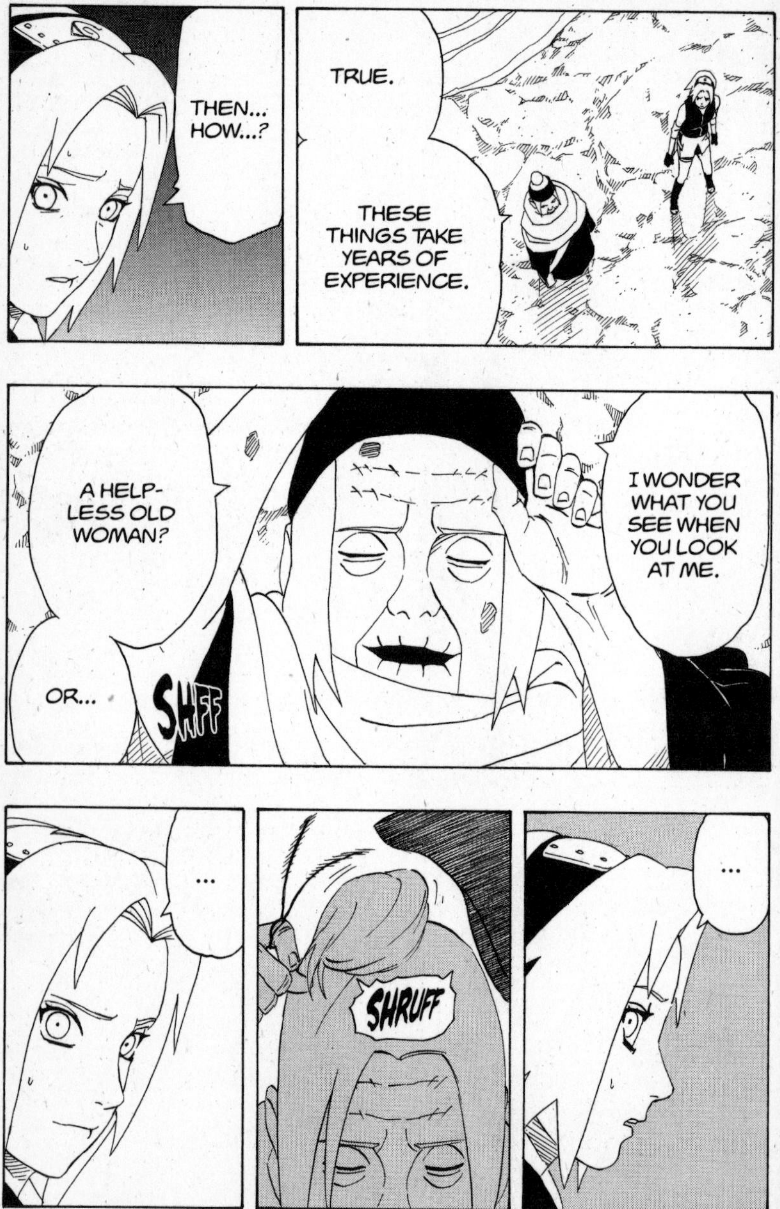
TRUE.
THESE THINGS TAKE YEARS OF EXPERIENCE.
THEN... HOW...?
I WONDER WHAT YOU SEE WHEN YOU LOOK AT ME.
A HELP-LESS OLD WOMAN?
OR...
SHFF
...
SHRUFF
...

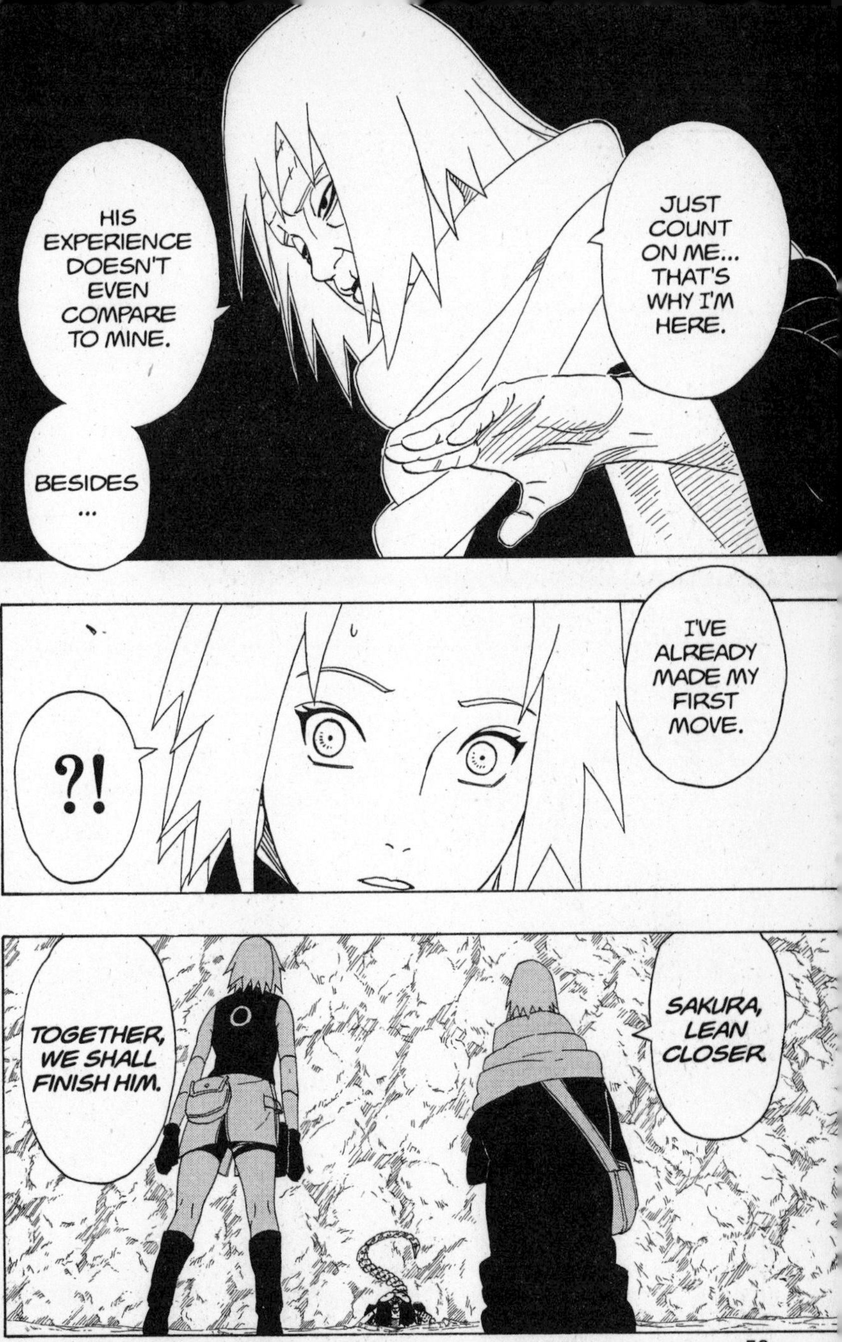
JUST COUNT ON ME... THAT'S WHY I'M HERE.
HIS EXPERIENCE DOESN'T EVEN COMPARE TO MINE.
BESIDES ...
I'VE ALREADY MADE MY FIRST MOVE.
?!
SAKURA, LEAN CLOSER.
TOGETHER, WE SHALL FINISH HIM.

READ THIS WAY

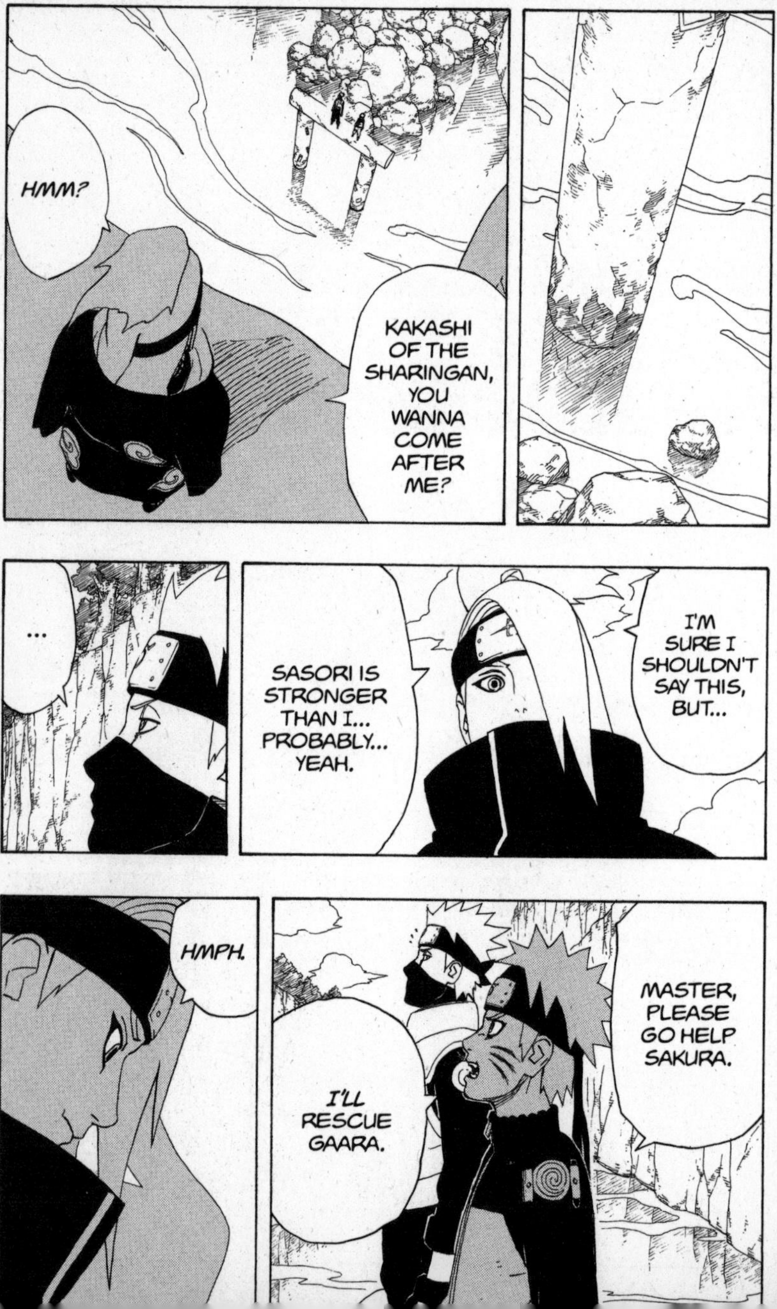
HMM?
KAKASHI OF THE SHARINGAN, YOU WANNA COME AFTER ME?
I'M SURE I SHOULDN'T SAY THIS, BUT...
SASORI IS STRONGER THAN I... PROBABLY... YEAH.
...
MASTER, PLEASE GO HELP SAKURA.
I'LL RESCUE GAARA.
HMPH.

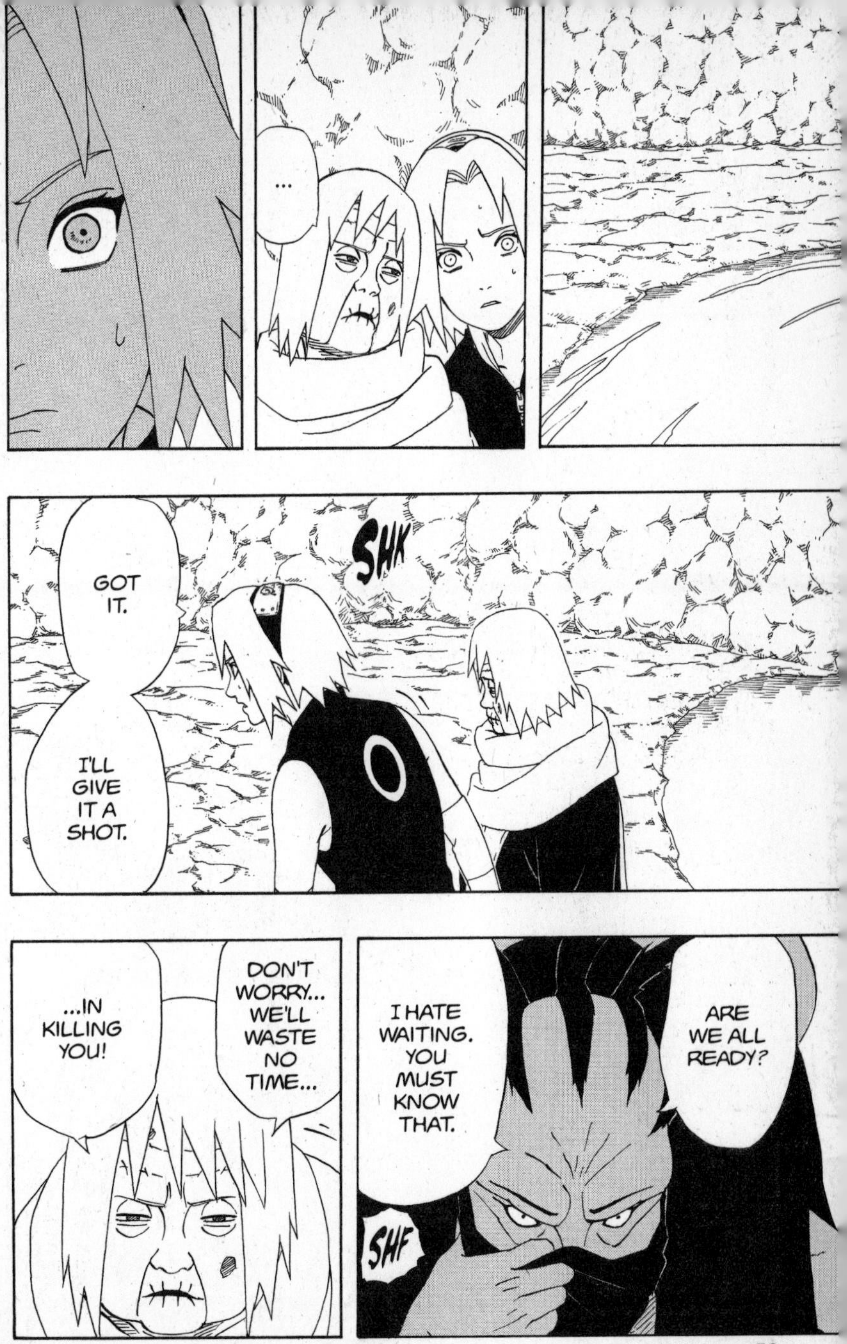
...
SHK
GOT IT.
I'LL GIVE IT A SHOT.
ARE WE ALL READY?
I HATE WAITING. YOU MUST KNOW THAT.
SHF
DON'T WORRY... WE'LL WASTE NO TIME...
...IN KILLING YOU!

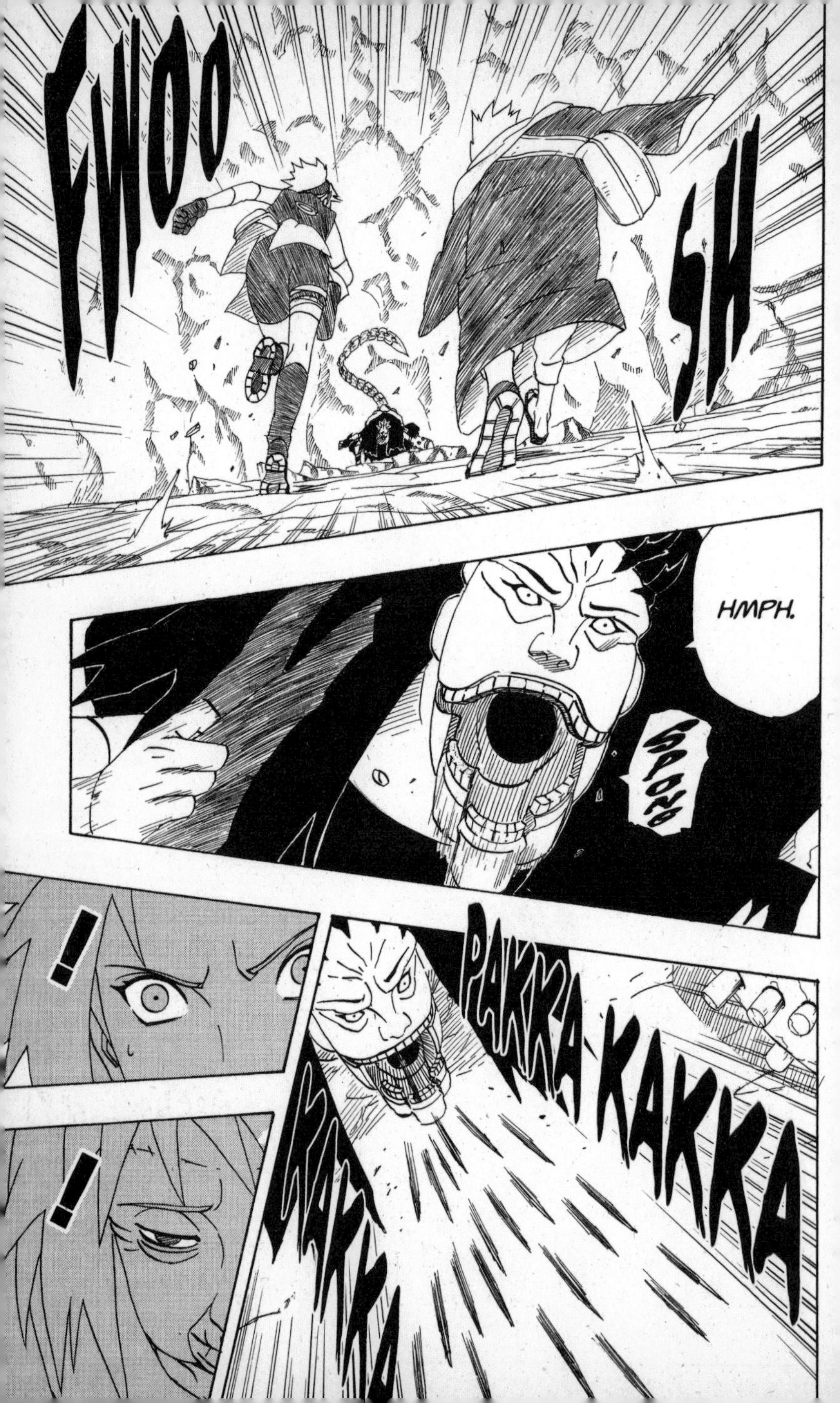
FWOOSH
HMPH.
SPOING
PAKKA-KAKKA
!
!

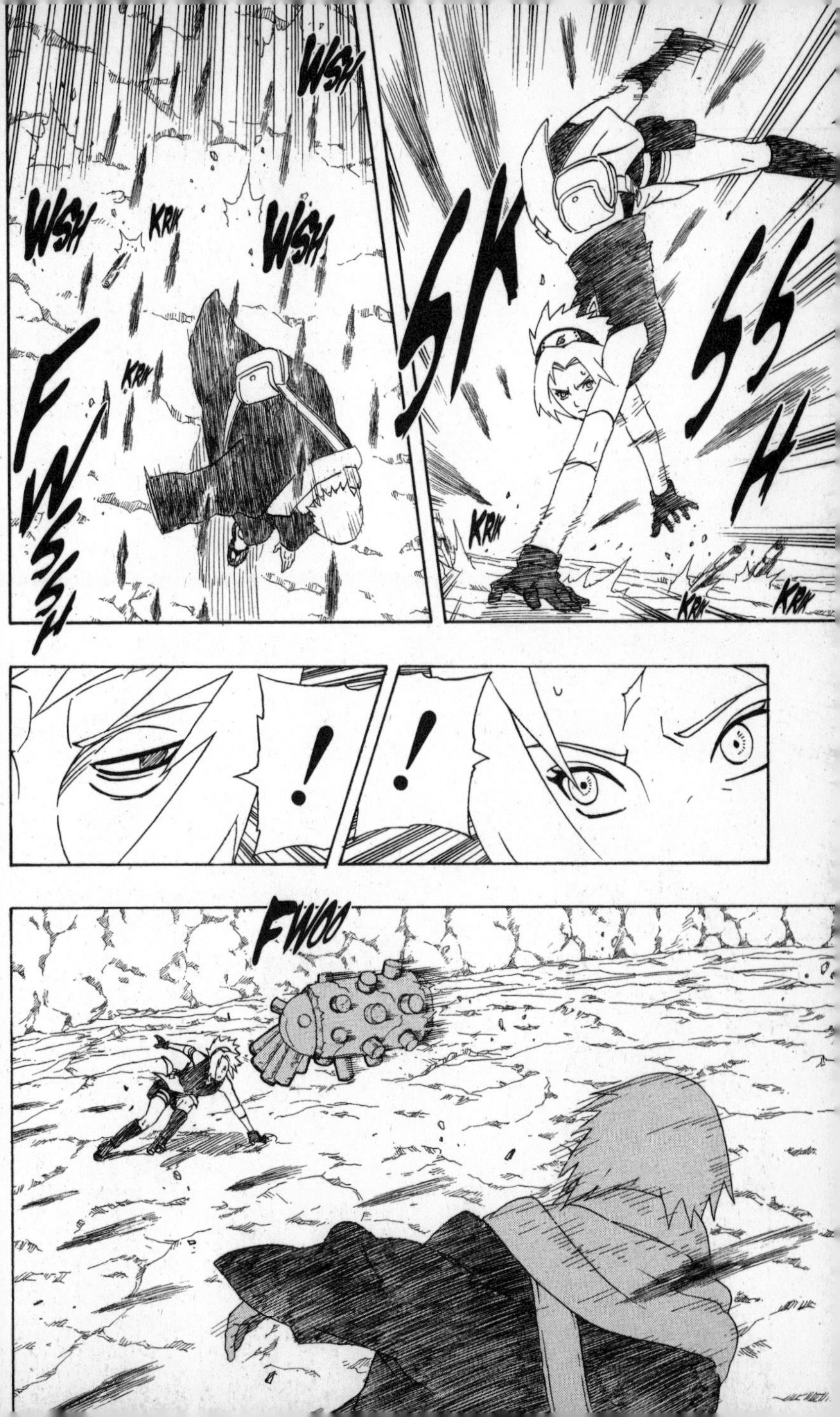
SK
SSSH
KRIK
KRIK
KRIK
WSH
WSH
KRIK
WSH
KRIK
FWSSH
!
!
FWOO

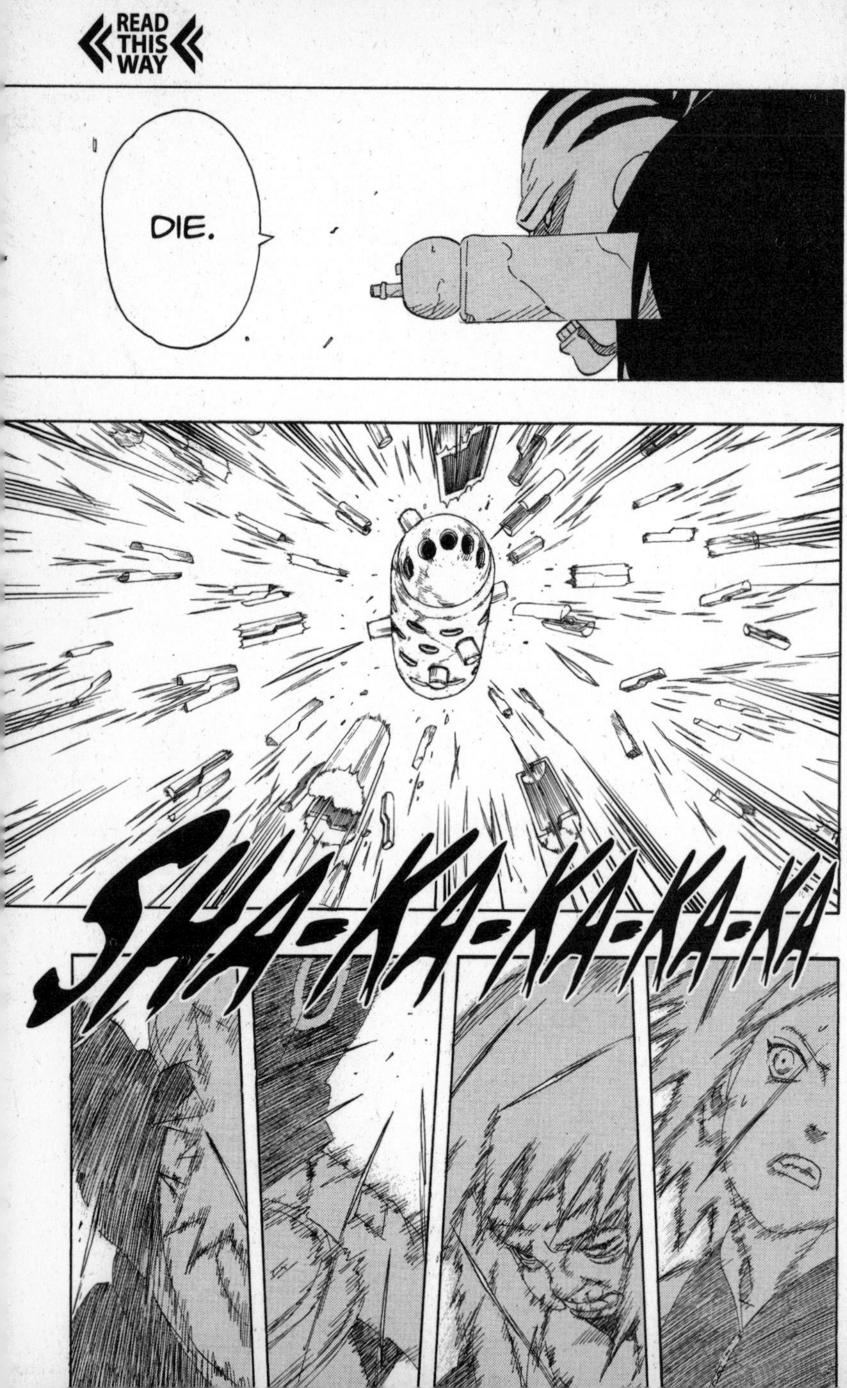
READ THIS WAY
DIE.
SHA-KA-KA-KA-KA

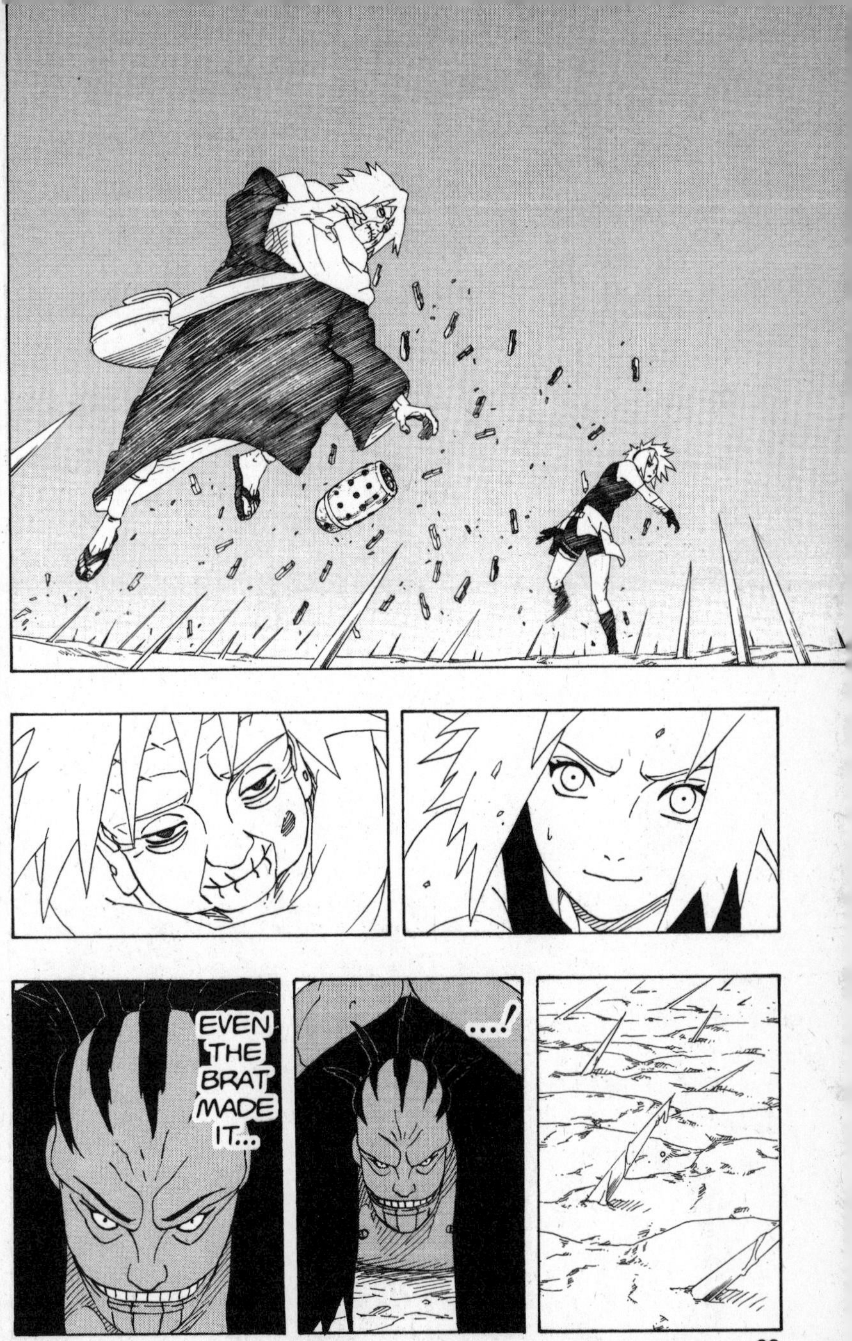
....!
EVEN THE BRAT MADE IT...

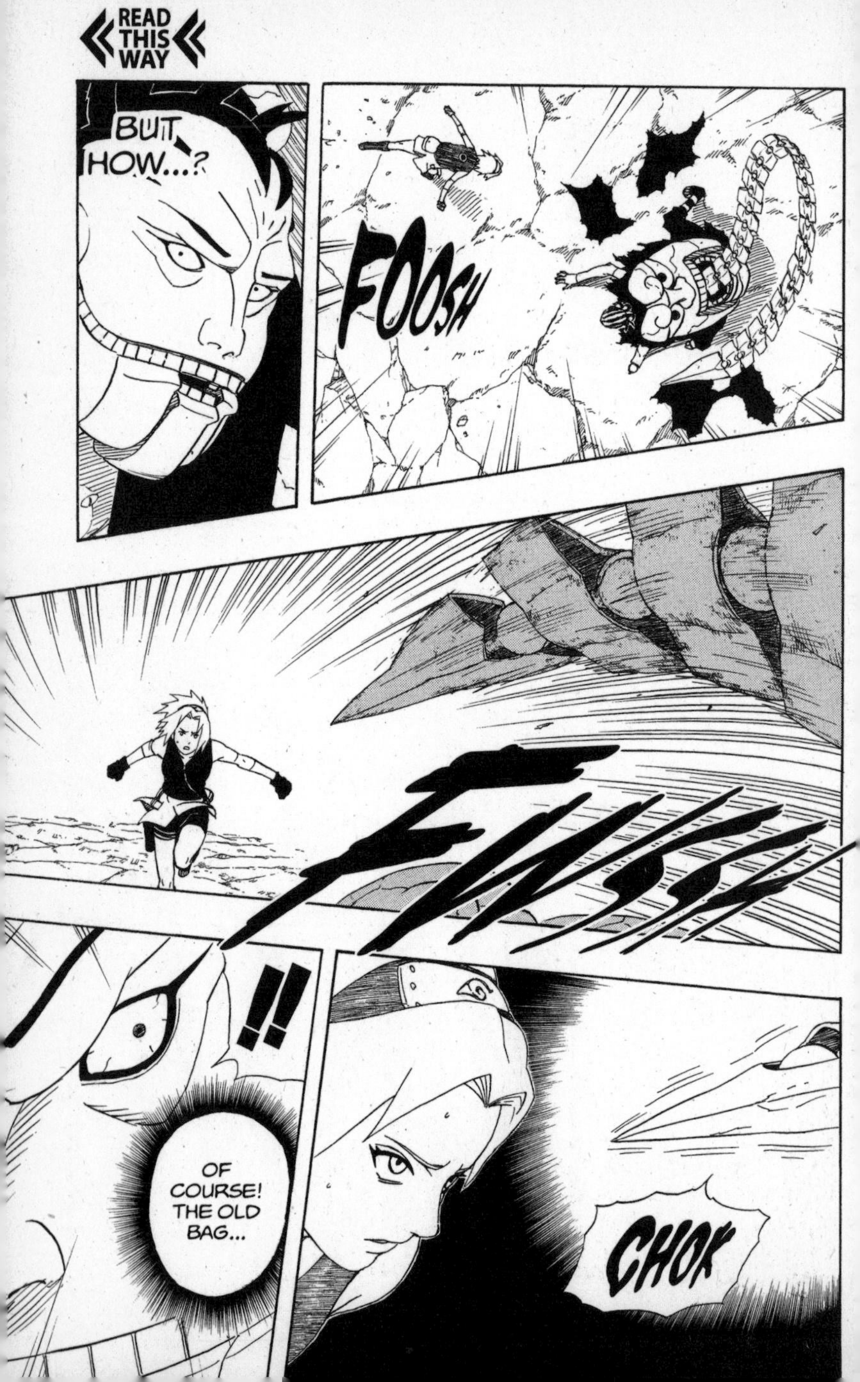
READ THIS WAY
FOOSH
BUT HOW...?
FWISSH
CHOK
!!
OF COURSE! THE OLD BAG...

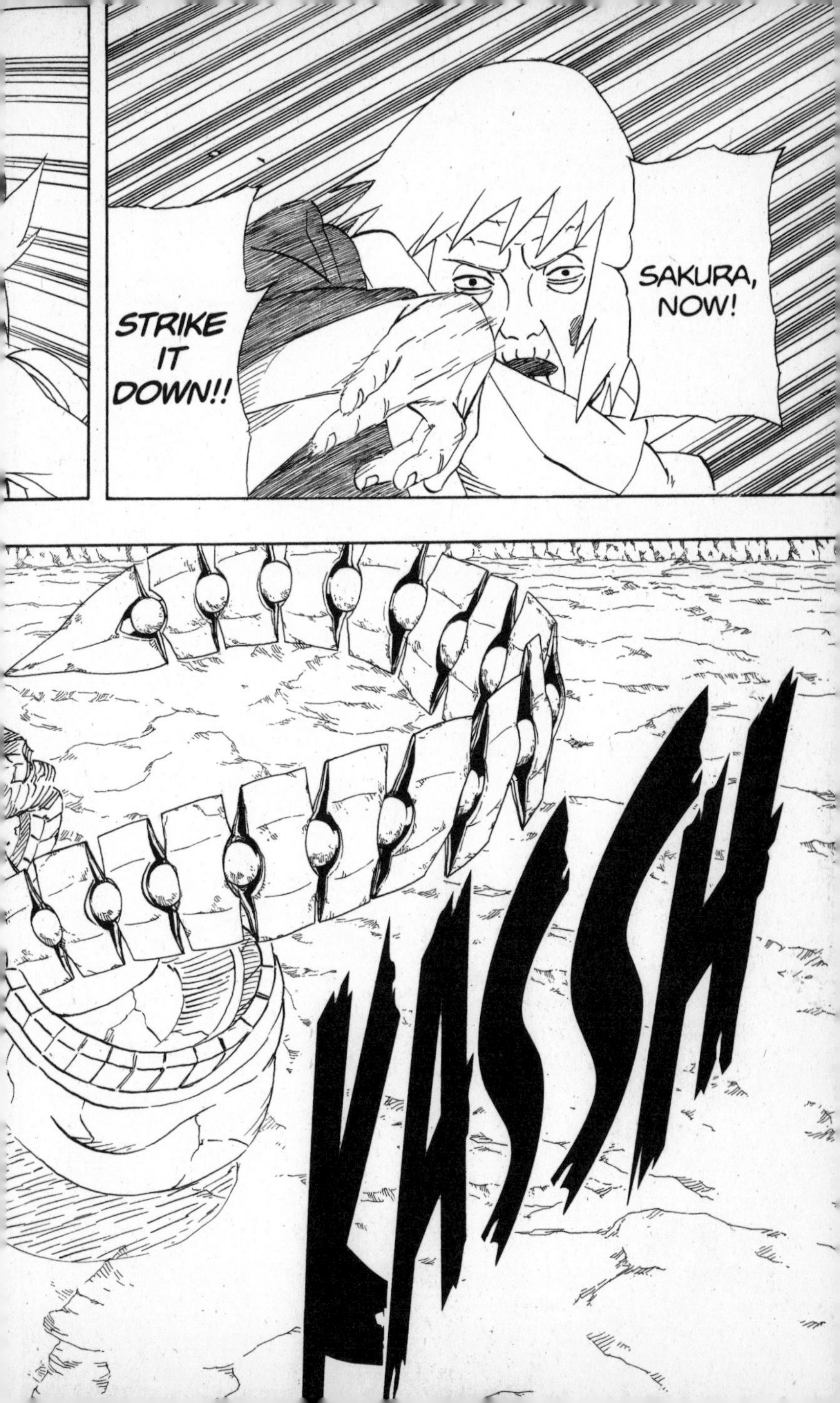
SAKURA, NOW!
STRIKE IT DOWN!!
KASSH

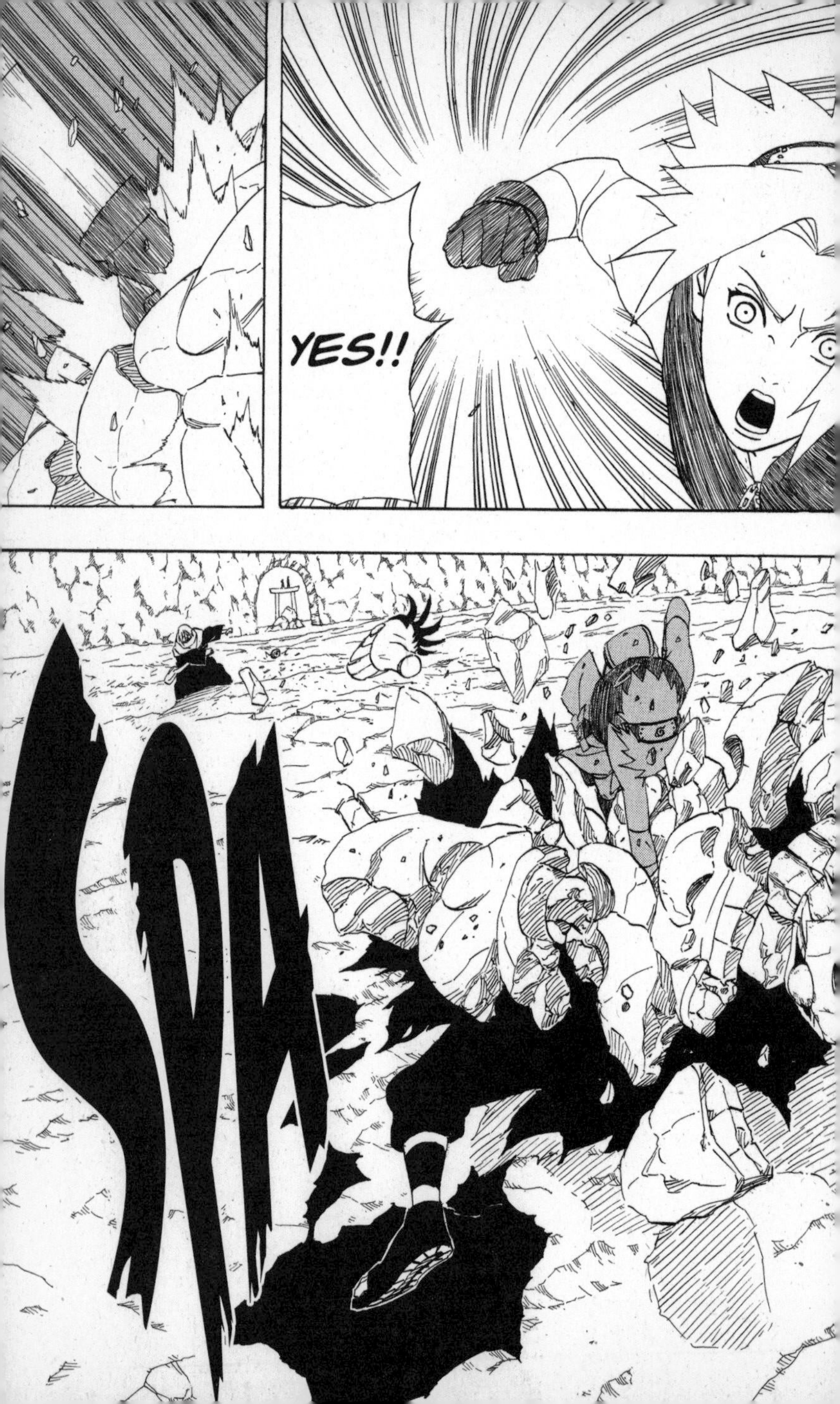
YES!!

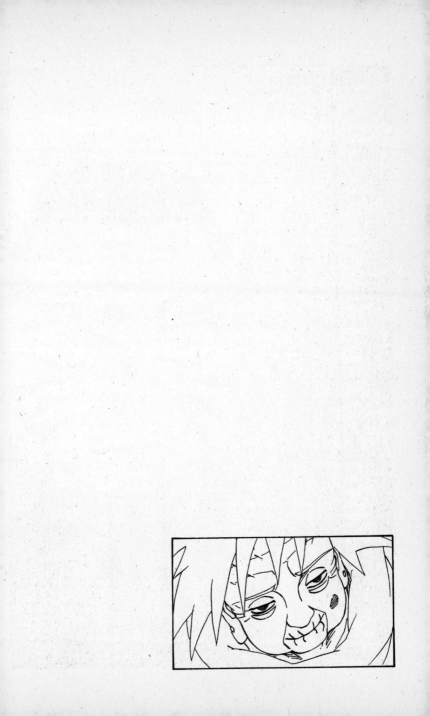

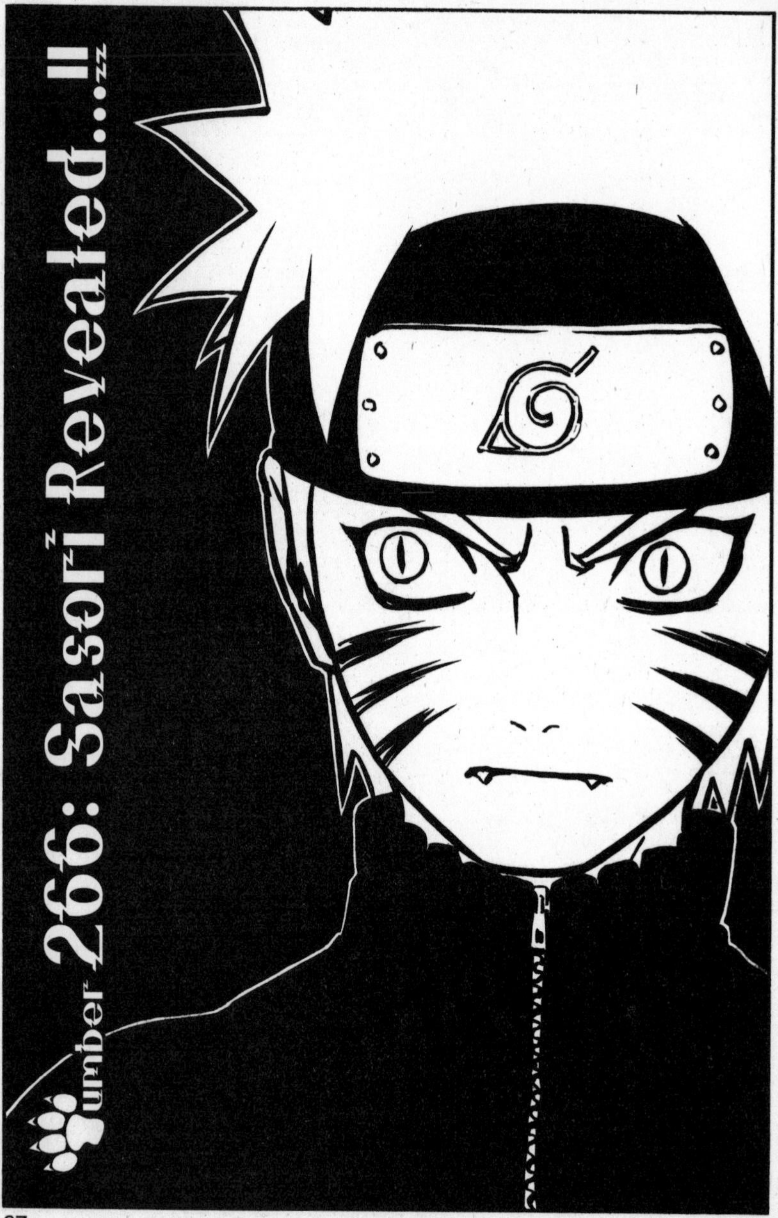
Number 266: Sasori Revealed…!!

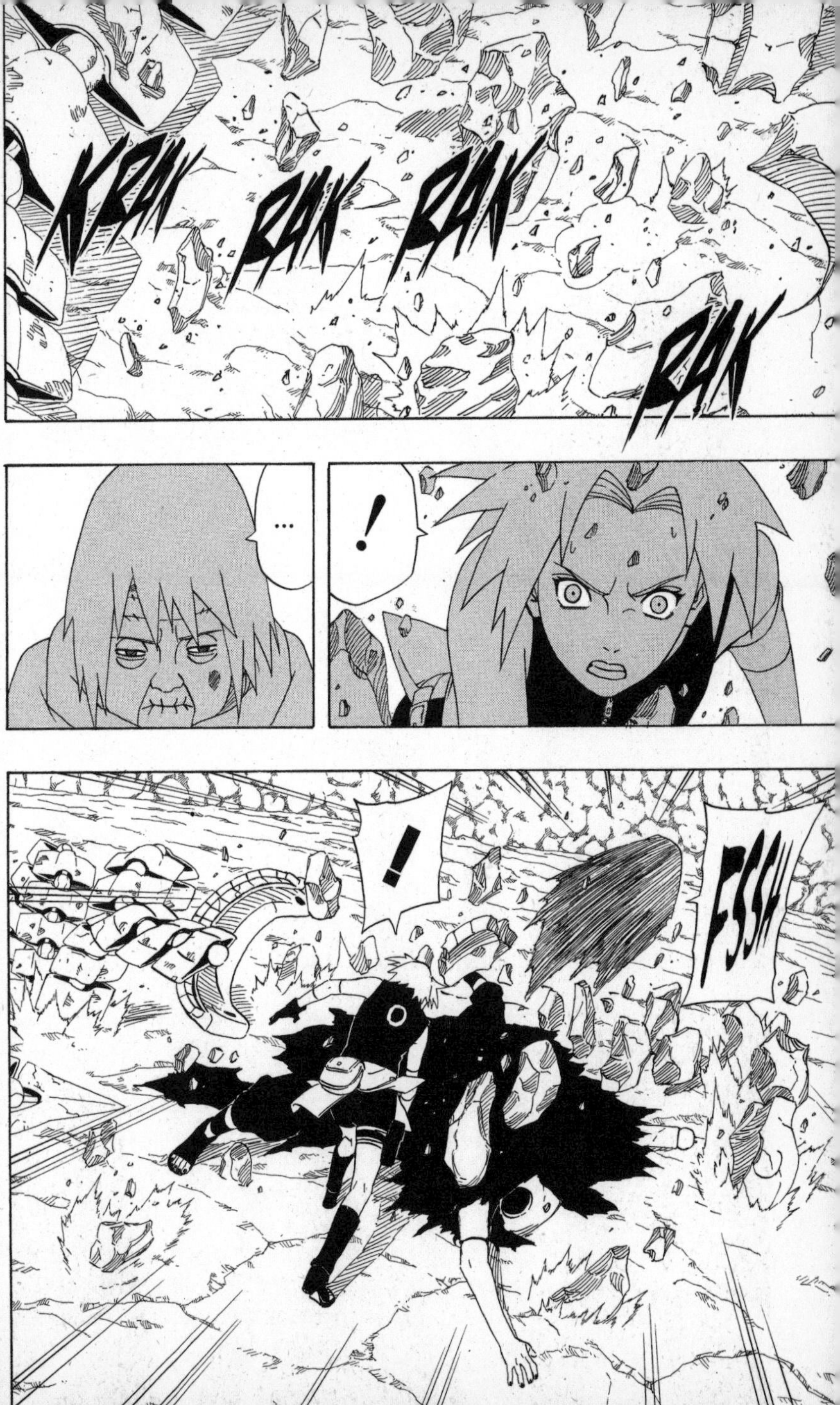

RAK
RAK
RAK
KRAK
!
...
FSSH
!

READ THIS WAY

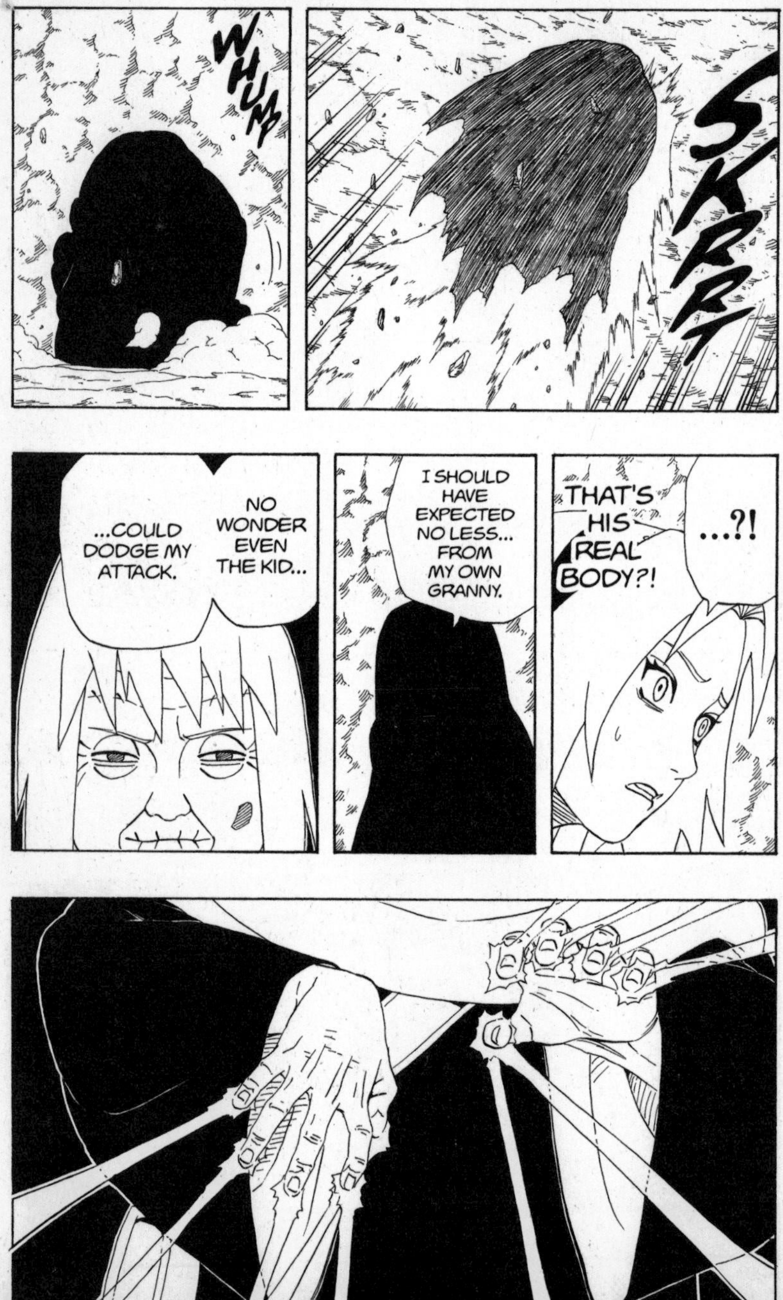
SKRRT
WHUM
...?!
THAT'S HIS REAL BODY?!
I SHOULD HAVE EXPECTED NO LESS... FROM MY OWN GRANNY.
NO WONDER EVEN THE KID...
...COULD DODGE MY ATTACK.

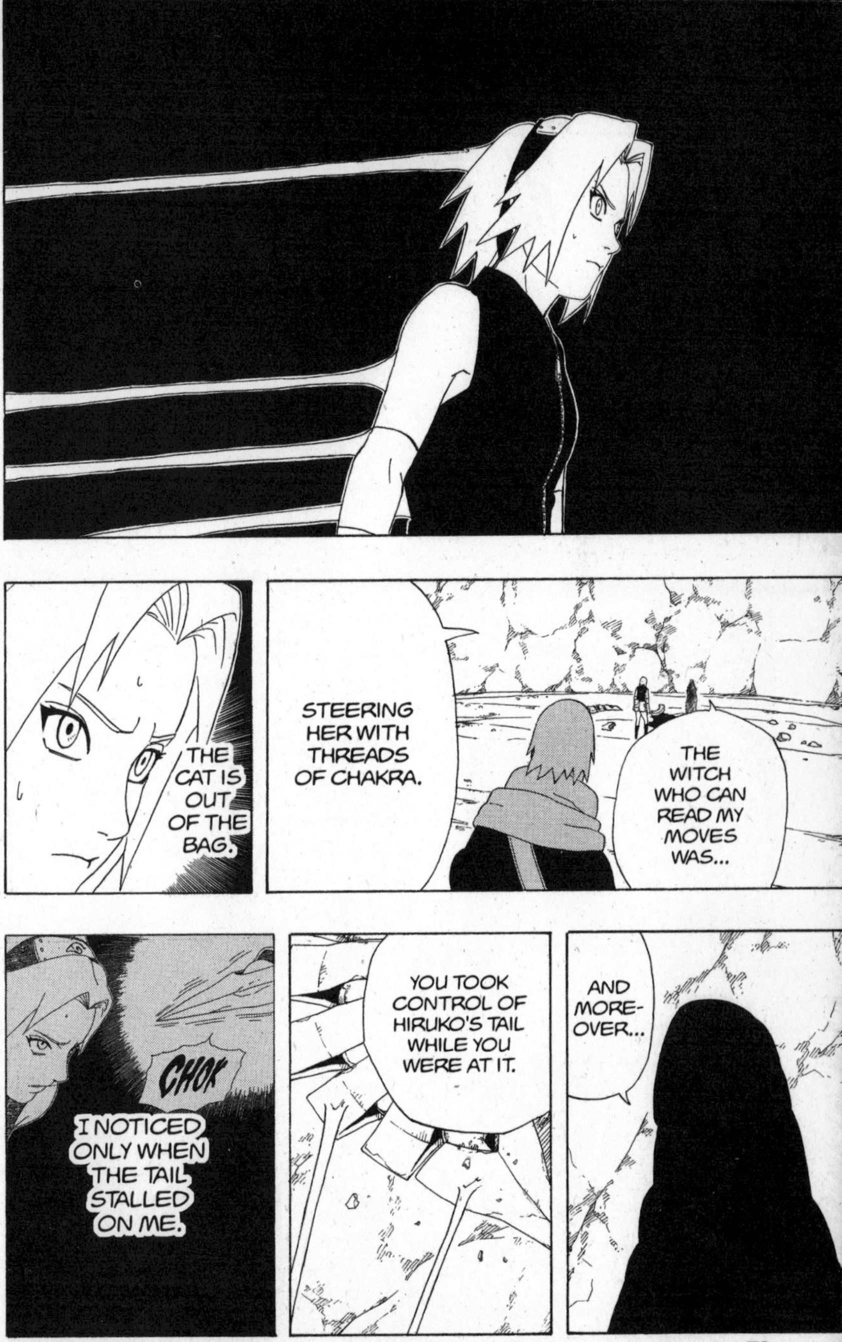
THE WITCH WHO CAN READ MY MOVES WAS...
STEERING HER WITH THREADS OF CHAKRA.
THE CAT IS OUT OF THE BAG.
AND MORE-OVER...
YOU TOOK CONTROL OF HIRUKO'S TAIL WHILE YOU WERE AT IT.
CHOK
I NOTICED ONLY WHEN THE TAIL STALLED ON ME.

READ THIS WAY

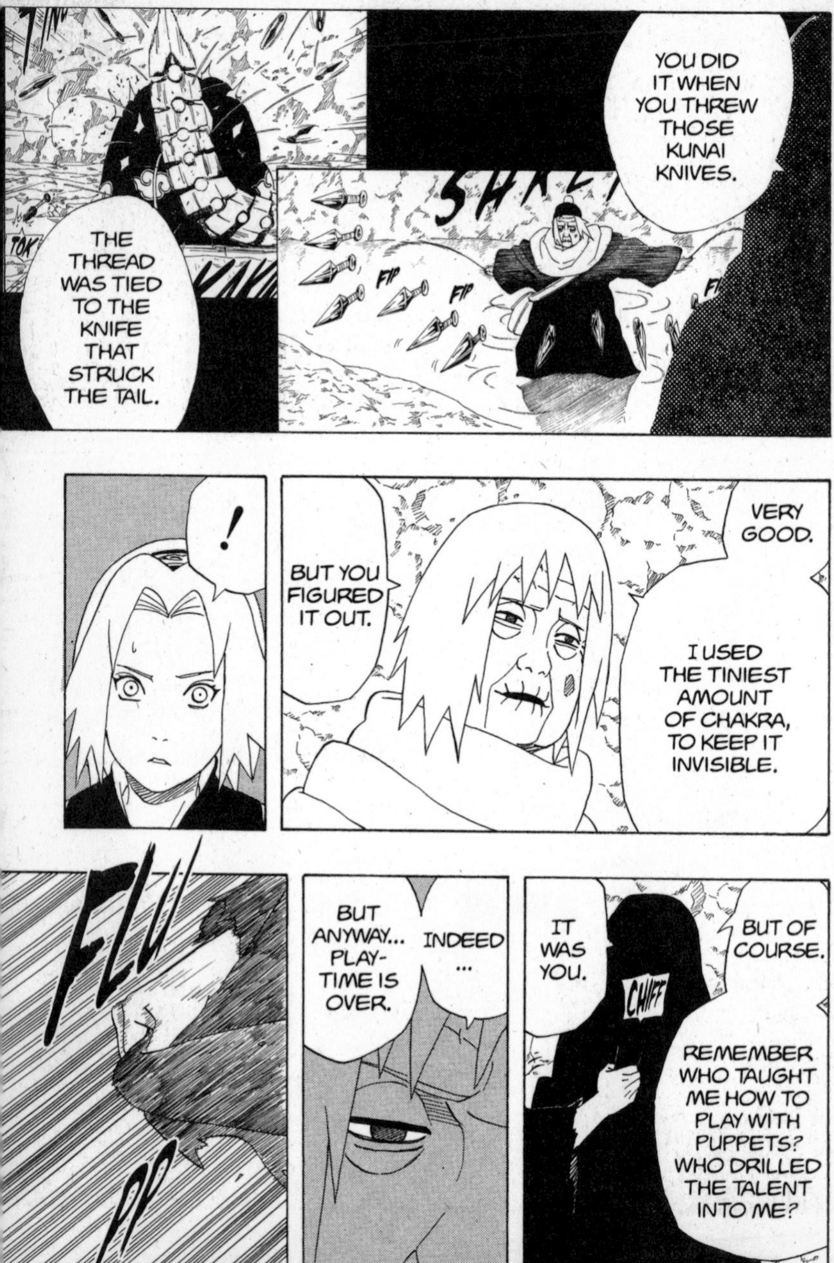
YOU DID IT WHEN YOU THREW THOSE KUNAI KNIVES.
FIP
FIP
THE THREAD WAS TIED TO THE KNIFE THAT STRUCK THE TAIL.
TOK
VERY GOOD.
I USED THE TINIEST AMOUNT OF CHAKRA, TO KEEP IT INVISIBLE.
BUT YOU FIGURED IT OUT.
!
BUT OF COURSE.
IT WAS YOU.
CHIFF
REMEMBER WHO TAUGHT ME HOW TO PLAY WITH PUPPETS? WHO DRILLED THE TALENT INTO ME?
INDEED...
BUT ANYWAY... PLAY-TIME IS OVER.
FLU
PP

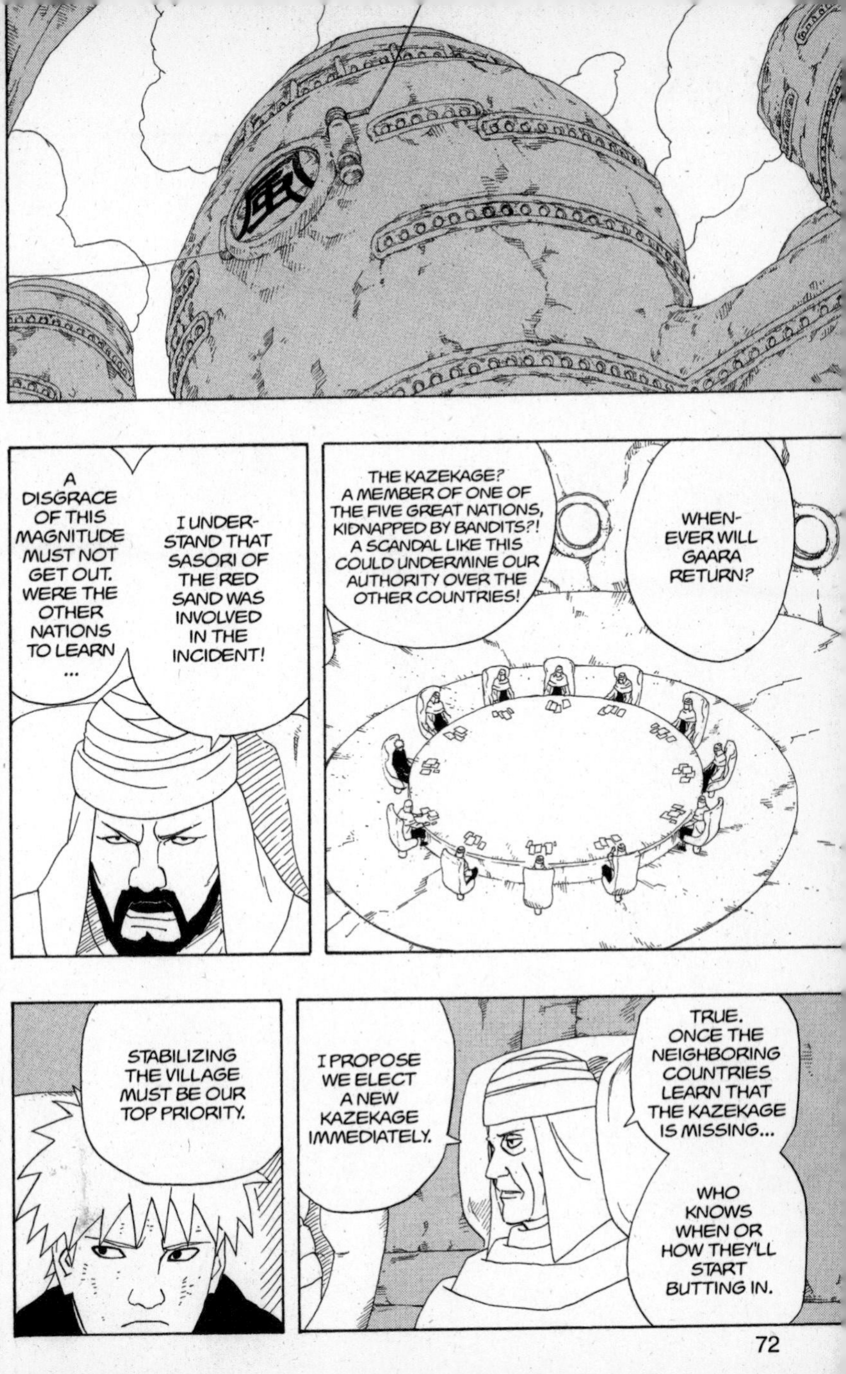

WHEN-EVER WILL GAARA RETURN?
THE KAZEKAGE? A MEMBER OF ONE OF THE FIVE GREAT NATIONS, KIDNAPPED BY BANDITS?! A SCANDAL LIKE THIS COULD UNDERMINE OUR AUTHORITY OVER THE OTHER COUNTRIES!
I UNDER-STAND THAT SASORI OF THE RED SAND WAS INVOLVED IN THE INCIDENT!
A DISGRACE OF THIS MAGNITUDE MUST NOT GET OUT. WERE THE OTHER NATIONS TO LEARN ...
TRUE. ONCE THE NEIGHBORING COUNTRIES LEARN THAT THE KAZEKAGE IS MISSING...
WHO KNOWS WHEN OR HOW THEY'LL START BUTTING IN.
I PROPOSE WE ELECT A NEW KAZEKAGE IMMEDIATELY.
STABILIZING THE VILLAGE MUST BE OUR TOP PRIORITY.

READ THIS WAY

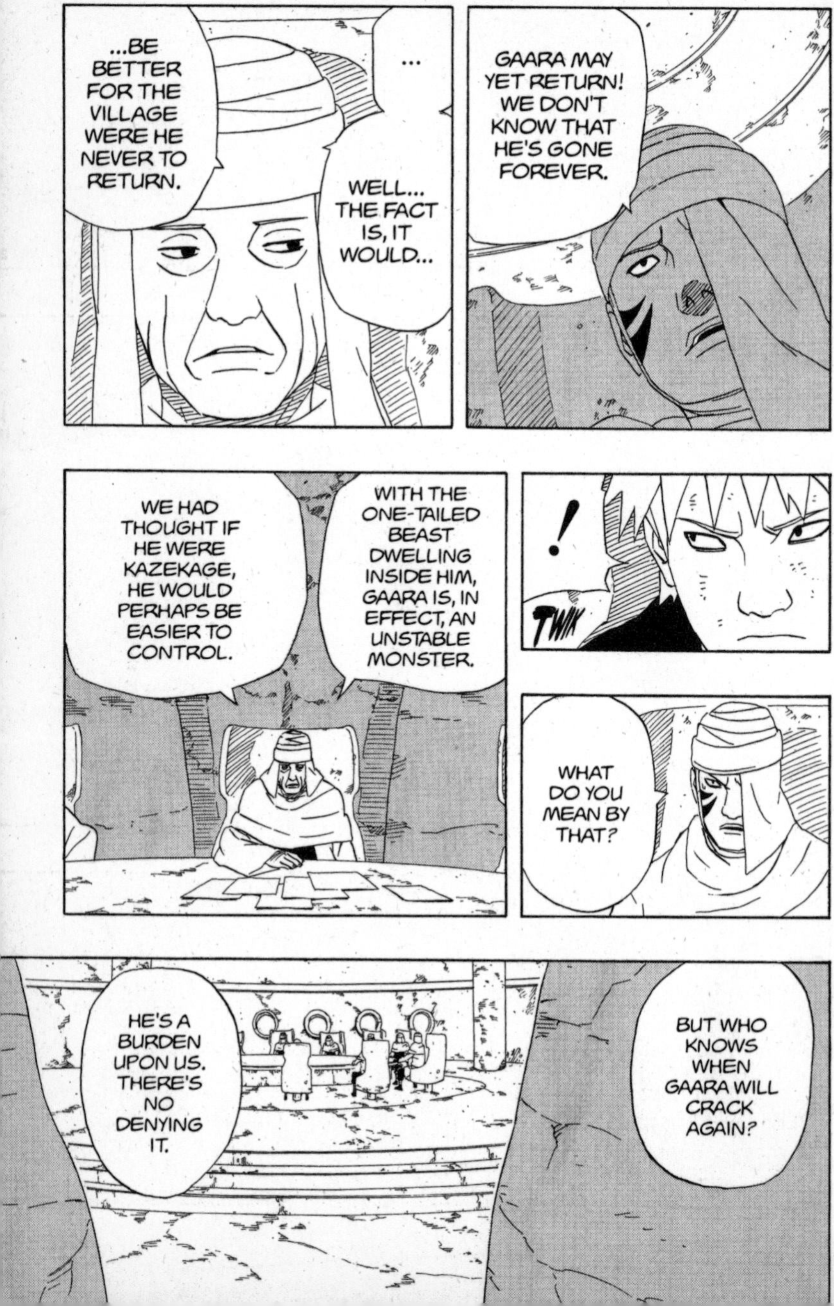
GAARA MAY YET RETURN! WE DON'T KNOW THAT HE'S GONE FOREVER.
...
WELL... THE FACT IS, IT WOULD...
...BE BETTER FOR THE VILLAGE WERE HE NEVER TO RETURN.
!
TWIK
WHAT DO YOU MEAN BY THAT?
WITH THE ONE-TAILED BEAST DWELLING INSIDE HIM, GAARA IS, IN EFFECT, AN UNSTABLE MONSTER.
WE HAD THOUGHT IF HE WERE KAZEKAGE, HE WOULD PERHAPS BE EASIER TO CONTROL.
BUT WHO KNOWS WHEN GAARA WILL CRACK AGAIN?
HE'S A BURDEN UPON US. THERE'S NO DENYING IT.

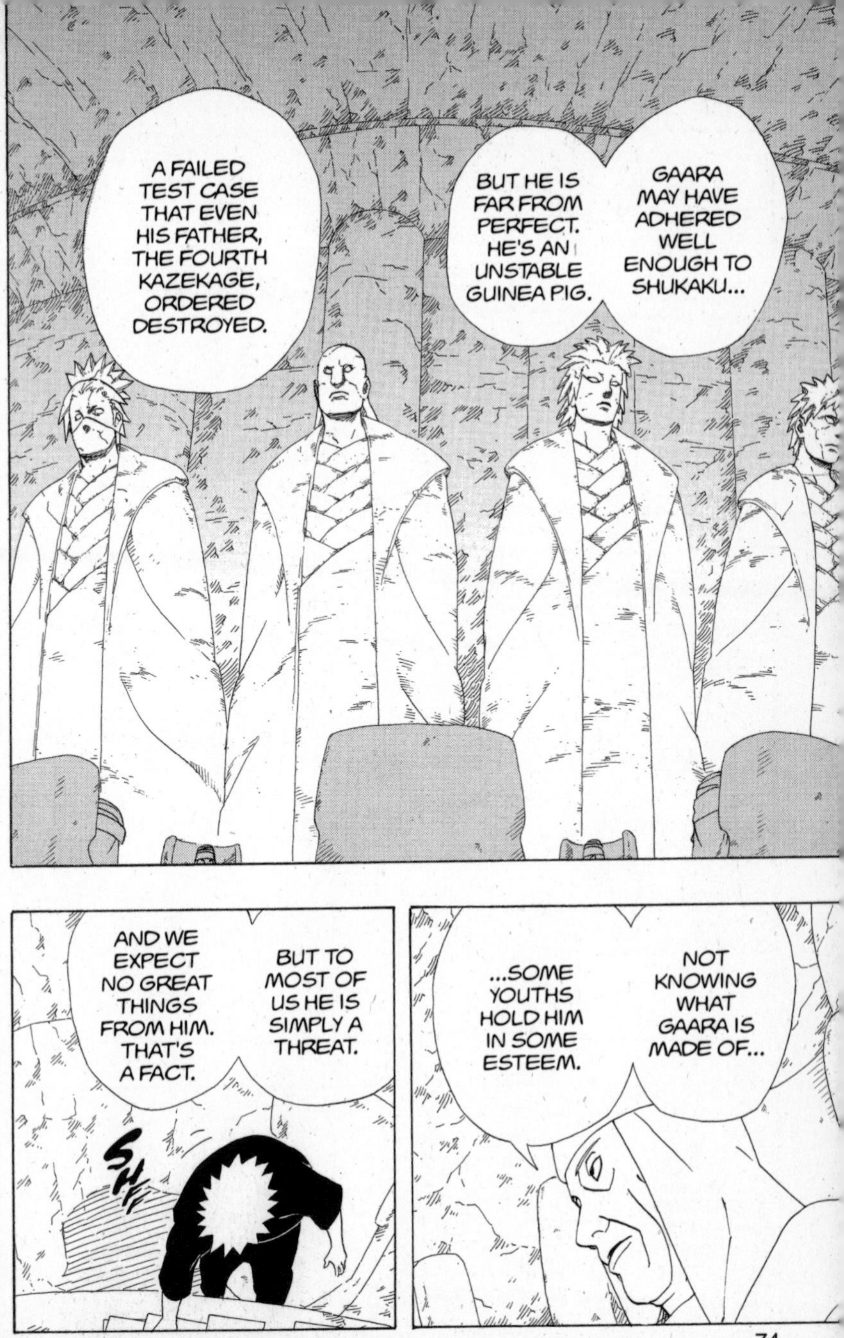
GAARA MAY HAVE ADHERED WELL ENOUGH TO SHUKAKU...
BUT HE IS FAR FROM PERFECT. HE'S AN UNSTABLE GUINEA PIG.
A FAILED TEST CASE THAT EVEN HIS FATHER, THE FOURTH KAZEKAGE, ORDERED DESTROYED.
NOT KNOWING WHAT GAARA IS MADE OF...
...SOME YOUTHS HOLD HIM IN SOME ESTEEM.
BUT TO MOST OF US HE IS SIMPLY A THREAT.
AND WE EXPECT NO GREAT THINGS FROM HIM. THAT'S A FACT.
SHFF

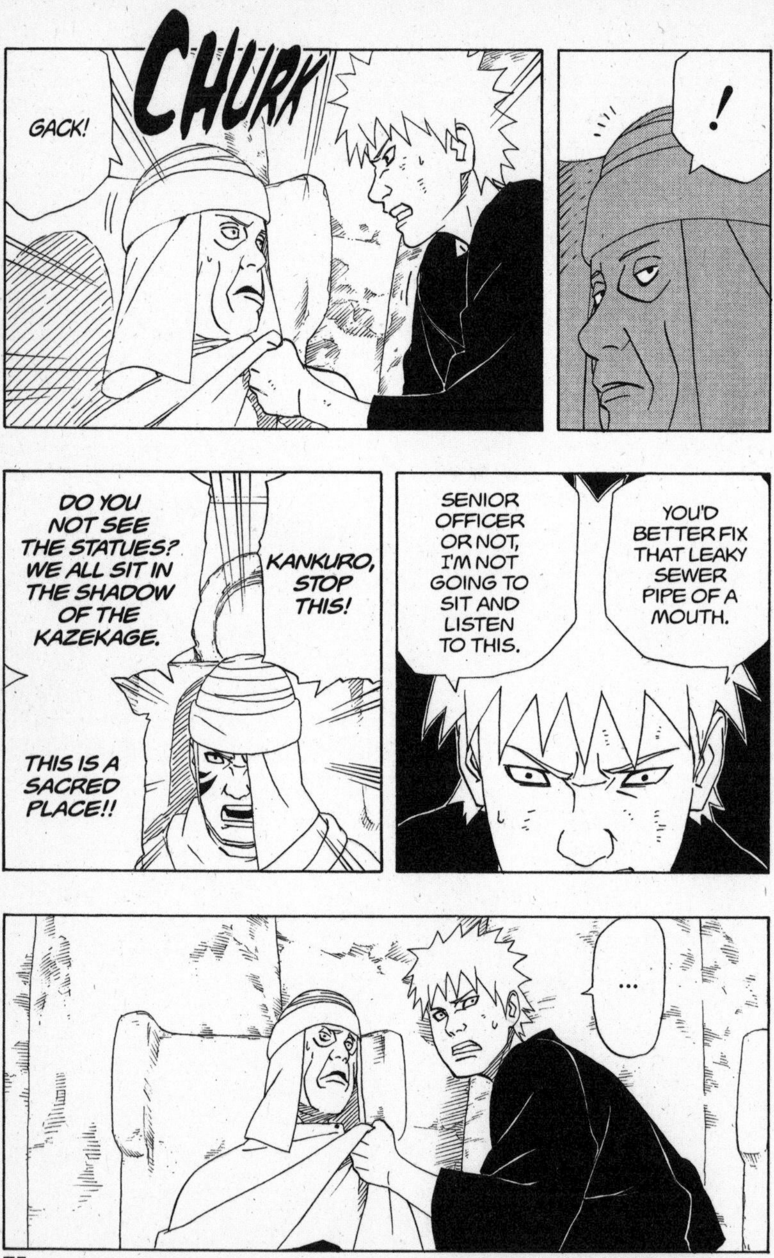
!
CHURK
GACK!
YOU'D BETTER FIX THAT LEAKY SEWER PIPE OF A MOUTH.
SENIOR OFFICER OR NOT, I'M NOT GOING TO SIT AND LISTEN TO THIS.
KANKURO, STOP THIS!
DO YOU NOT SEE THE STATUES? WE ALL SIT IN THE SHADOW OF THE KAZEKAGE.
THIS IS A SACRED PLACE!!
...

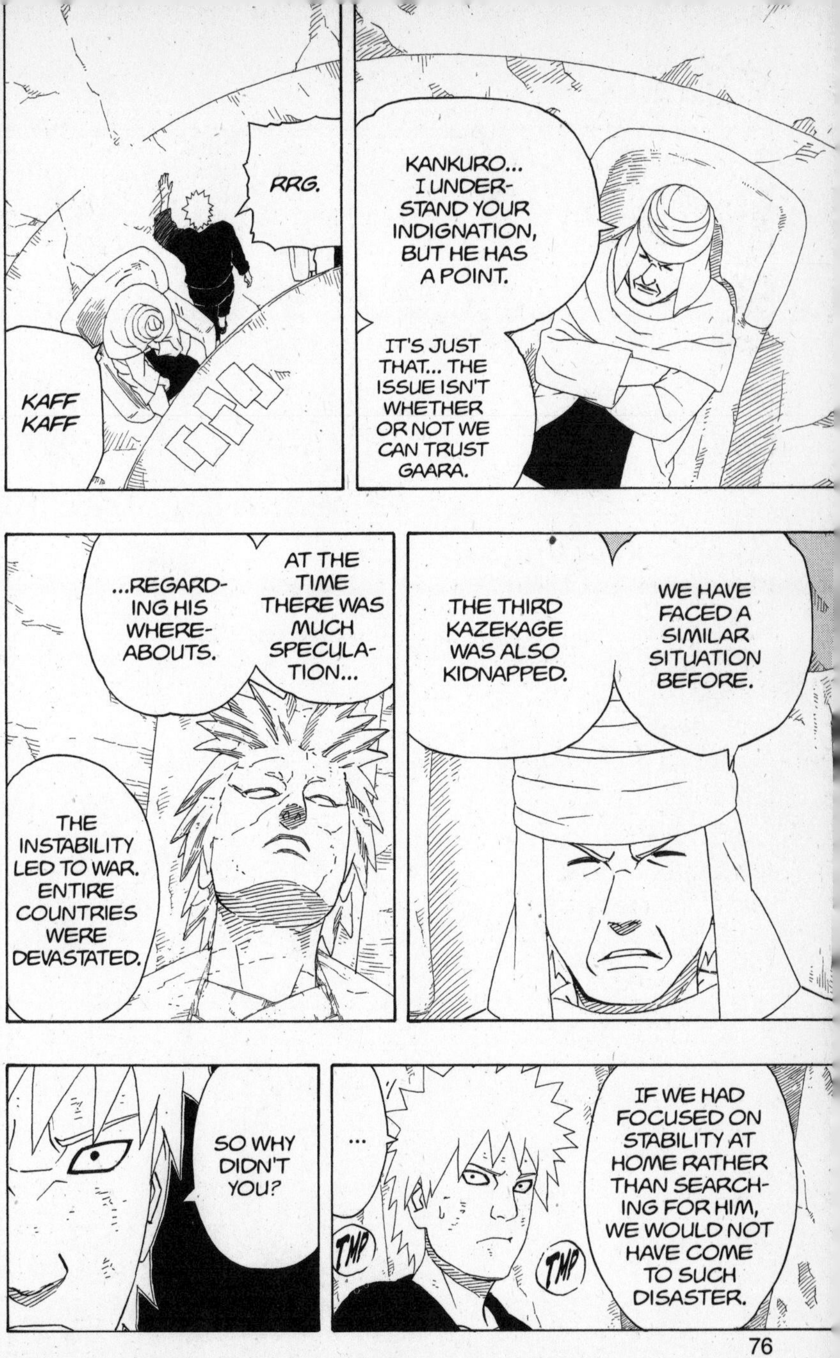
KANKURO... I UNDERSTAND YOUR INDIGNATION, BUT HE HAS A POINT.
IT'S JUST THAT... THE ISSUE ISN'T WHETHER OR NOT WE CAN TRUST GAARA.
RRG.
KAFF KAFF
WE HAVE FACED A SIMILAR SITUATION BEFORE.
THE THIRD KAZEKAGE WAS ALSO KIDNAPPED.
AT THE TIME THERE WAS MUCH SPECULATION...
...REGARDING HIS WHEREABOUTS.
THE INSTABILITY LED TO WAR. ENTIRE COUNTRIES WERE DEVASTATED.
IF WE HAD FOCUSED ON STABILITY AT HOME RATHER THAN SEARCHING FOR HIM, WE WOULD NOT HAVE COME TO SUCH DISASTER.
TMP
TMP
...
SO WHY DIDN'T YOU?

READ THIS WAY

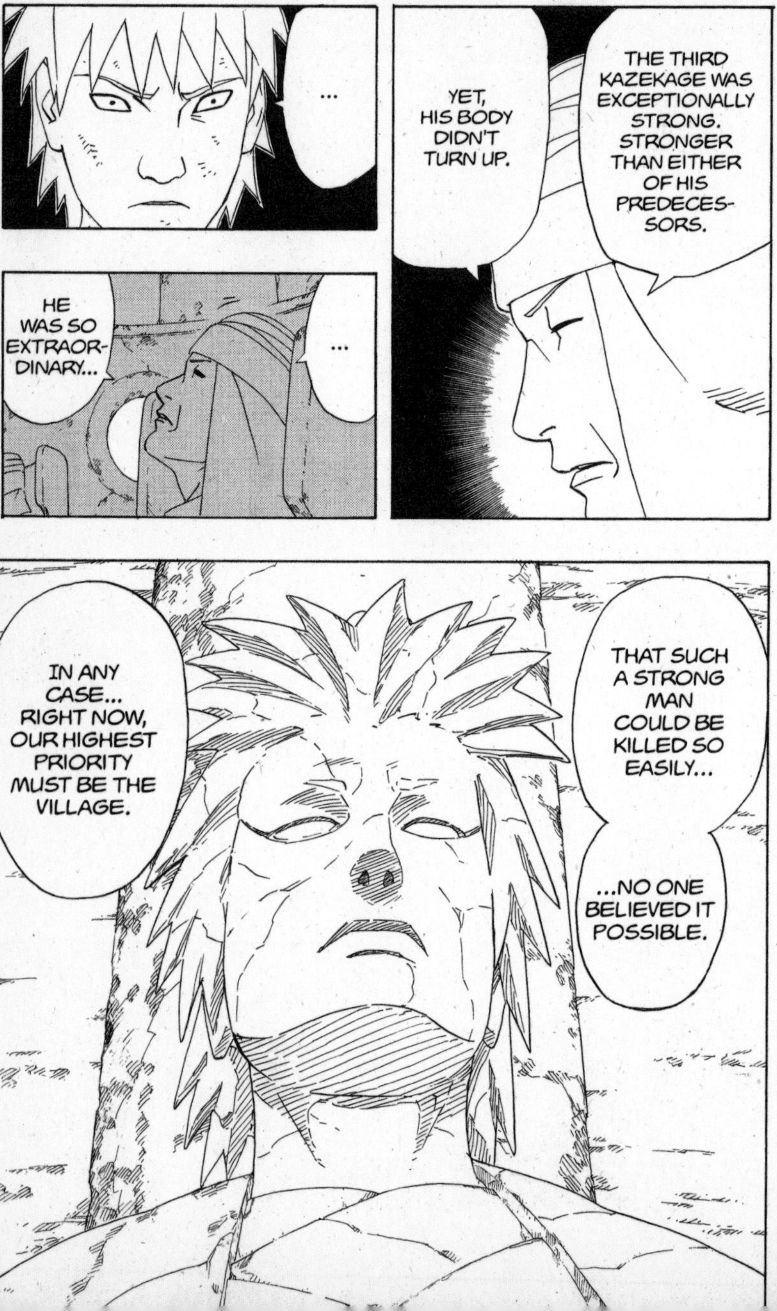
THE THIRD KAZEKAGE WAS EXCEPTIONALLY STRONG. STRONGER THAN EITHER OF HIS PREDECESSORS.
YET, HIS BODY DIDN'T TURN UP.
...
...
HE WAS SO EXTRAORDINARY...
THAT SUCH A STRONG MAN COULD BE KILLED SO EASILY...
...NO ONE BELIEVED IT POSSIBLE.
IN ANY CASE... RIGHT NOW, OUR HIGHEST PRIORITY MUST BE THE VILLAGE.

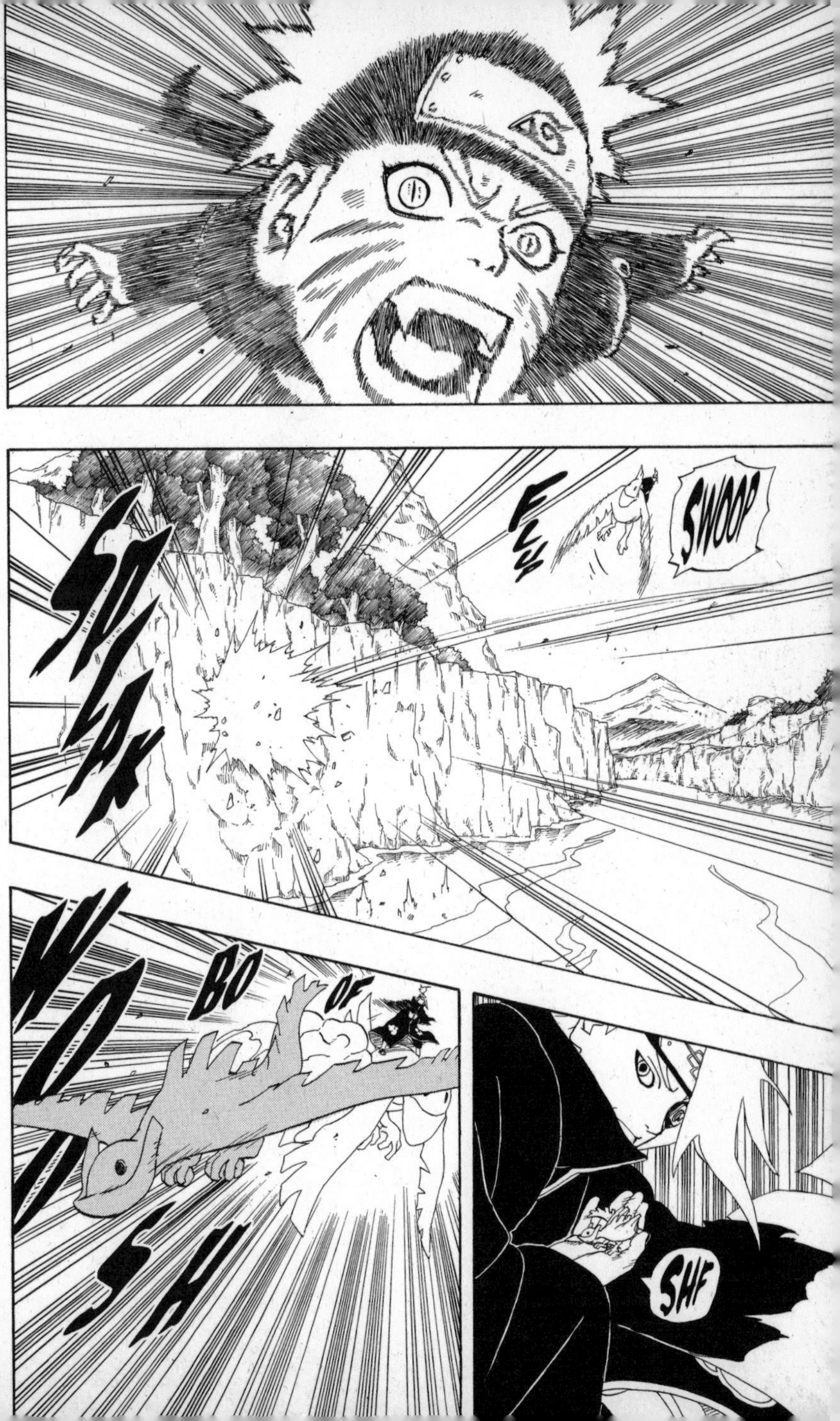
SWOOP
FLAP
SPLAK
SHF
BOOF
WHOOSH

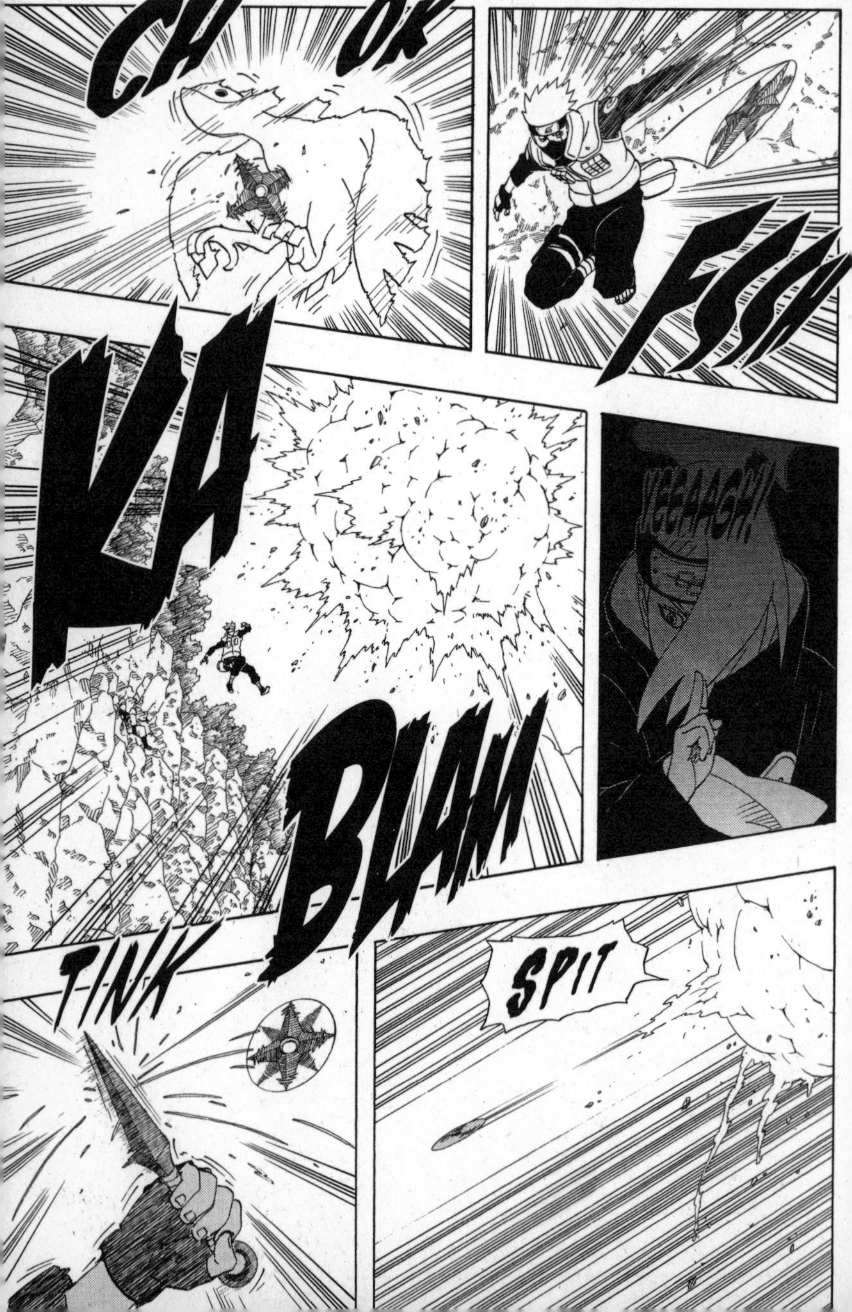
FSH
CH OK
KA BLAM
SPIT
TINK

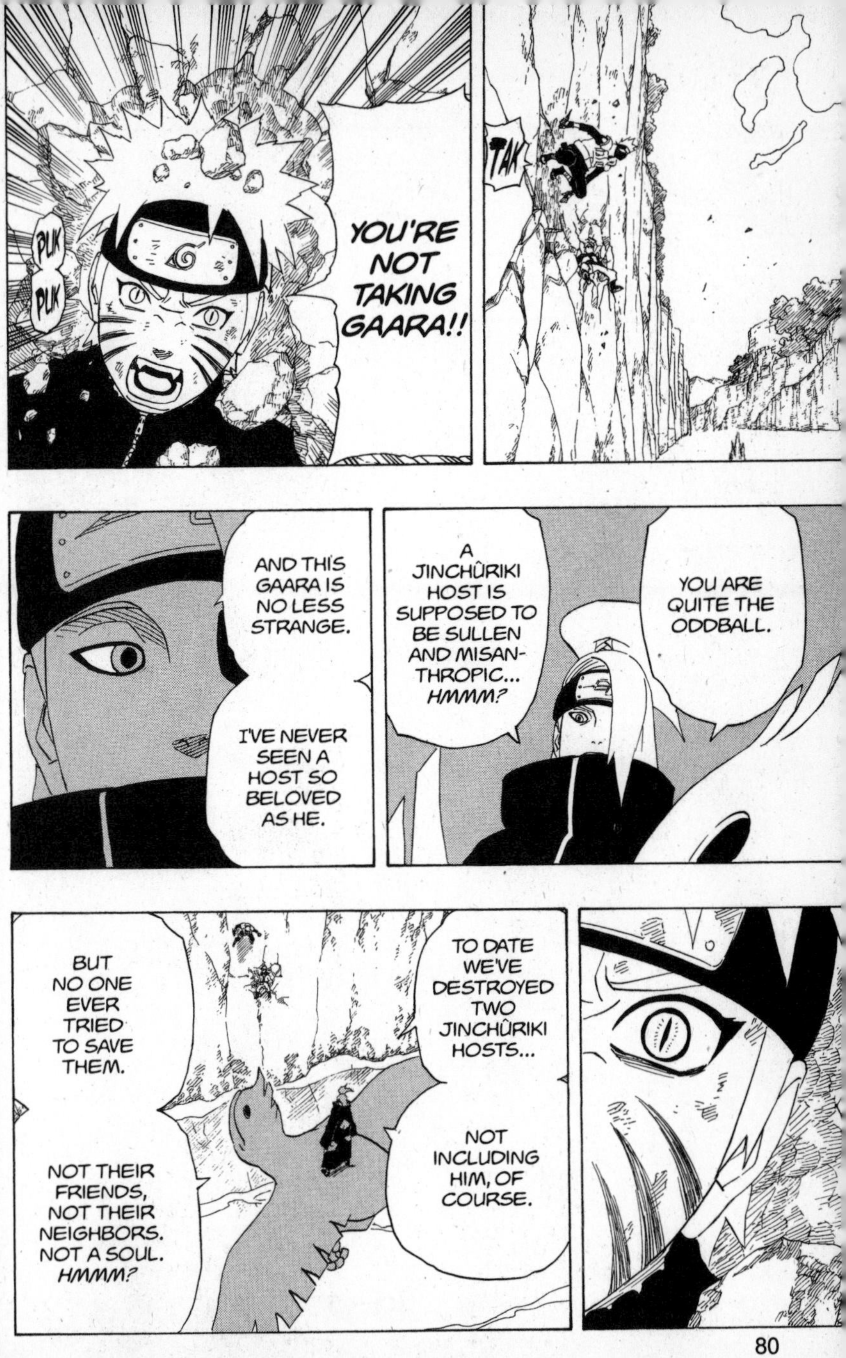
TAK
PUK
PUK
YOU'RE NOT TAKING GAARA!!
YOU ARE QUITE THE ODDBALL.
A JINCHÛRIKI HOST IS SUPPOSED TO BE SULLEN AND MISANTHROPIC... *HMMM?*
AND THIS GAARA IS NO LESS STRANGE.
I'VE NEVER SEEN A HOST SO BELOVED AS HE.
TO DATE WE'VE DESTROYED TWO JINCHÛRIKI HOSTS...
NOT INCLUDING HIM, OF COURSE.
BUT NO ONE EVER TRIED TO SAVE THEM.
NOT THEIR FRIENDS, NOT THEIR NEIGHBORS. NOT A SOUL. *HMMM?*

READ THIS WAY

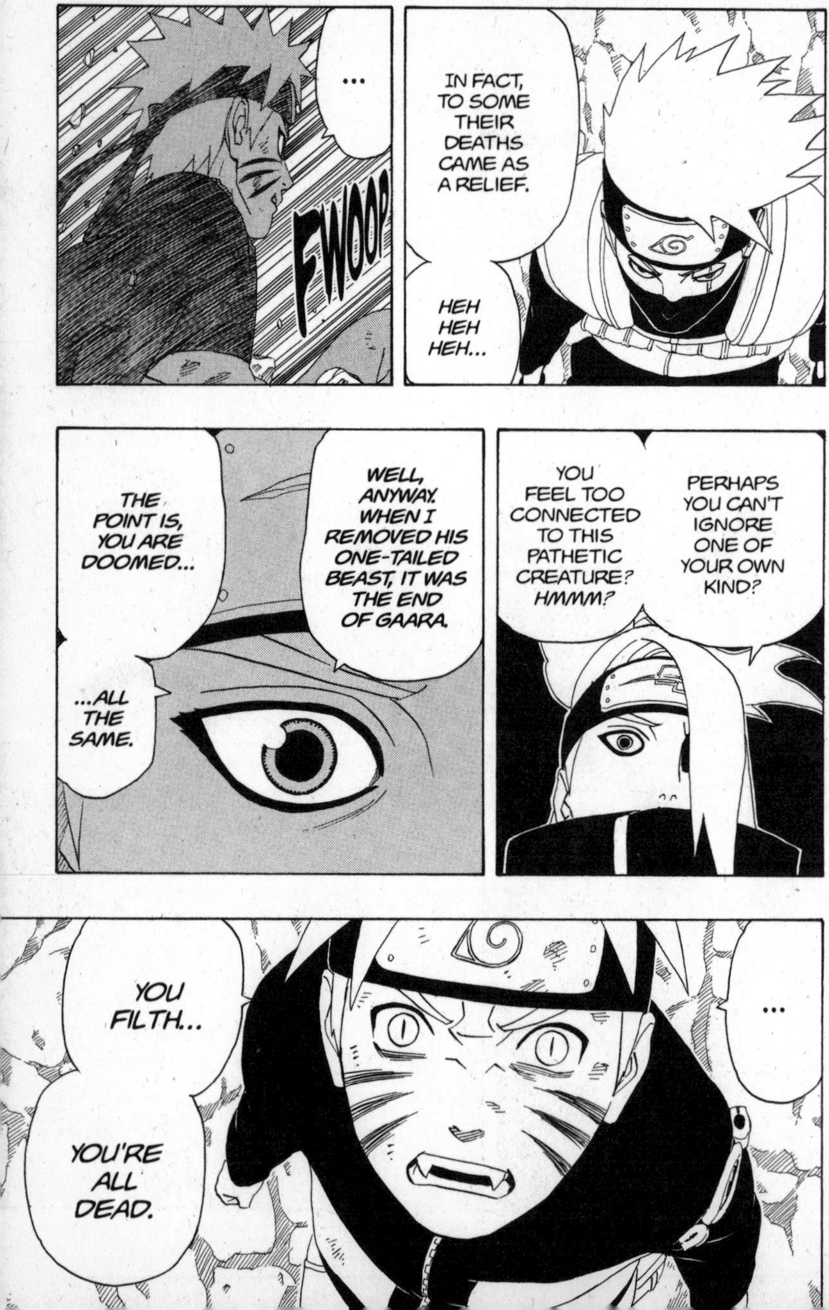

IN FACT, TO SOME THEIR DEATHS CAME AS A RELIEF.
HEH HEH HEH...
...
FWOOP
PERHAPS YOU CAN'T IGNORE ONE OF YOUR OWN KIND?
YOU FEEL TOO CONNECTED TO THIS PATHETIC CREATURE? HMMM?
WELL, ANYWAY. WHEN I REMOVED HIS ONE-TAILED BEAST, IT WAS THE END OF GAARA.
THE POINT IS, YOU ARE DOOMED...
...ALL THE SAME.
...
YOU FILTH...
YOU'RE ALL DEAD.

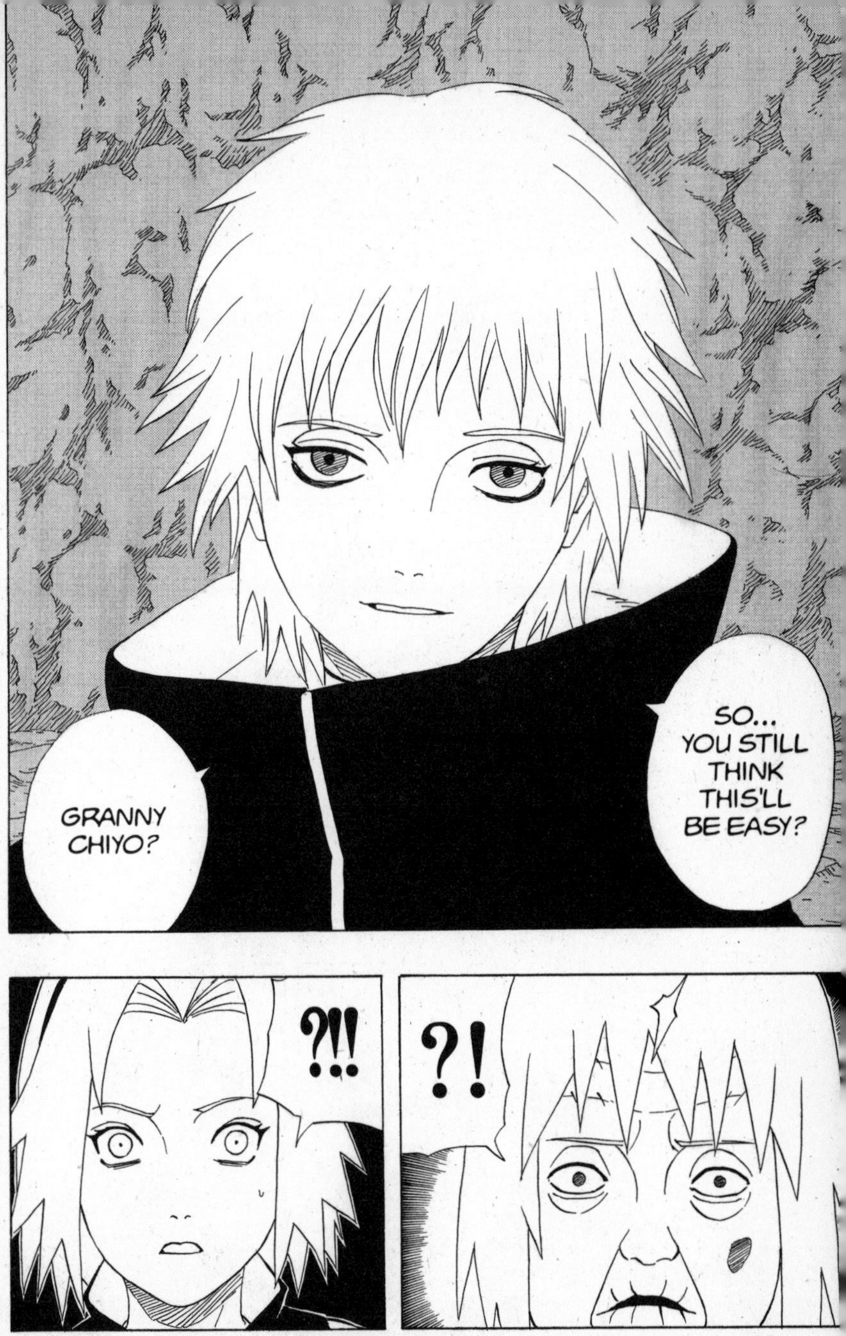
SO... YOU STILL THINK THIS'LL BE EASY?
GRANNY CHIYO?
?!
?!!

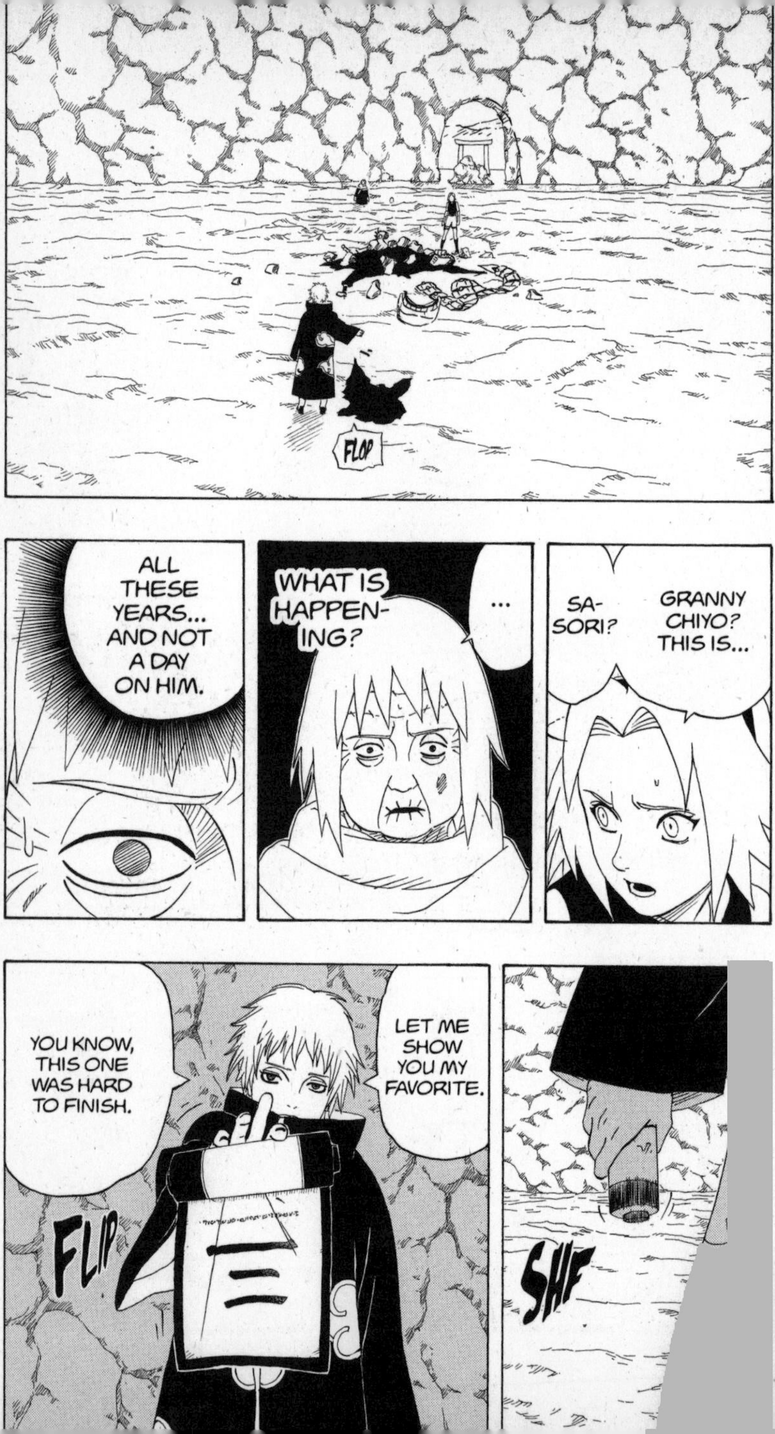
FLOP
GRANNY CHIYO? THIS IS...
SA-SORI?
...
WHAT IS HAPPEN-ING?
ALL THESE YEARS... AND NOT A DAY ON HIM.
SHF
LET ME SHOW YOU MY FAVORITE.
YOU KNOW, THIS ONE WAS HARD TO FINISH.
FLIP

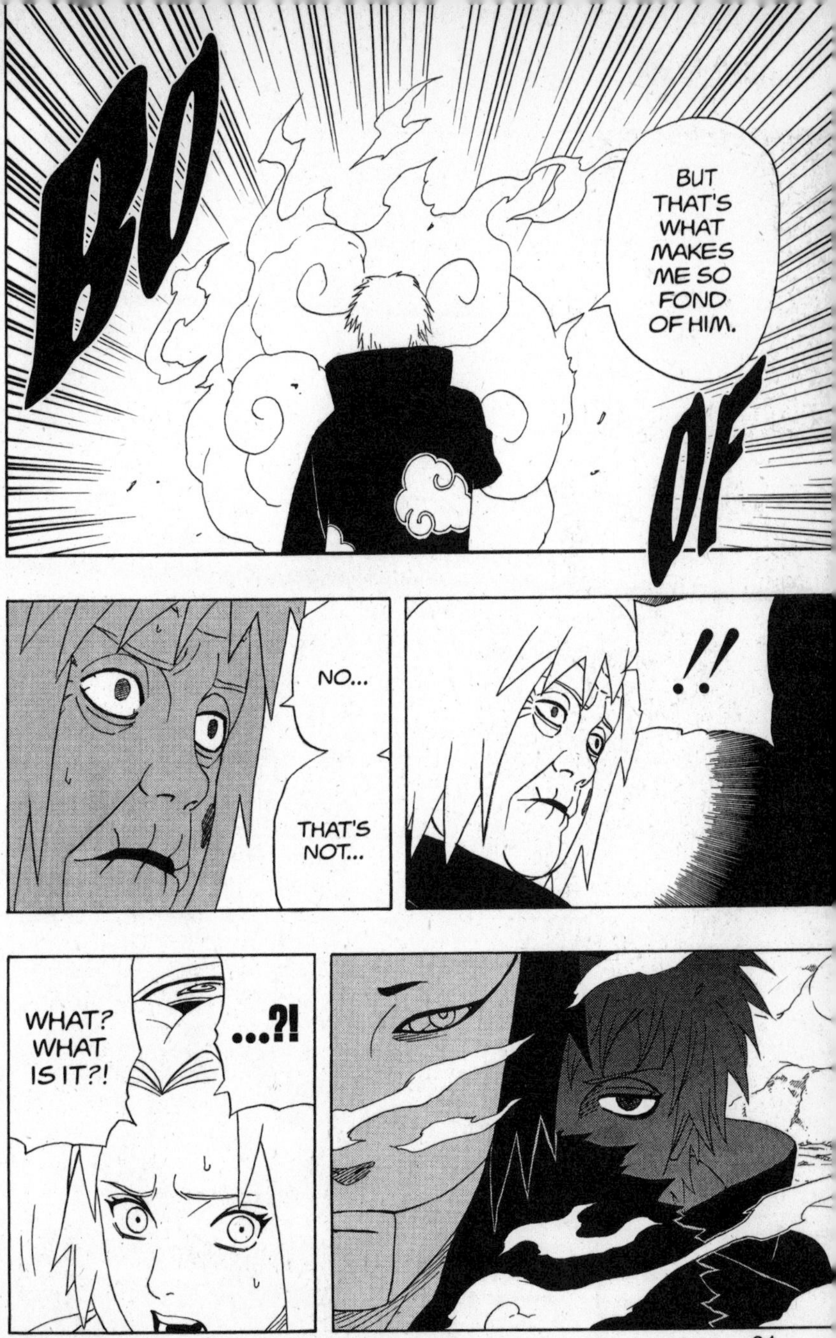
BUT THAT'S WHAT MAKES ME SO FOND OF HIM.
BO
OF
!!
NO...
THAT'S NOT...
...?!
WHAT? WHAT IS IT?!

READ THIS WAY

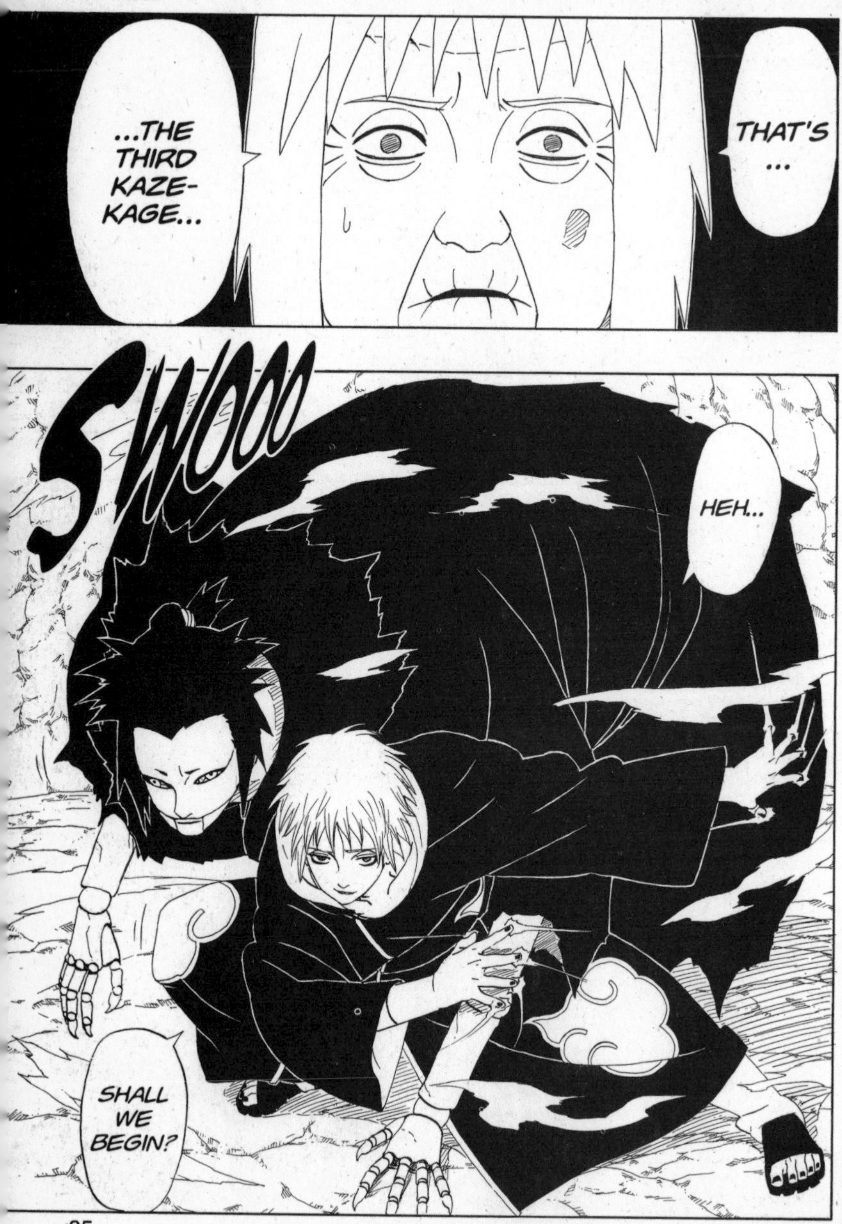
THAT'S ...
...THE THIRD KAZE-KAGE...
HEH...
SWOOO
SHALL WE BEGIN?

NARUTO

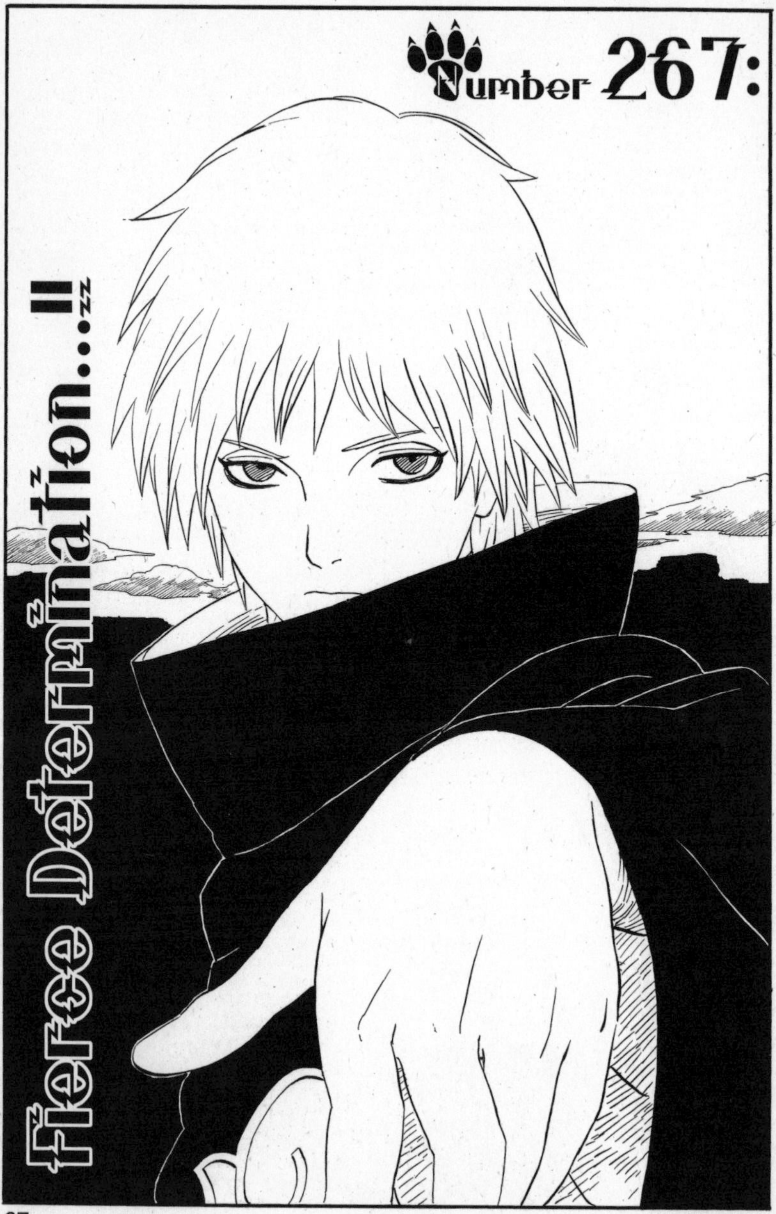
Number 267:
Fierce Determination...!!

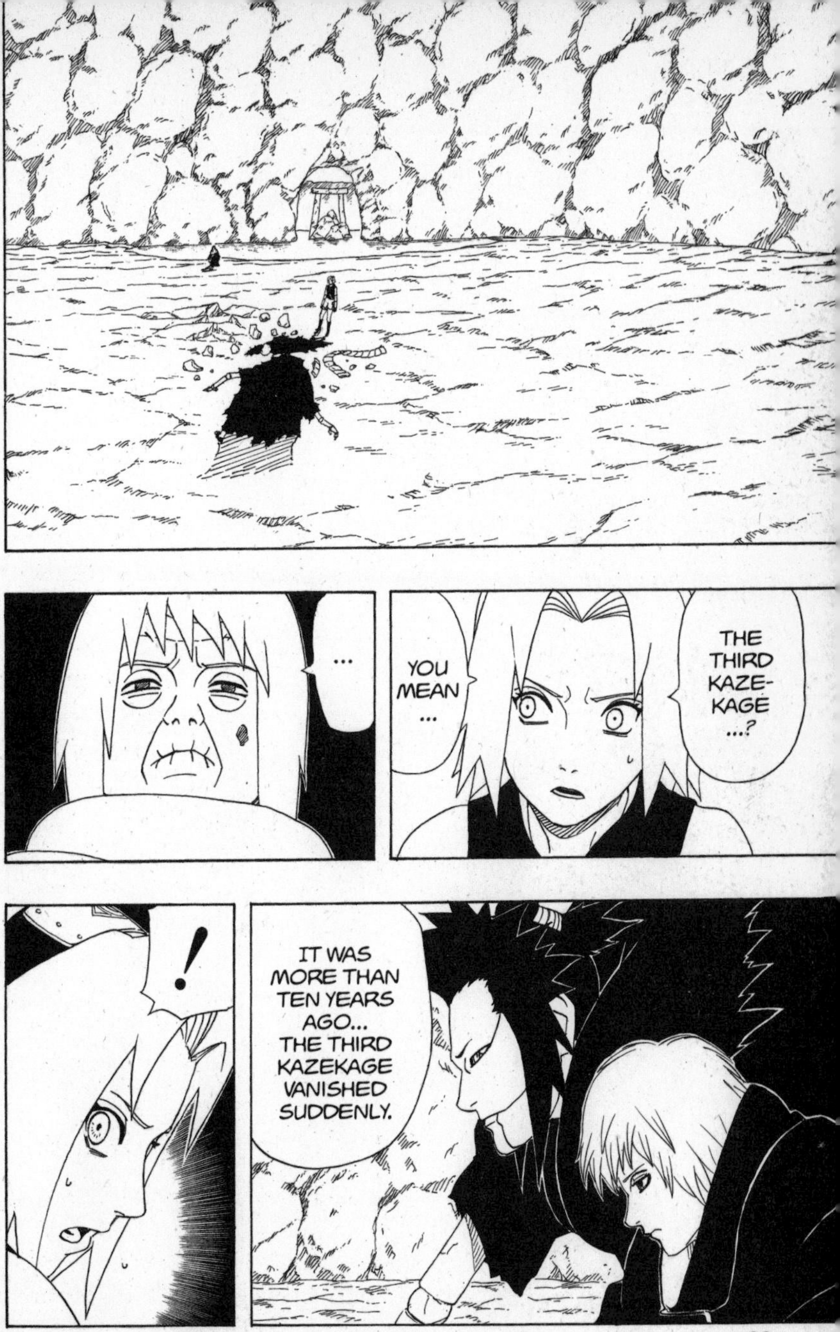
THE THIRD KAZE-KAGE ...?
YOU MEAN ...
...
IT WAS MORE THAN TEN YEARS AGO... THE THIRD KAZEKAGE VANISHED SUDDENLY.
!

READ THIS WAY

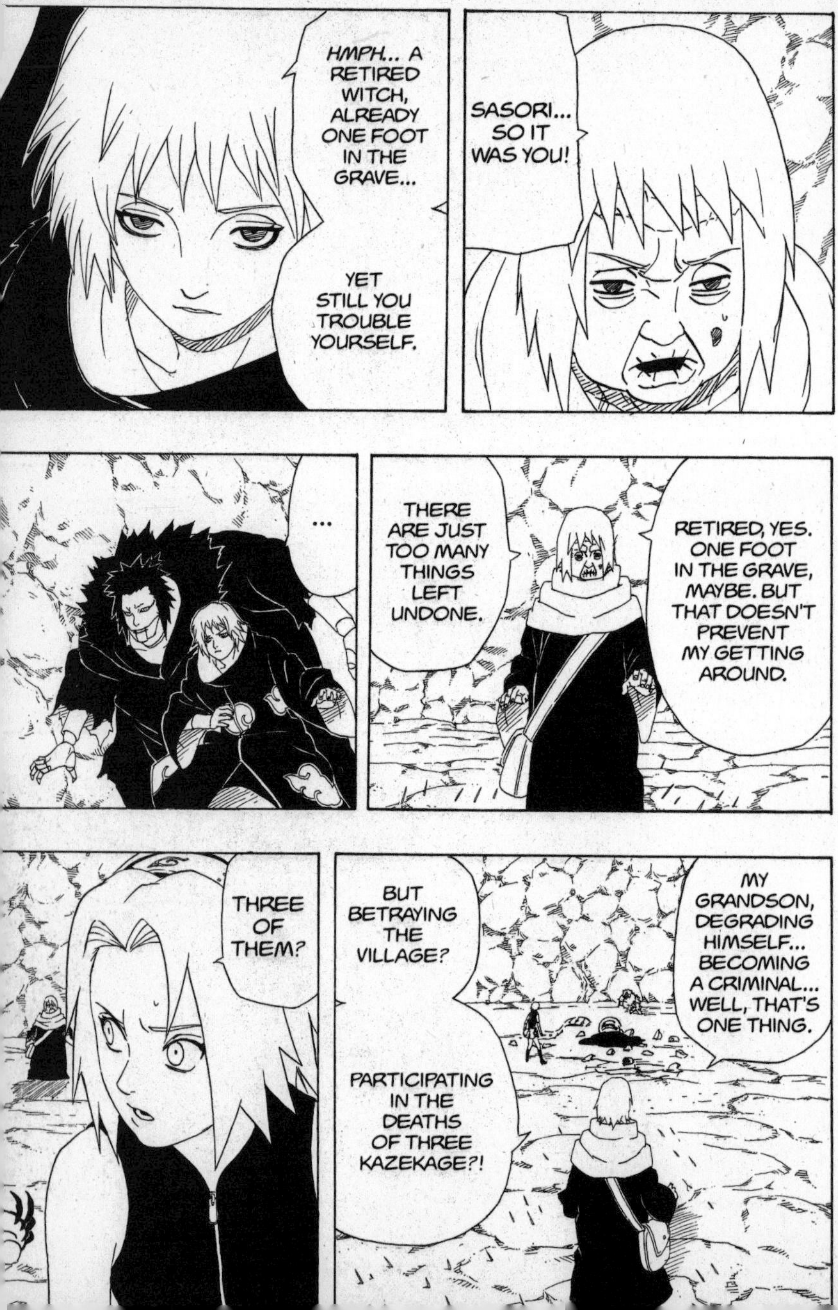
SASORI... SO IT WAS YOU!
HMPH... A RETIRED WITCH, ALREADY ONE FOOT IN THE GRAVE...
YET STILL YOU TROUBLE YOURSELF.
RETIRED, YES. ONE FOOT IN THE GRAVE, MAYBE. BUT THAT DOESN'T PREVENT MY GETTING AROUND.
THERE ARE JUST TOO MANY THINGS LEFT UNDONE.
...
MY GRANDSON, DEGRADING HIMSELF... BECOMING A CRIMINAL... WELL, THAT'S ONE THING.
BUT BETRAYING THE VILLAGE?
PARTICIPATING IN THE DEATHS OF THREE KAZEKAGE?!
THREE OF THEM?

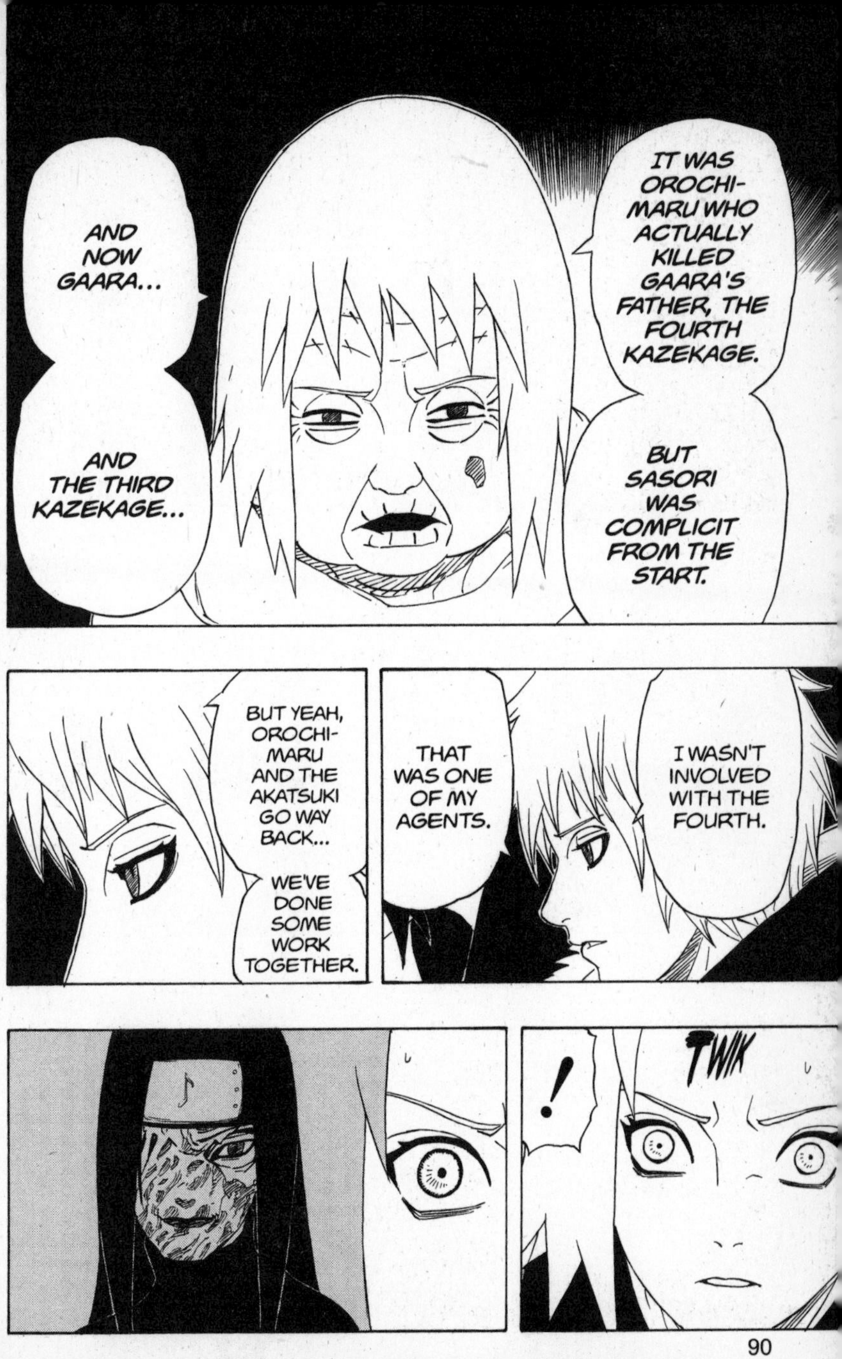
IT WAS OROCHI-MARU WHO ACTUALLY KILLED GAARA'S FATHER, THE FOURTH KAZEKAGE.
BUT SASORI WAS COMPLICIT FROM THE START.
AND NOW GAARA...
AND THE THIRD KAZEKAGE...
I WASN'T INVOLVED WITH THE FOURTH.
THAT WAS ONE OF MY AGENTS.
BUT YEAH, OROCHI-MARU AND THE AKATSUKI GO WAY BACK...
WE'VE DONE SOME WORK TOGETHER.
TWIK
!

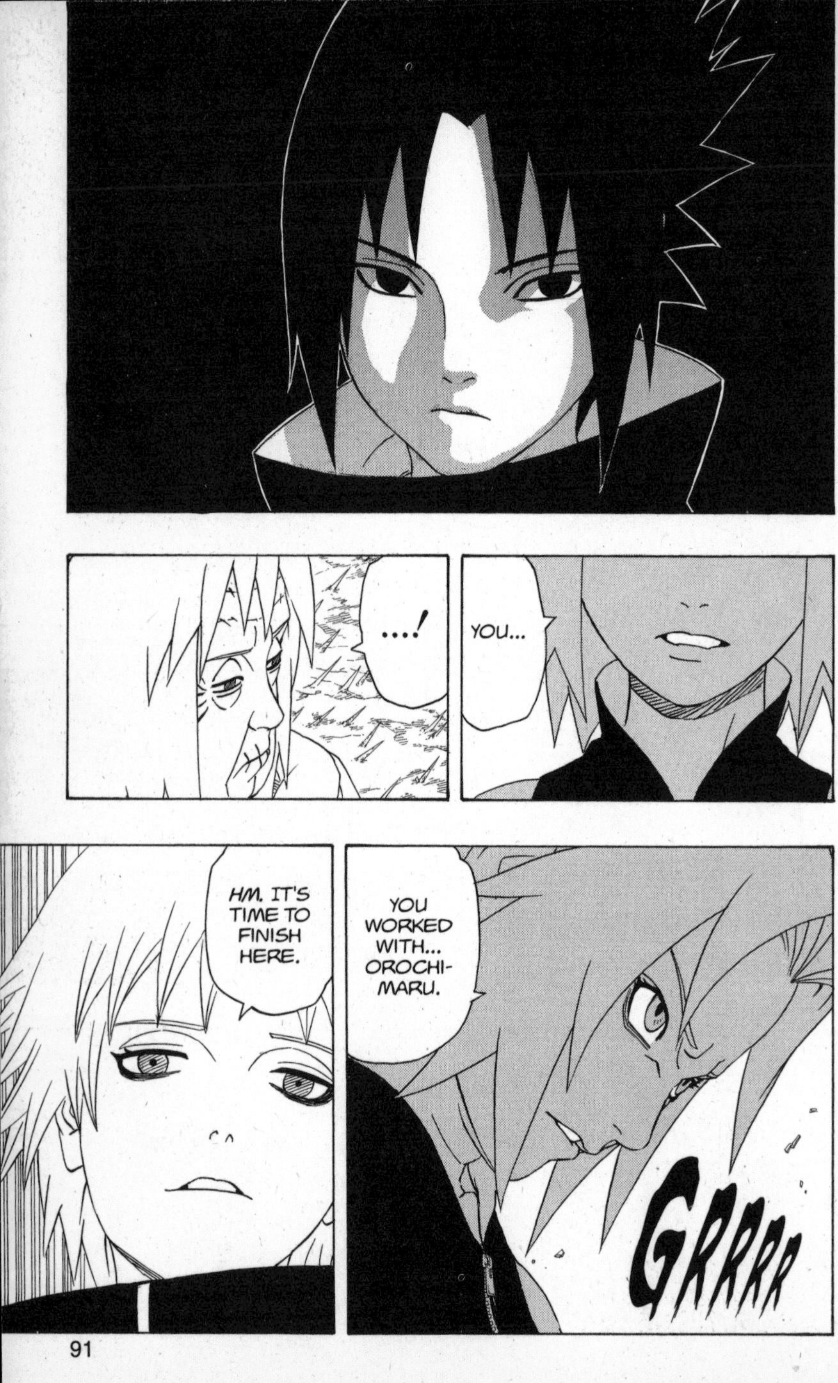
YOU...
...!
YOU WORKED WITH... OROCHI-MARU.
GRRRR
HM. IT'S TIME TO FINISH HERE.

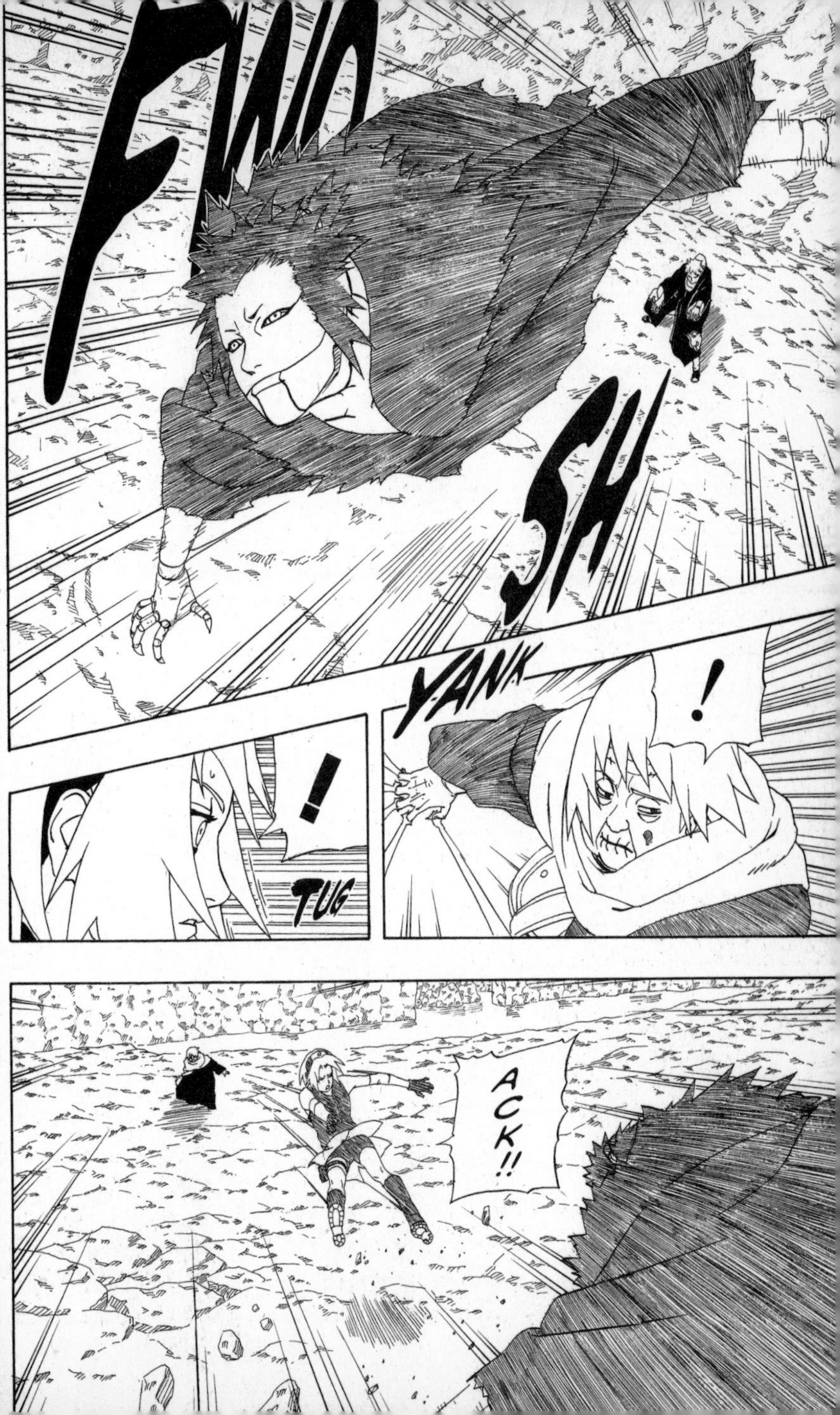
FWIP
SH
YANK
!
!
TUG
ACK!!

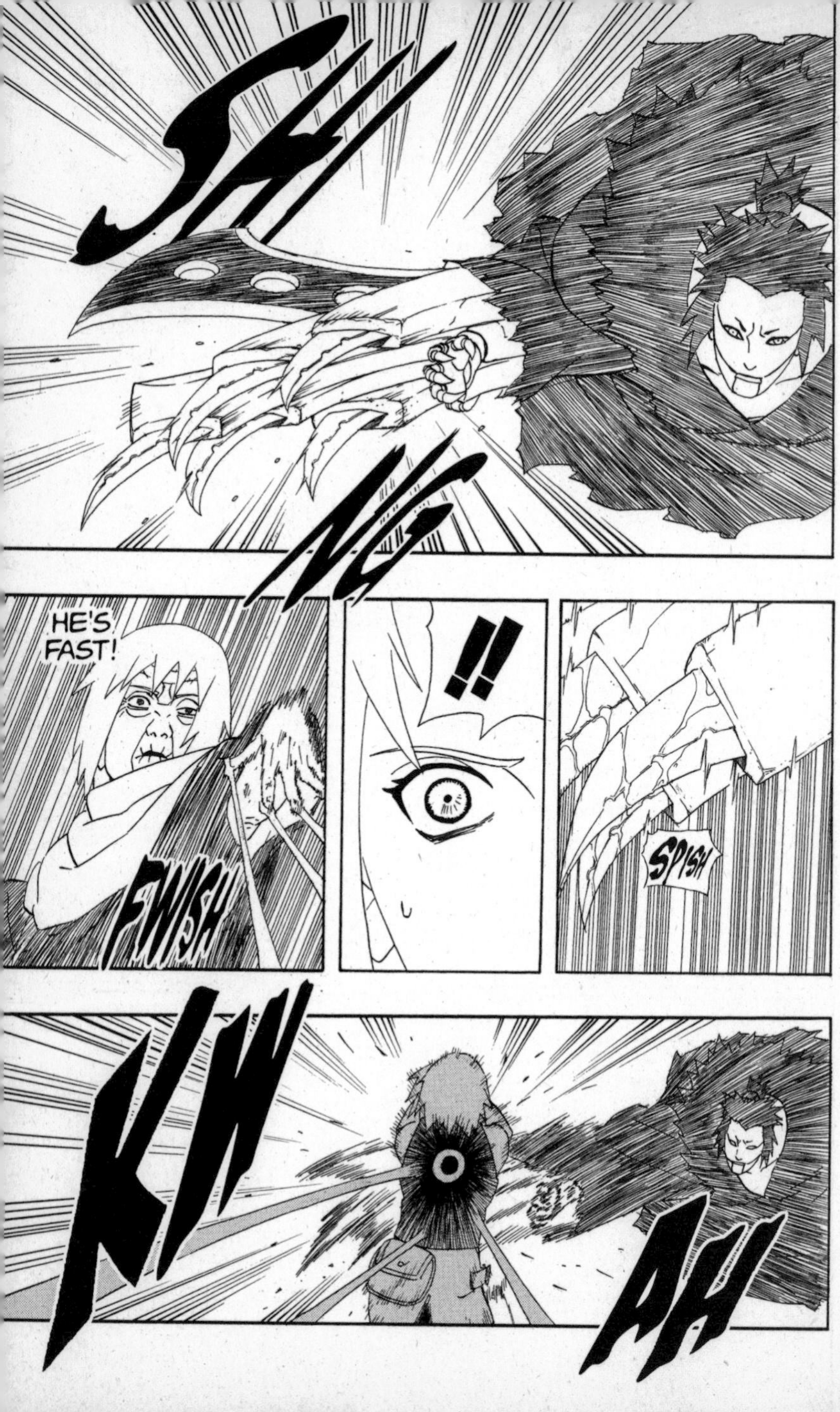
SHNG
SPISH
!!
HE'S FAST!
FWISH
KHAH

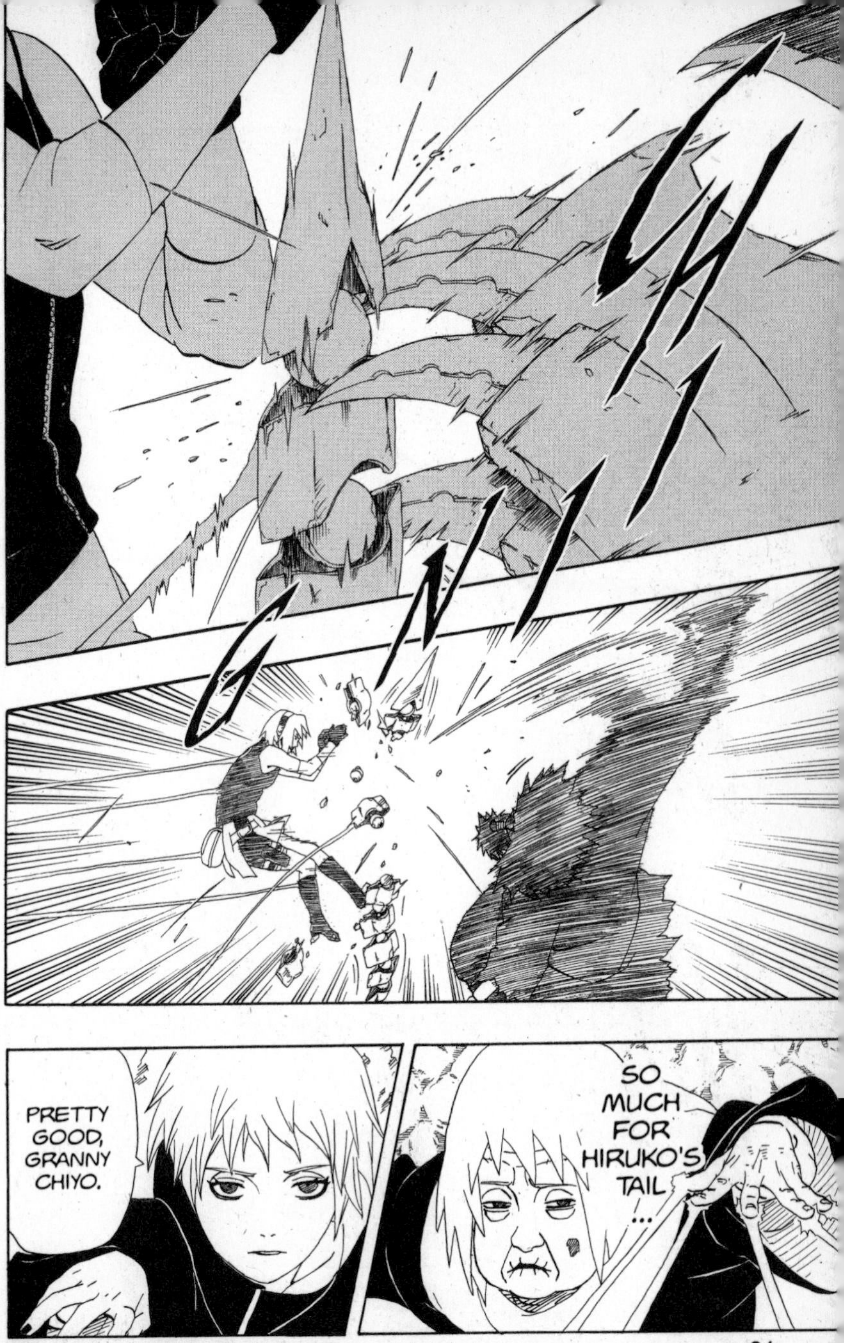
GNNN
SO MUCH FOR HIRUKO'S TAIL ...
PRETTY GOOD, GRANNY CHIYO.

READ THIS WAY

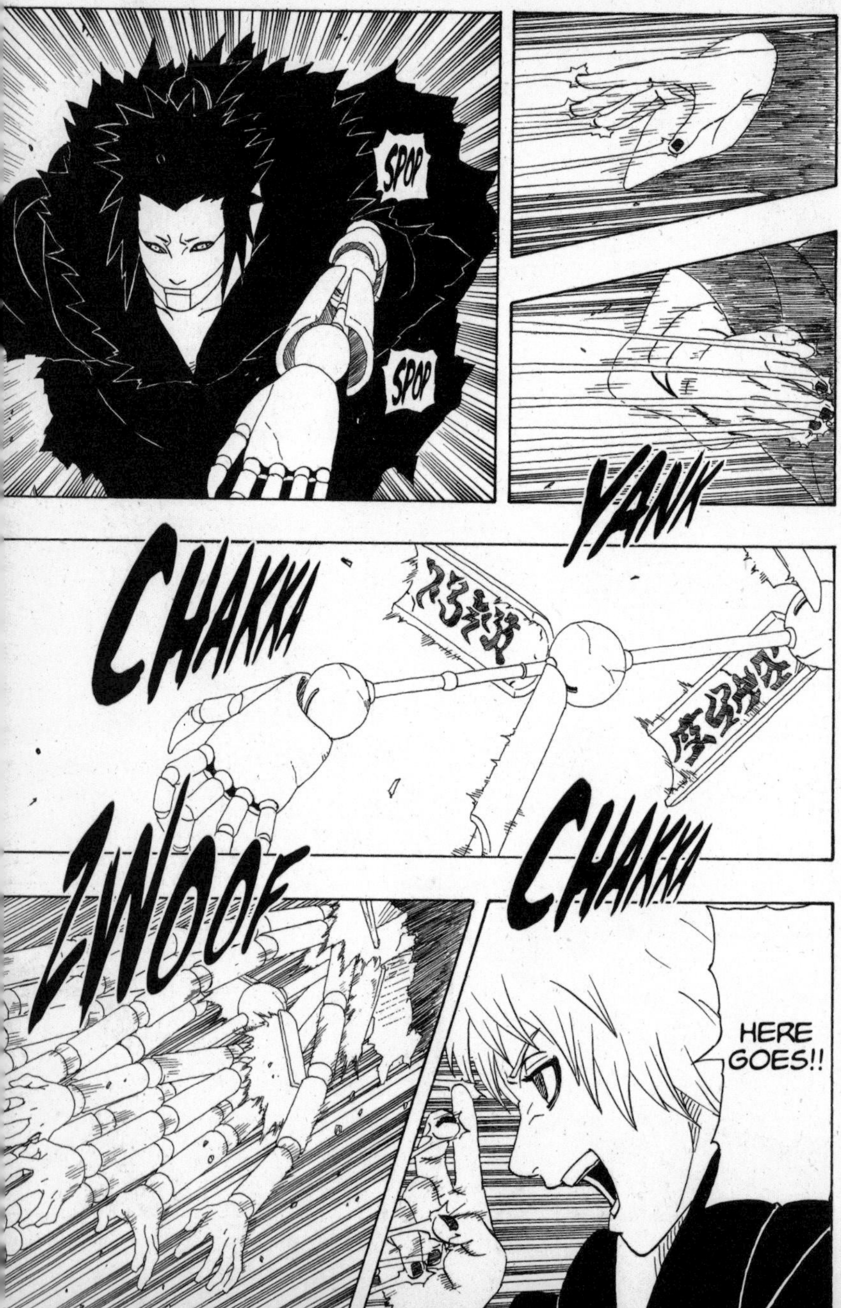
YANK
SPOP
SPOP
CHAKKA
CHAKKA
HERE GOES!!
ZWOOF

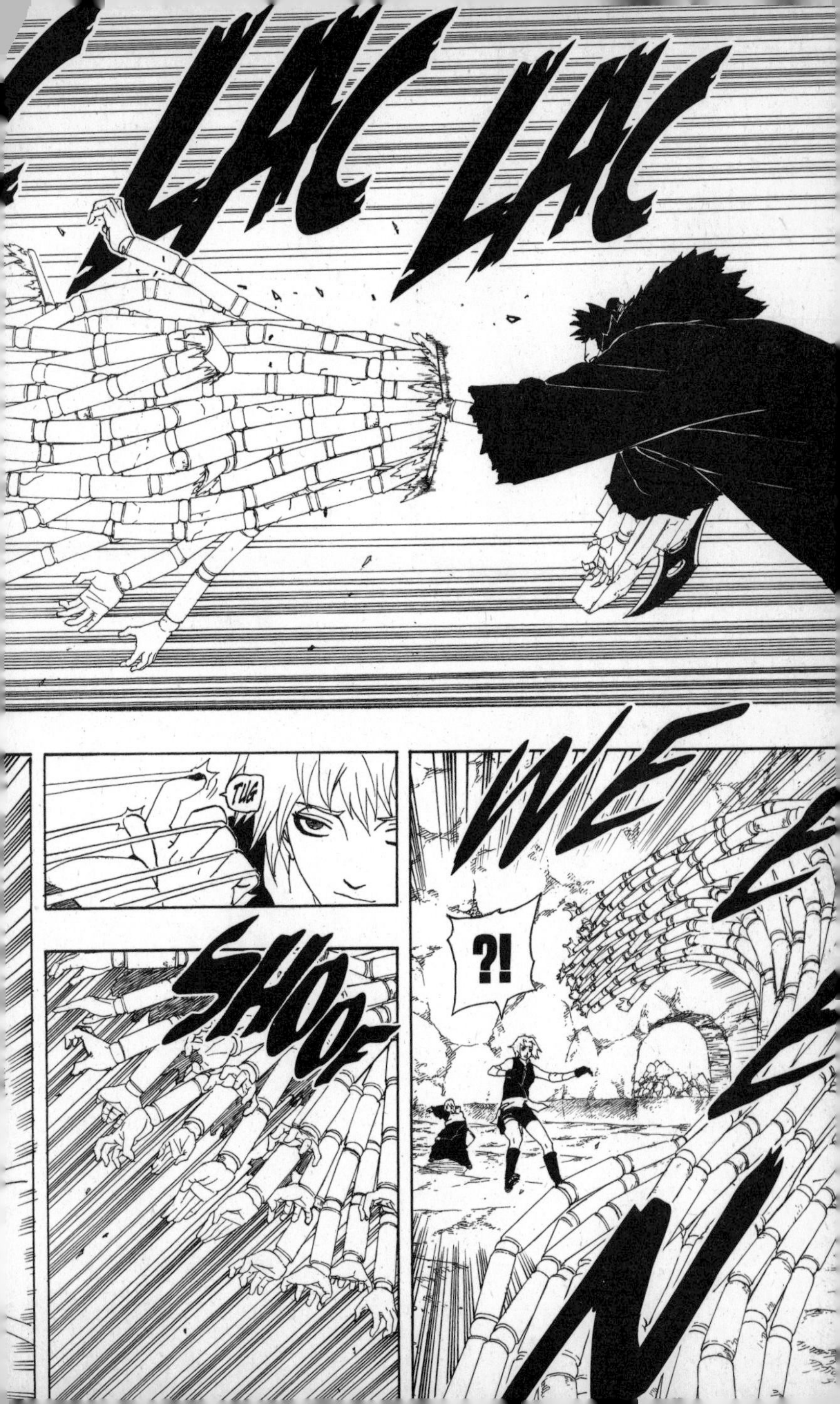
C LAC LAC
WE
?!
TUG
SHOOF

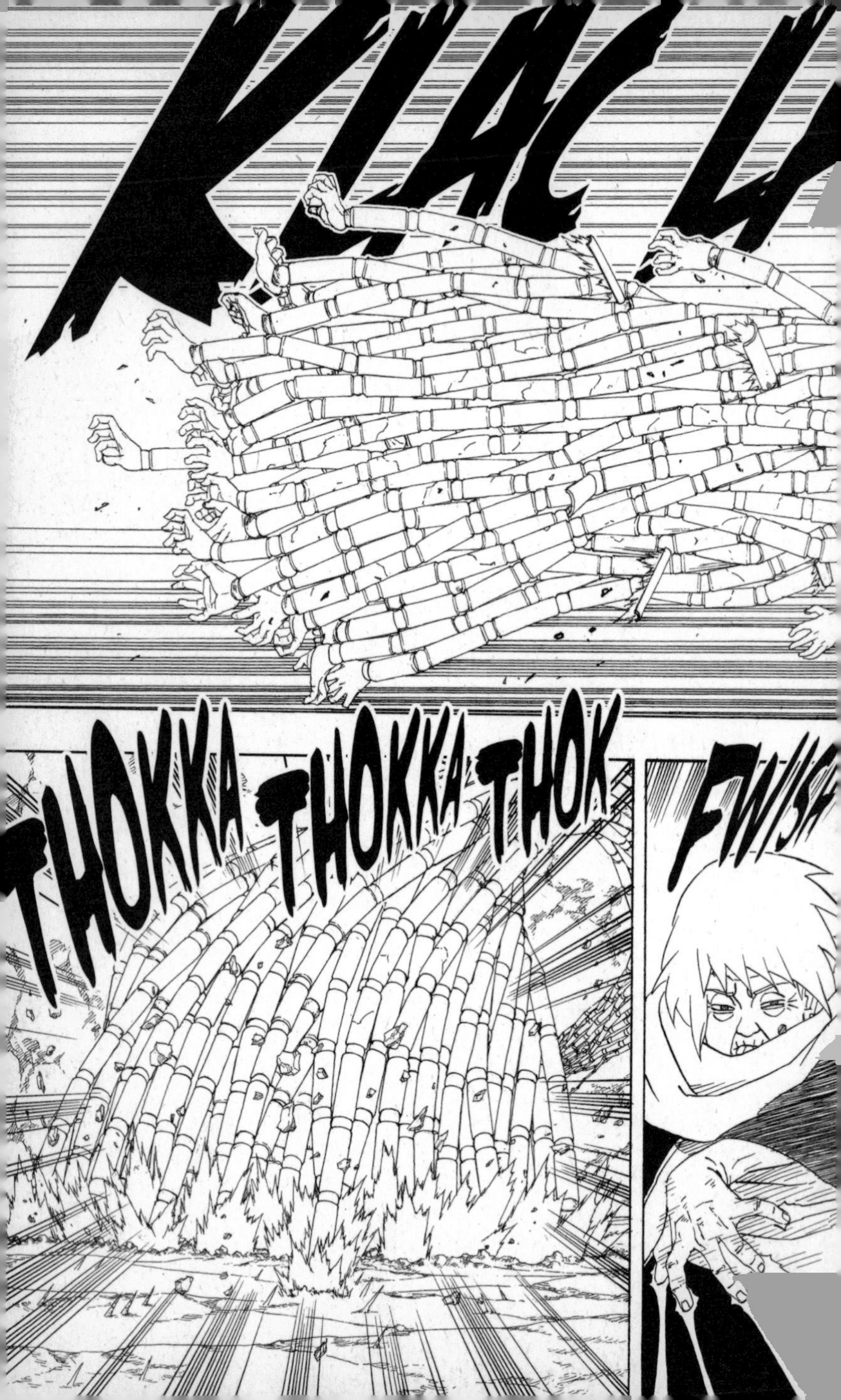
KLACK
FWISH
THOKKA THOKKA THOK

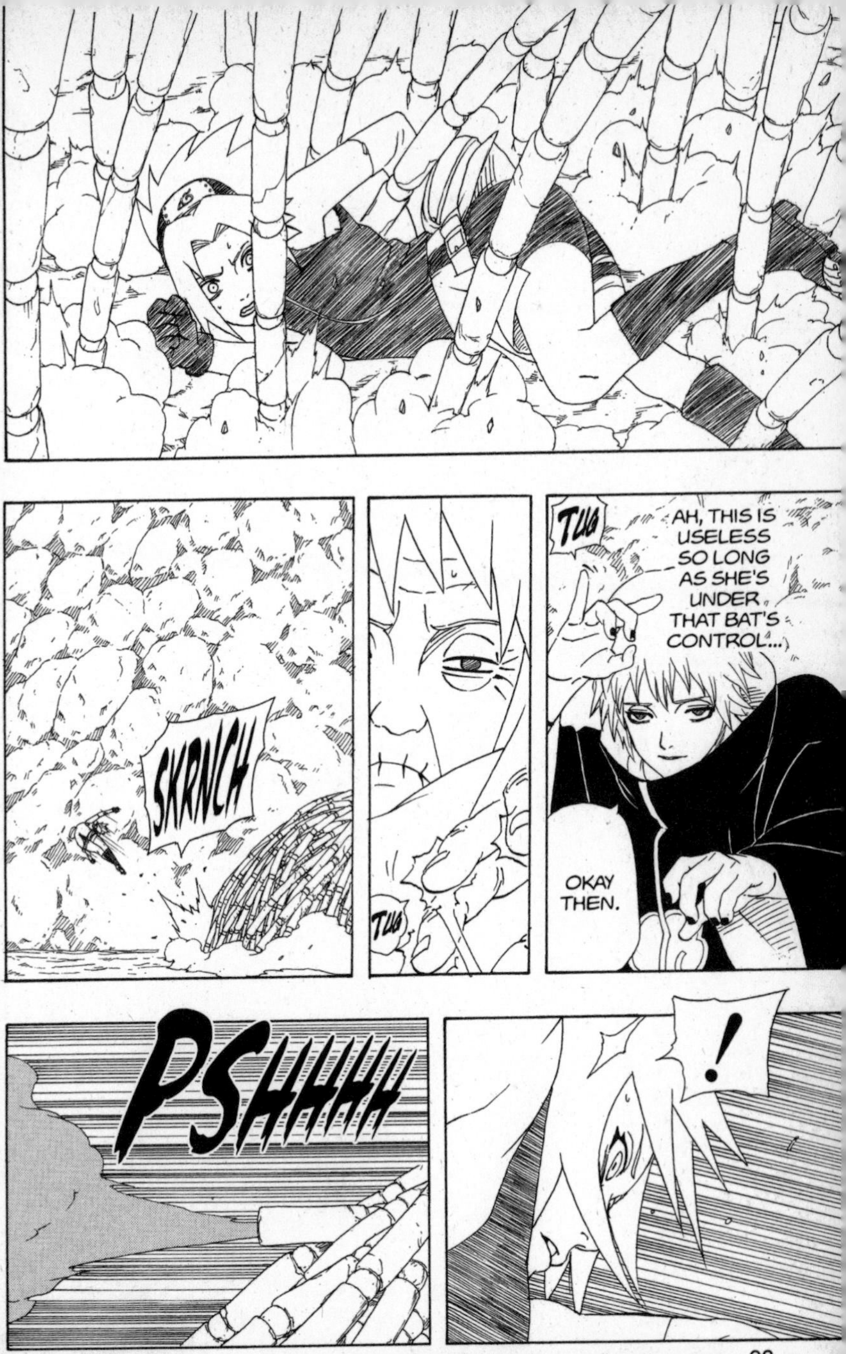
TUG
AH, THIS IS USELESS SO LONG AS SHE'S UNDER THAT BAT'S CONTROL...
OKAY THEN.
TUG
SKRNCH
!
PSHHHH

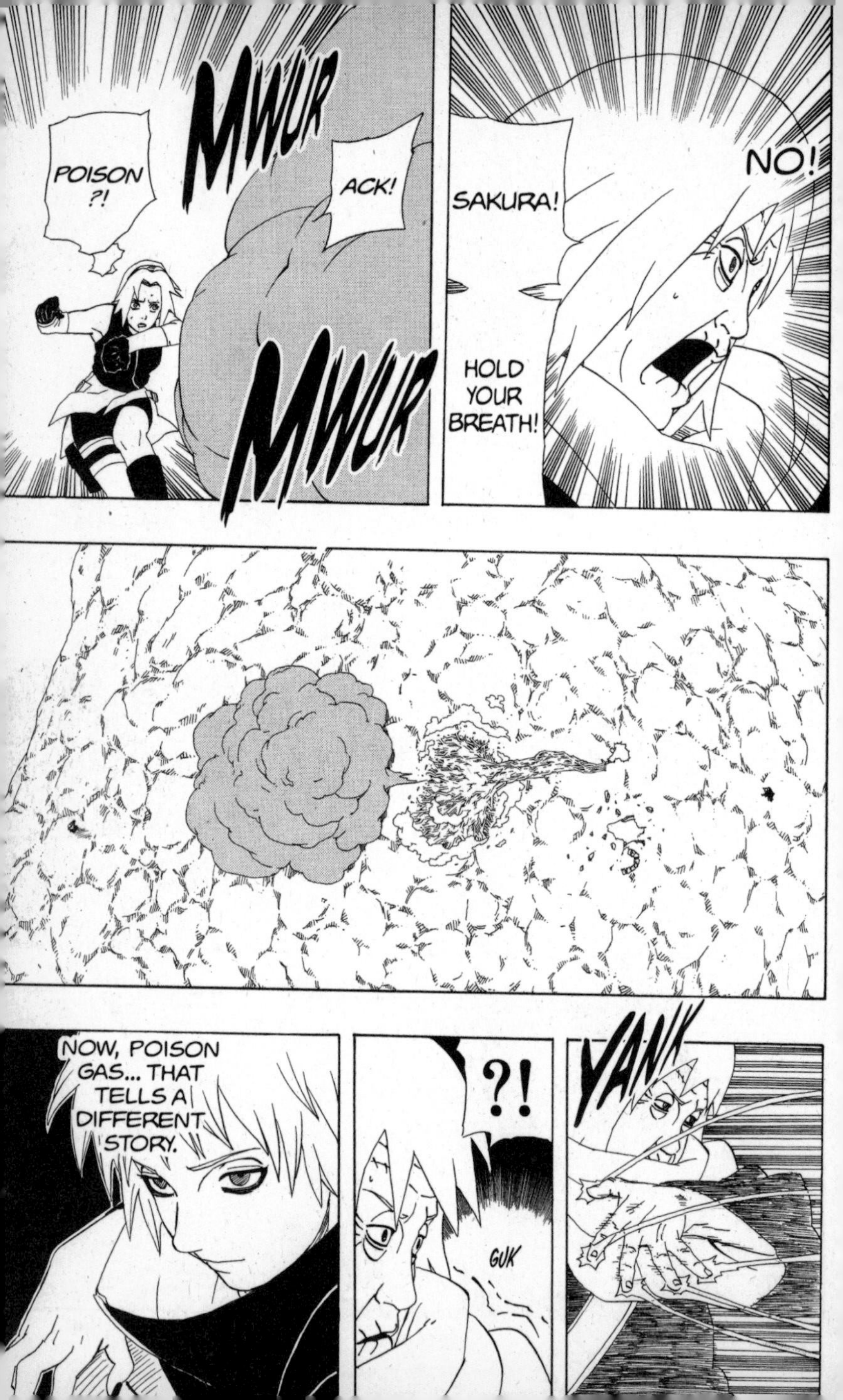
NO!
SAKURA!
HOLD YOUR BREATH!
ACK!
MWUR
POISON ?!
MWUR
YANK
?!
GUK
NOW, POISON GAS... THAT TELLS A DIFFERENT STORY.

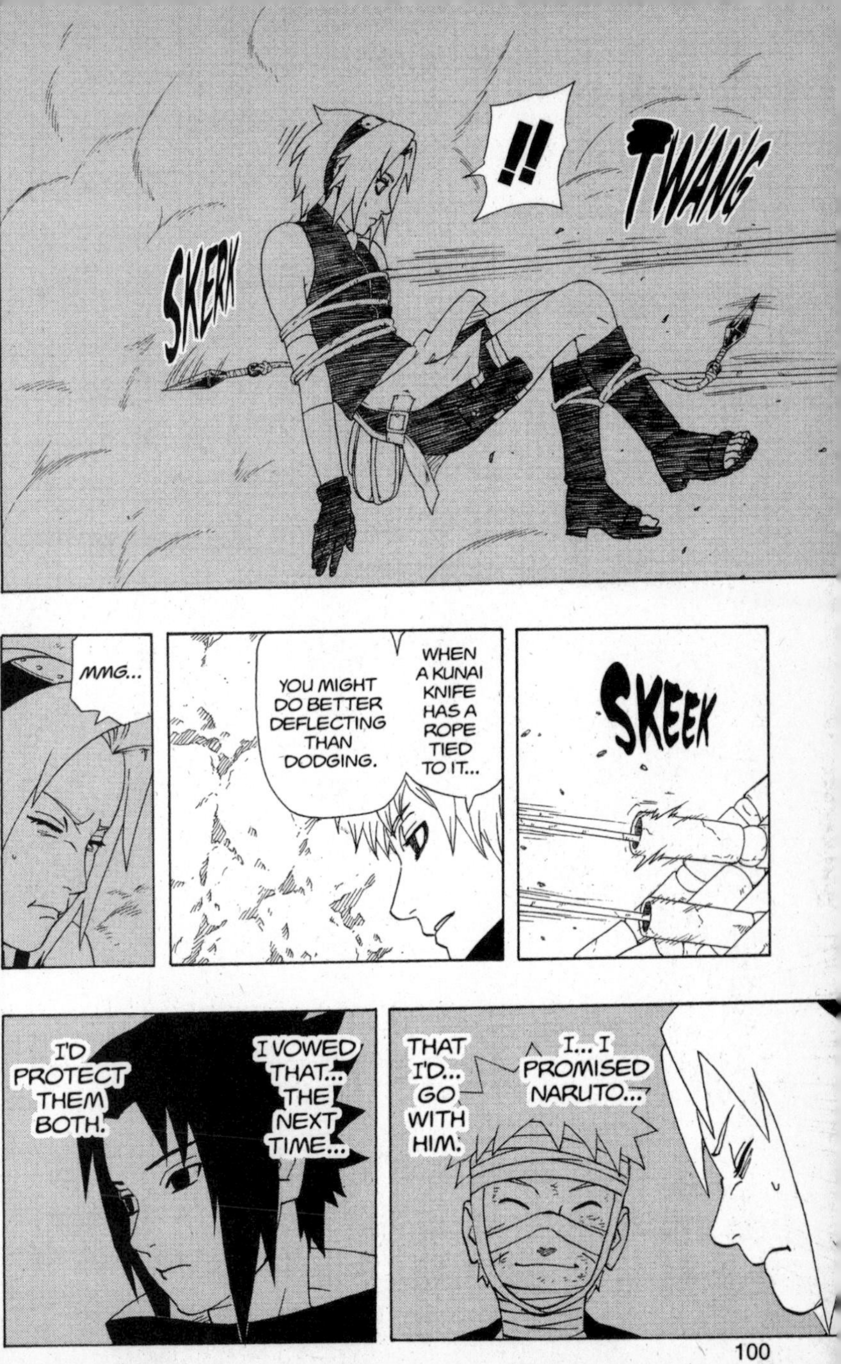
TWANG
!!
SKERK
SKEEK
WHEN A KUNAI KNIFE HAS A ROPE TIED TO IT...
YOU MIGHT DO BETTER DEFLECTING THAN DODGING.
MMG...
I... I PROMISED NARUTO...
THAT I'D... GO WITH HIM.
I VOWED THAT... THE NEXT TIME...
I'D PROTECT THEM BOTH.

READ THIS WAY

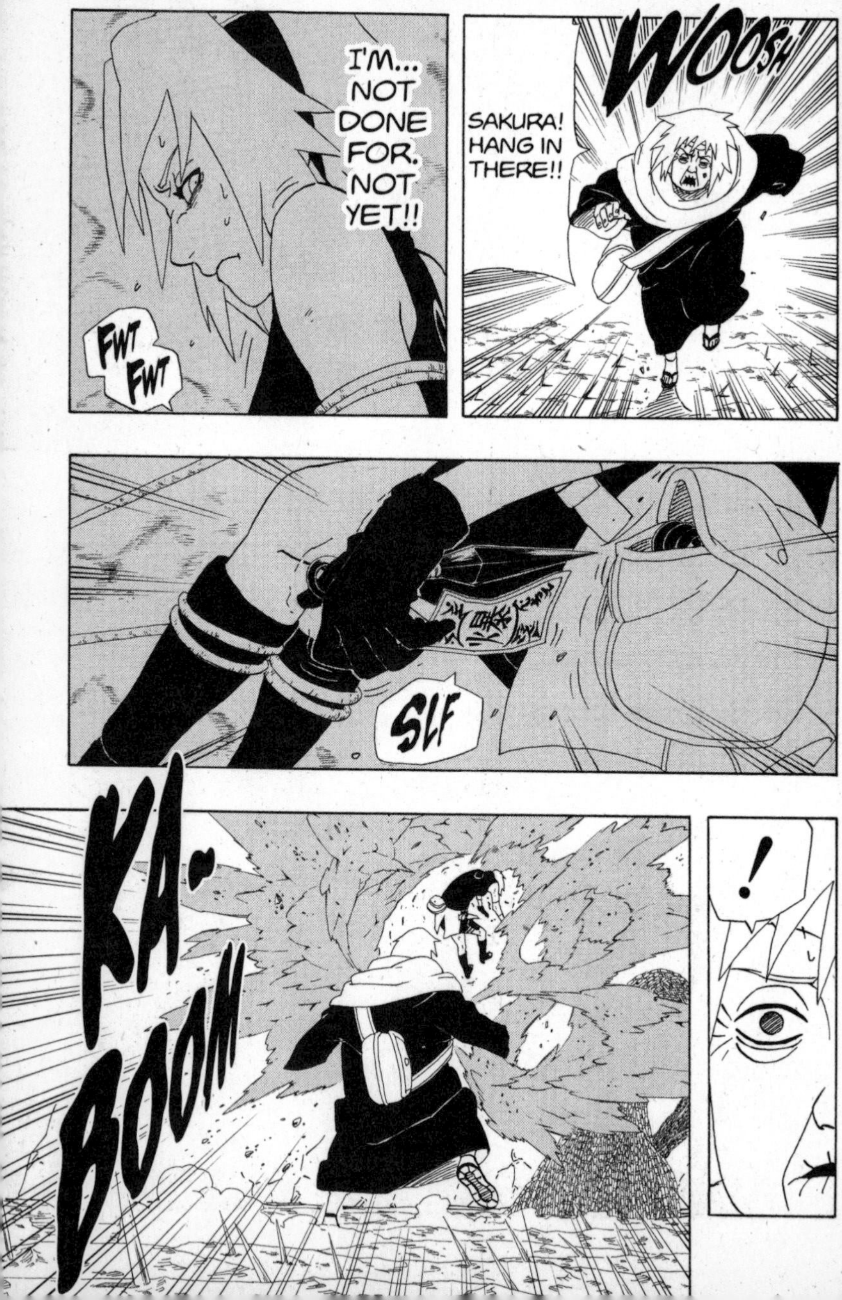
WOOSH
SAKURA! HANG IN THERE!!
I'M... NOT DONE FOR. NOT YET!!
FWT FWT
SLF
!
KA-BOOM

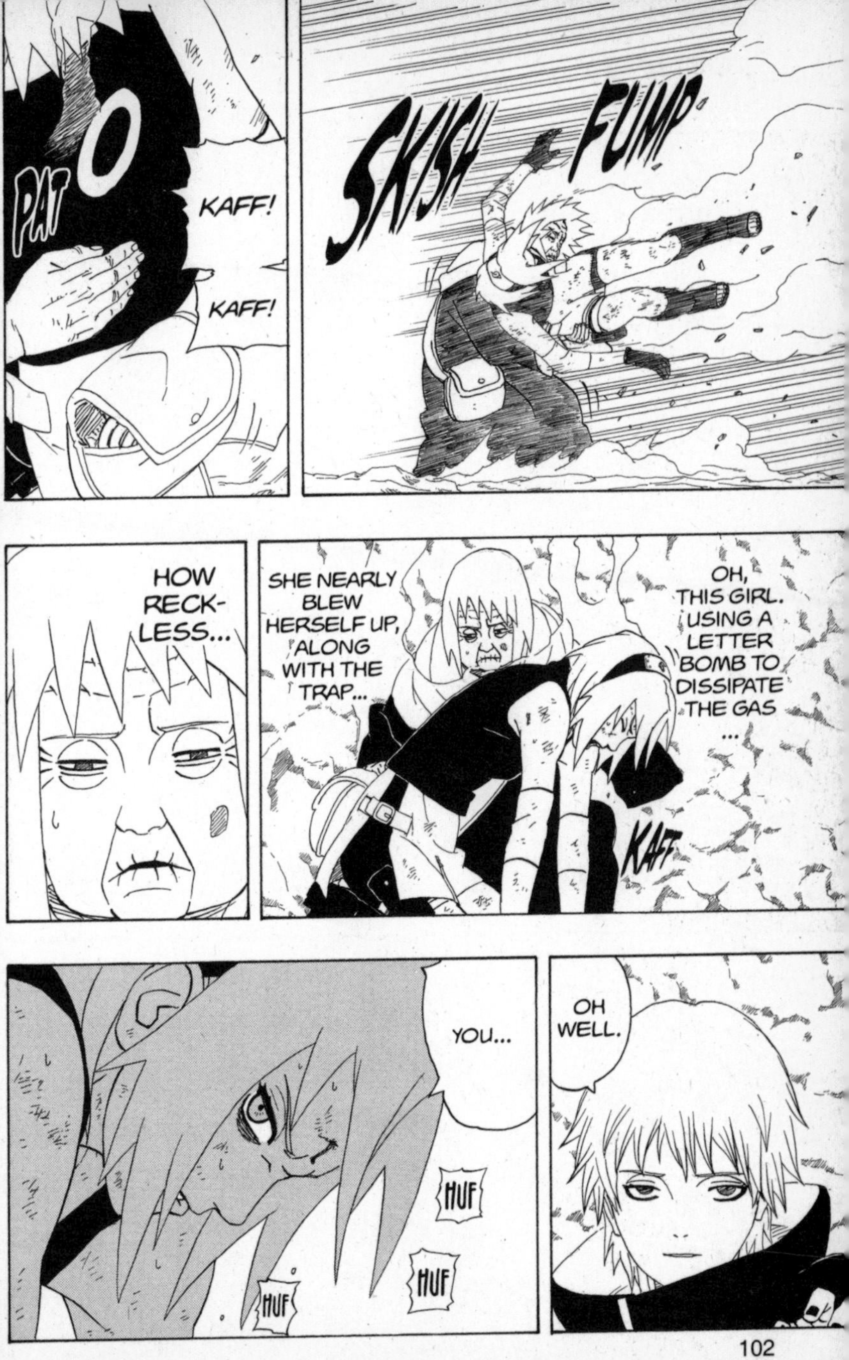
SKISH
FUMP
PAT
KAFF!
KAFF!
OH, THIS GIRL. USING A LETTER BOMB TO DISSIPATE THE GAS...
SHE NEARLY BLEW HERSELF UP, ALONG WITH THE TRAP...
KAFF
HOW RECK-LESS...
OH WELL.
YOU...
HUF
HUF
HUF

READ THIS WAY

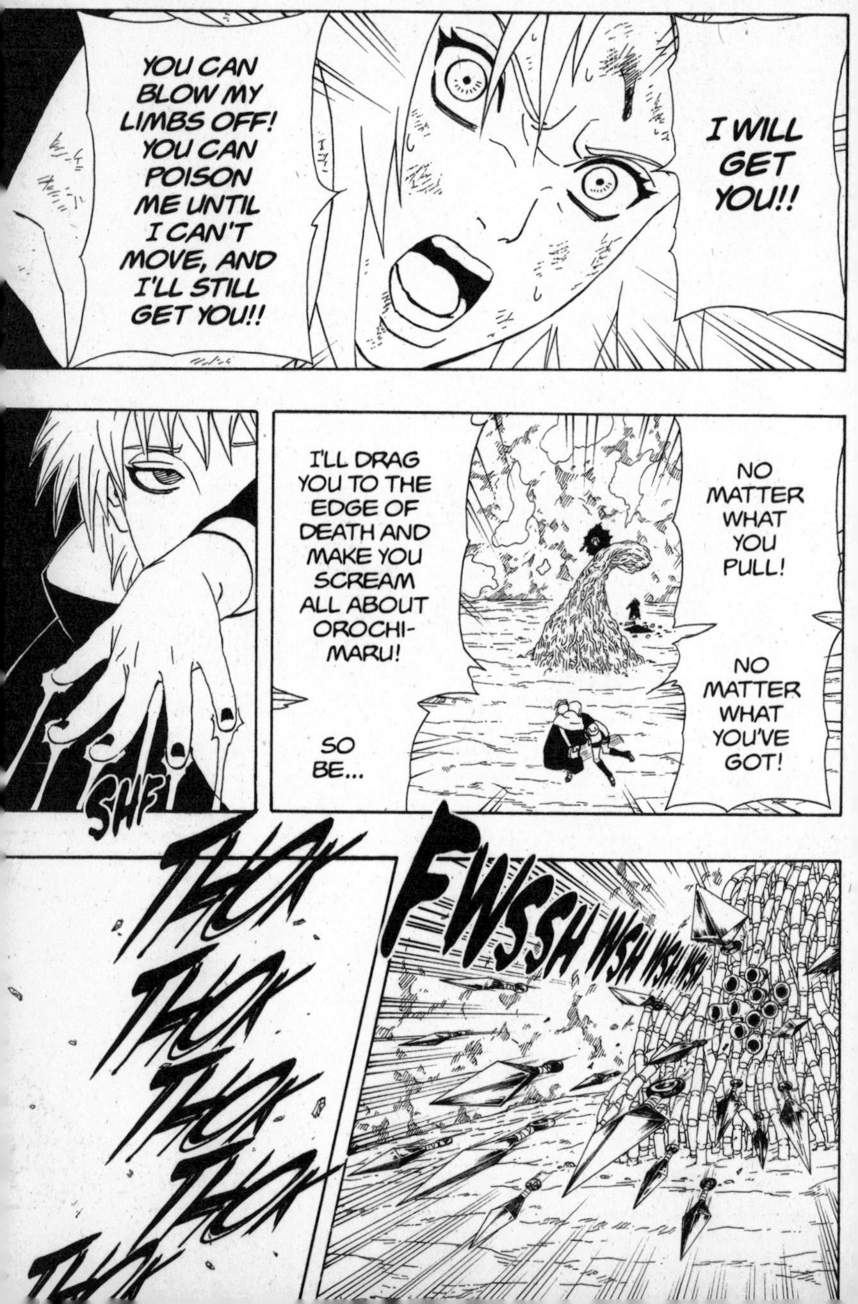
I WILL GET YOU!!
YOU CAN BLOW MY LIMBS OFF! YOU CAN POISON ME UNTIL I CAN'T MOVE, AND I'LL STILL GET YOU!!
NO MATTER WHAT YOU PULL!
NO MATTER WHAT YOU'VE GOT!
I'LL DRAG YOU TO THE EDGE OF DEATH AND MAKE YOU SCREAM ALL ABOUT OROCHI-MARU!
SO BE...
SHF
FWSSH WSH WSH WSH
THOK THOK THOK THOK

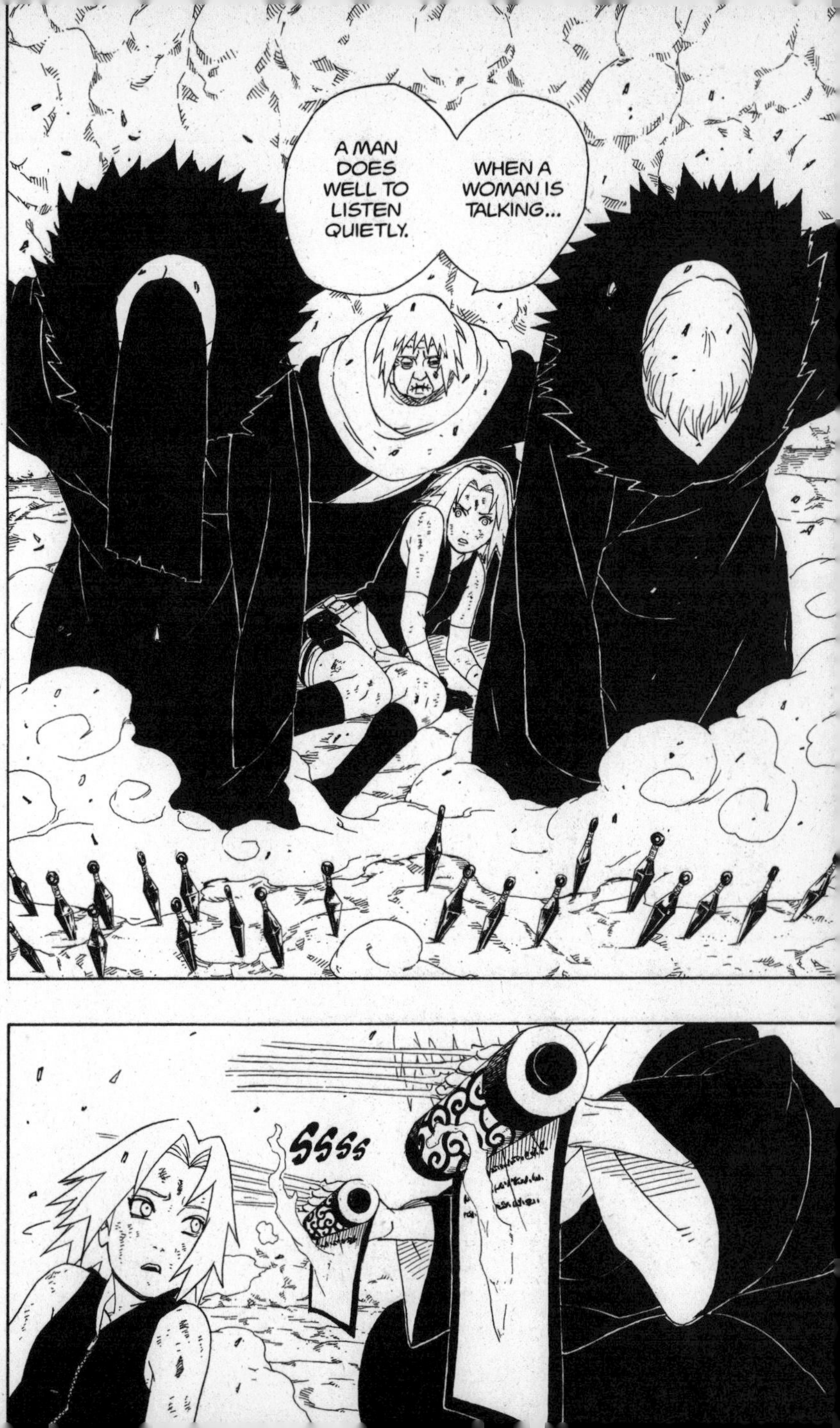

WHEN A WOMAN IS TALKING...
A MAN DOES WELL TO LISTEN QUIETLY.
SSSS

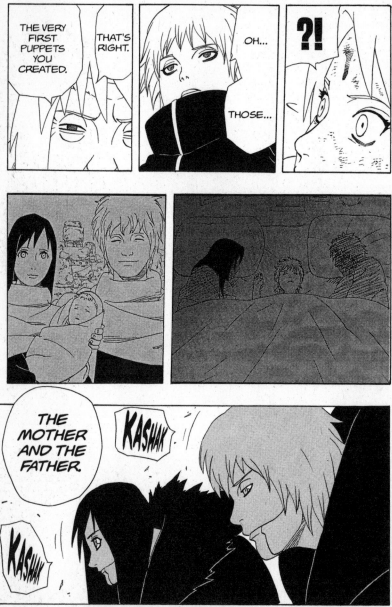

THE VERY FIRST PUPPETS YOU CREATED.

THAT'S RIGHT.

OH...

THOSE...

?!

THE MOTHER AND THE FATHER.

KASHAK

KASHAK

NARUTO

Number 268: Puppet Masters!!

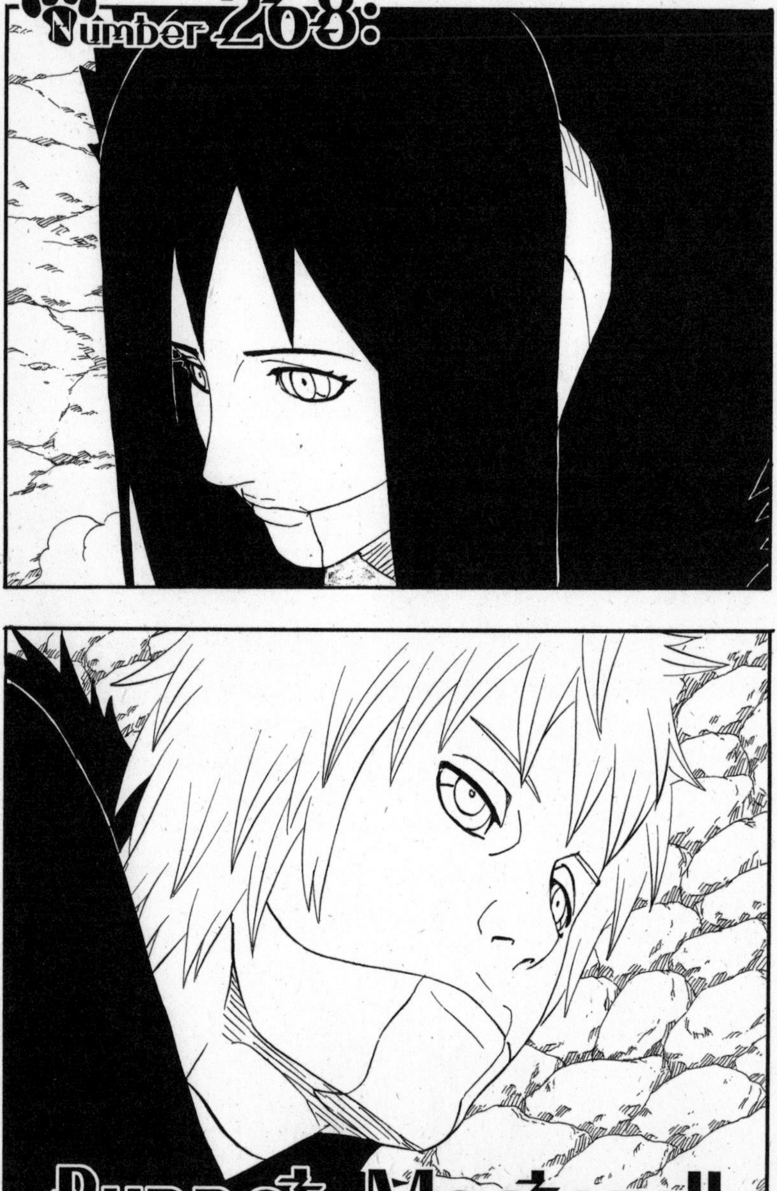

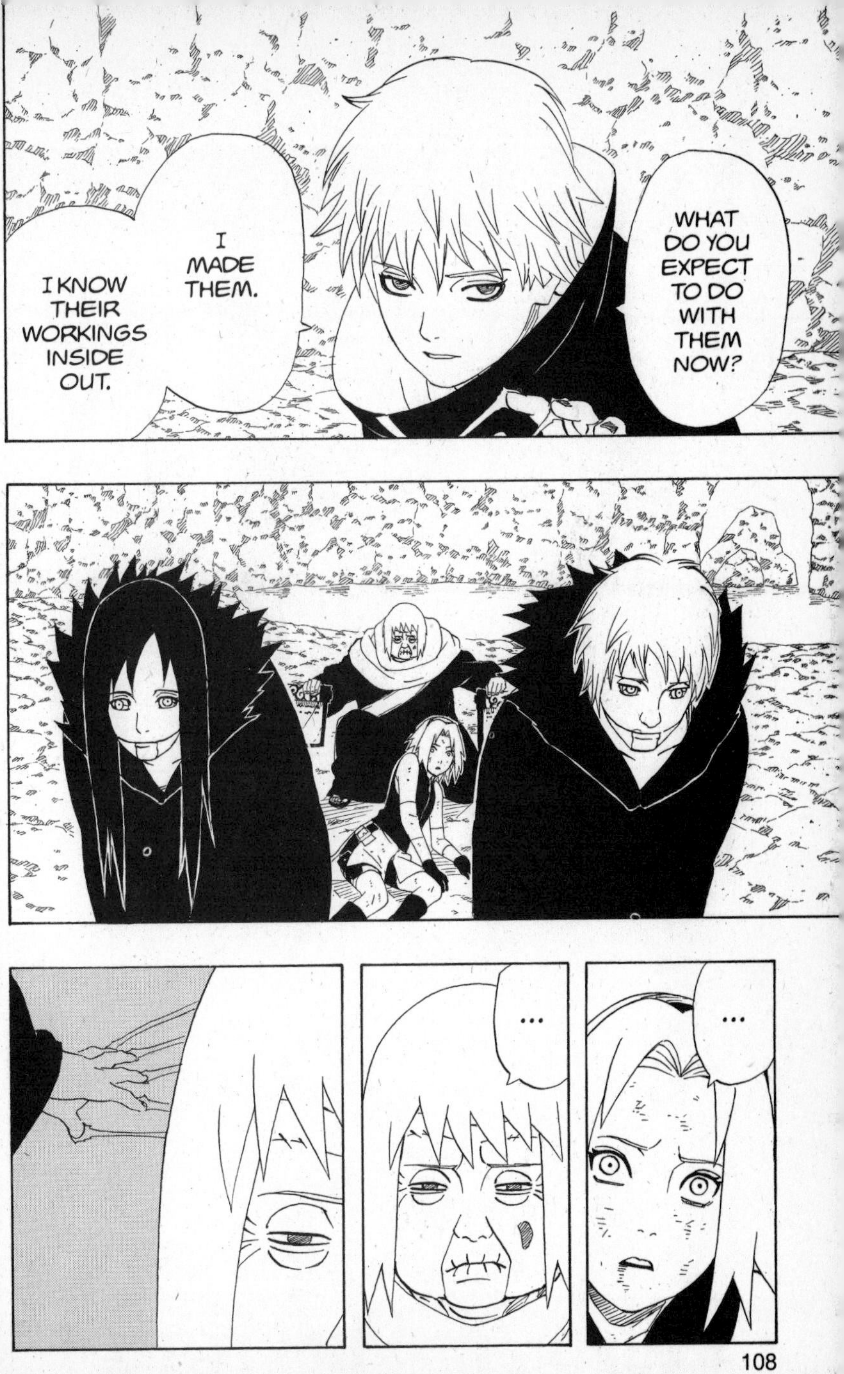
WHAT DO YOU EXPECT TO DO WITH THEM NOW?
I MADE THEM.
I KNOW THEIR WORKINGS INSIDE OUT.
...
...

READ THIS WAY

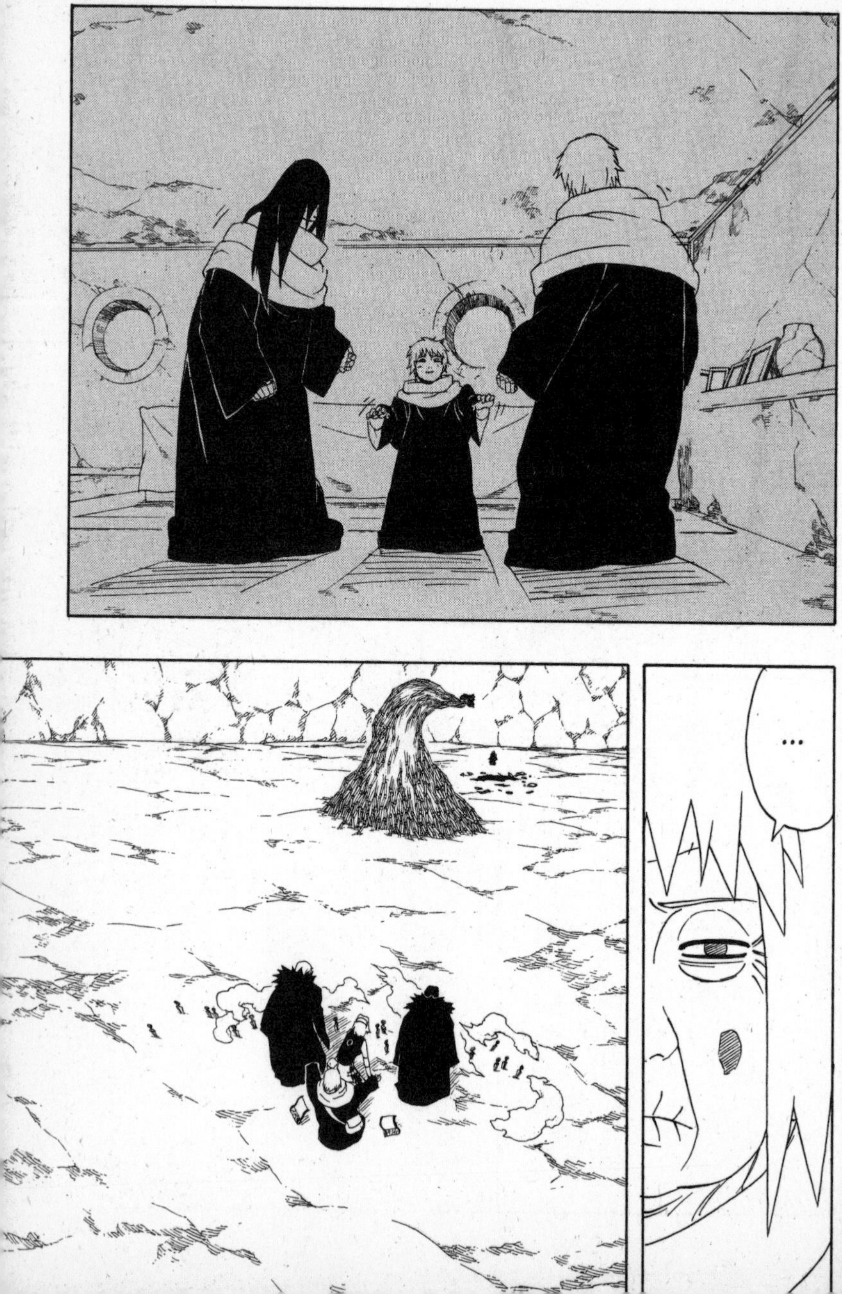
...

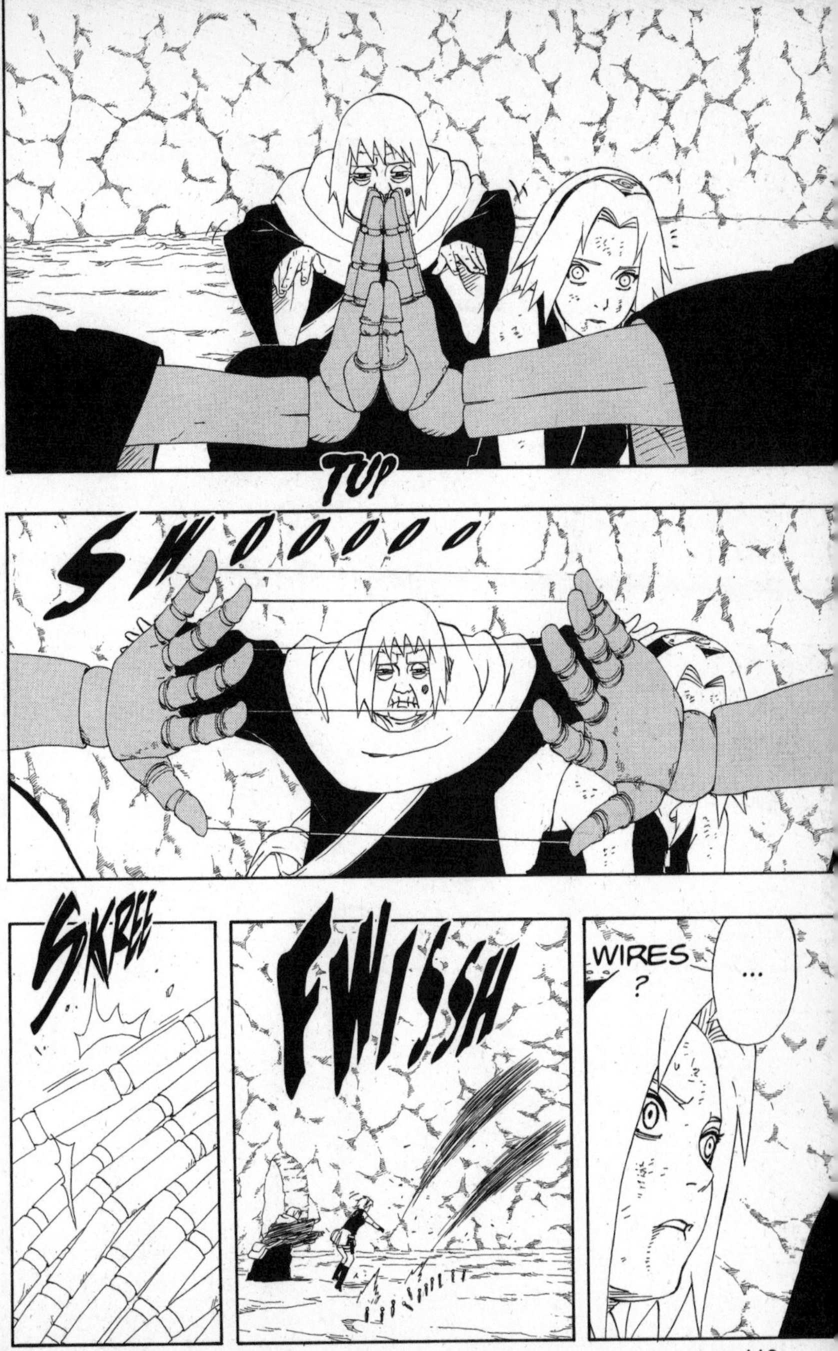
TUP
SWOOOOOO
WIRES?
...
FWISSH
SKREE

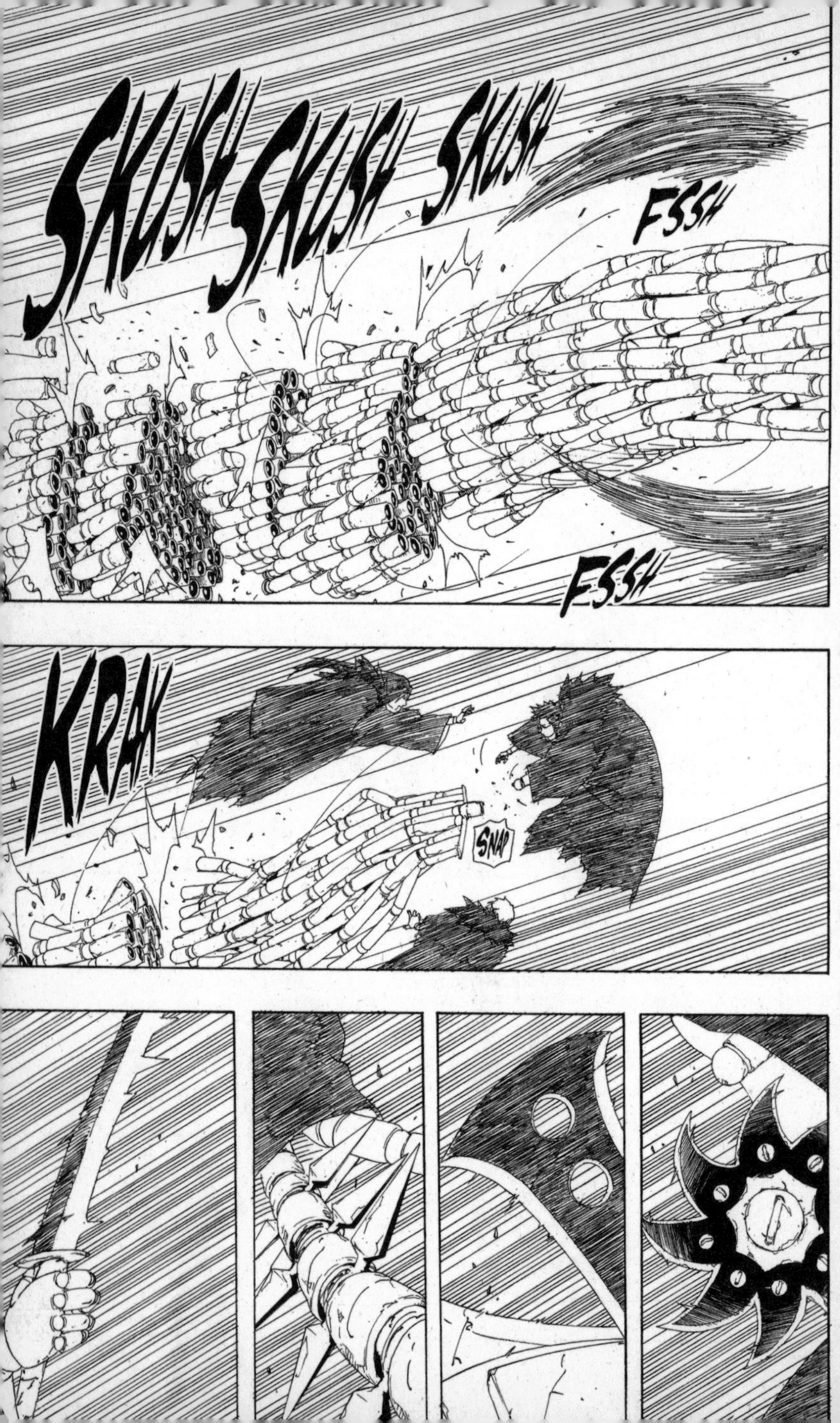
SKLISH SKLISH SKLISH
FSSH
FSSH
KRAK
SNAP

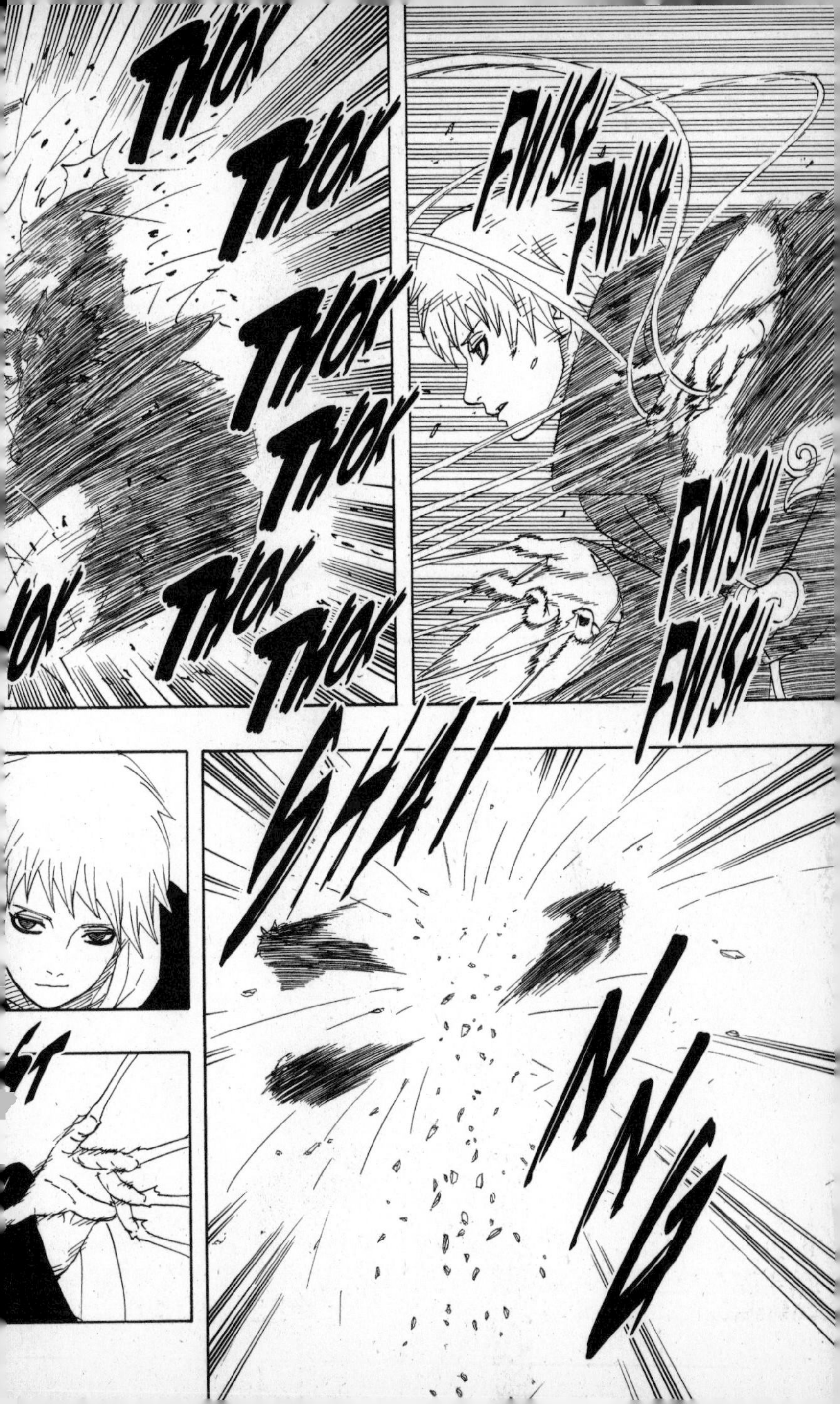
FWISH
FWISH
FWISH
FWISH
THOK
THOK
THOK
THOK
THOK
THOK
SHAA
NNNG

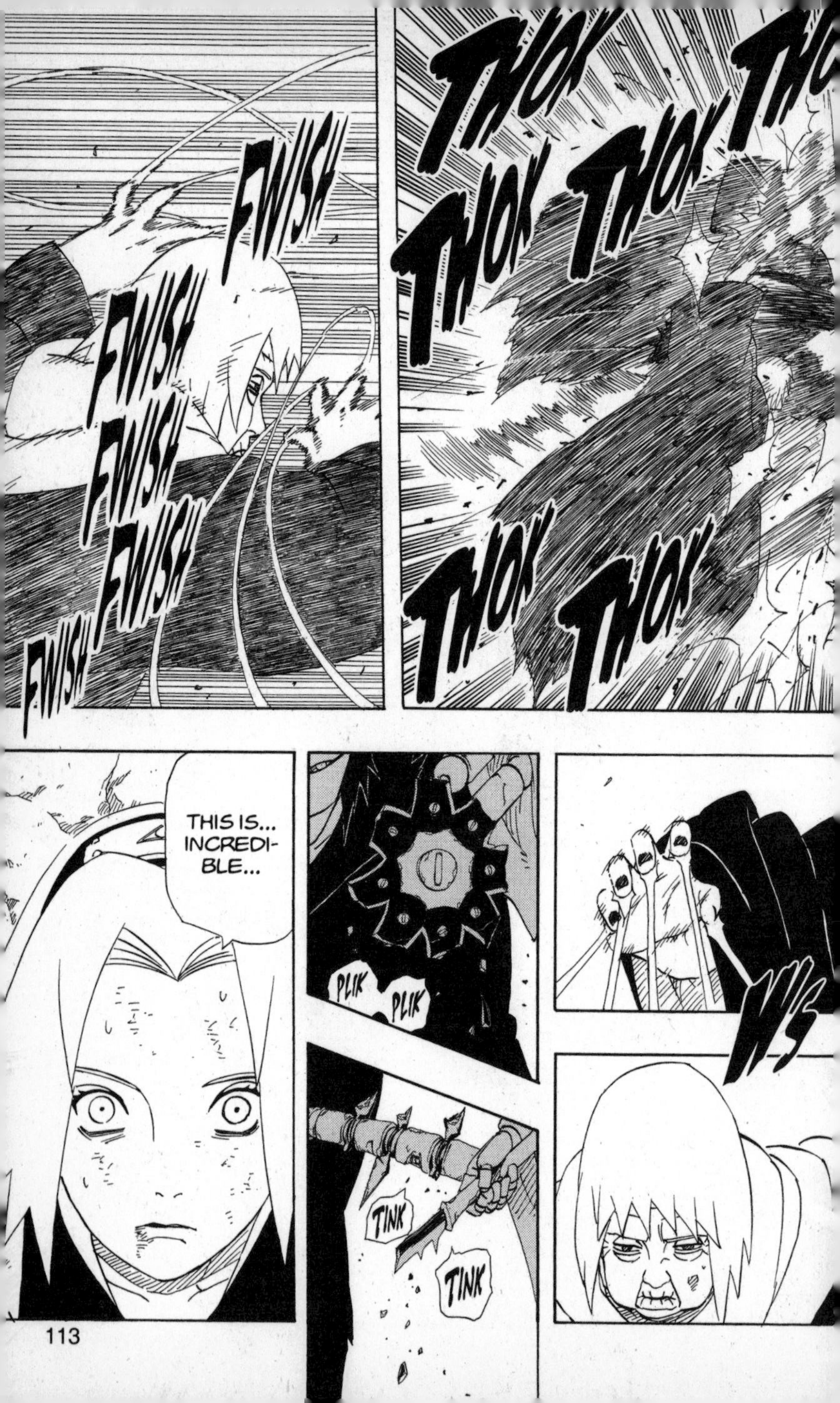
THOK
THOK
THOK
THOK
THOK
THOK
FWISH
FWISH
FWISH
FWISH
FWISH
WHS
PLIK
PLIK
TINK
TINK
THIS IS... INCREDIBLE...

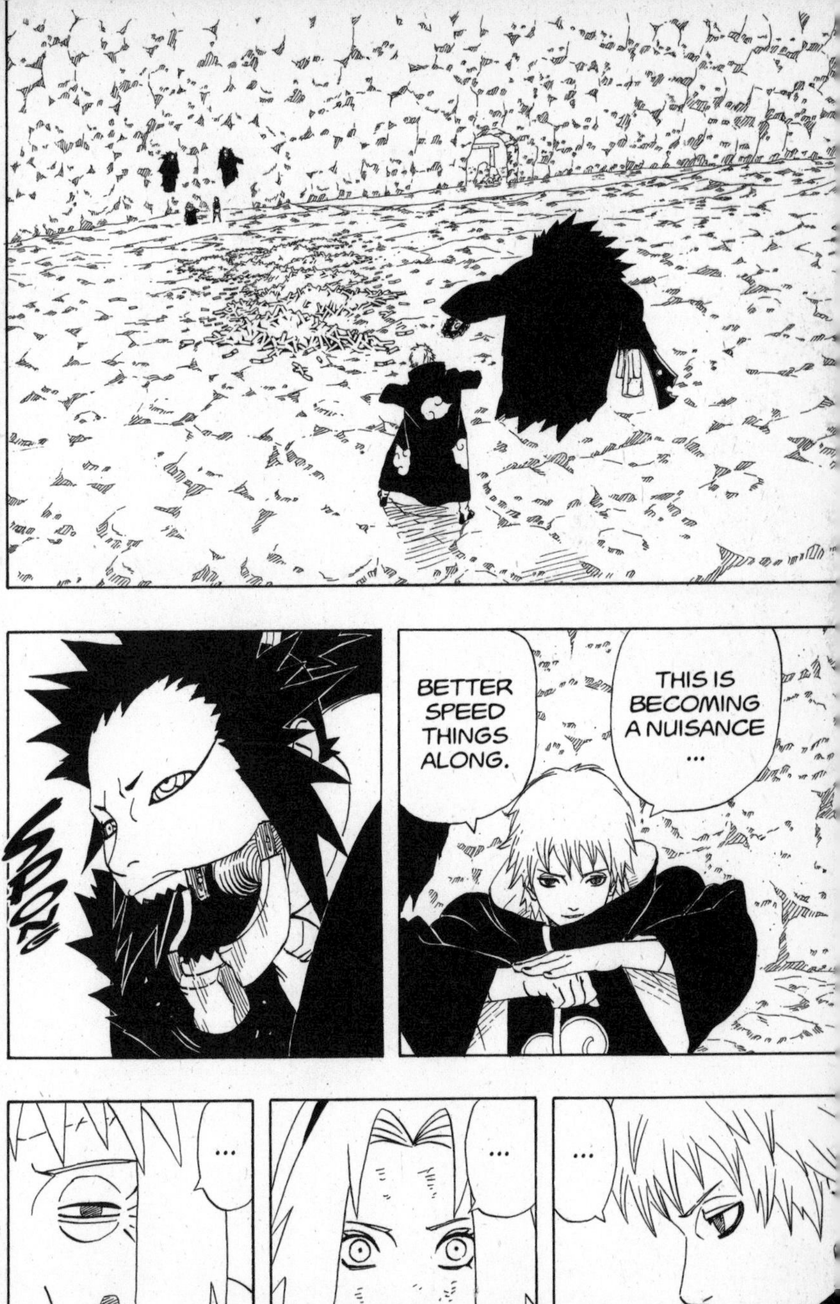
THIS IS BECOMING A NUISANCE ...
BETTER SPEED THINGS ALONG.
...
...
...

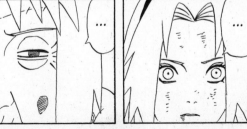

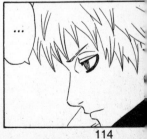

READ THIS WAY

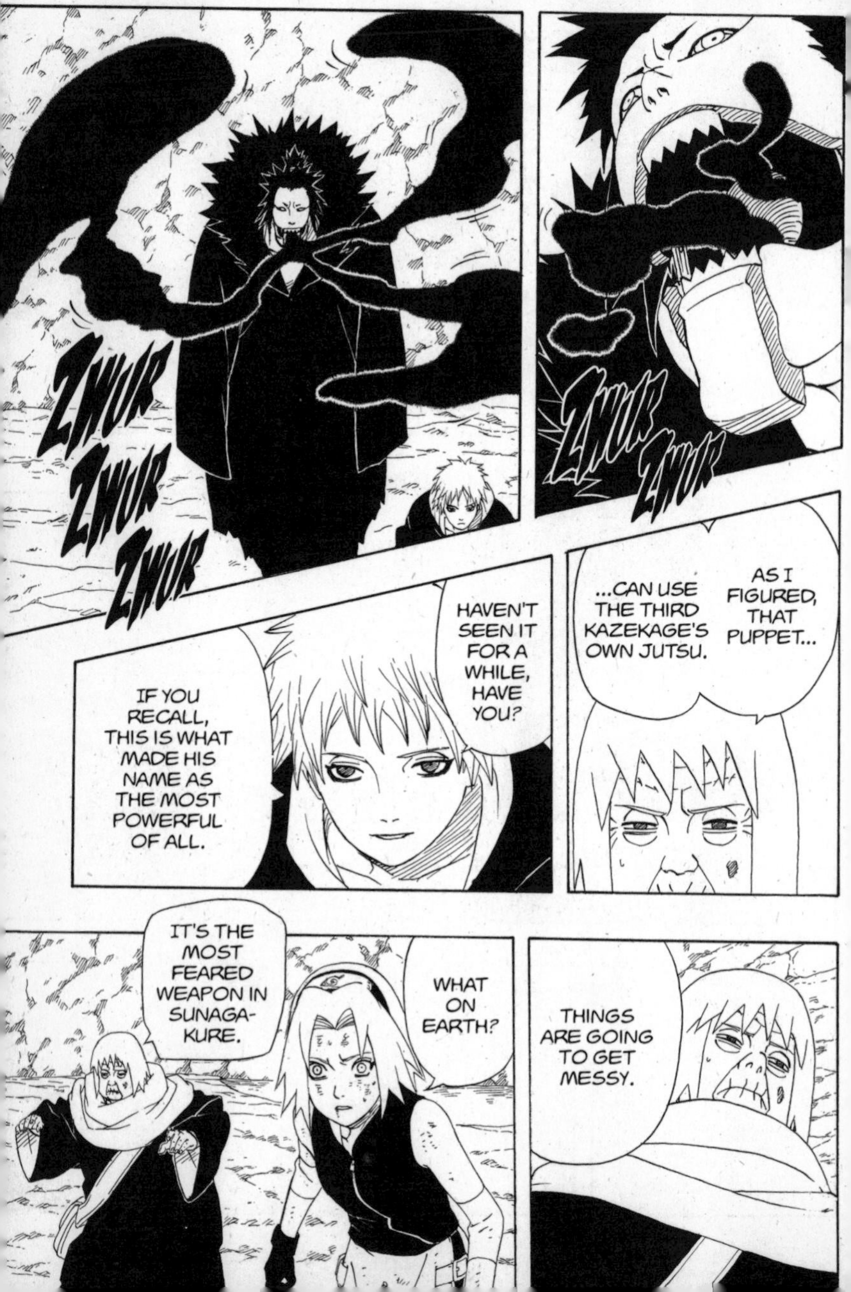
ZWUR ZWUR
ZWUR ZWUR ZWUR
AS I FIGURED, THAT PUPPET...
...CAN USE THE THIRD KAZEKAGE'S OWN JUTSU.
HAVEN'T SEEN IT FOR A WHILE, HAVE YOU?
IF YOU RECALL, THIS IS WHAT MADE HIS NAME AS THE MOST POWERFUL OF ALL.
THINGS ARE GOING TO GET MESSY.
WHAT ON EARTH?
IT'S THE MOST FEARED WEAPON IN SUNAGA-KURE.

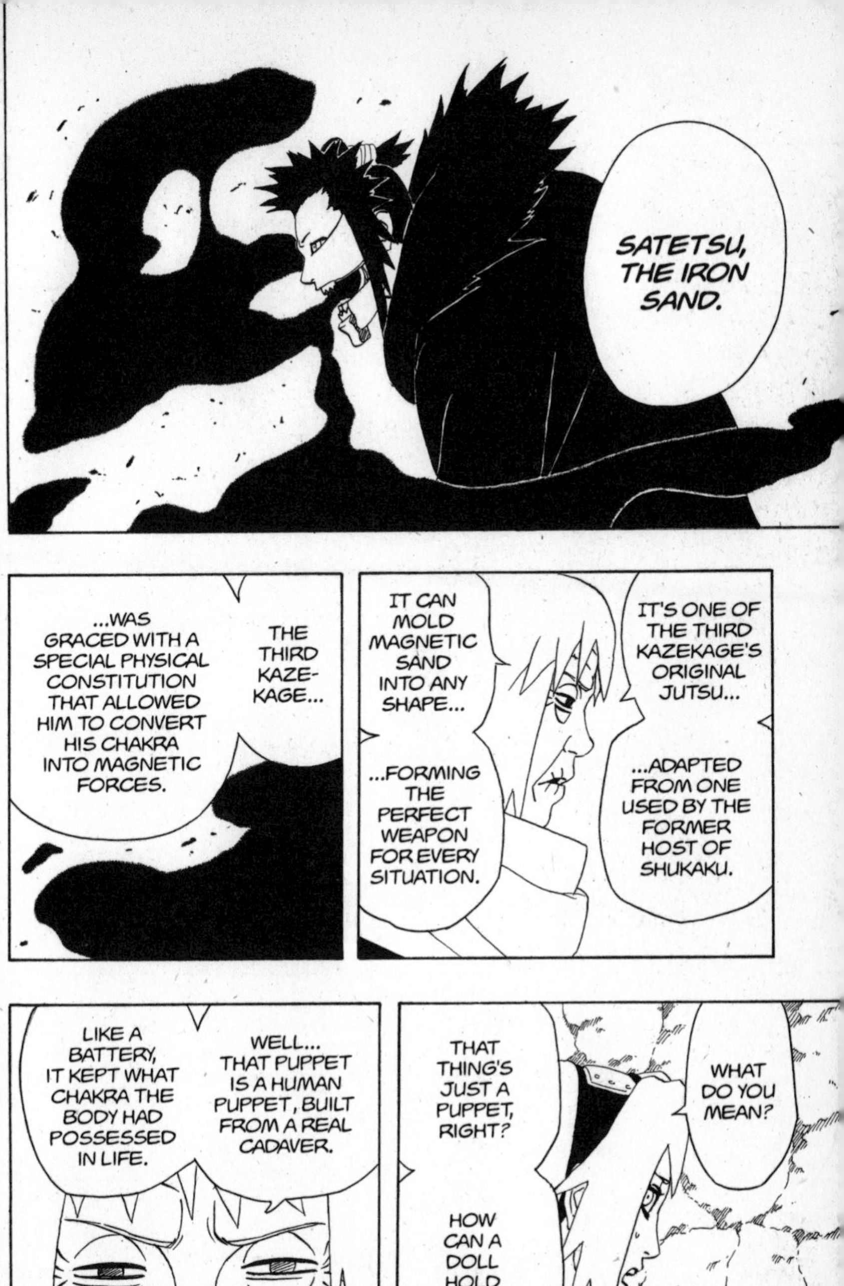
SATETSU, THE IRON SAND.
IT'S ONE OF THE THIRD KAZEKAGE'S ORIGINAL JUTSU...
...ADAPTED FROM ONE USED BY THE FORMER HOST OF SHUKAKU.
IT CAN MOLD MAGNETIC SAND INTO ANY SHAPE...
...FORMING THE PERFECT WEAPON FOR EVERY SITUATION.
THE THIRD KAZE-KAGE...
...WAS GRACED WITH A SPECIAL PHYSICAL CONSTITUTION THAT ALLOWED HIM TO CONVERT HIS CHAKRA INTO MAGNETIC FORCES.
WHAT DO YOU MEAN?
THAT THING'S JUST A PUPPET, RIGHT?
HOW CAN A DOLL HOLD CHAKRA?
WELL... THAT PUPPET IS A HUMAN PUPPET, BUILT FROM A REAL CADAVER.
LIKE A BATTERY, IT KEPT WHAT CHAKRA THE BODY HAD POSSESSED IN LIFE.

READ THIS WAY

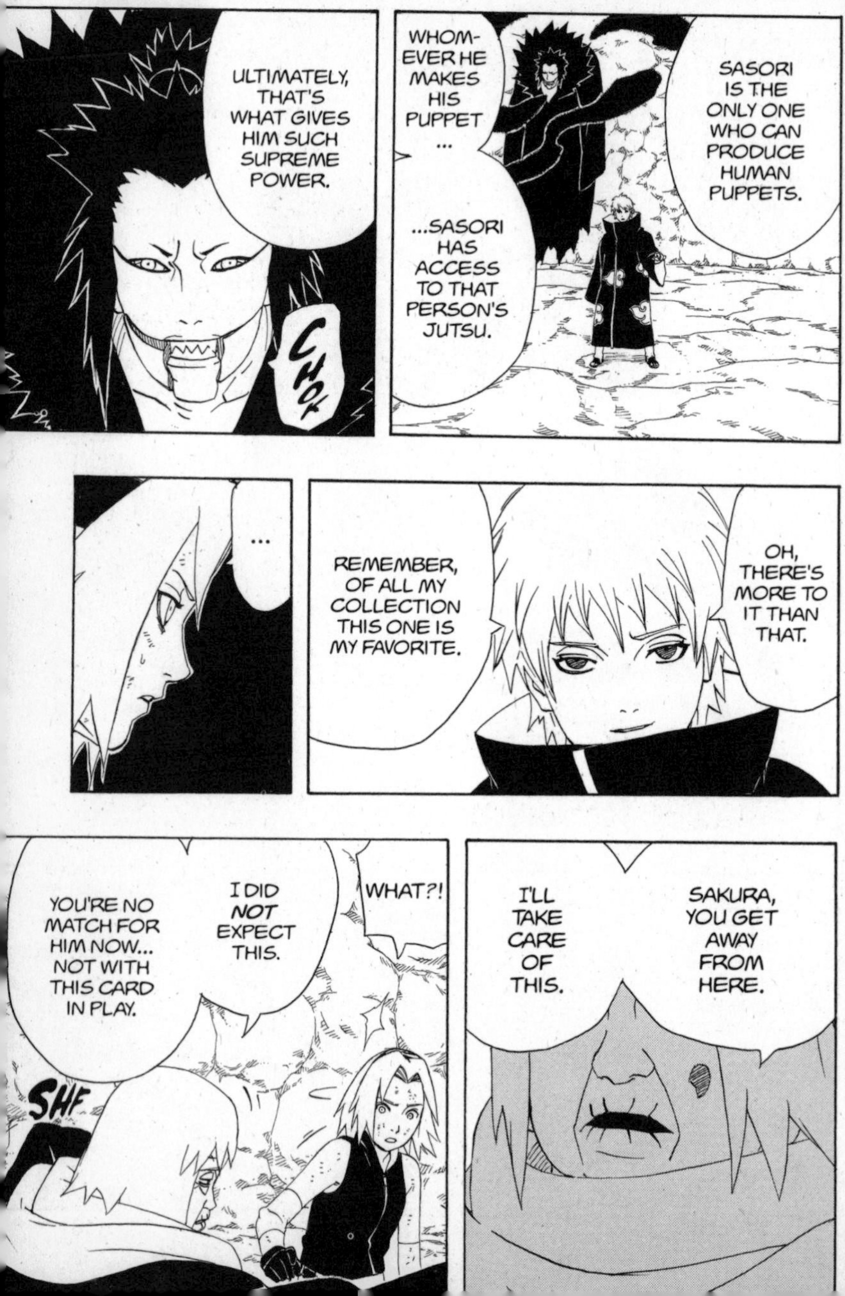
SASORI IS THE ONLY ONE WHO CAN PRODUCE HUMAN PUPPETS.
WHOMEVER HE MAKES HIS PUPPET ...
...SASORI HAS ACCESS TO THAT PERSON'S JUTSU.
ULTIMATELY, THAT'S WHAT GIVES HIM SUCH SUPREME POWER.
CHOK
OH, THERE'S MORE TO IT THAN THAT.
REMEMBER, OF ALL MY COLLECTION THIS ONE IS MY FAVORITE.
...
SAKURA, YOU GET AWAY FROM HERE.
I'LL TAKE CARE OF THIS.
WHAT?!
I DID *NOT* EXPECT THIS.
YOU'RE NO MATCH FOR HIM NOW... NOT WITH THIS CARD IN PLAY.
SHF

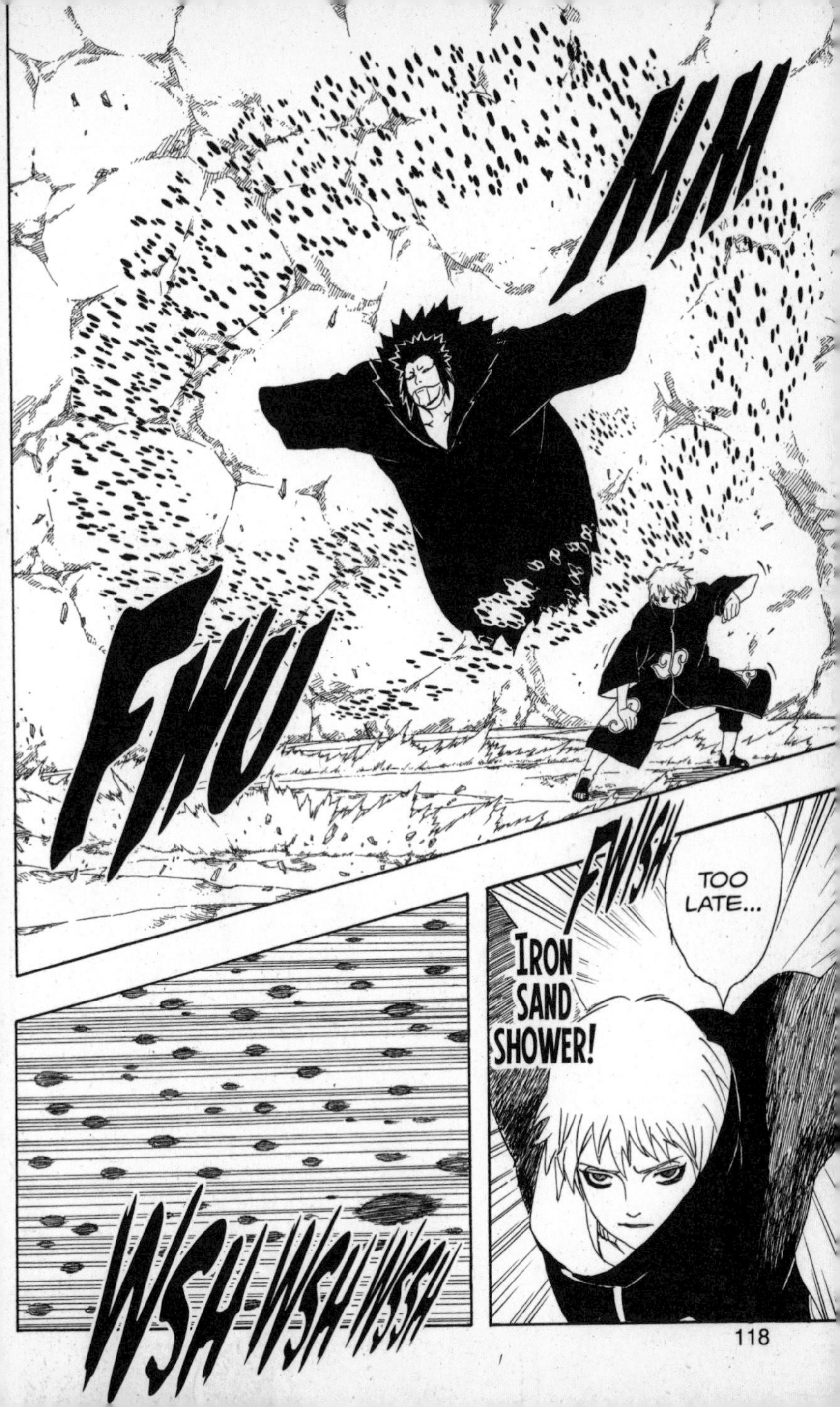
FWM
FWU
TOO LATE...
FWISH
IRON SAND SHOWER!
WSH WSH WSH

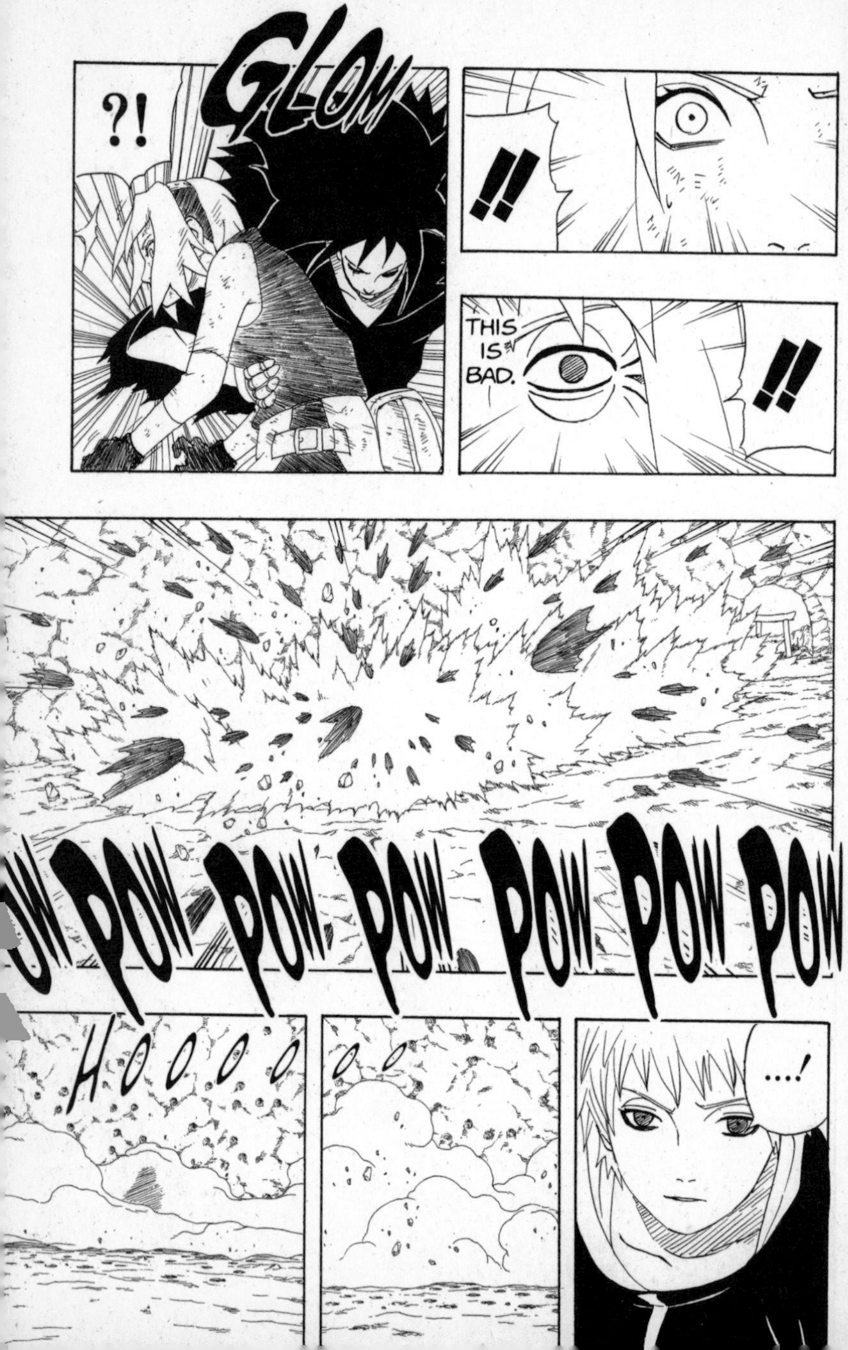
!!
THIS IS BAD.
!!
GLOW
?!
OW POW POW POW POW POW POW
...!
HOOOOOO

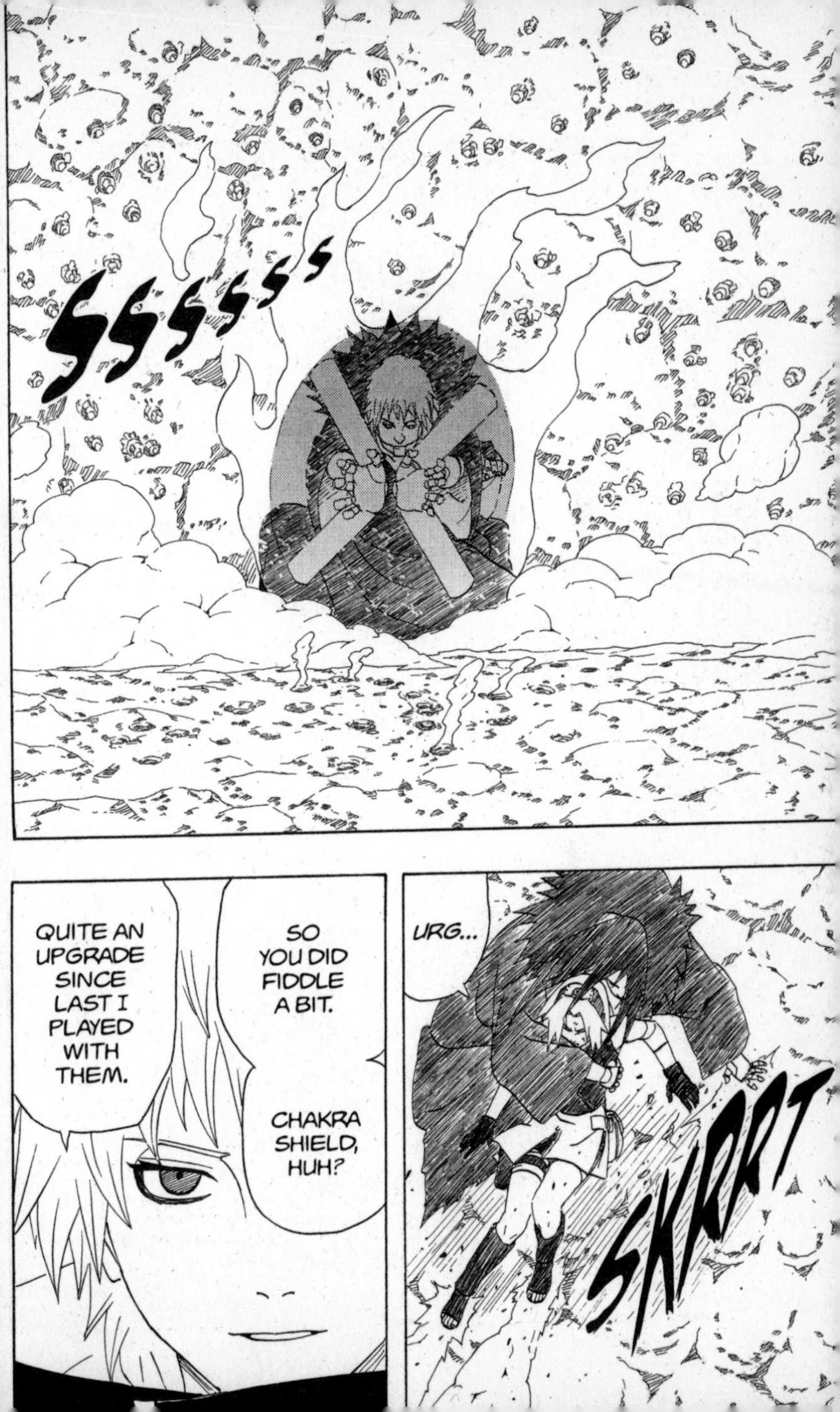
SSSSSS
URG...
SKRRT
SO YOU DID FIDDLE A BIT.
CHAKRA SHIELD, HUH?
QUITE AN UPGRADE SINCE LAST I PLAYED WITH THEM.

READ THIS WAY

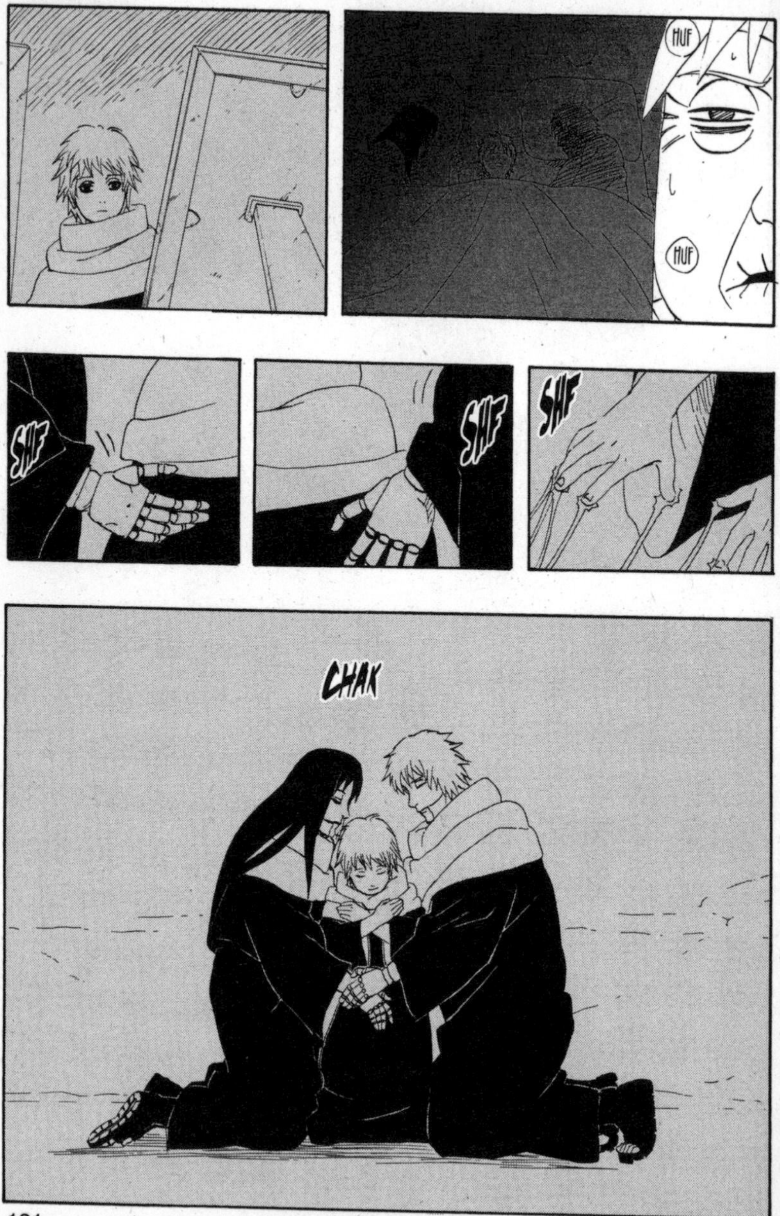

HUF
HUF
SHF
SHF
SHF
CHAK

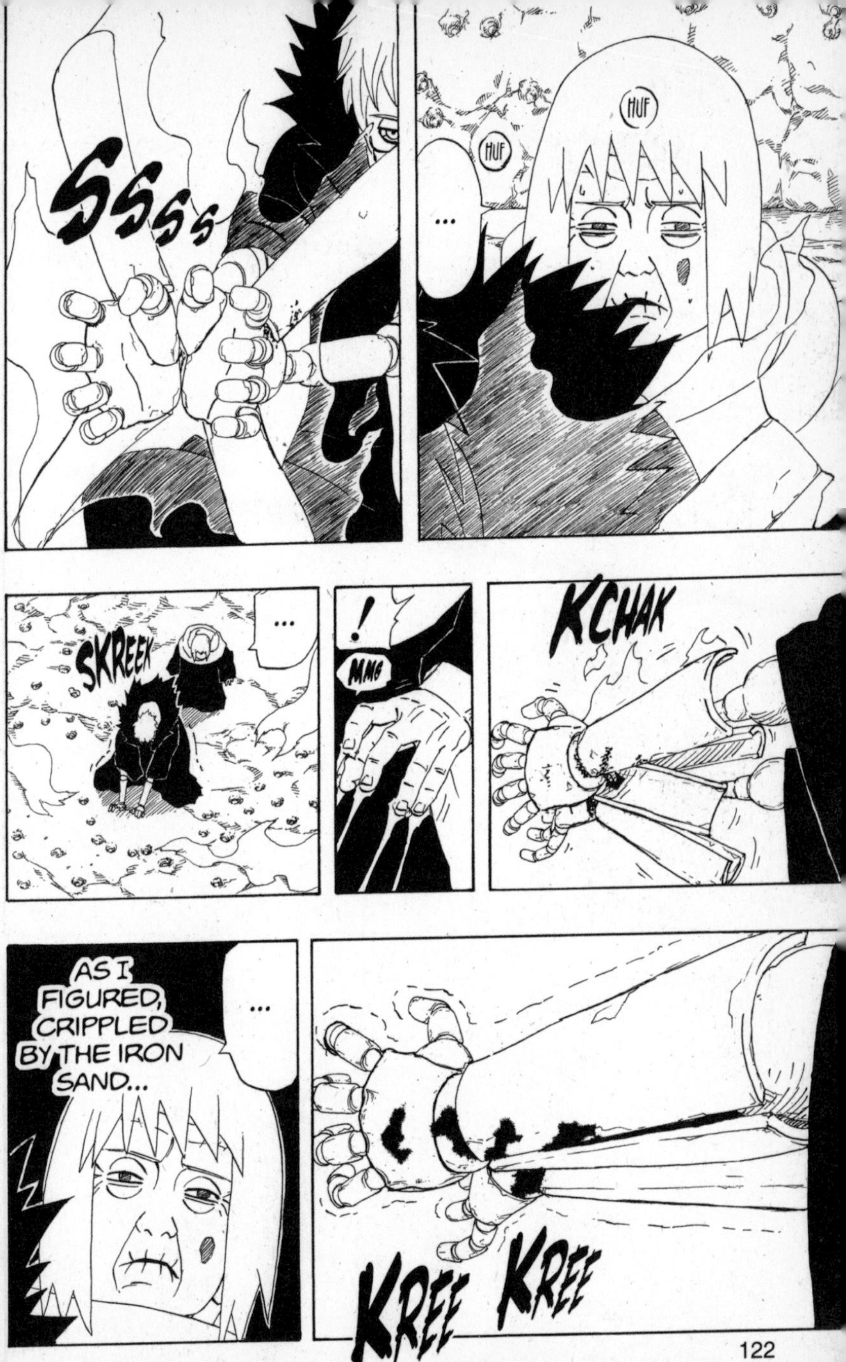
HUF
HUF
...
SSSS
KCHAK
!
MMG
...
SKREEK
KREE KREE
...
AS I FIGURED, CRIPPLED BY THE IRON SAND...

READ THIS WAY

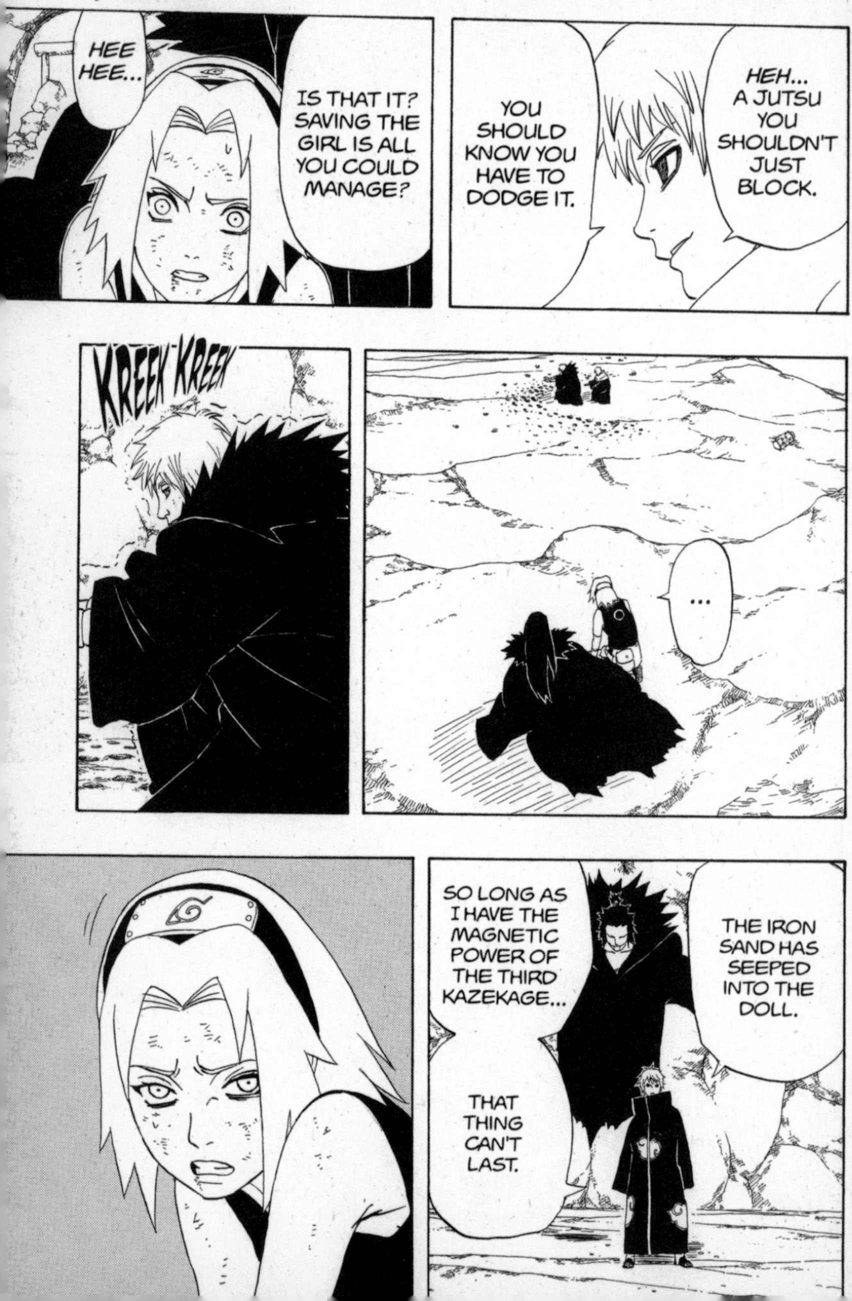
HEH... A JUTSU YOU SHOULDN'T JUST BLOCK.
YOU SHOULD KNOW YOU HAVE TO DODGE IT.
IS THAT IT? SAVING THE GIRL IS ALL YOU COULD MANAGE?
HEE HEE...
...
KREEK KREEK
THE IRON SAND HAS SEEPED INTO THE DOLL.
SO LONG AS I HAVE THE MAGNETIC POWER OF THE THIRD KAZEKAGE...
THAT THING CAN'T LAST.

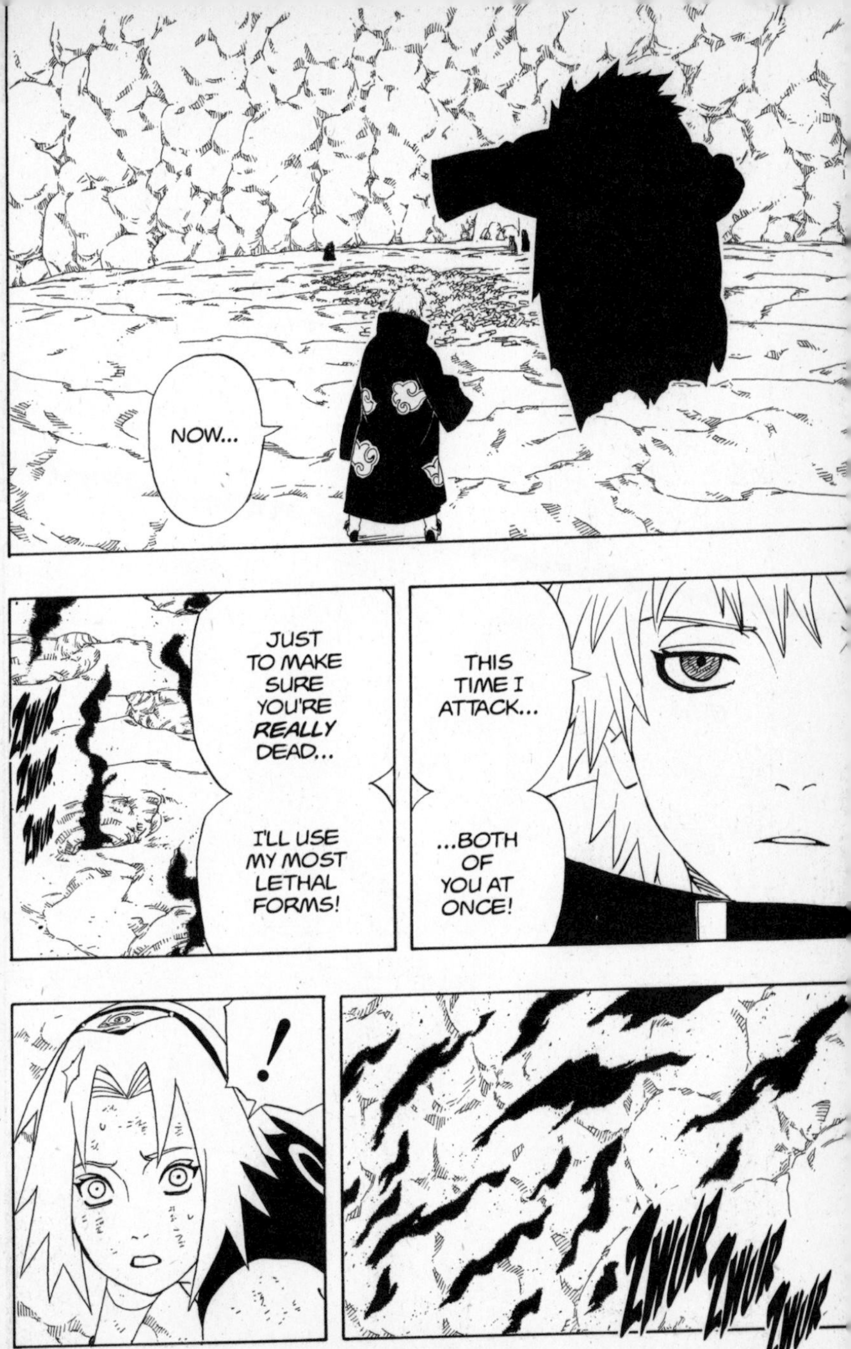
NOW...
THIS TIME I ATTACK...
...BOTH OF YOU AT ONCE!
JUST TO MAKE SURE YOU'RE *REALLY* DEAD...
I'LL USE MY MOST LETHAL FORMS!
ZWUR ZWUR ZWUR
ZWUR ZWUR ZWUR
!

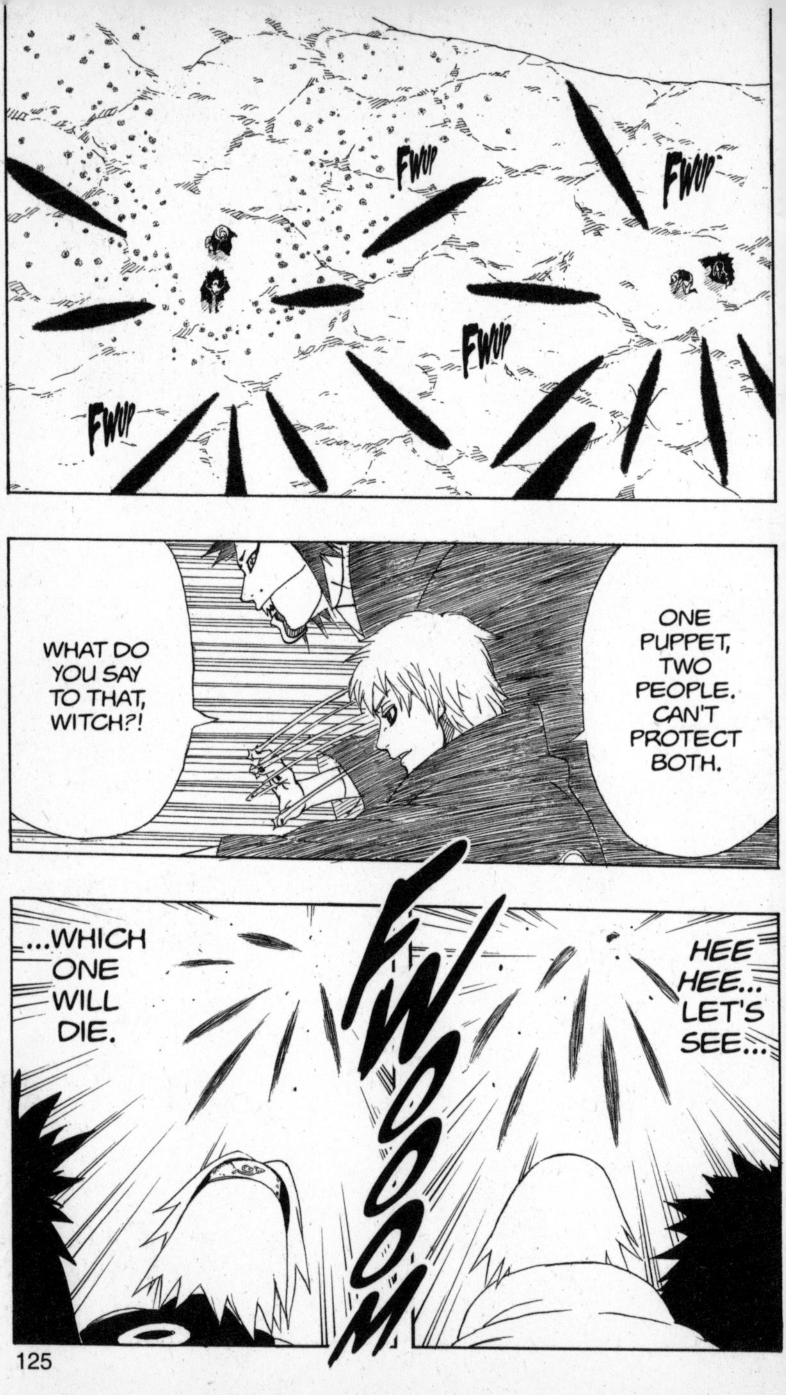
FWUP
FWUP
FWUP
FWUP
ONE PUPPET, TWO PEOPLE. CAN'T PROTECT BOTH.
WHAT DO YOU SAY TO THAT, WITCH?!
HEE HEE... LET'S SEE...
...WHICH ONE WILL DIE.
FWOOOOM

NARUTO

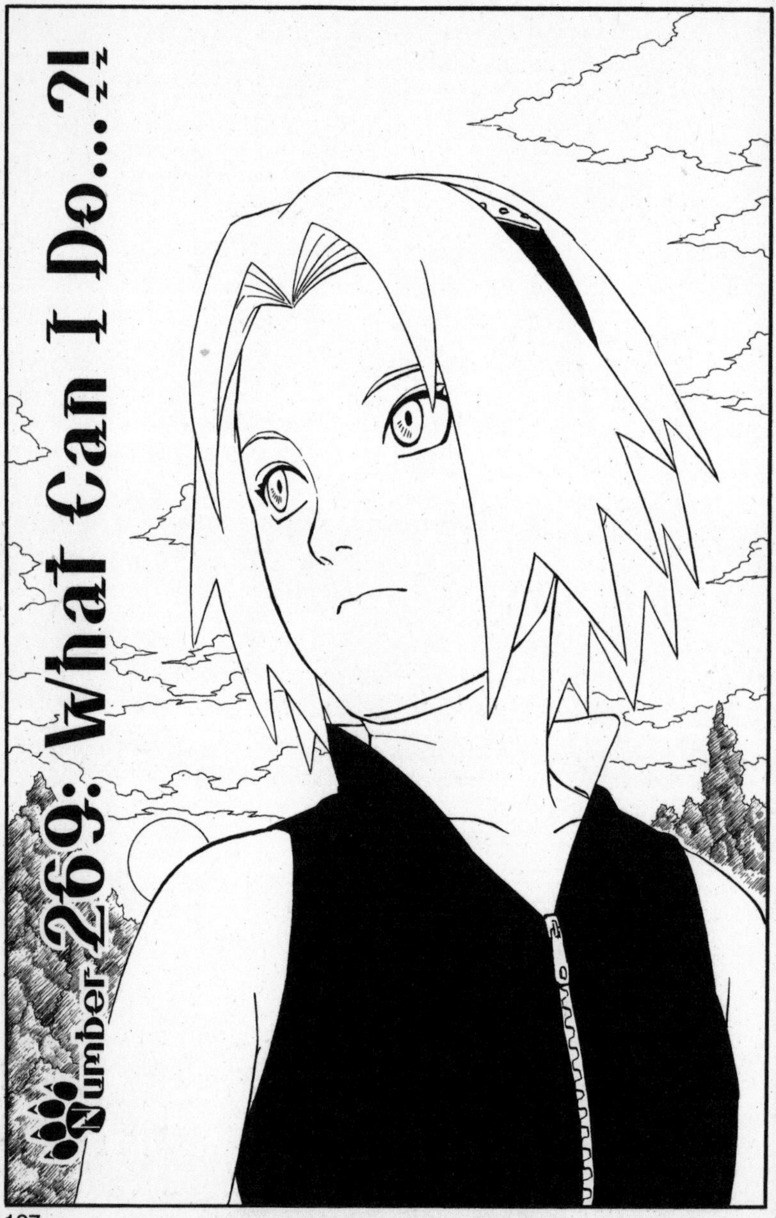
Number 269: What Can I Do...?!

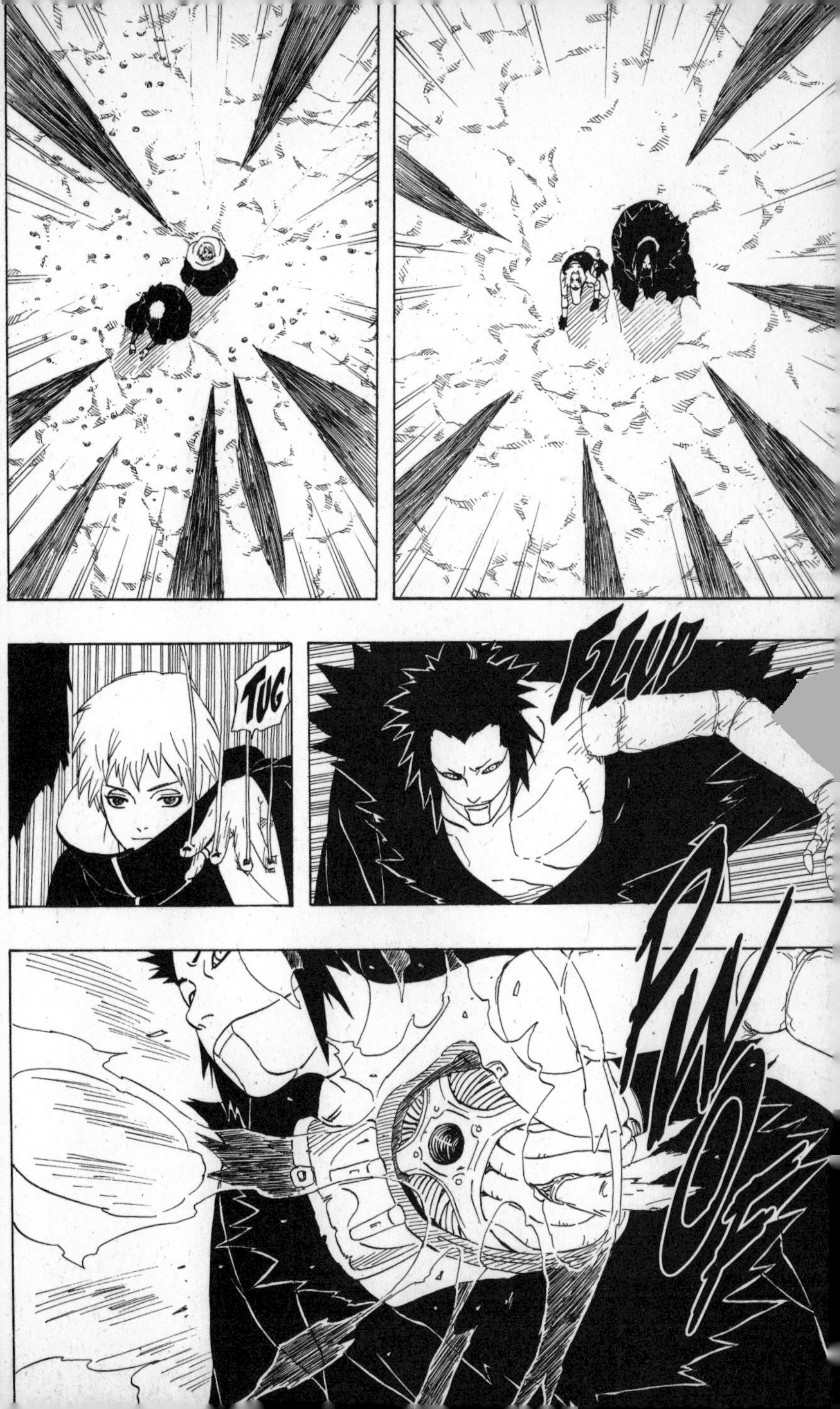
TUG
FLUP

READ THIS WAY

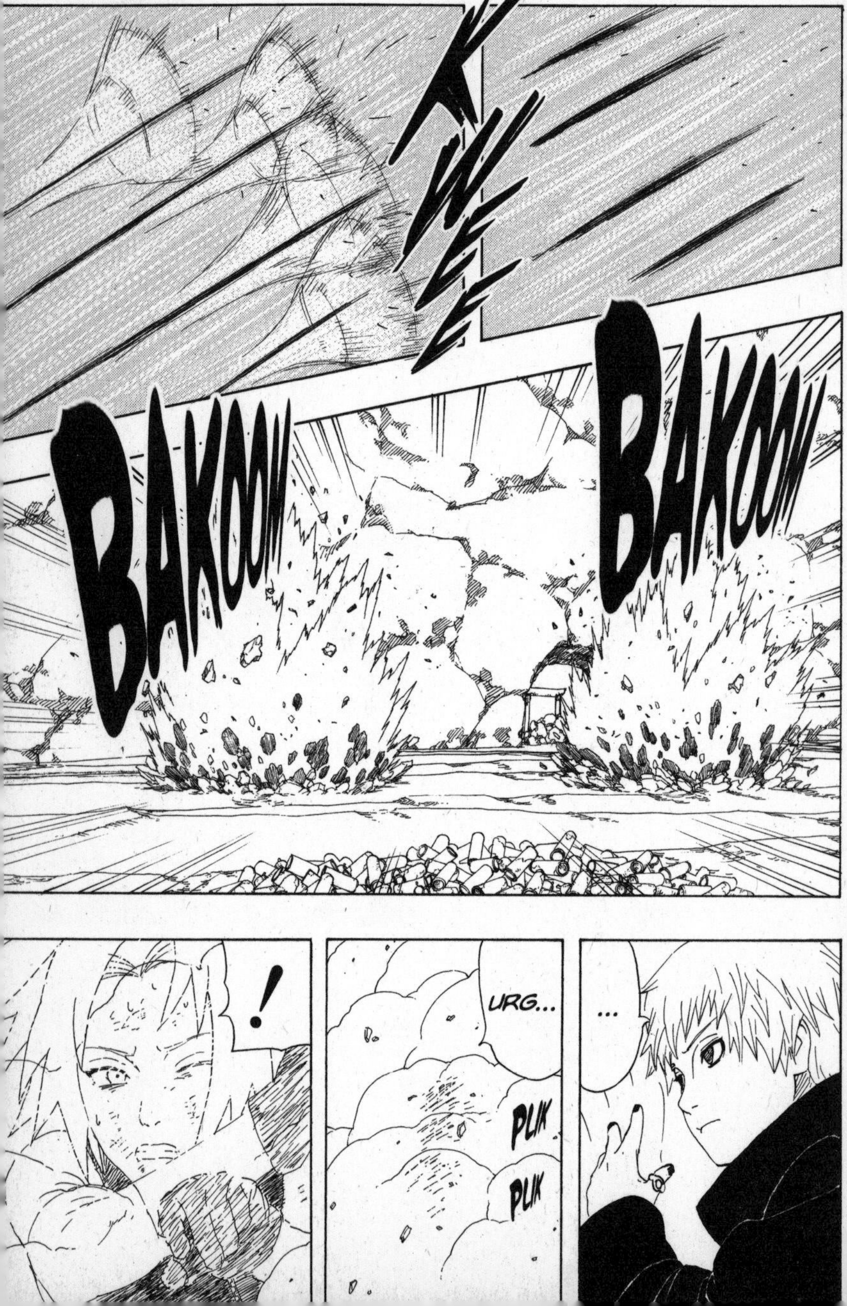
KWEEE
BAKOOM
BAKOOM
...
URG...
PLIK
PLIK
!

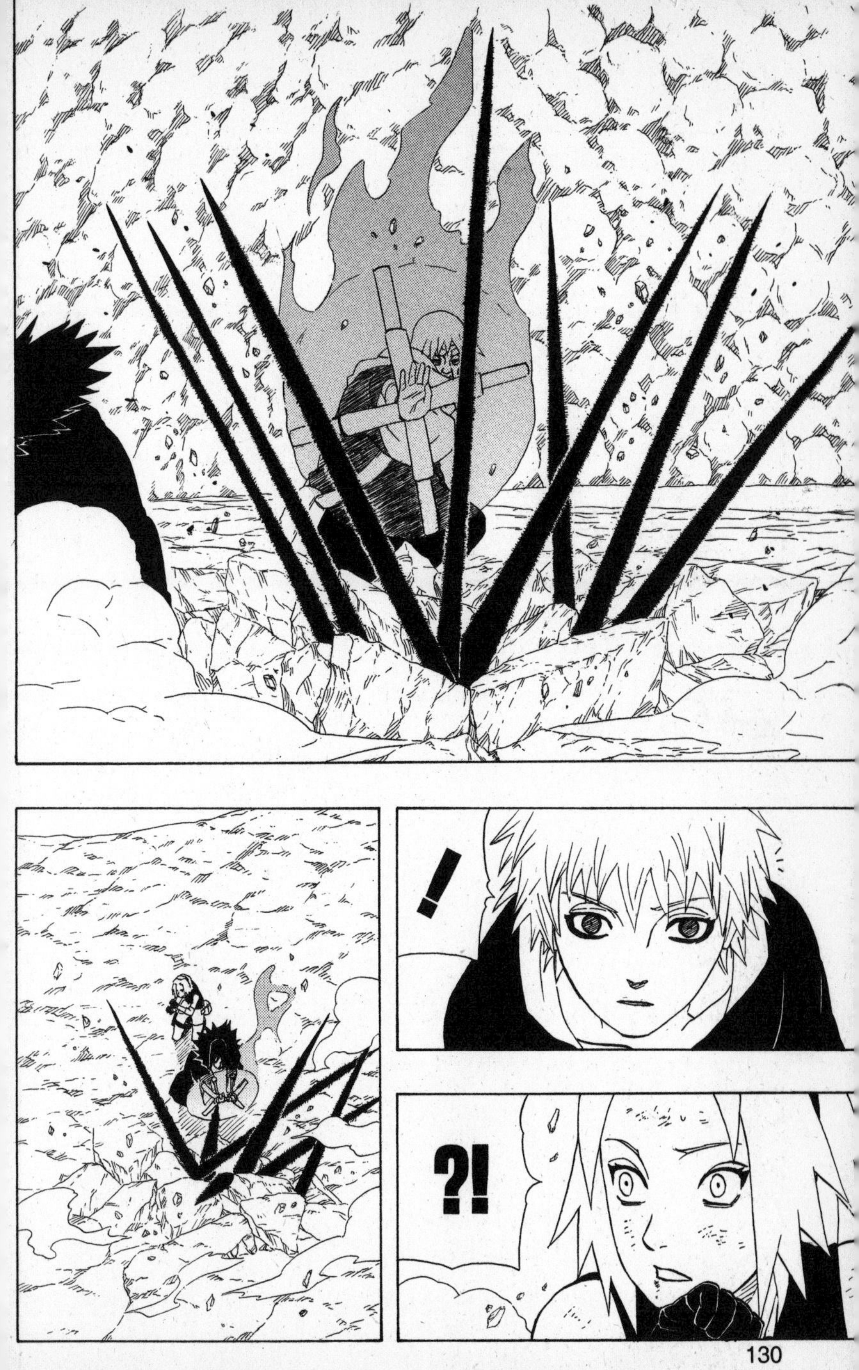
!
?!

READ THIS WAY

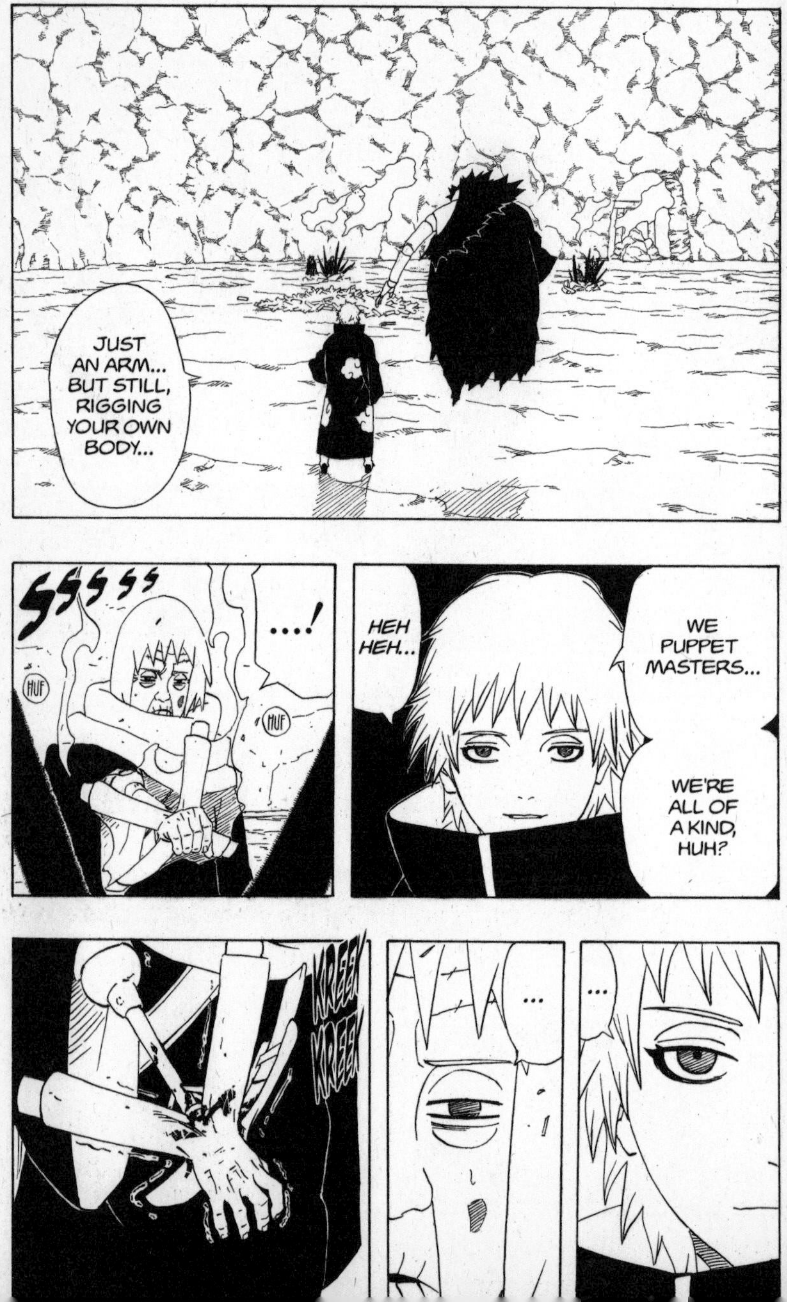
JUST AN ARM... BUT STILL, RIGGING YOUR OWN BODY...
HEH HEH...
WE PUPPET MASTERS...
WE'RE ALL OF A KIND, HUH?
SSSSS
HUF
...!
HUF
...
...
KREEK
KREEK

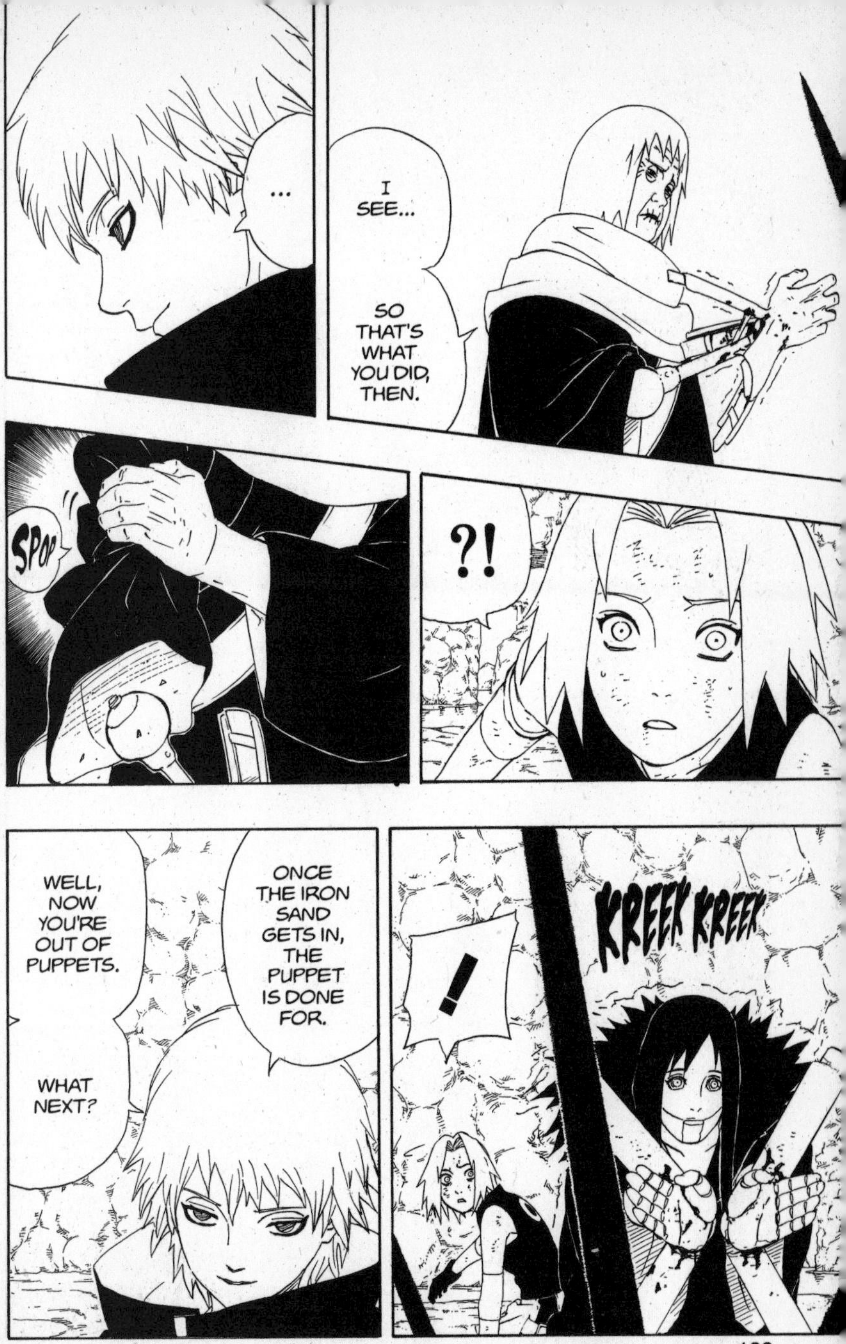
I SEE...
SO THAT'S WHAT YOU DID, THEN.
...
?!
SPOP
KREEK KREEK
!
ONCE THE IRON SAND GETS IN, THE PUPPET IS DONE FOR.
WELL, NOW YOU'RE OUT OF PUPPETS.
WHAT NEXT?

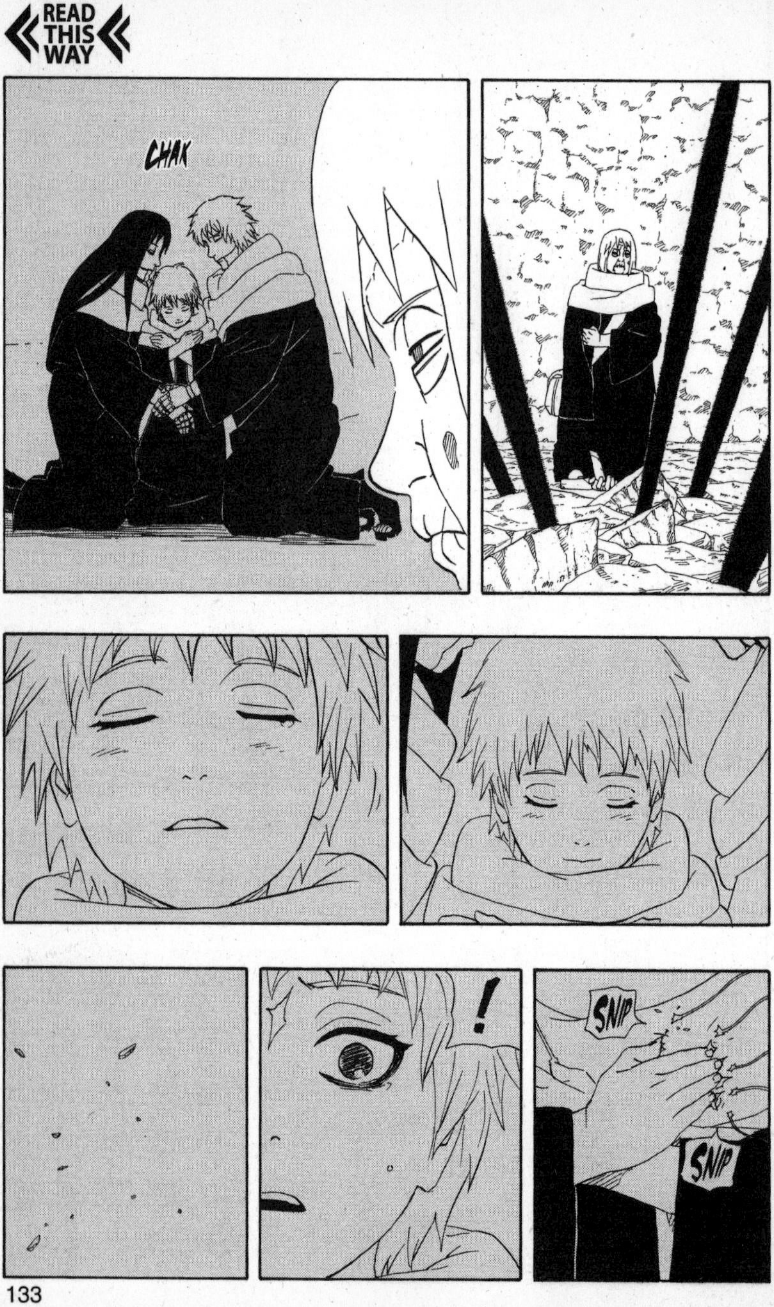
READ THIS WAY
CHAK
!
SNIP
SNIP

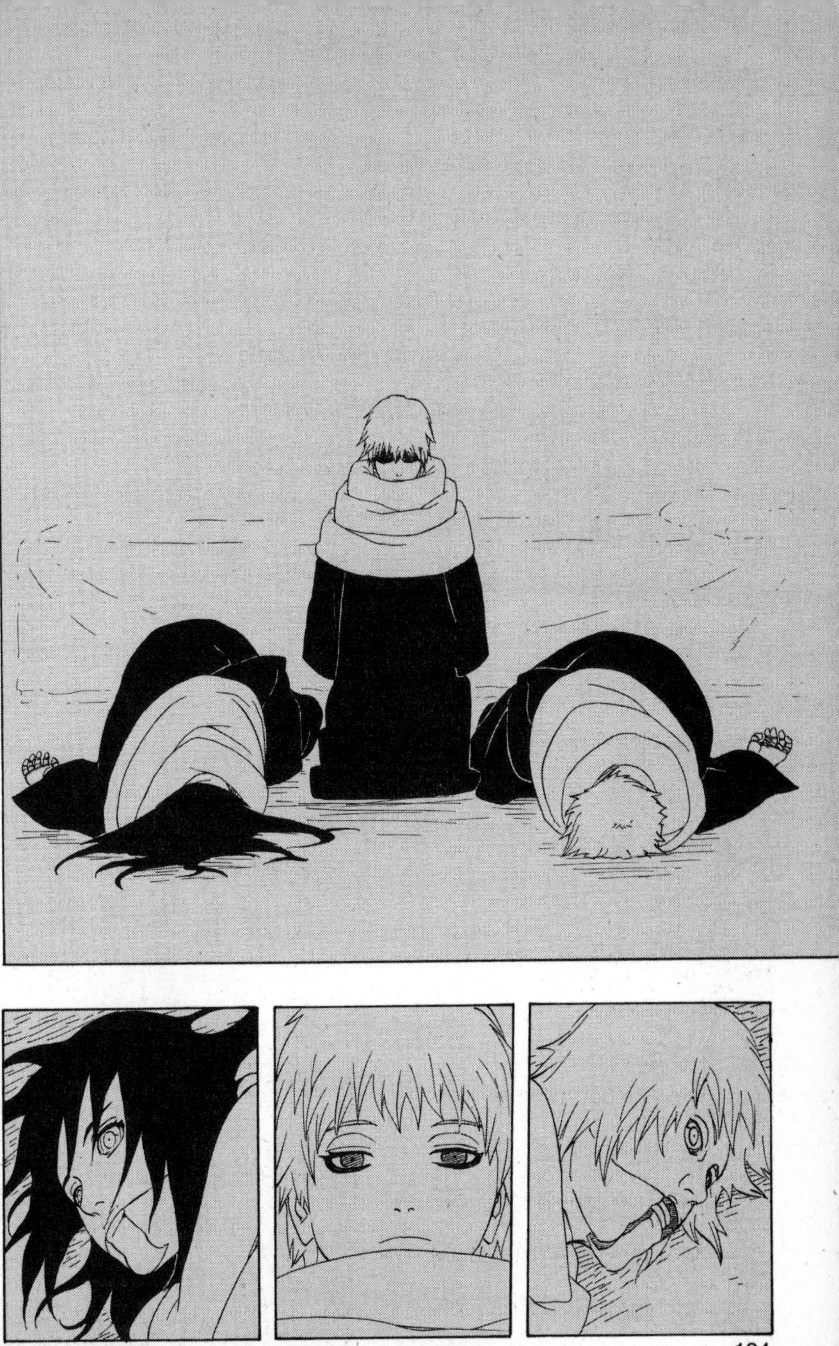

READ THIS WAY

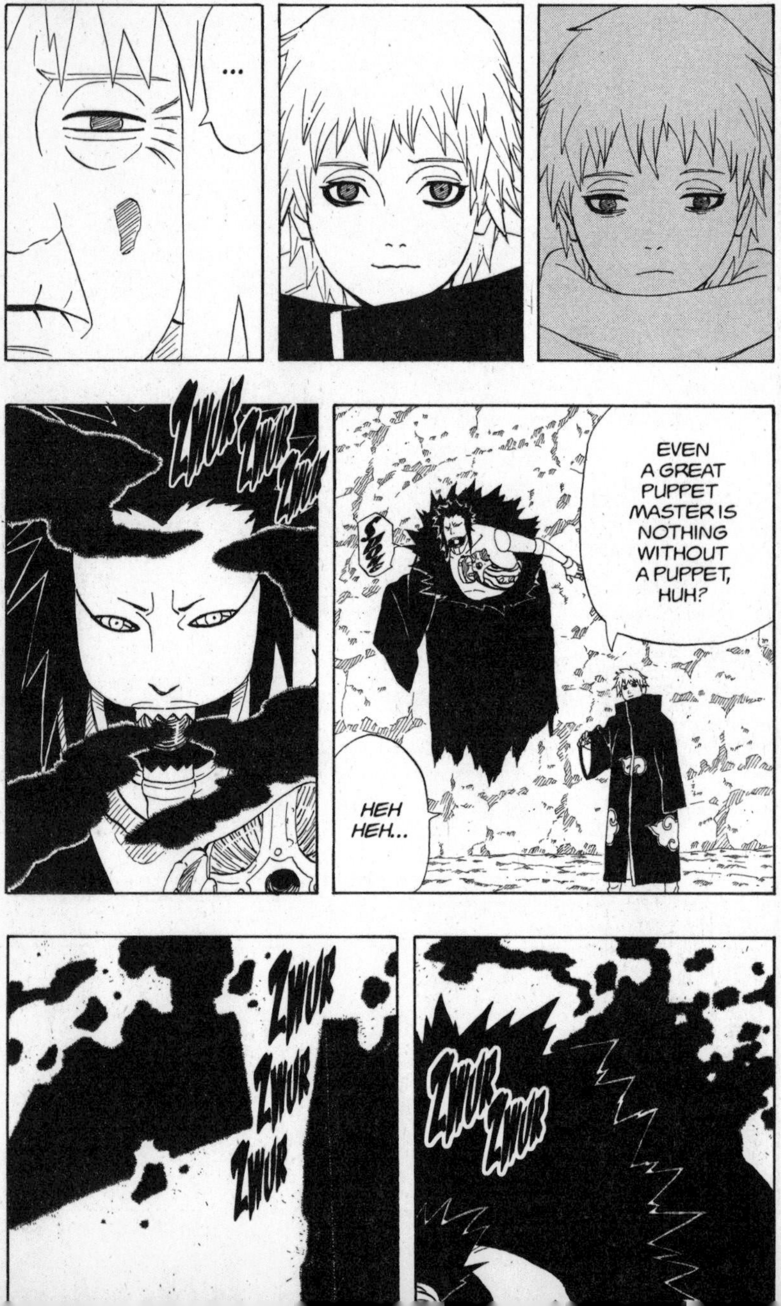
...
EVEN A GREAT PUPPET MASTER IS NOTHING WITHOUT A PUPPET, HUH?
HEH HEH...
ZWUR ZWUR ZWUR
ZWUR ZWUR
ZWUR ZWUR ZWUR ZWUR

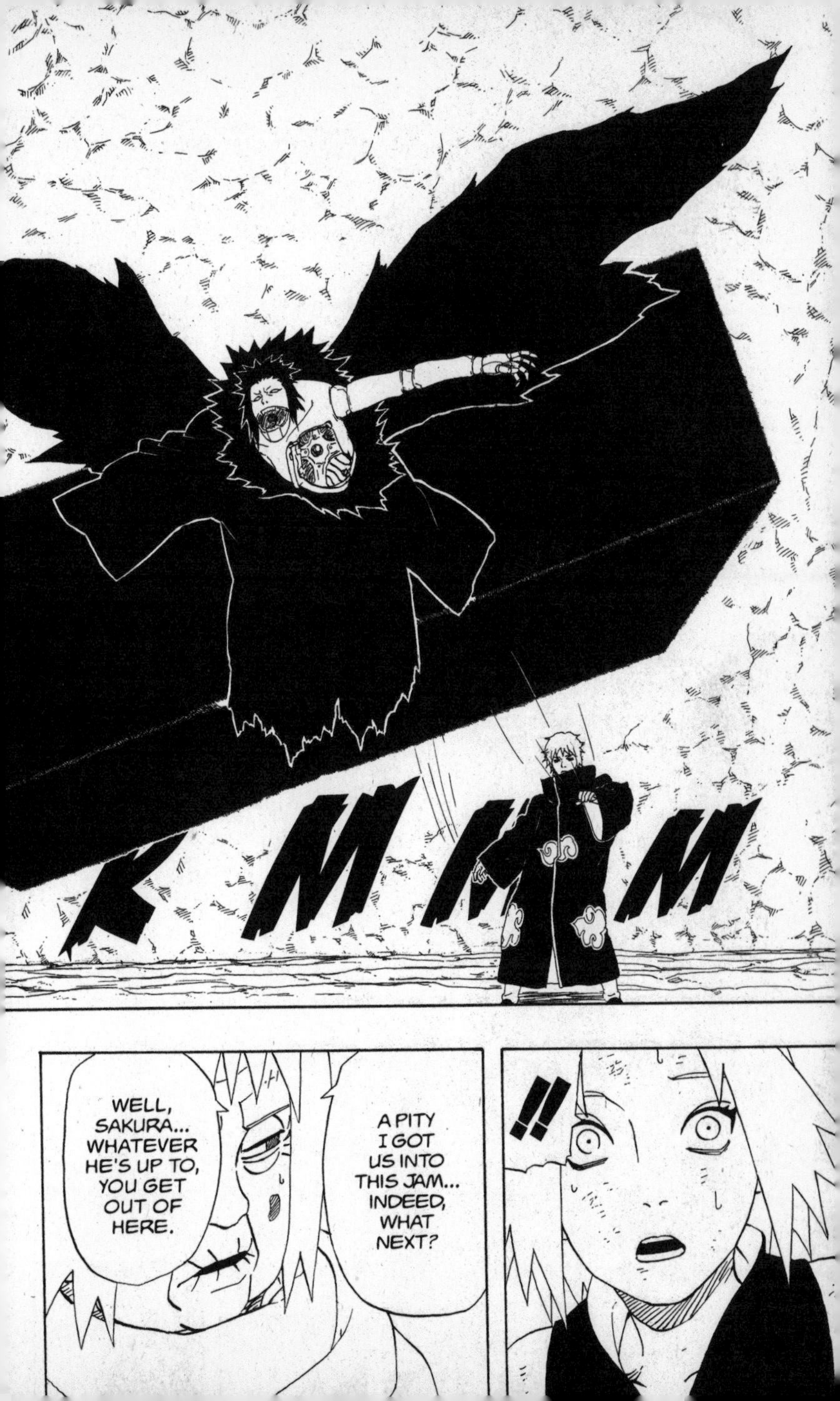
KMMMM
!!
A PITY I GOT US INTO THIS JAM... INDEED, WHAT NEXT?
WELL, SAKURA... WHATEVER HE'S UP TO, YOU GET OUT OF HERE.

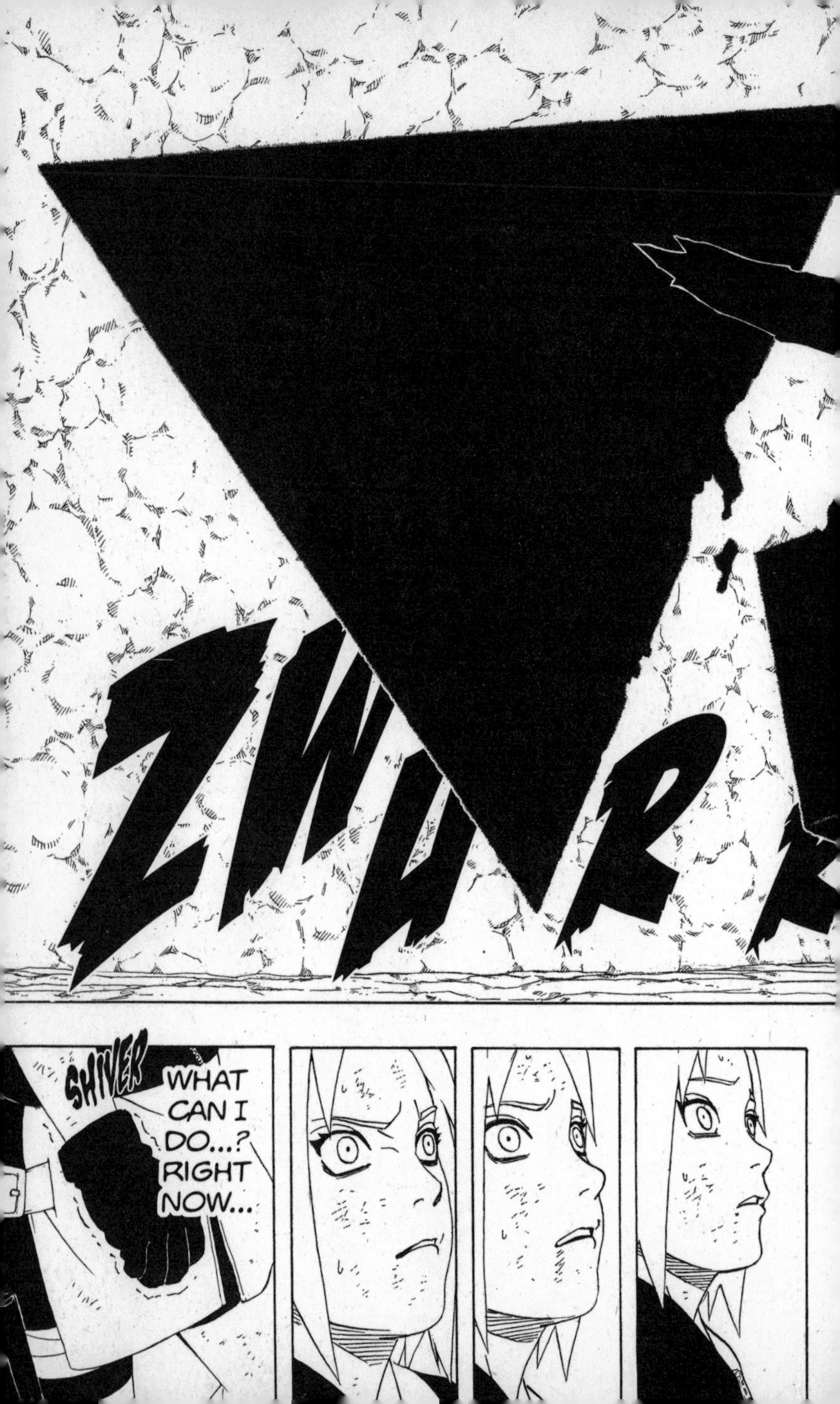
ZWUR
WHAT CAN I DO...? RIGHT NOW...
SHIVER

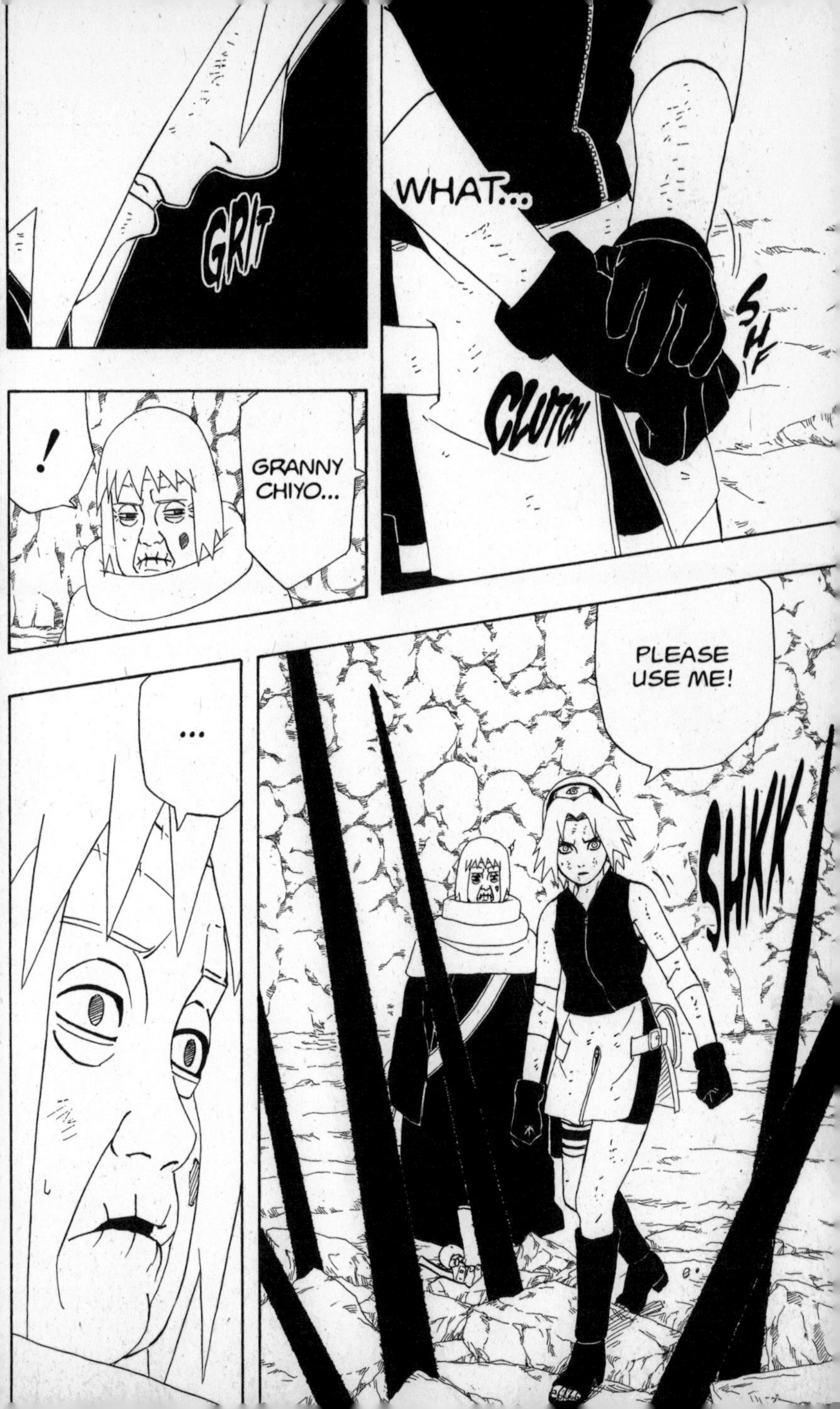

WHAT...
SHF
CLUTCH
GRIT
!
GRANNY CHIYO...
PLEASE USE ME!
SHKK
...

READ THIS WAY

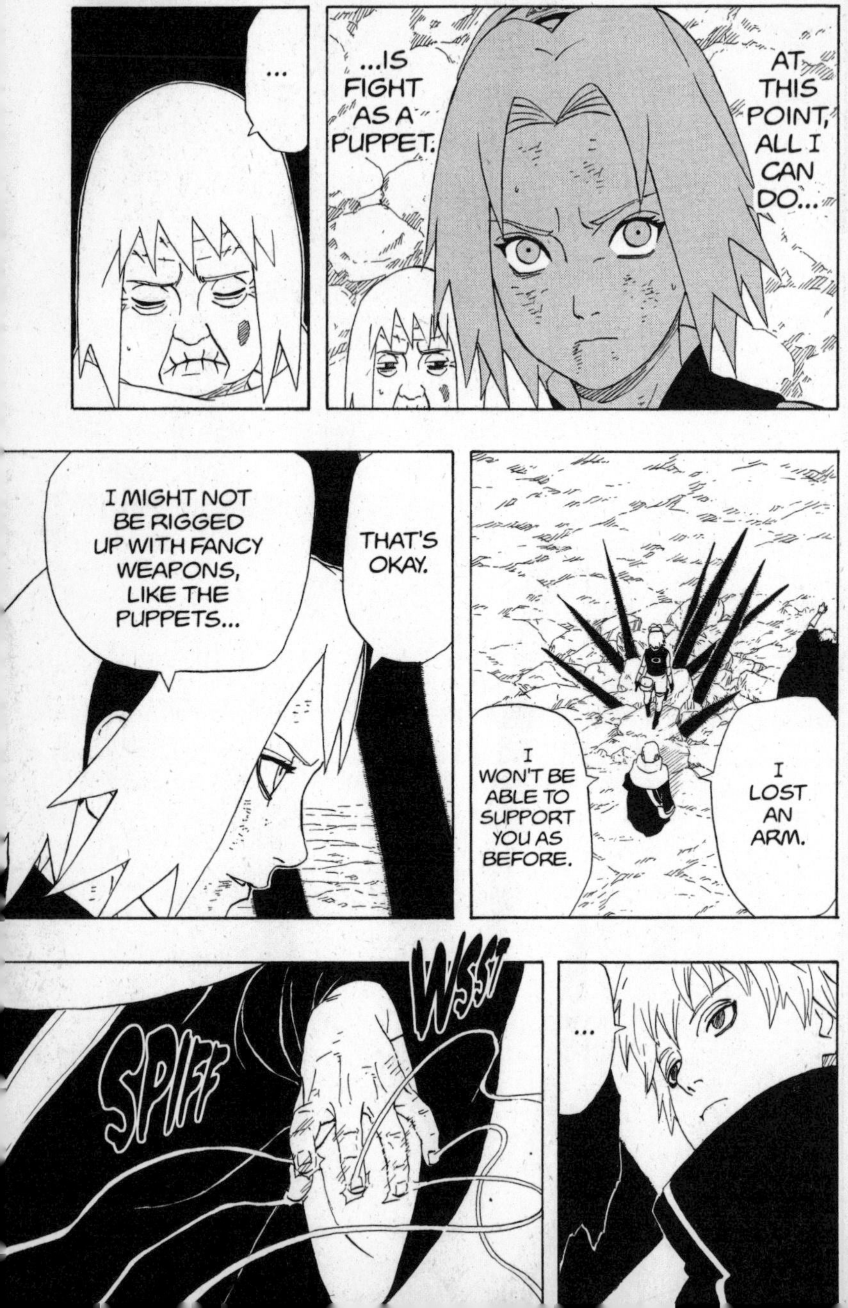

AT THIS POINT, ALL I CAN DO...
...IS FIGHT AS A PUPPET.
...
I LOST AN ARM.
I WON'T BE ABLE TO SUPPORT YOU AS BEFORE.
THAT'S OKAY.
I MIGHT NOT BE RIGGED UP WITH FANCY WEAPONS, LIKE THE PUPPETS...
...
WSST
SPIFF

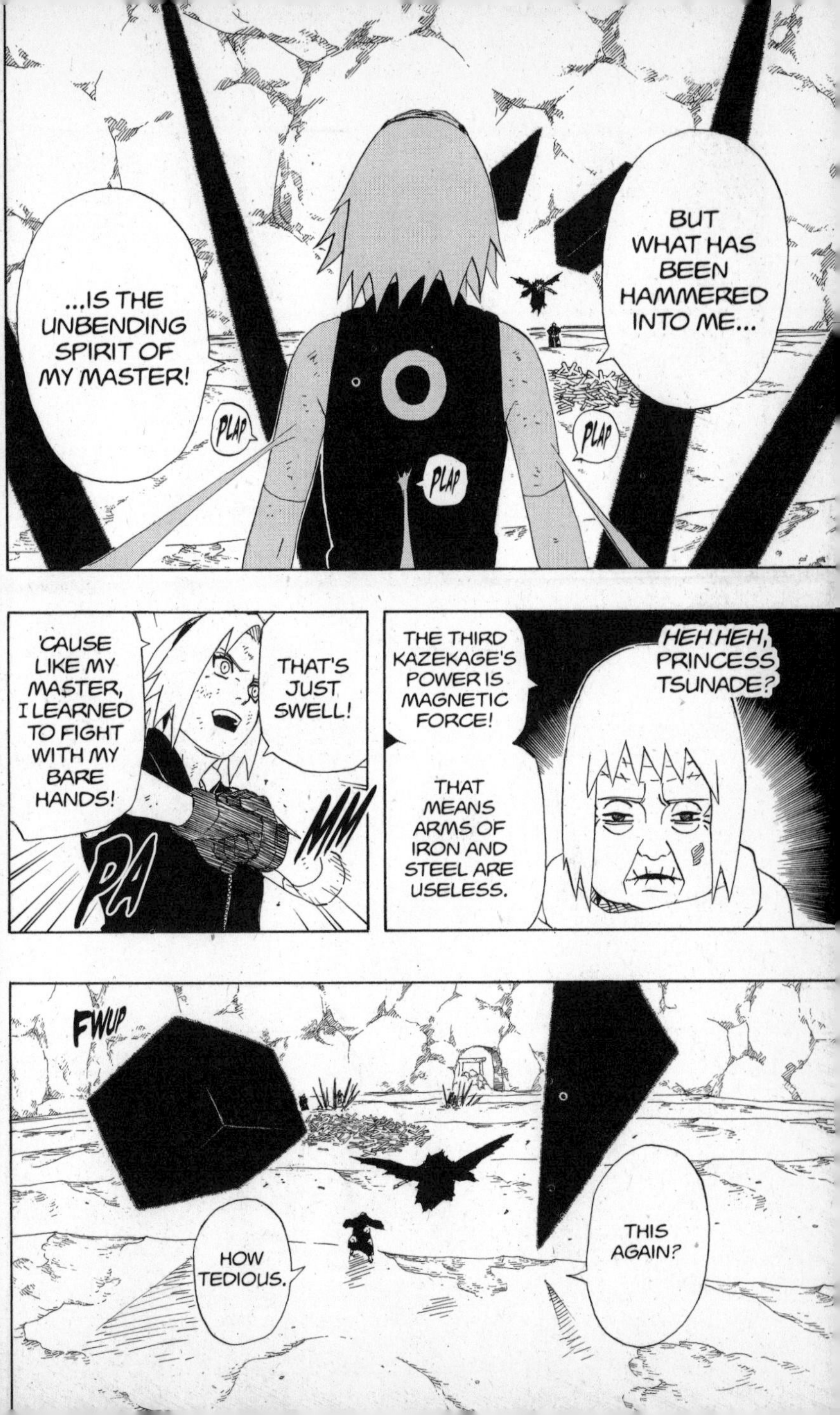
BUT WHAT HAS BEEN HAMMERED INTO ME...
...IS THE UNBENDING SPIRIT OF MY MASTER!
PLAP
PLAP
PLAP
HEH HEH, PRINCESS TSUNADE?
THE THIRD KAZEKAGE'S POWER IS MAGNETIC FORCE!
THAT MEANS ARMS OF IRON AND STEEL ARE USELESS.
THAT'S JUST SWELL!
'CAUSE LIKE MY MASTER, I LEARNED TO FIGHT WITH MY BARE HANDS!
MM
PA
FWUP
THIS AGAIN?
HOW TEDIOUS.

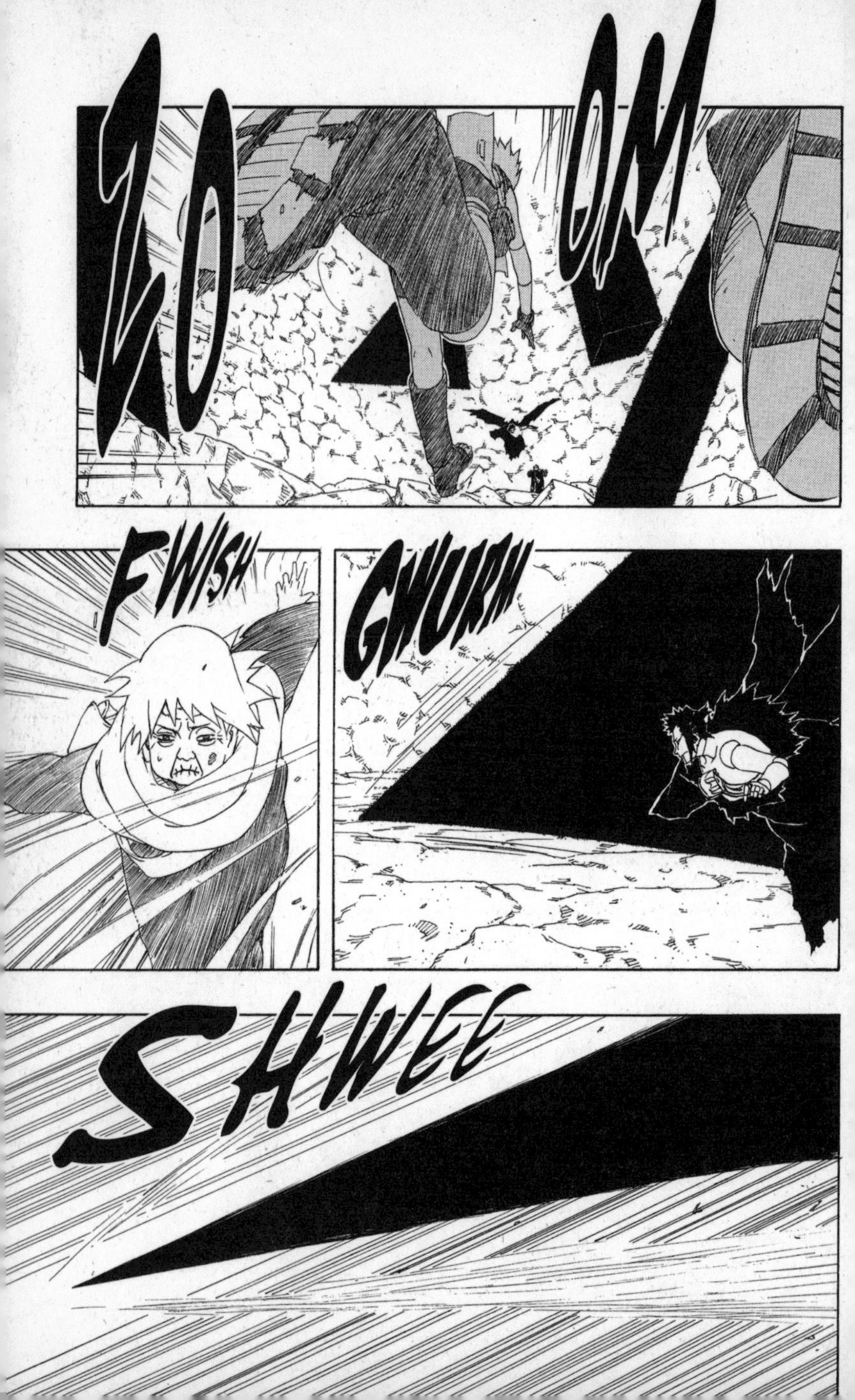
ZOOM
GWUSH
FWISH
SHWEE

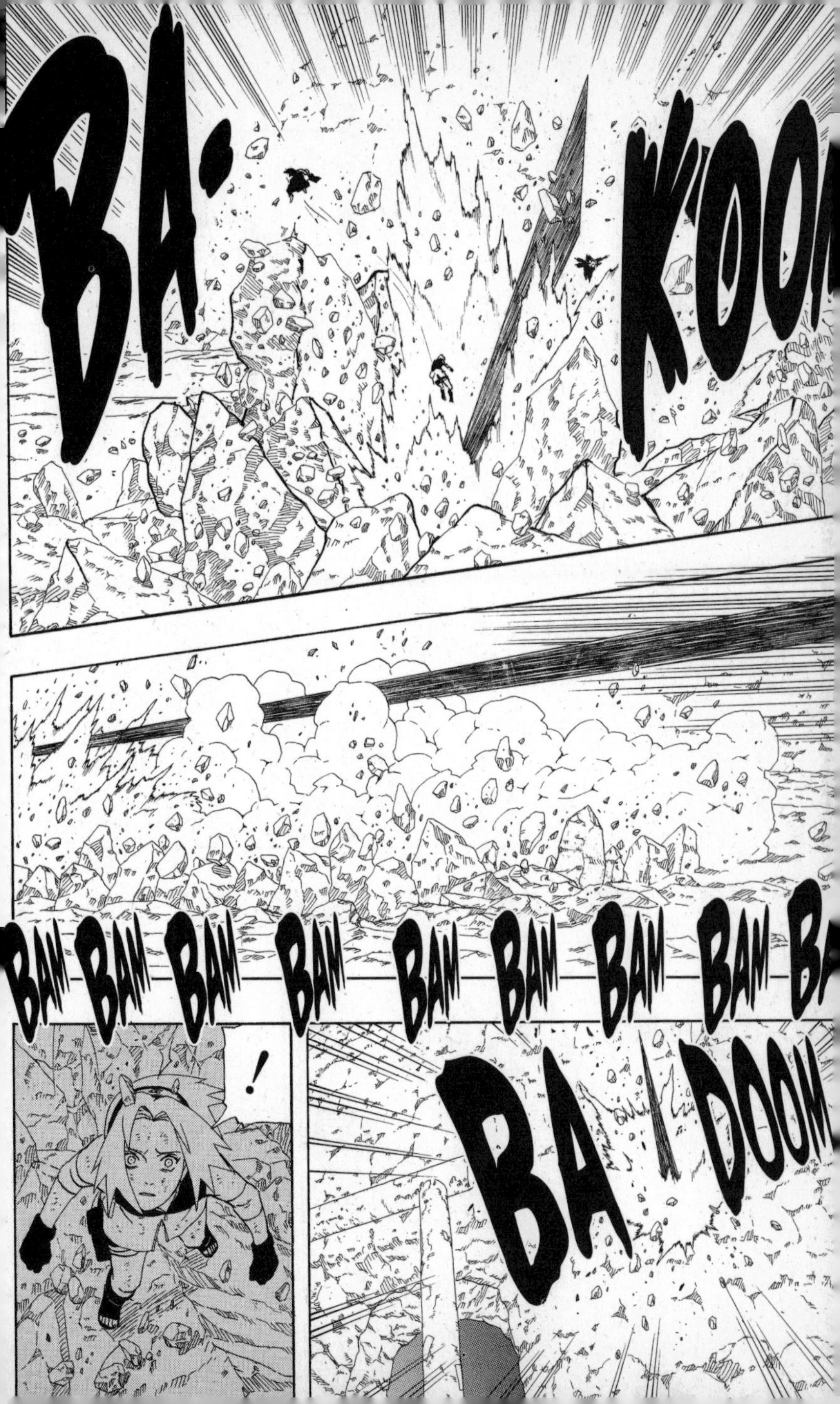
BA-K'OOM
BAM BAM BAM BAM BAM BAM BAM BAM BAM
BA-DOOM
!

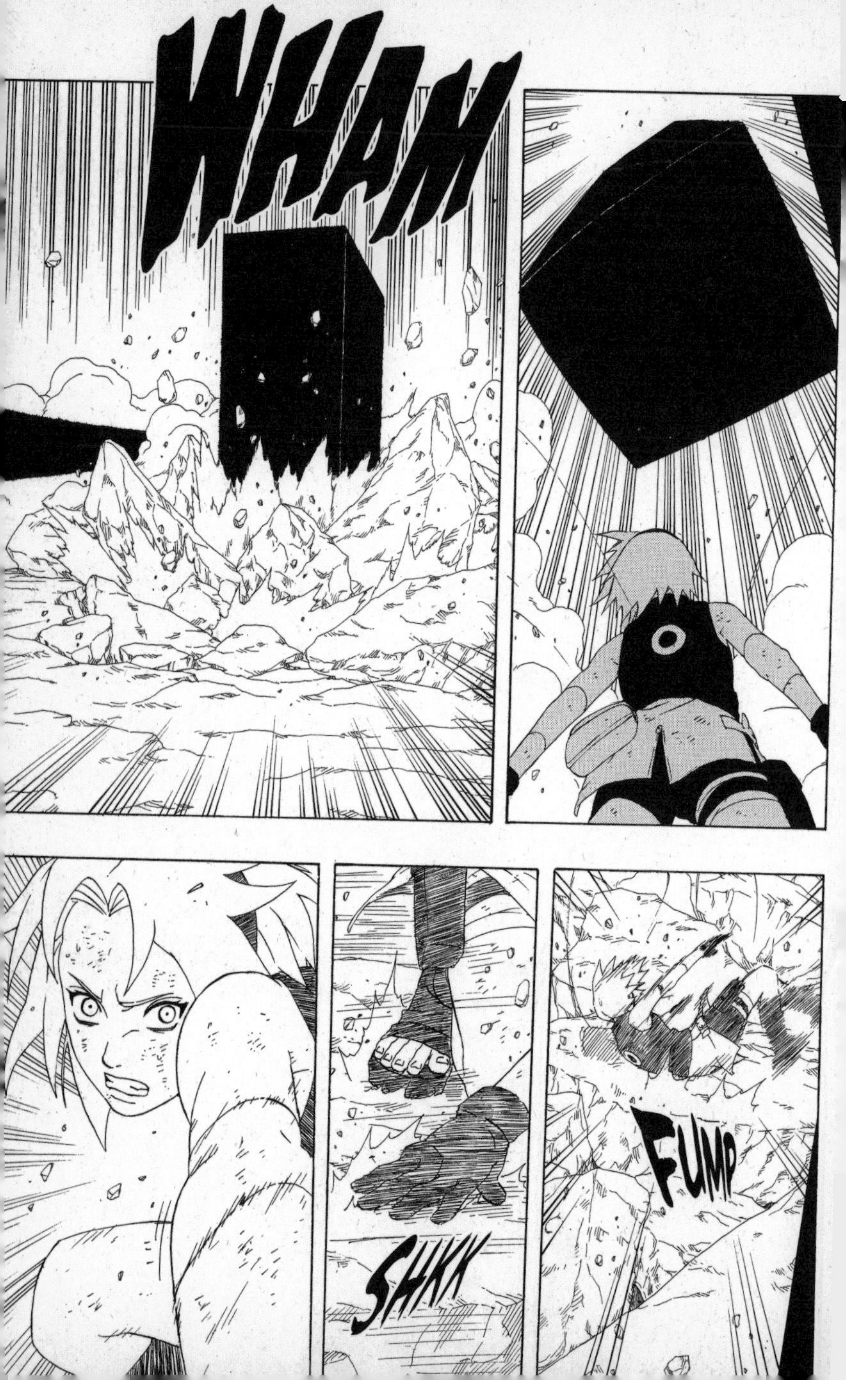
WHAM
FUMP
SHKK

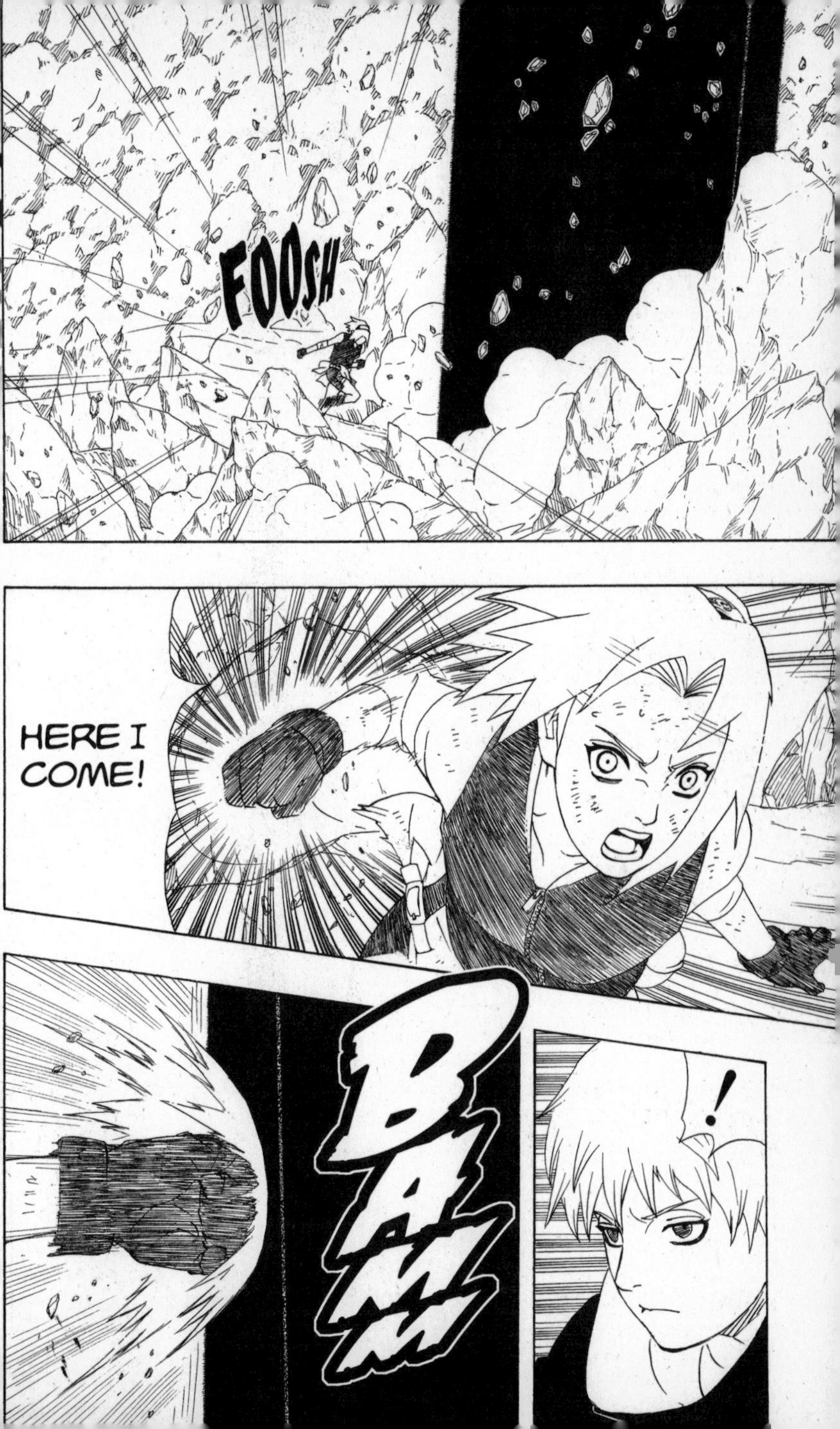
FOOSH
HERE I COME!
BAMM
!

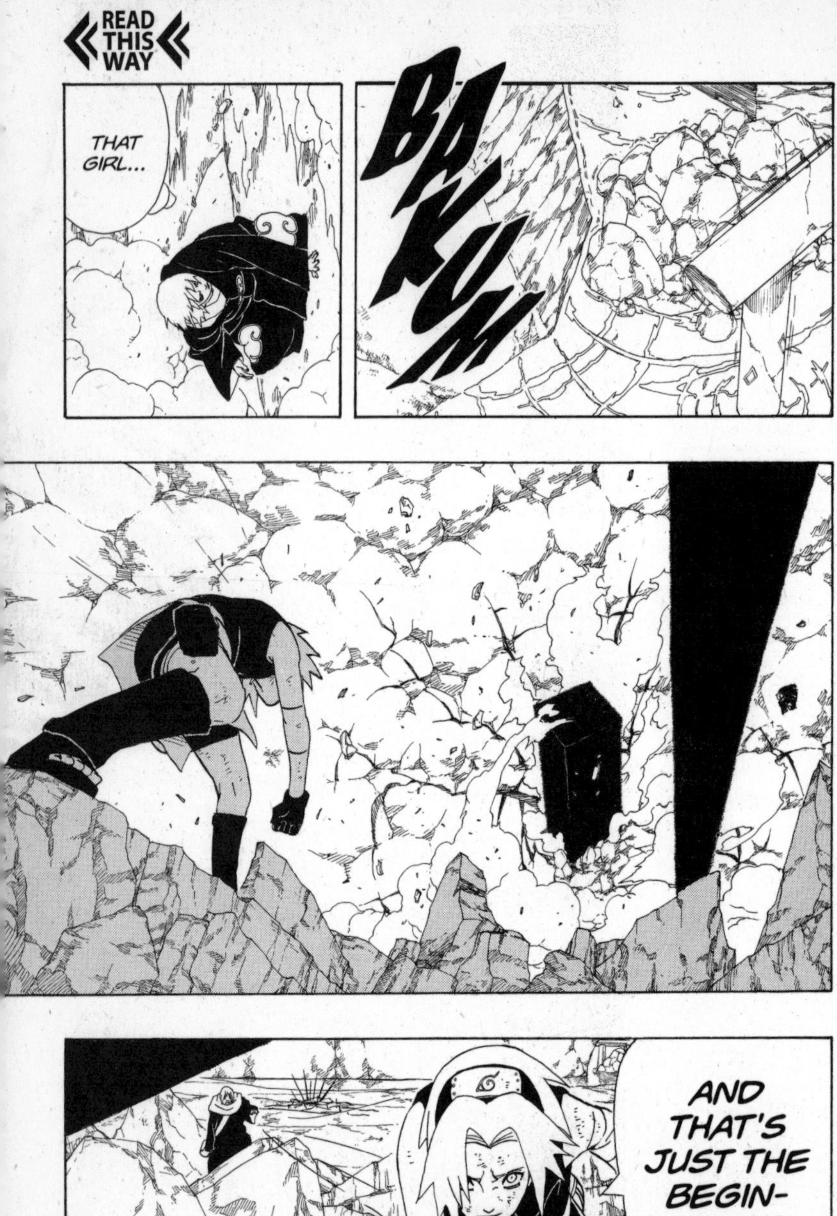
READ THIS WAY
BA-KUM
THAT GIRL...
AND THAT'S JUST THE BEGIN-NING!!

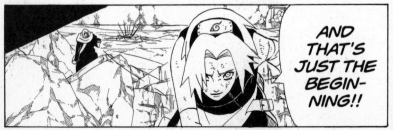

NARUTO

Number 270: Miscalculation...!!

SHKK
HUF
HUF

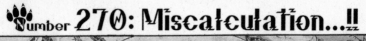

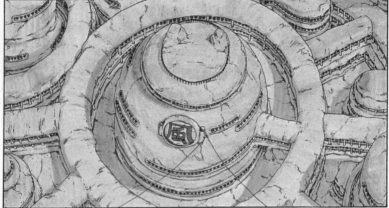

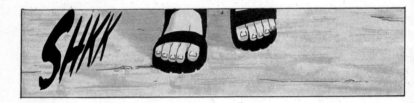

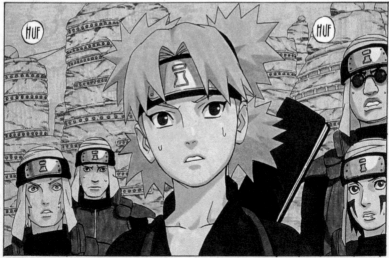

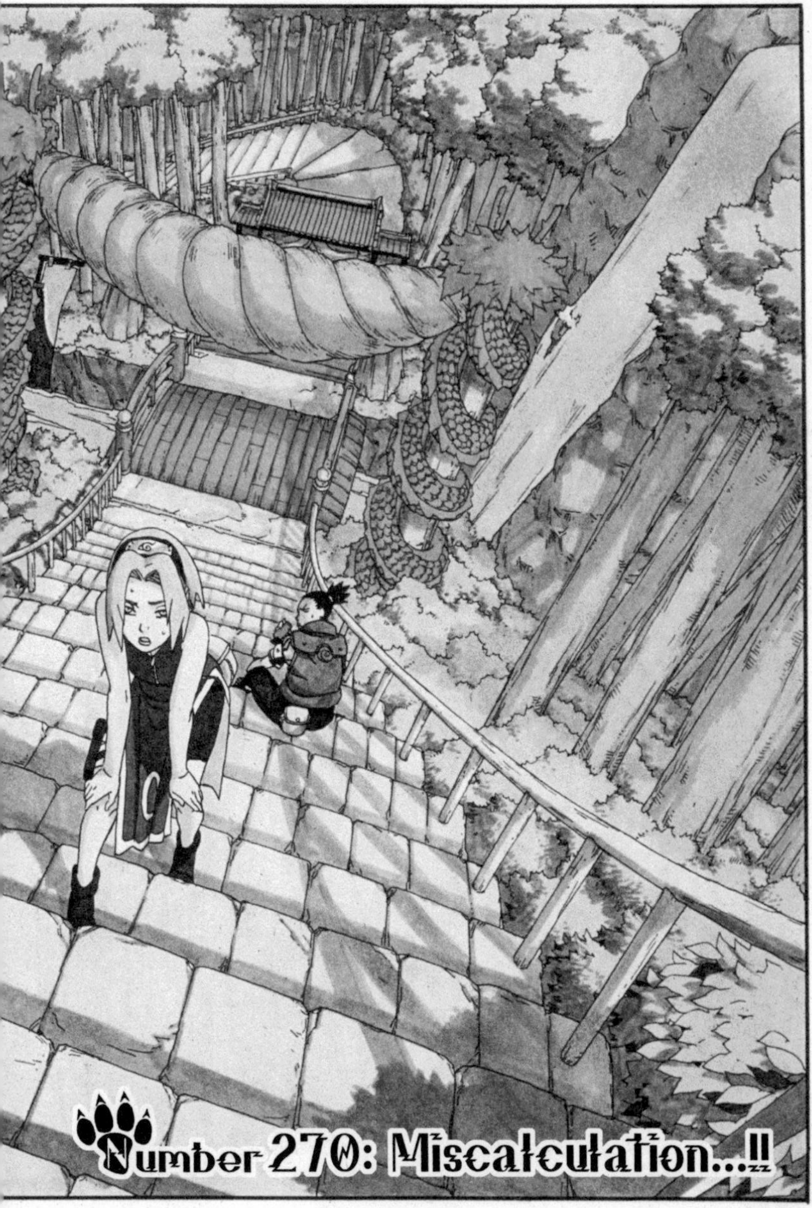
Number 270: Miscalculation...!!

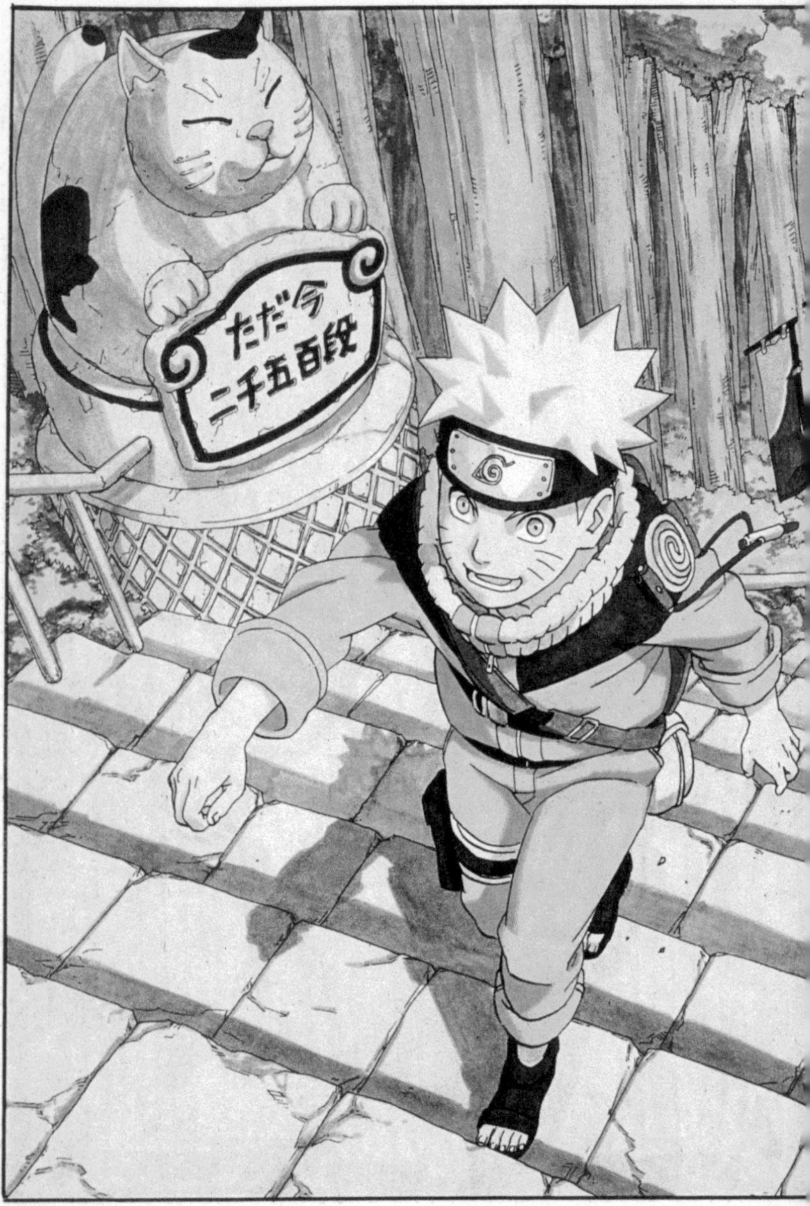
ただ今
二千五百段

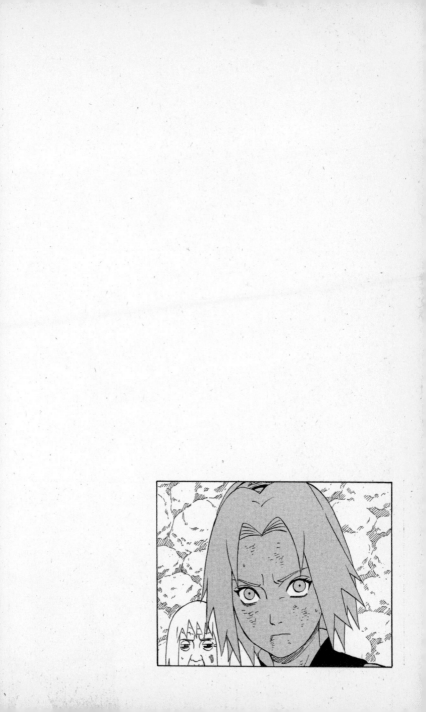

READ THIS WAY

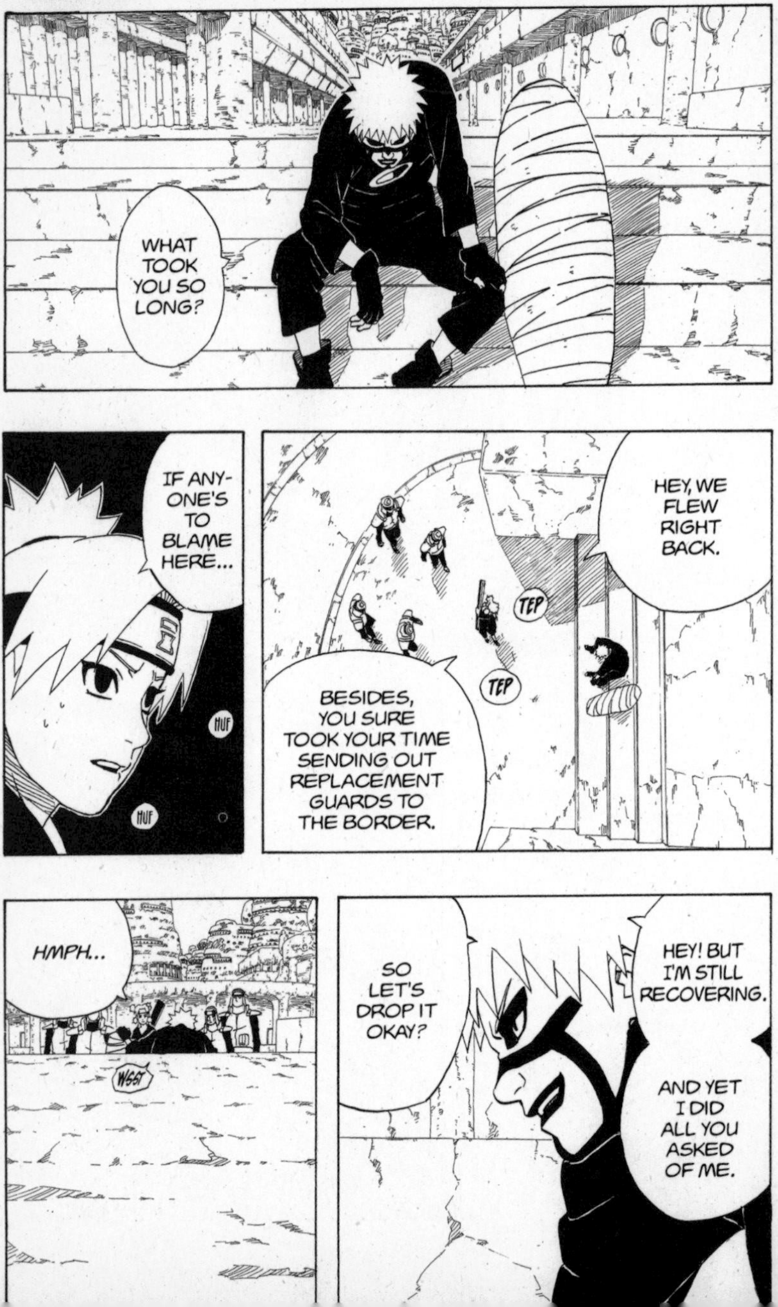
WHAT TOOK YOU SO LONG?
HEY, WE FLEW RIGHT BACK.
TEP
TEP
BESIDES, YOU SURE TOOK YOUR TIME SENDING OUT REPLACEMENT GUARDS TO THE BORDER.
IF ANY-ONE'S TO BLAME HERE...
HUF
HUF
HEY! BUT I'M STILL RECOVERING.
AND YET I DID ALL YOU ASKED OF ME.
SO LET'S DROP IT OKAY?
HMPH...
WSST

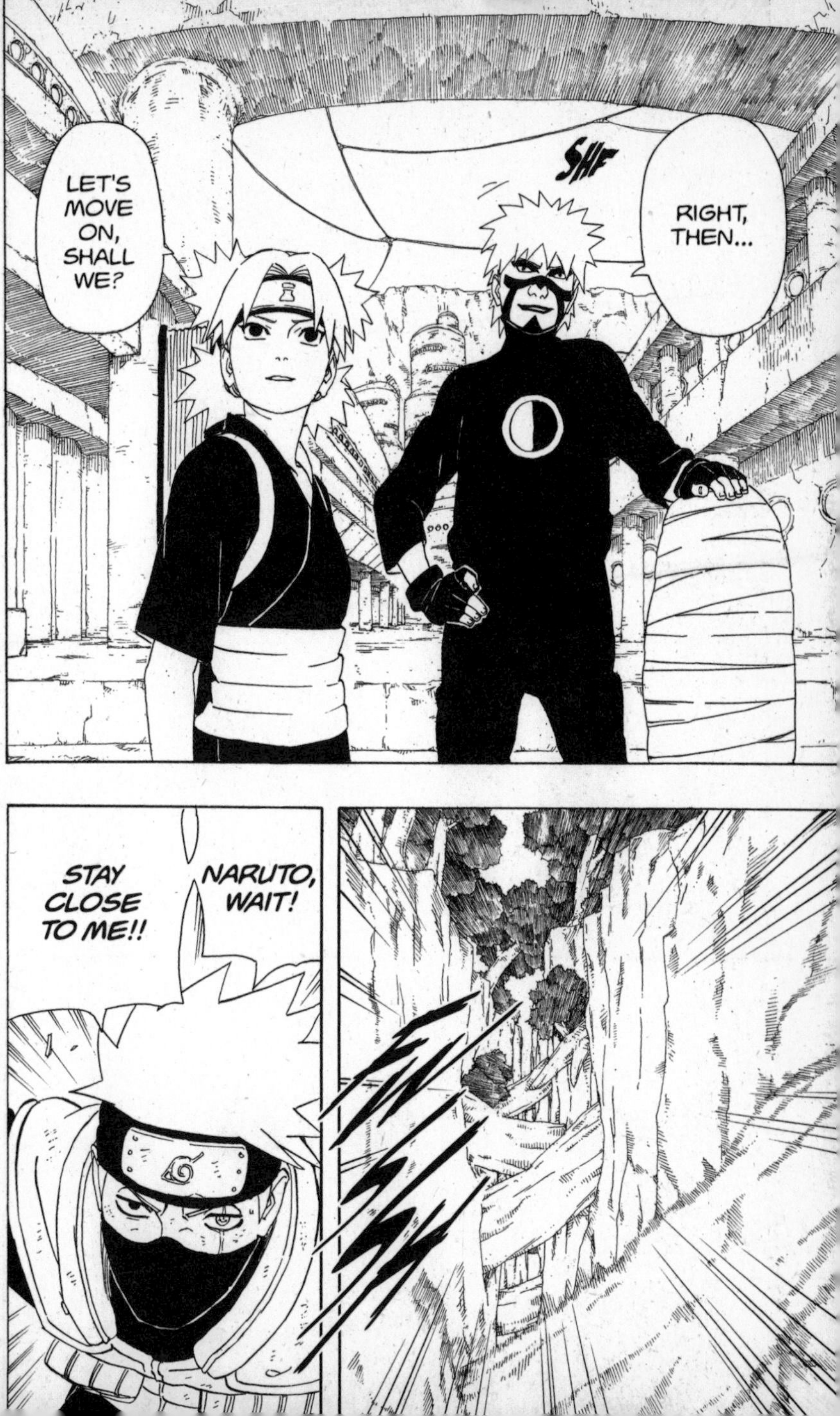
RIGHT, THEN...
SHF
LET'S MOVE ON, SHALL WE?
NARUTO, WAIT!
STAY CLOSE TO ME!!

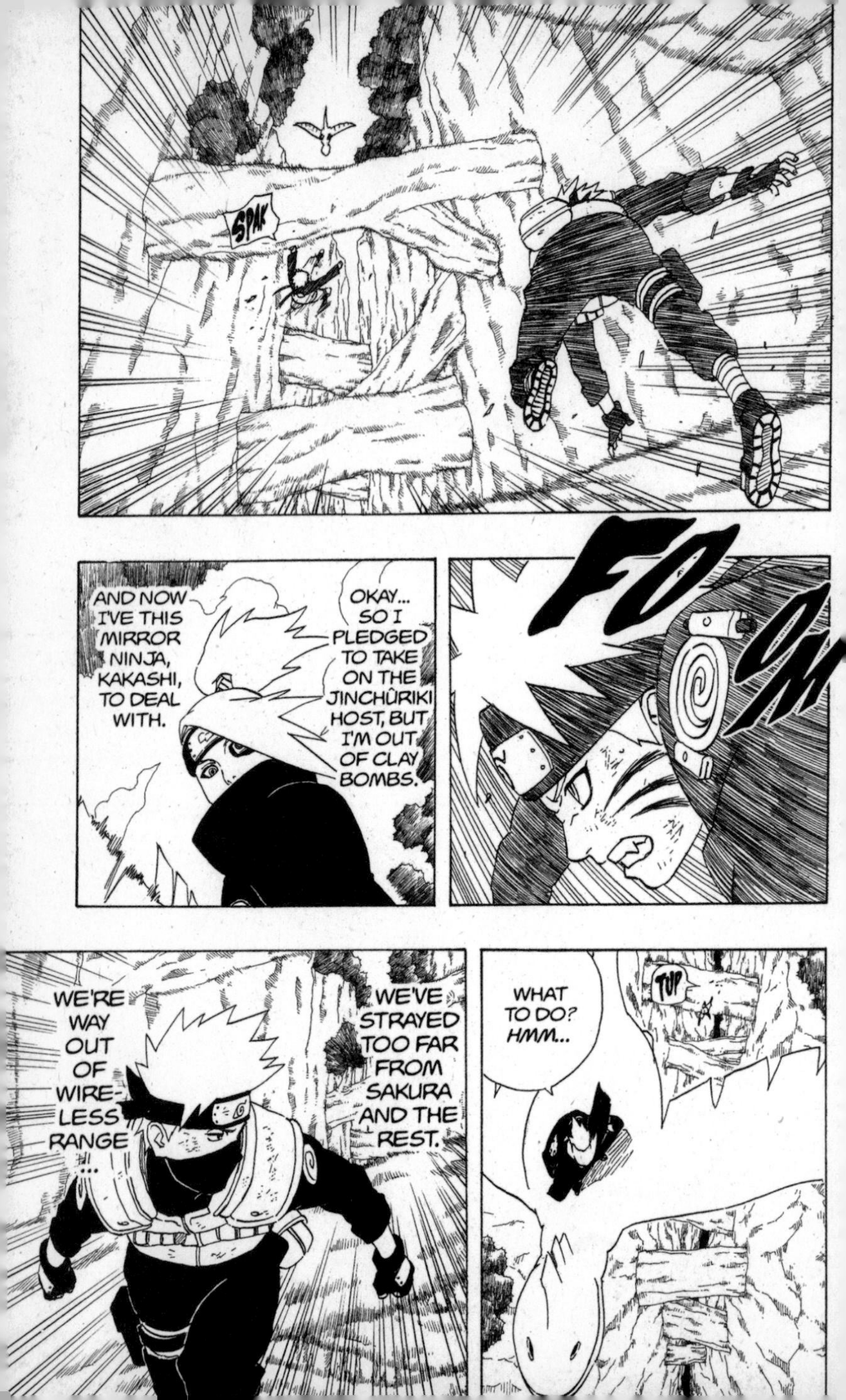
SPAK
FOOM
OKAY... SO I PLEDGED TO TAKE ON THE JINCHÛRIKI HOST, BUT I'M OUT OF CLAY BOMBS.
AND NOW I'VE THIS MIRROR NINJA, KAKASHI, TO DEAL WITH.
TUP
WHAT TO DO? HMM...
WE'VE STRAYED TOO FAR FROM SAKURA AND THE REST.
WE'RE WAY OUT OF WIRELESS RANGE...

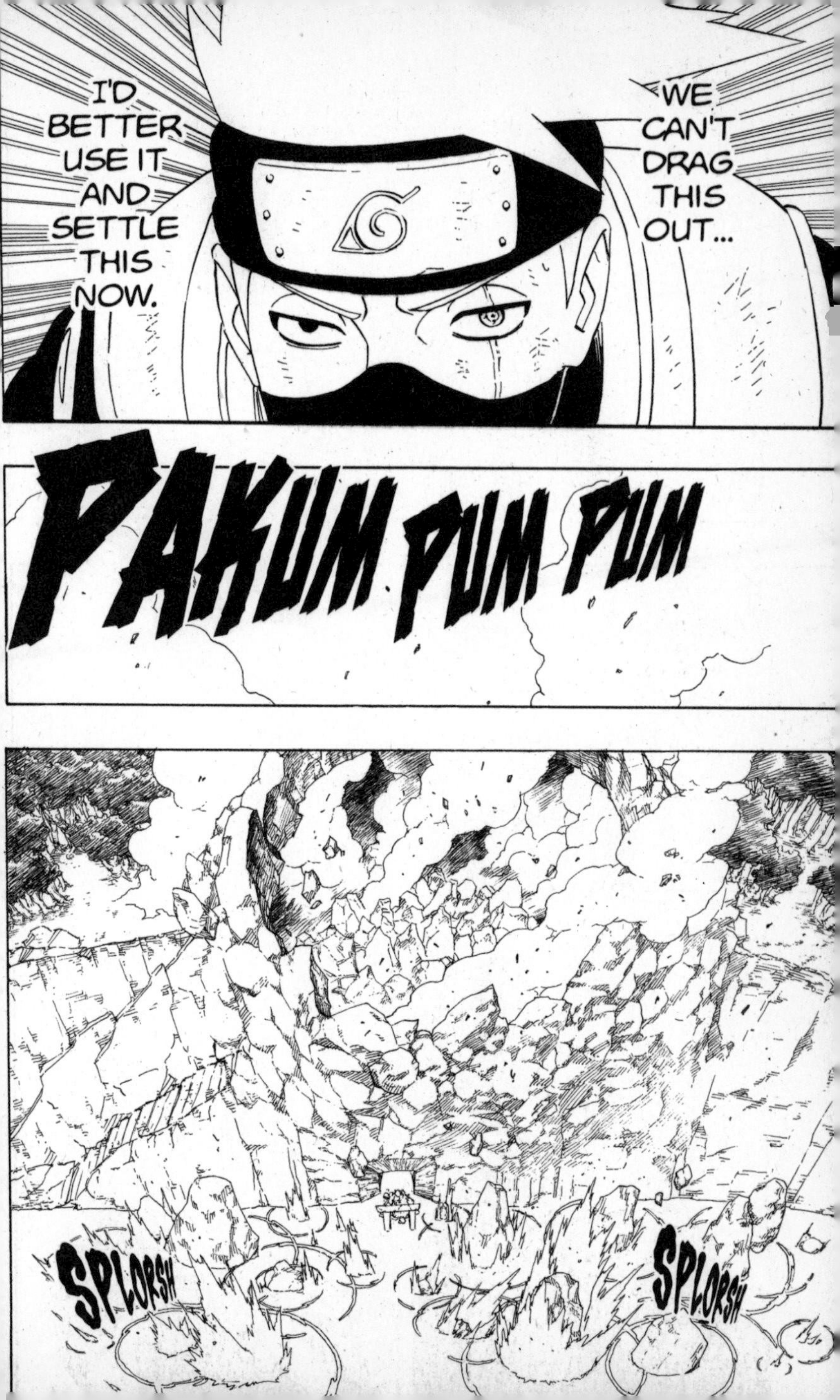
WE CAN'T DRAG THIS OUT...
I'D BETTER USE IT AND SETTLE THIS NOW.
PAKUM PUM PUM
SPLORSH
SPLORSH

READ THIS WAY

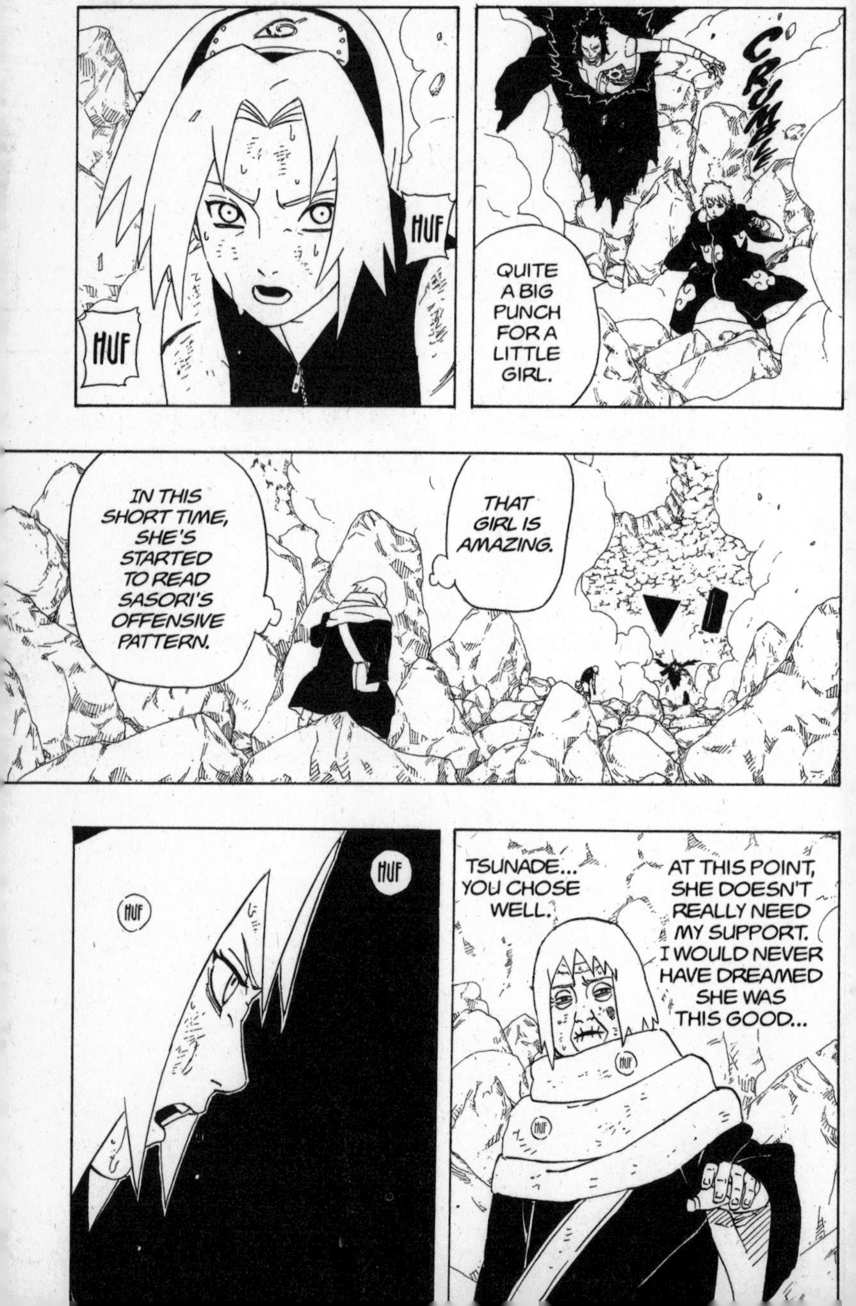
CRUMBLE
QUITE A BIG PUNCH FOR A LITTLE GIRL.
HUF
HUF
THAT GIRL IS AMAZING.
IN THIS SHORT TIME, SHE'S STARTED TO READ SASORI'S OFFENSIVE PATTERN.
AT THIS POINT, SHE DOESN'T REALLY NEED MY SUPPORT. I WOULD NEVER HAVE DREAMED SHE WAS THIS GOOD...
TSUNADE... YOU CHOSE WELL.
HUF
HUF
HUF
HUF

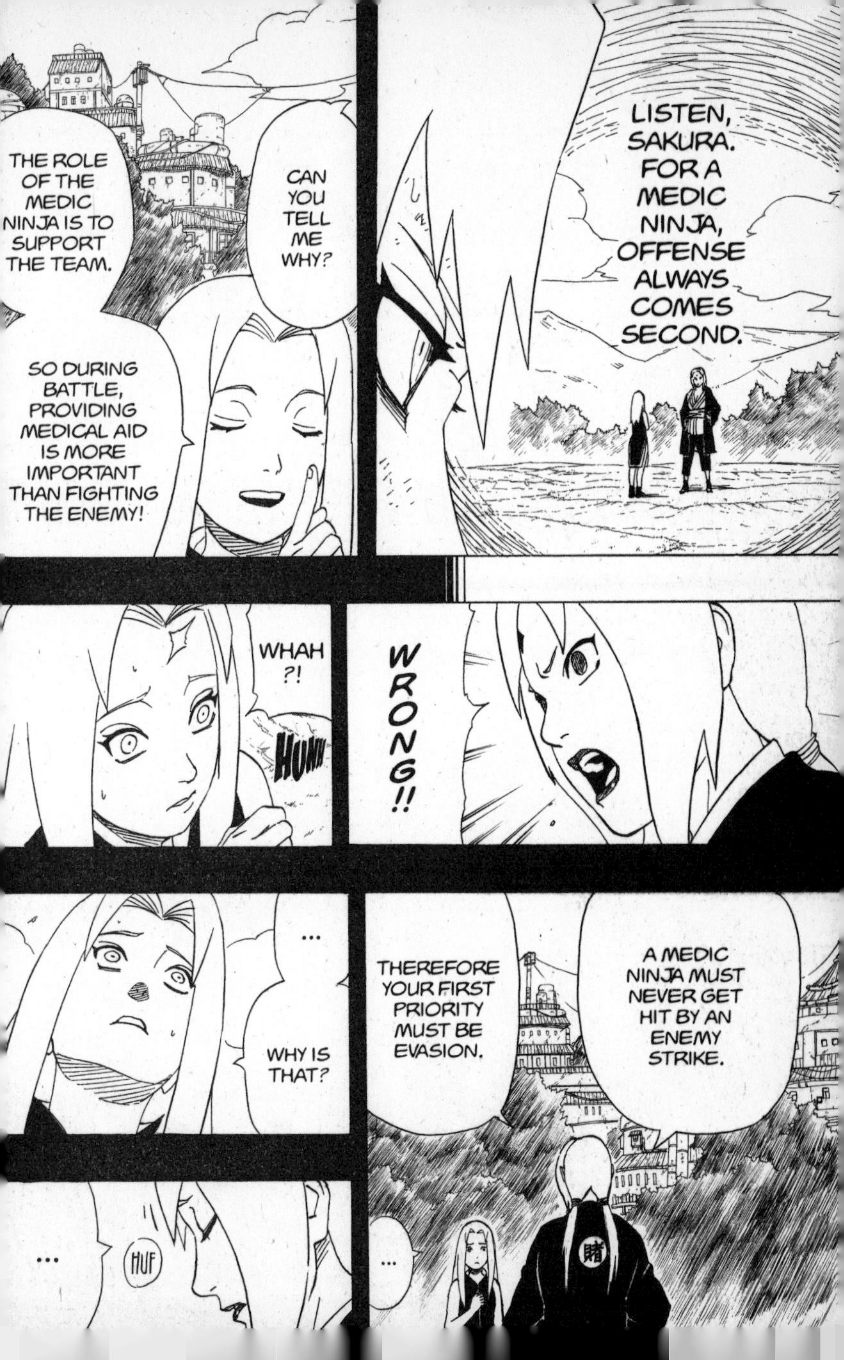

LISTEN, SAKURA. FOR A MEDIC NINJA, OFFENSE ALWAYS COMES SECOND.
CAN YOU TELL ME WHY?
THE ROLE OF THE MEDIC NINJA IS TO SUPPORT THE TEAM.
SO DURING BATTLE, PROVIDING MEDICAL AID IS MORE IMPORTANT THAN FIGHTING THE ENEMY!
WRONG!!
WHAH?!
HUNH
A MEDIC NINJA MUST NEVER GET HIT BY AN ENEMY STRIKE.
THEREFORE YOUR FIRST PRIORITY MUST BE EVASION.
...
...
WHY IS THAT?
HUF
...

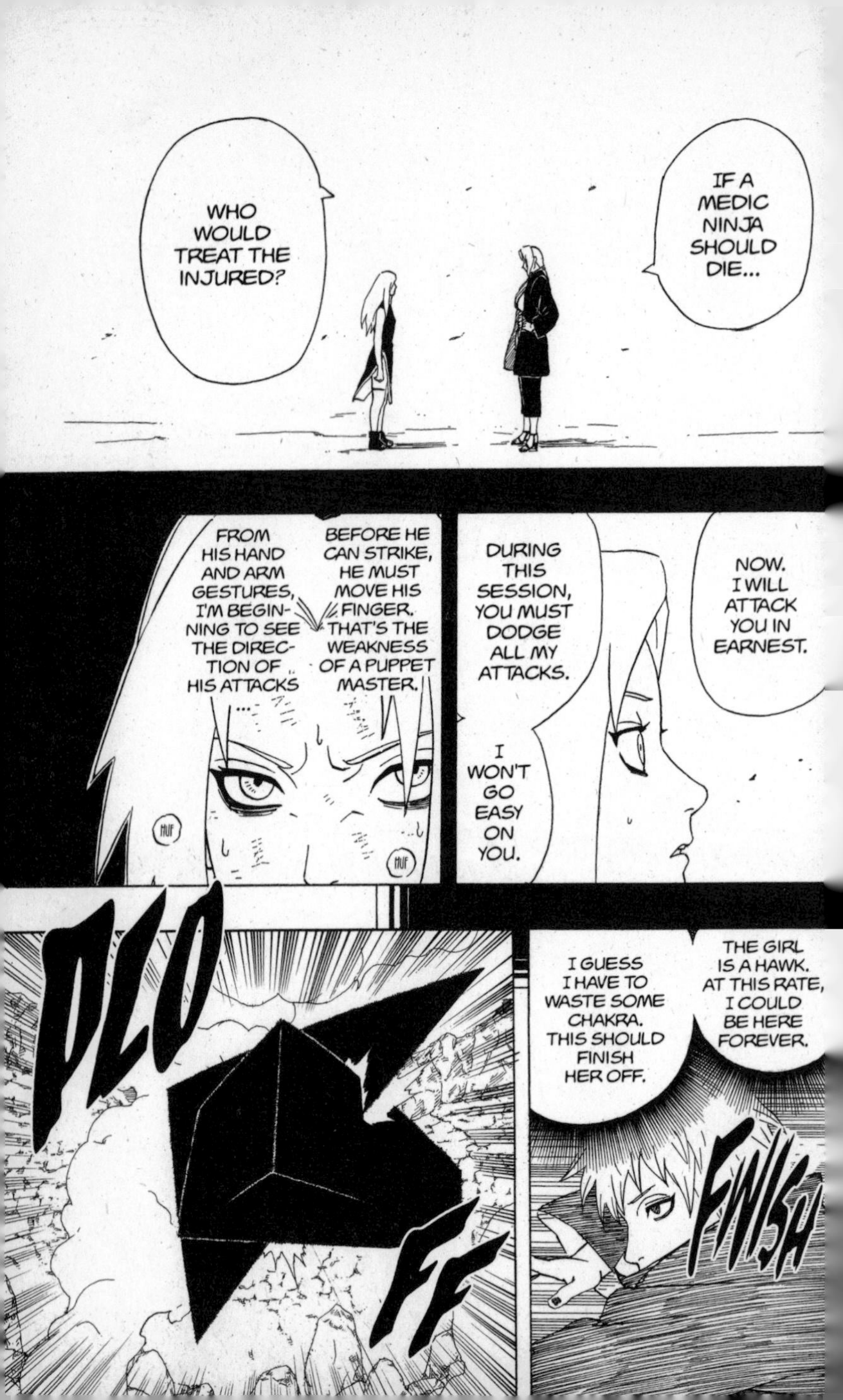
IF A MEDIC NINJA SHOULD DIE...
WHO WOULD TREAT THE INJURED?
NOW. I WILL ATTACK YOU IN EARNEST.
DURING THIS SESSION, YOU MUST DODGE ALL MY ATTACKS.
I WON'T GO EASY ON YOU.
BEFORE HE CAN STRIKE, HE MUST MOVE HIS FINGER. THAT'S THE WEAKNESS OF A PUPPET MASTER.
FROM HIS HAND AND ARM GESTURES, I'M BEGINNING TO SEE THE DIRECTION OF HIS ATTACKS...
HUF
HUF
THE GIRL IS A HAWK. AT THIS RATE, I COULD BE HERE FOREVER.
I GUESS I HAVE TO WASTE SOME CHAKRA. THIS SHOULD FINISH HER OFF.
FINISH
DLOFF

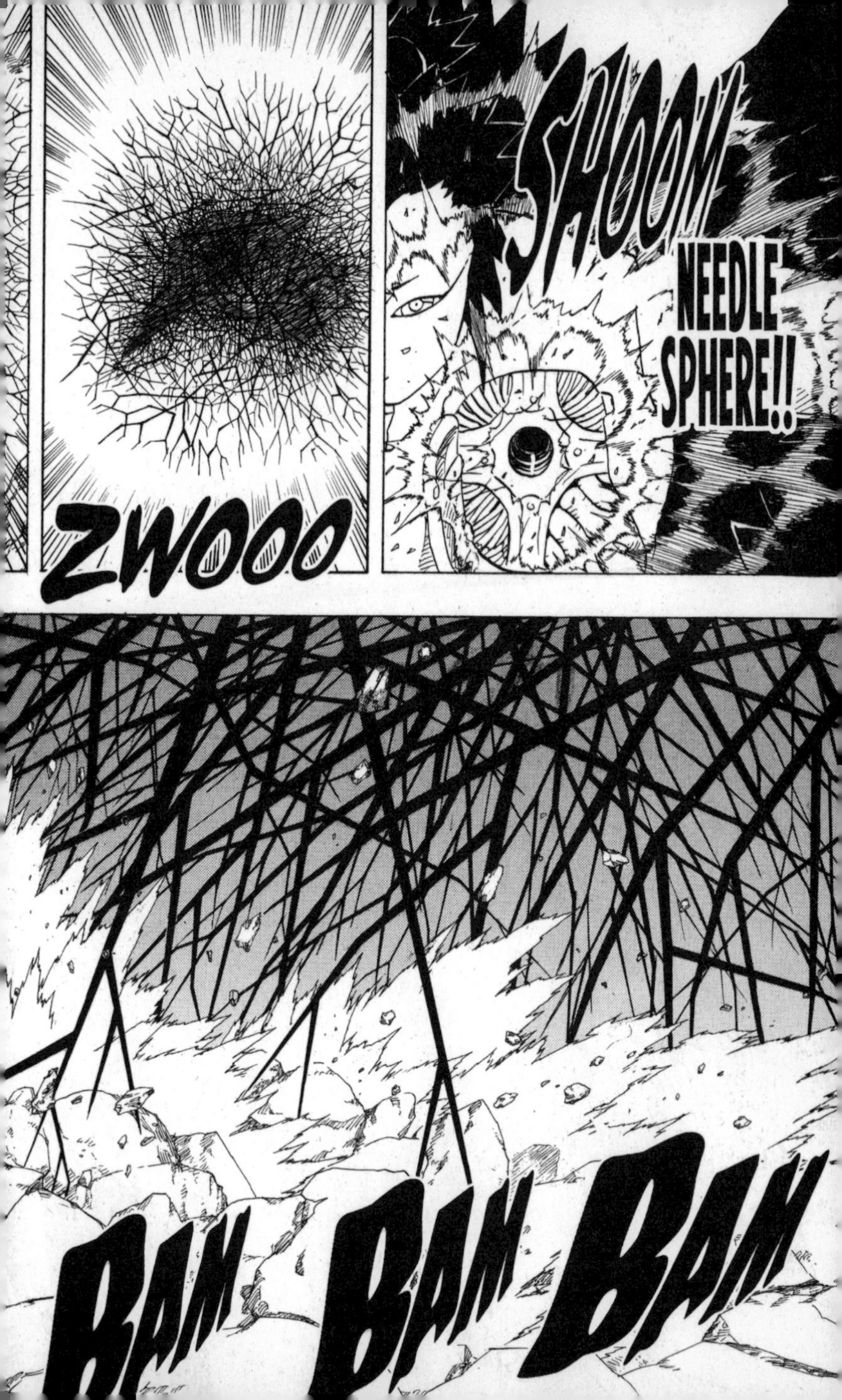
SHOOM
NEEDLE SPHERE!!
ZWOOO
BAM BAM BAM

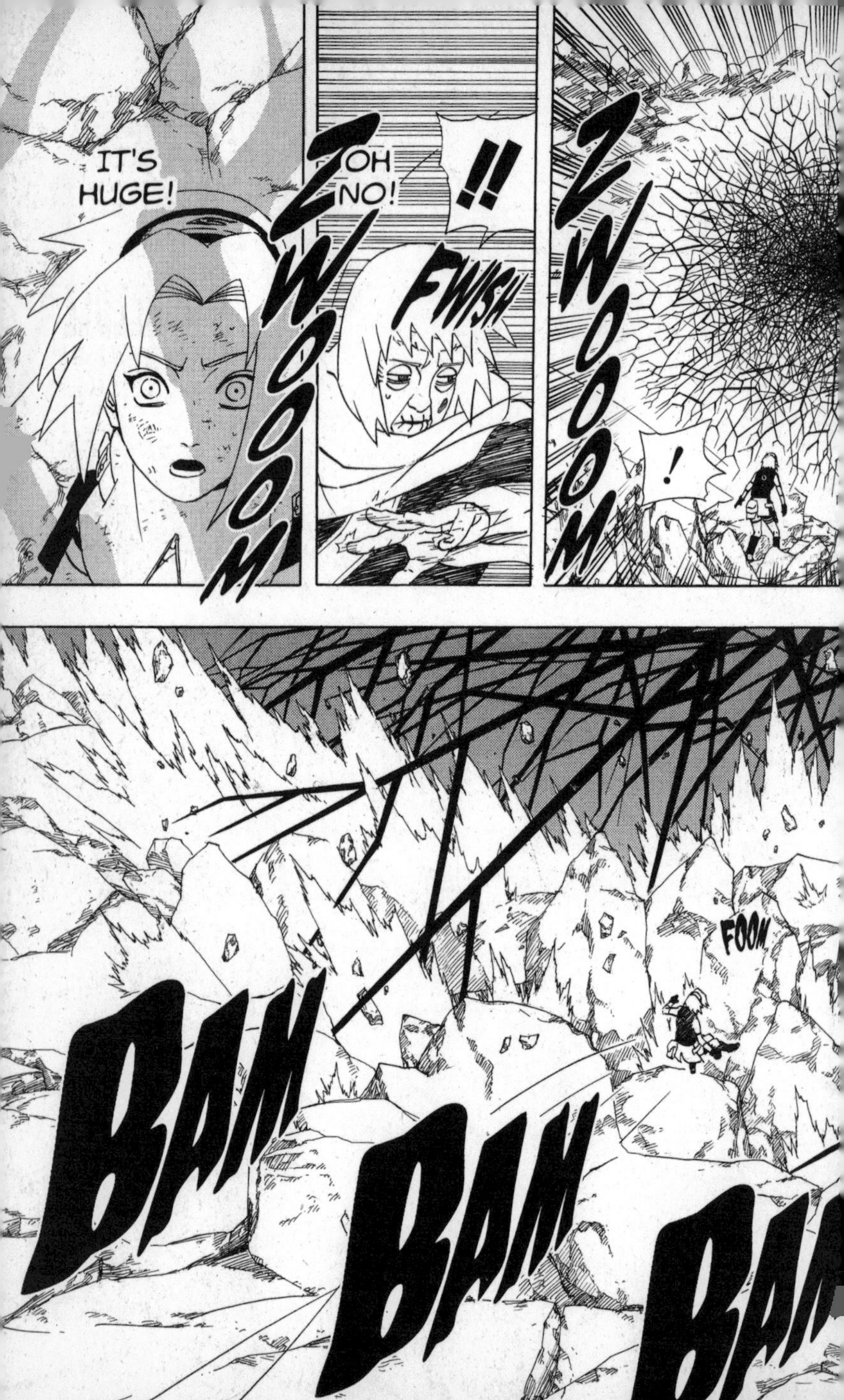
ZWOOOOM
!
OH NO!
!!
FWISH
ZWOOOOM
IT'S HUGE!
ZWOOOOM
FOOM
BAM
BAM
BAM

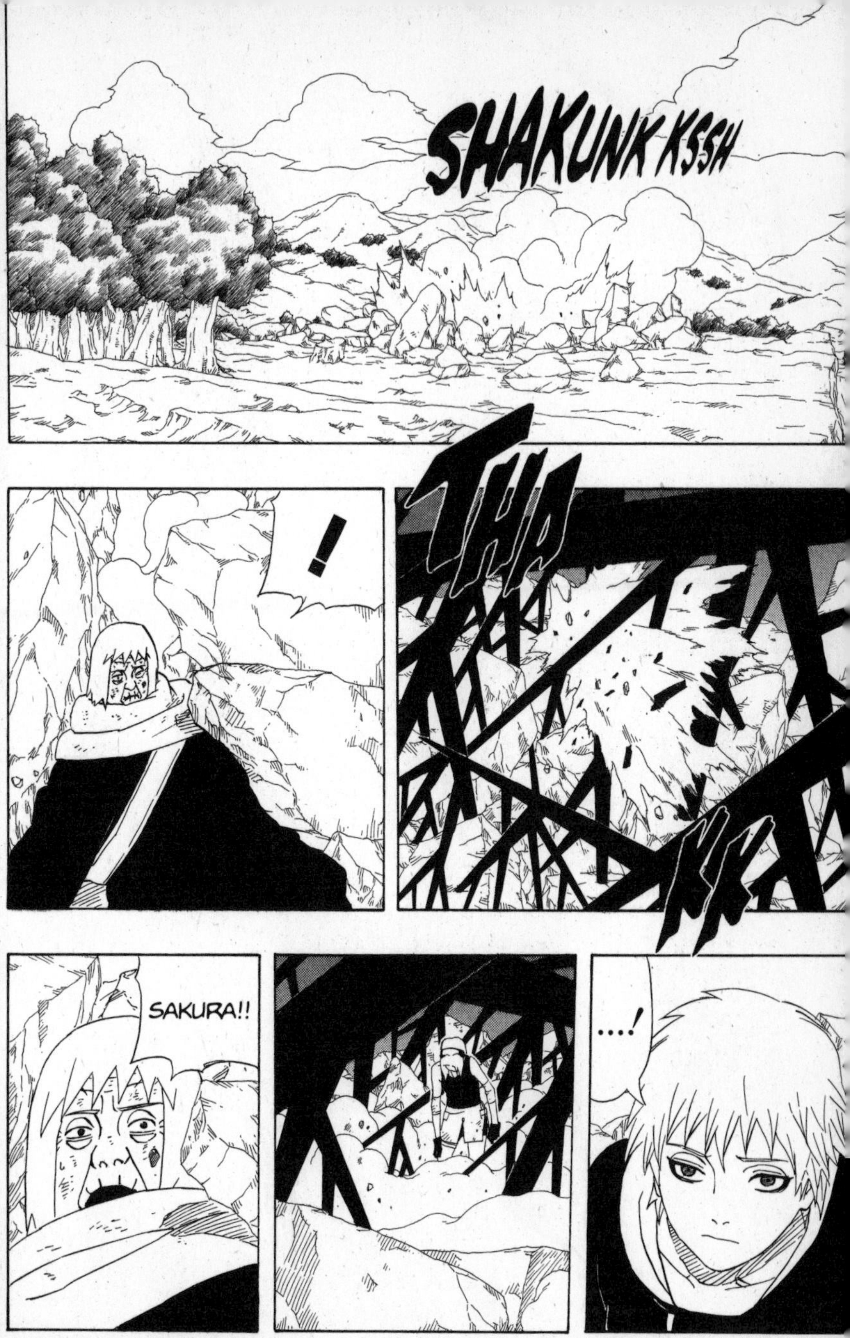
SHAKUNK KSSH
THA
NK
!
....!
SAKURA!!

READ THIS WAY

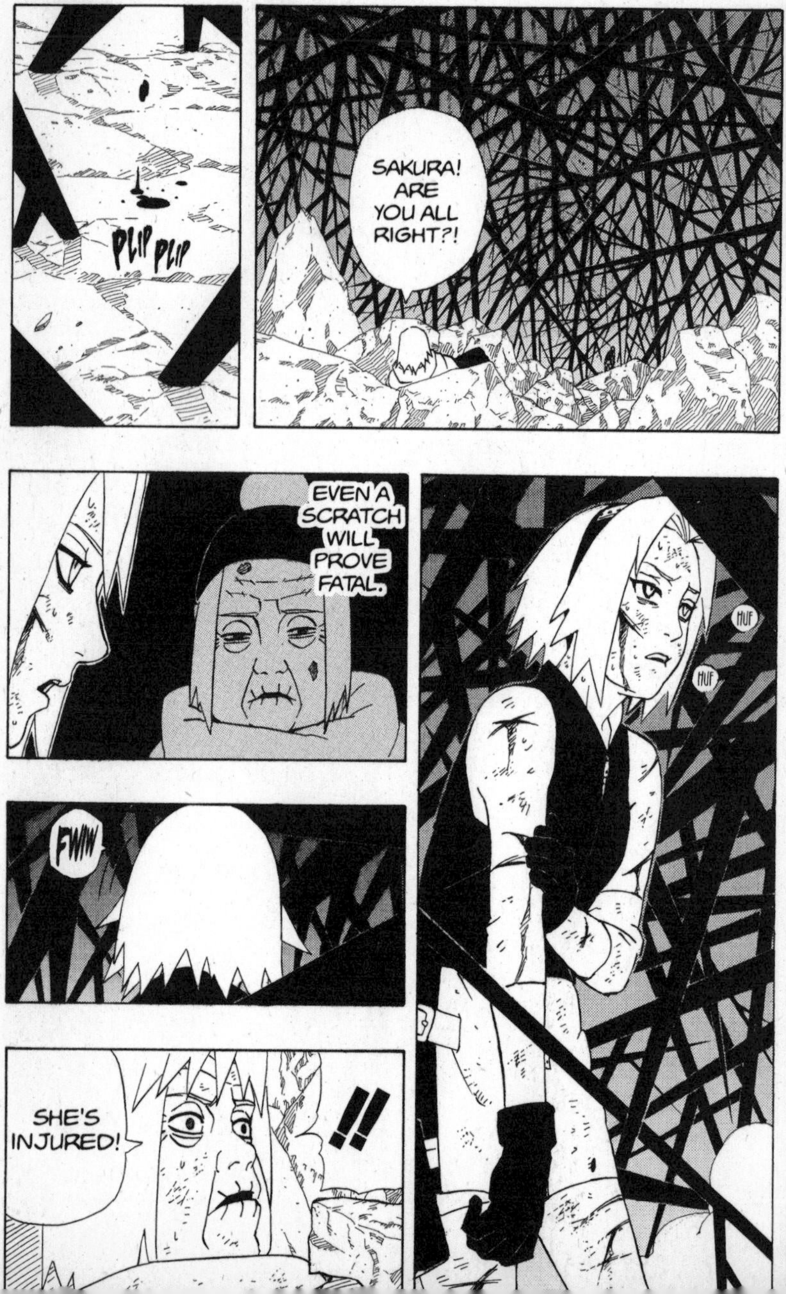
SAKURA! ARE YOU ALL RIGHT?!
PLIP PLIP
HUF
HUF
EVEN A SCRATCH WILL PROVE FATAL.
FWIW
SHE'S INJURED!
!!

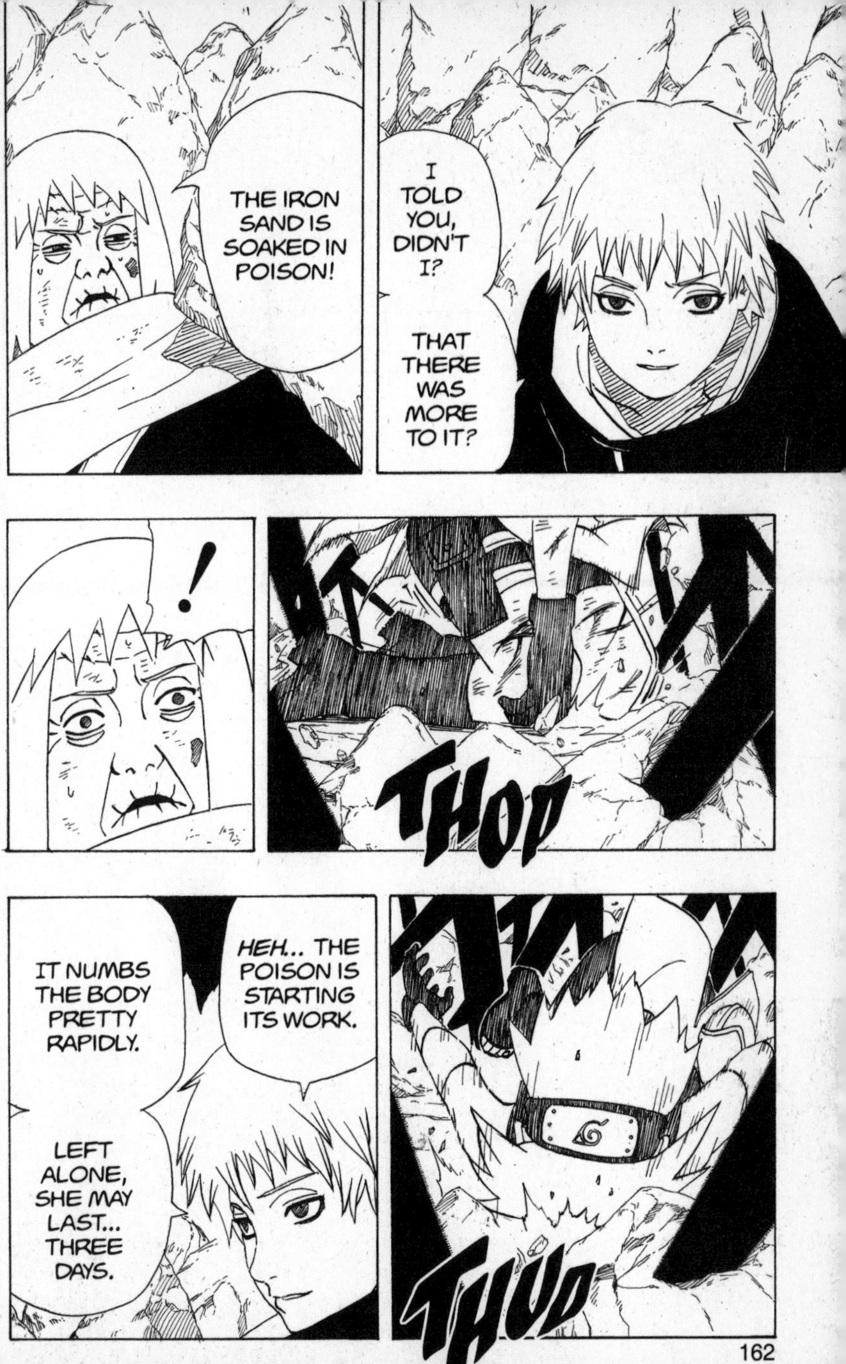
I TOLD YOU, DIDN'T I?
THAT THERE WAS MORE TO IT?
THE IRON SAND IS SOAKED IN POISON!
THOP
!
THUD
HEH... THE POISON IS STARTING ITS WORK.
IT NUMBS THE BODY PRETTY RAPIDLY.
LEFT ALONE, SHE MAY LAST... THREE DAYS.

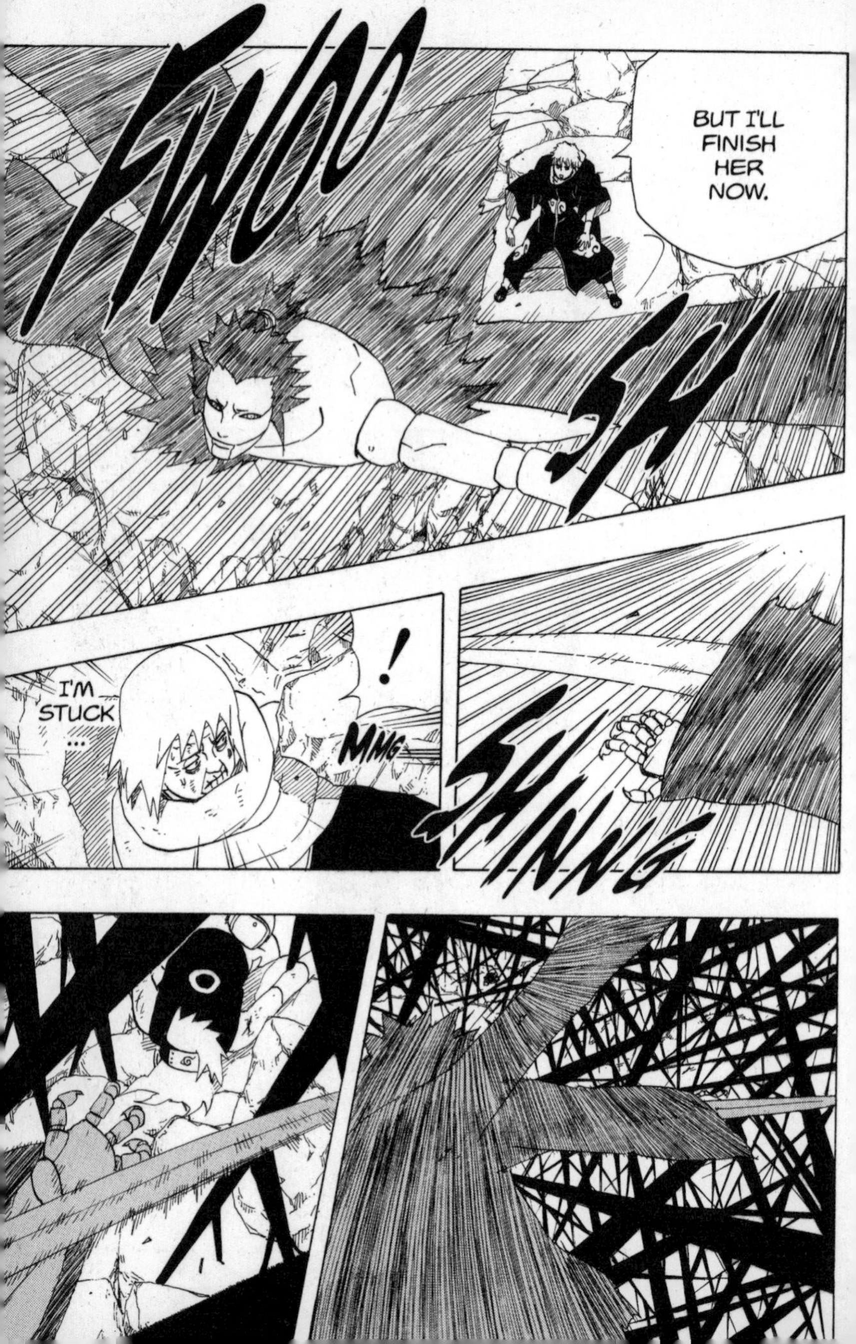
BUT I'LL FINISH HER NOW.
FWOO
SH
SHING
!
MMG
I'M STUCK ...

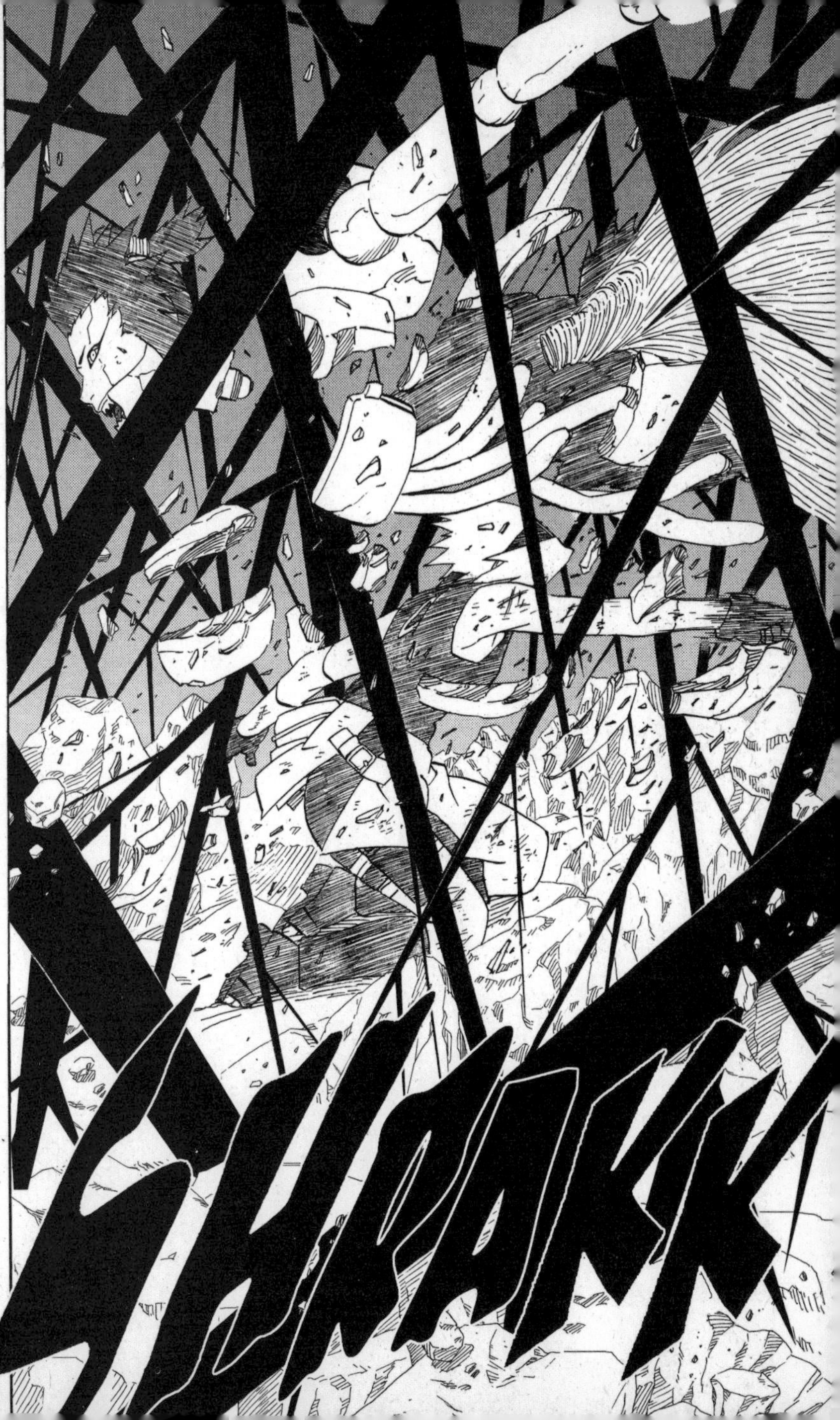

READ THIS WAY

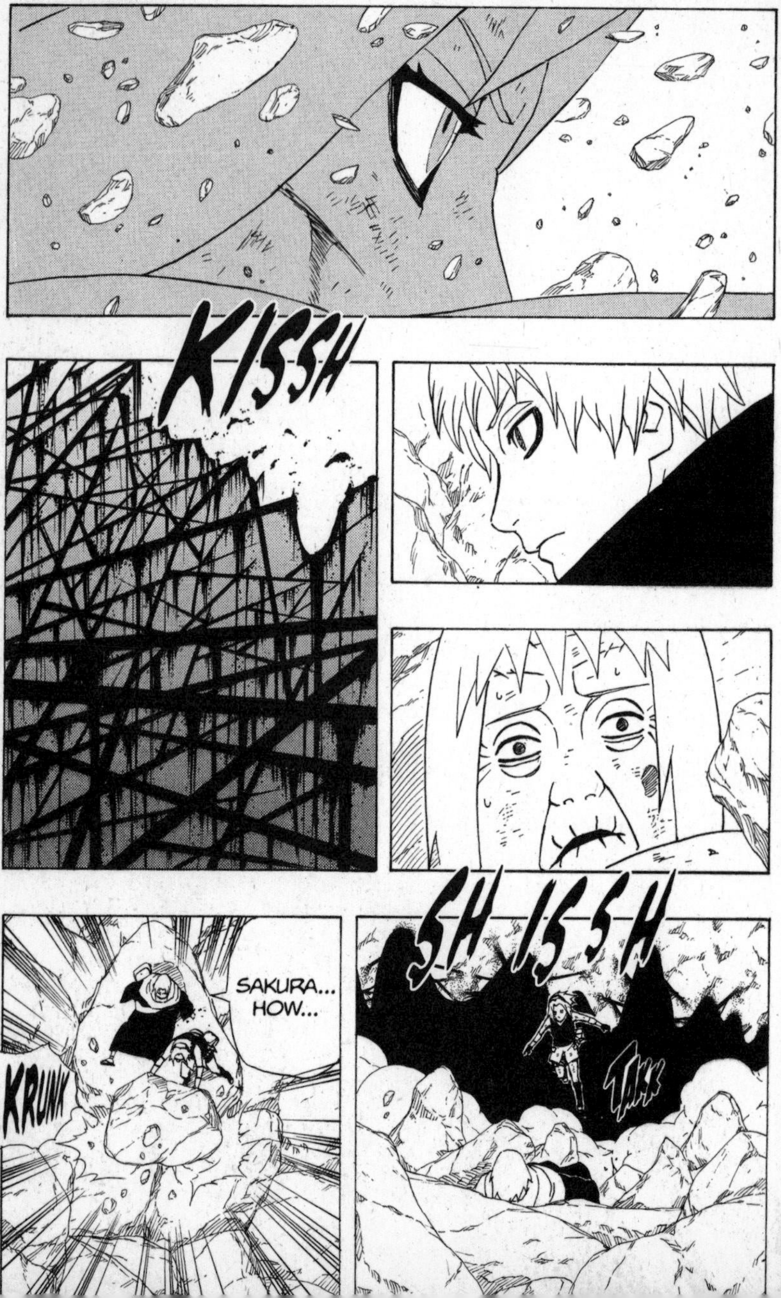
KISSH
SHISSH
TAKK
SAKURA... HOW...
KRUNK

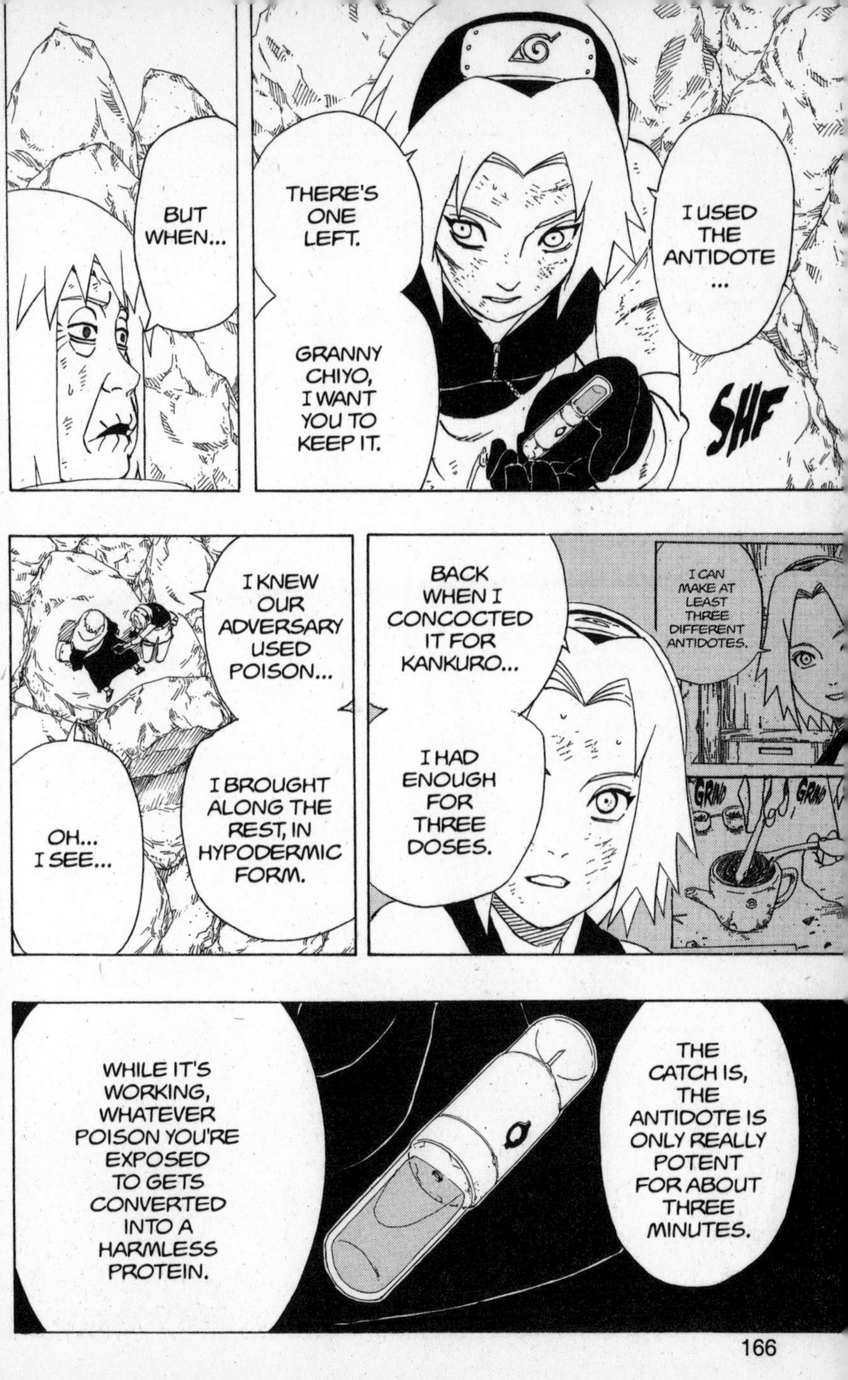
I USED THE ANTIDOTE ...
SHF
THERE'S ONE LEFT.
GRANNY CHIYO, I WANT YOU TO KEEP IT.
BUT WHEN...
I CAN MAKE AT LEAST THREE DIFFERENT ANTIDOTES.
GRIND, GRIND
BACK WHEN I CONCOCTED IT FOR KANKURO...
I HAD ENOUGH FOR THREE DOSES.
I KNEW OUR ADVERSARY USED POISON...
I BROUGHT ALONG THE REST, IN HYPODERMIC FORM.
OH... I SEE...
THE CATCH IS, THE ANTIDOTE IS ONLY REALLY POTENT FOR ABOUT THREE MINUTES.
WHILE IT'S WORKING, WHATEVER POISON YOU'RE EXPOSED TO GETS CONVERTED INTO A HARMLESS PROTEIN.

READ THIS WAY

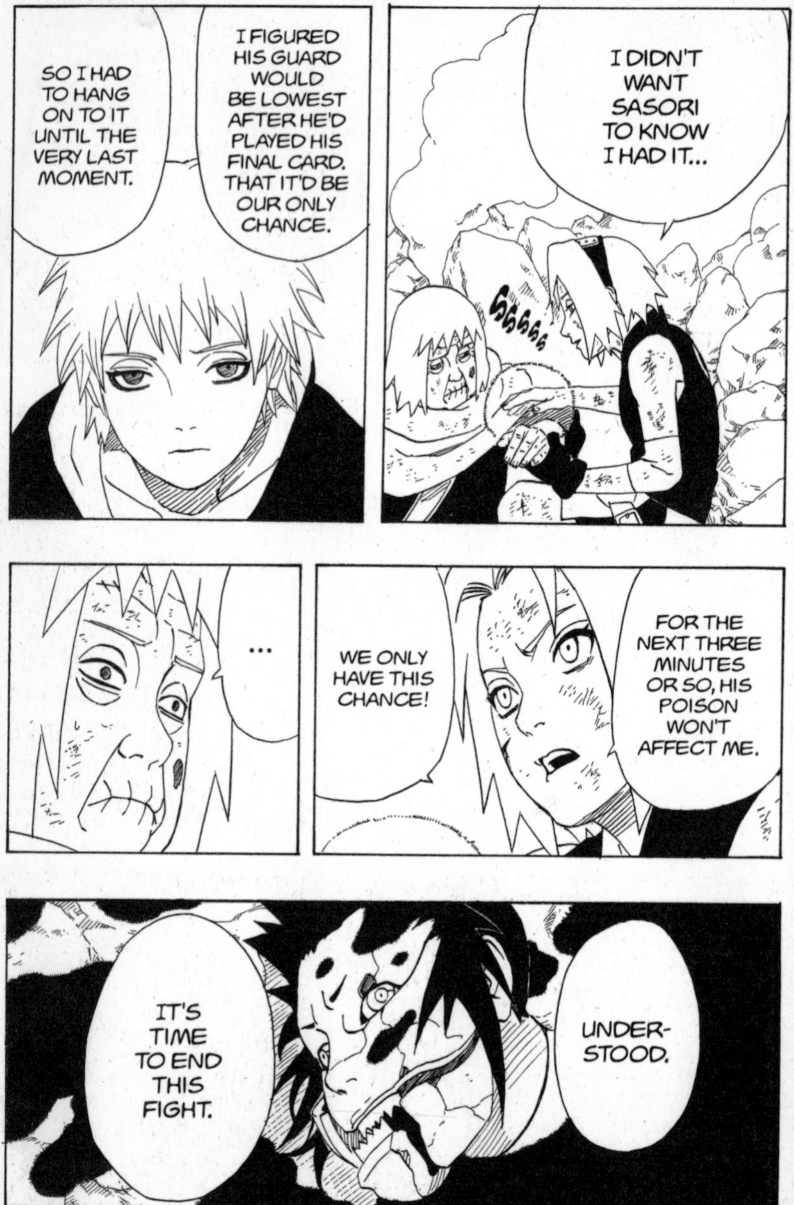
I DIDN'T WANT SASORI TO KNOW I HAD IT...
SSSSS
I FIGURED HIS GUARD WOULD BE LOWEST AFTER HE'D PLAYED HIS FINAL CARD. THAT IT'D BE OUR ONLY CHANCE.
SO I HAD TO HANG ON TO IT UNTIL THE VERY LAST MOMENT.
FOR THE NEXT THREE MINUTES OR SO, HIS POISON WON'T AFFECT ME.
WE ONLY HAVE THIS CHANCE!
...
UNDER-STOOD.
IT'S TIME TO END THIS FIGHT.

NARUTO

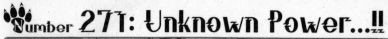

Number 271: Unknown Power...!!

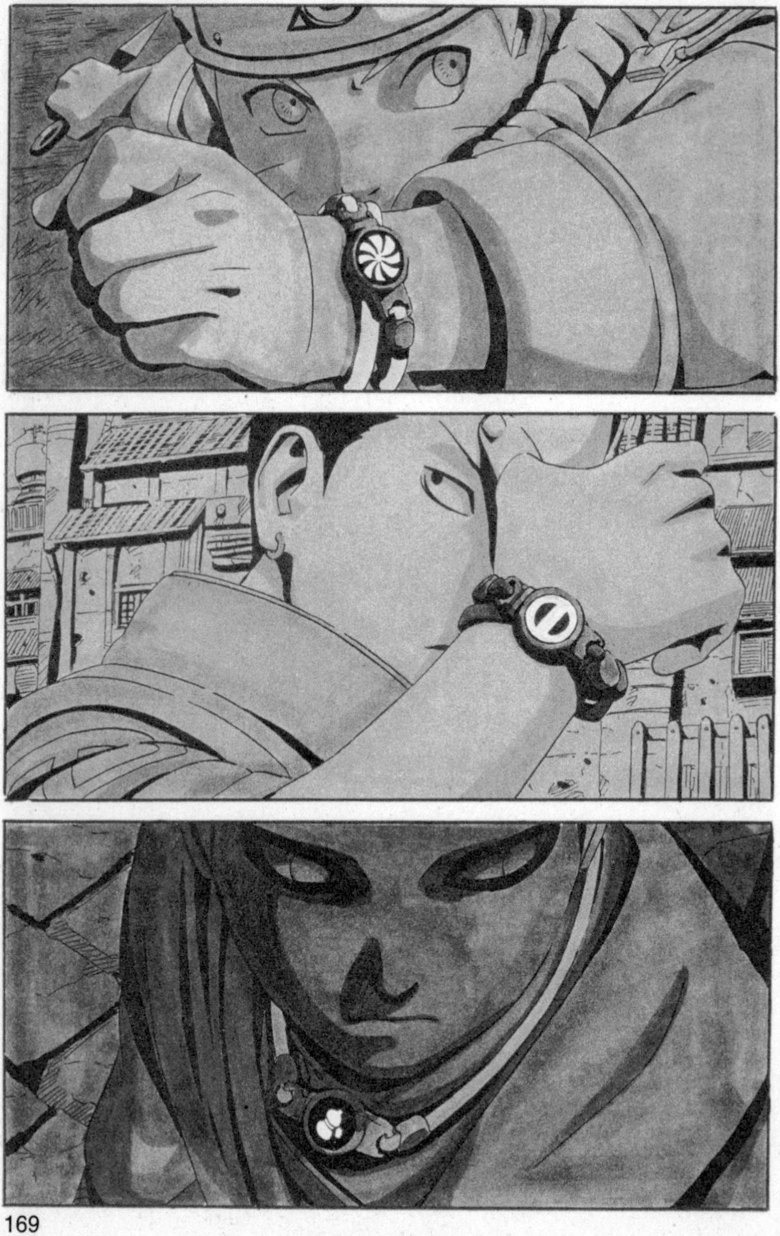

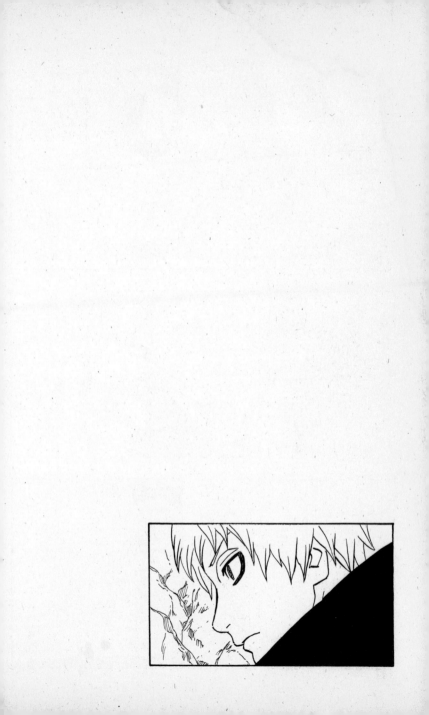

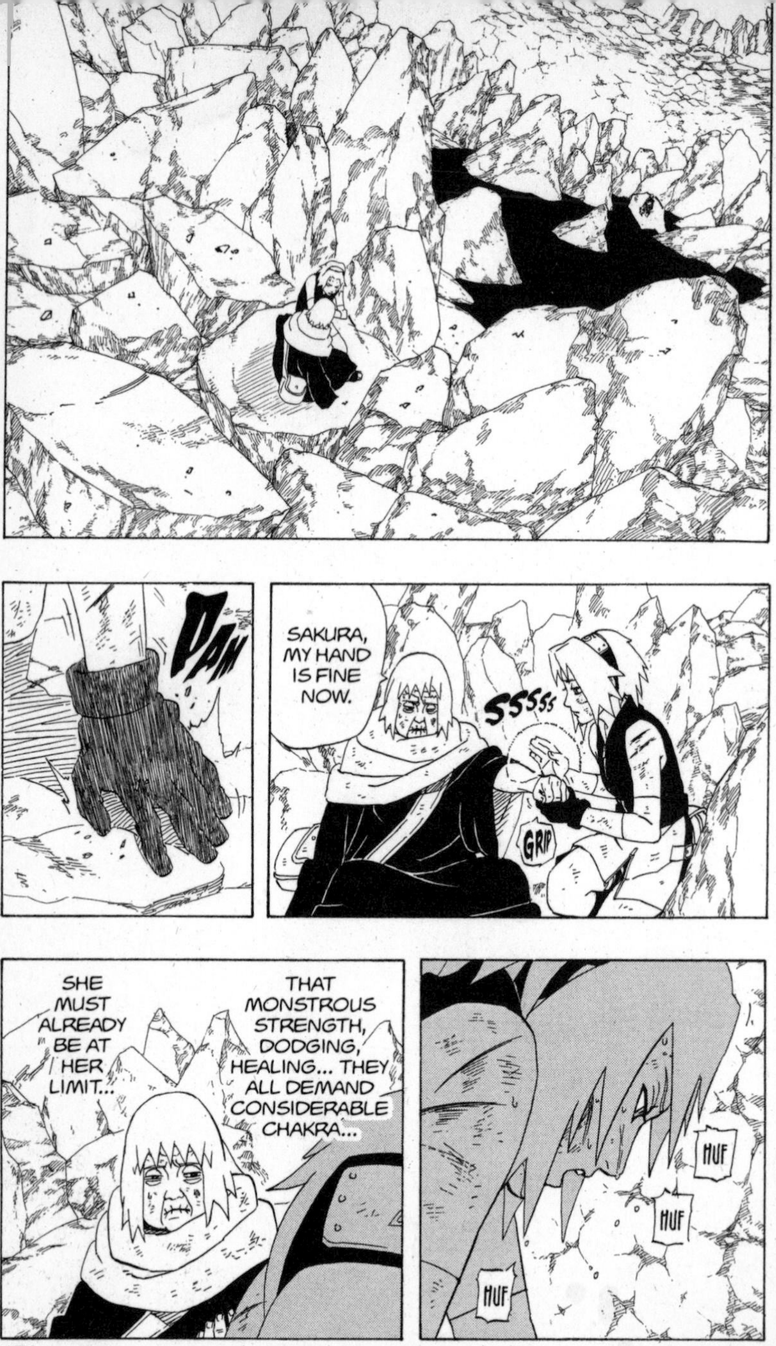
SAKURA, MY HAND IS FINE NOW.
SSSSS
GRIP
DAM
HUF
HUF
HUF
THAT MONSTROUS STRENGTH, DODGING, HEALING... THEY ALL DEMAND CONSIDERABLE CHAKRA...
SHE MUST ALREADY BE AT HER LIMIT...

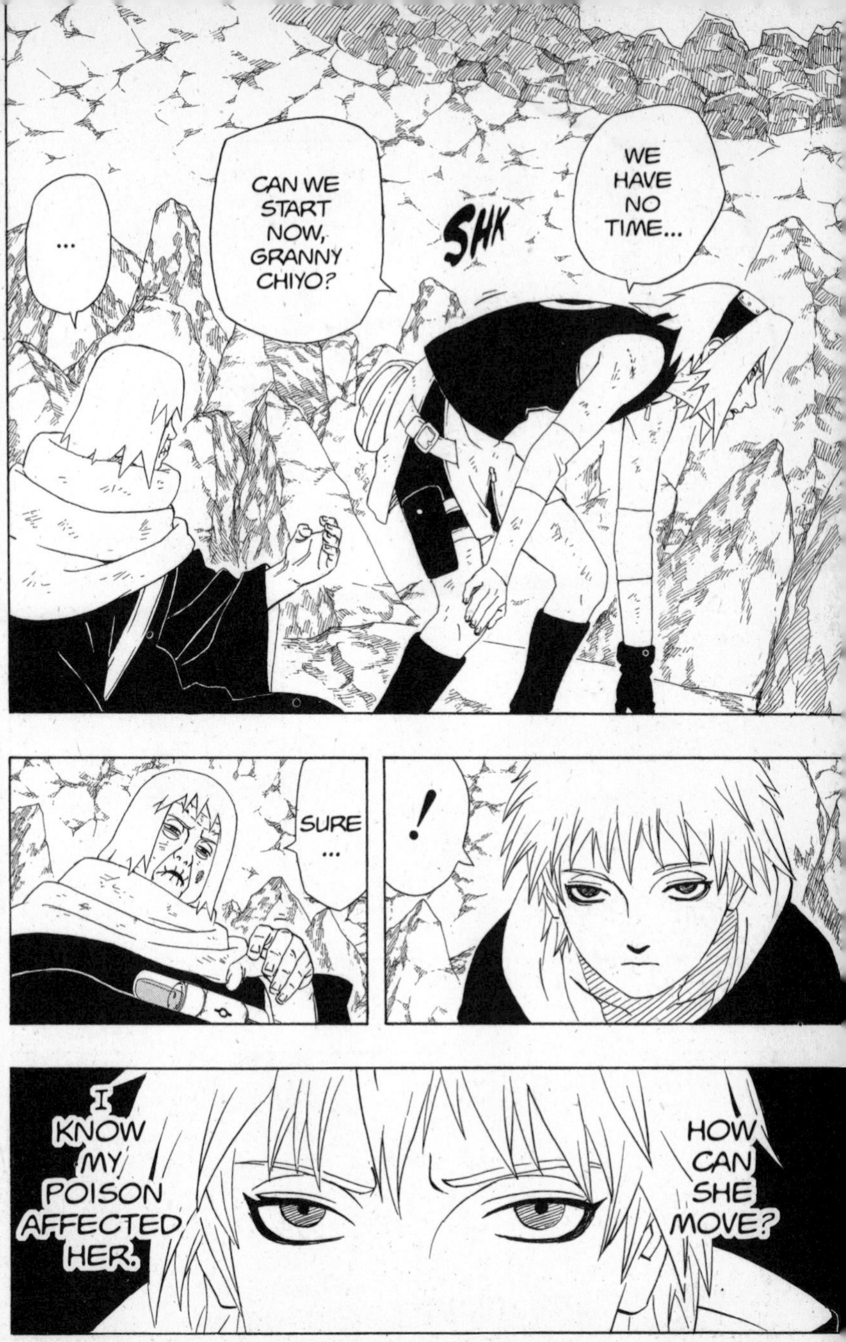
WE HAVE NO TIME...
SHK
CAN WE START NOW, GRANNY CHIYO?
...
!
SURE ...
HOW CAN SHE MOVE?
I KNOW MY POISON AFFECTED HER.

READ THIS WAY

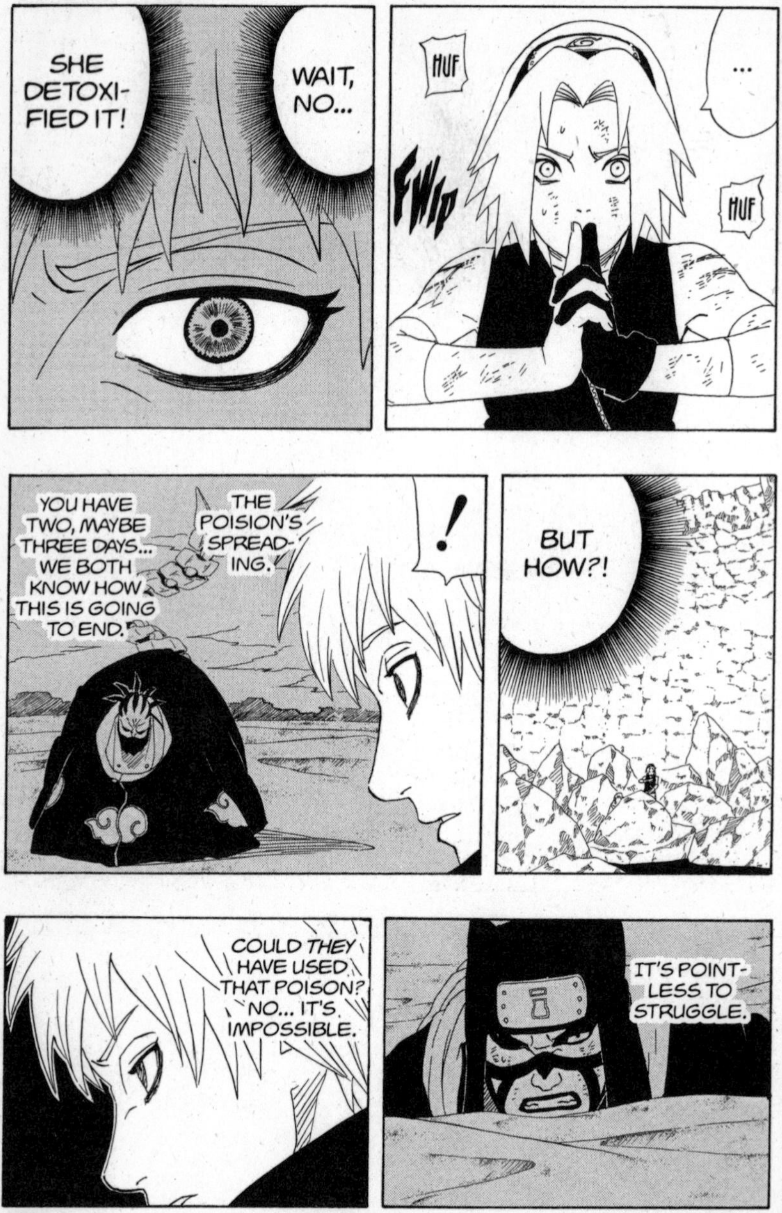
...
HUF
FWIP
HUF
WAIT, NO...
SHE DETOXI-FIED IT!
BUT HOW?!
!
THE POISION'S SPREAD-ING.
YOU HAVE TWO, MAYBE THREE DAYS... WE BOTH KNOW HOW THIS IS GOING TO END.
IT'S POINT-LESS TO STRUGGLE.
COULD THEY HAVE USED THAT POISON? NO... IT'S IMPOSSIBLE.

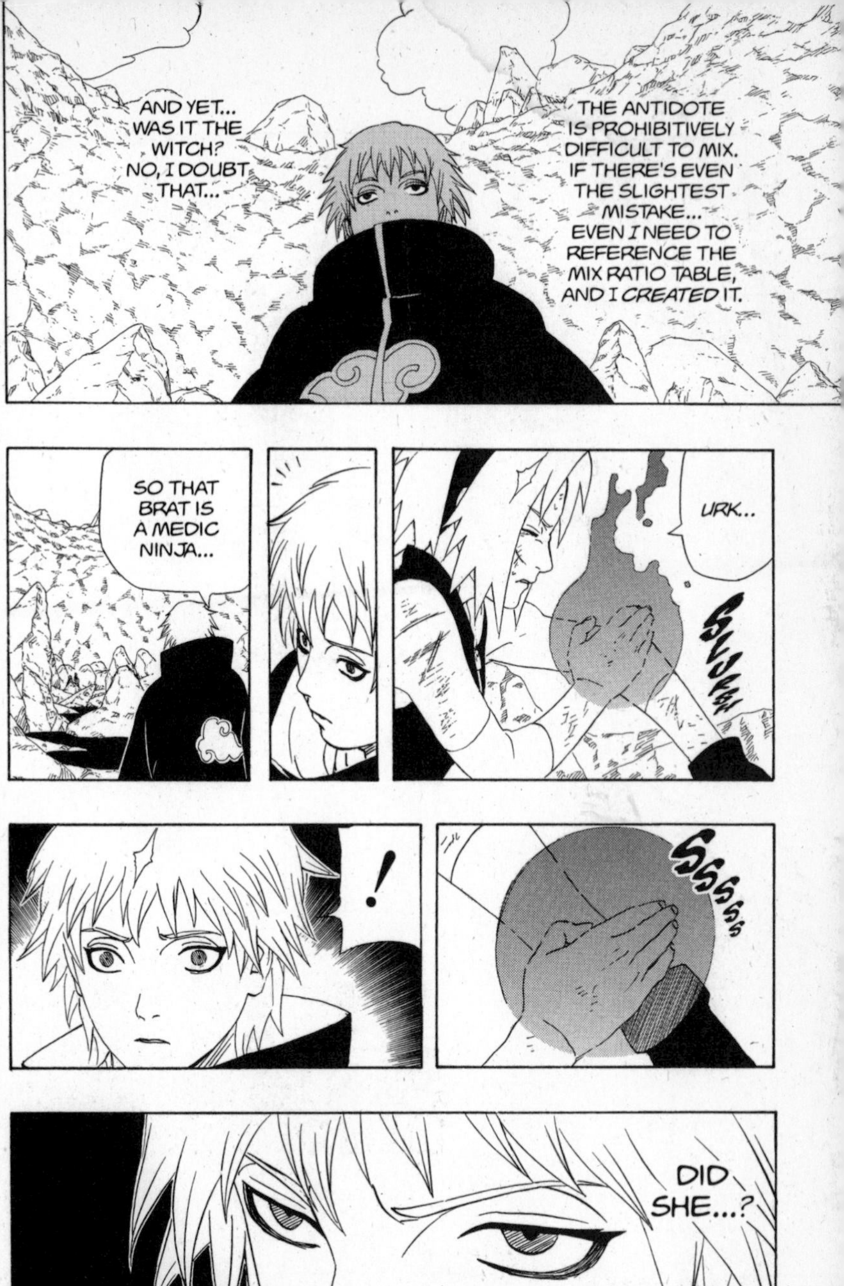
THE ANTIDOTE IS PROHIBITIVELY DIFFICULT TO MIX. IF THERE'S EVEN THE SLIGHTEST MISTAKE... EVEN *I* NEED TO REFERENCE THE MIX RATIO TABLE, AND I *CREATED* IT.
AND YET... WAS IT THE WITCH? NO, I DOUBT THAT...
URK...
SLURK
SO THAT BRAT IS A MEDIC NINJA...
SSSsss
!
DID SHE...?

READ THIS WAY

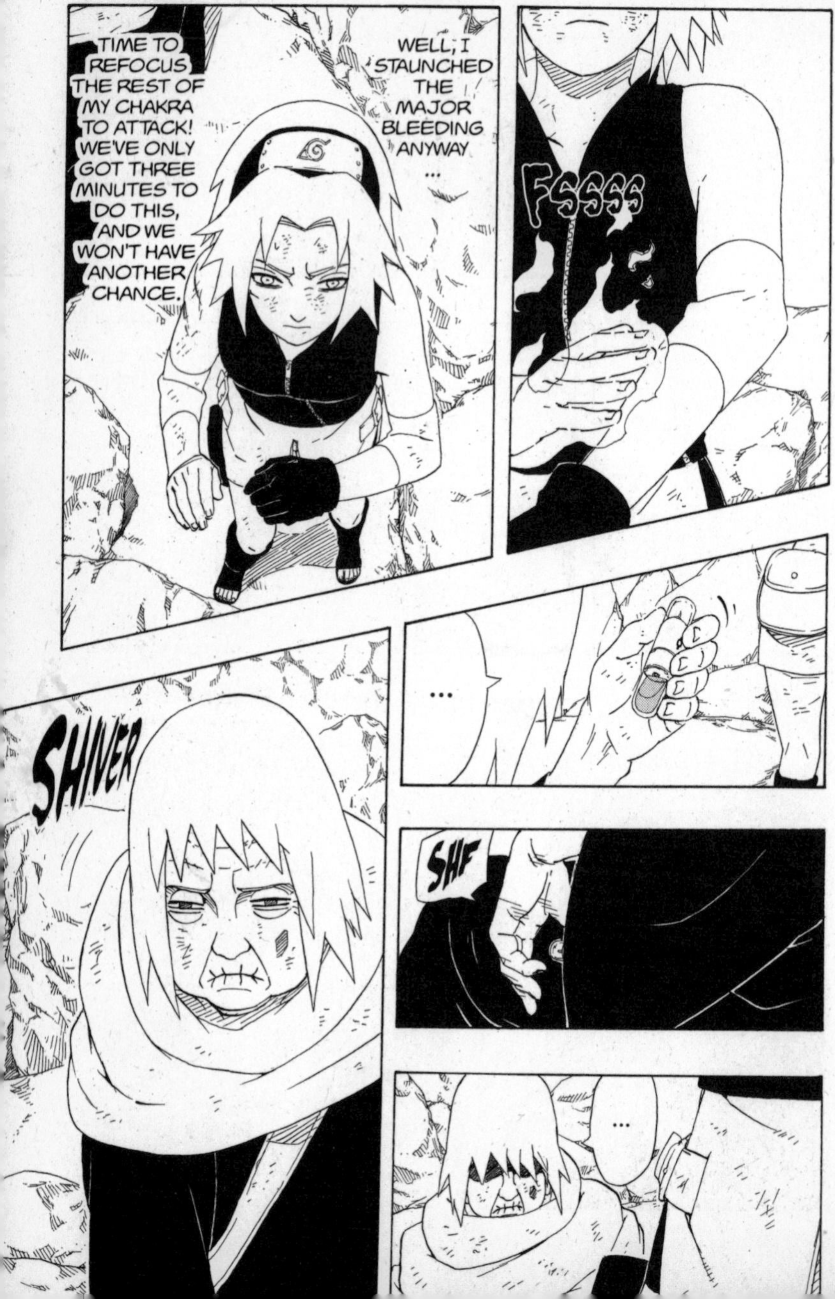
FSSSS
WELL, I STAUNCHED THE MAJOR BLEEDING ANYWAY ...
TIME TO REFOCUS THE REST OF MY CHAKRA TO ATTACK! WE'VE ONLY GOT THREE MINUTES TO DO THIS, AND WE WON'T HAVE ANOTHER CHANCE.
...
SHF
...
SHIVER

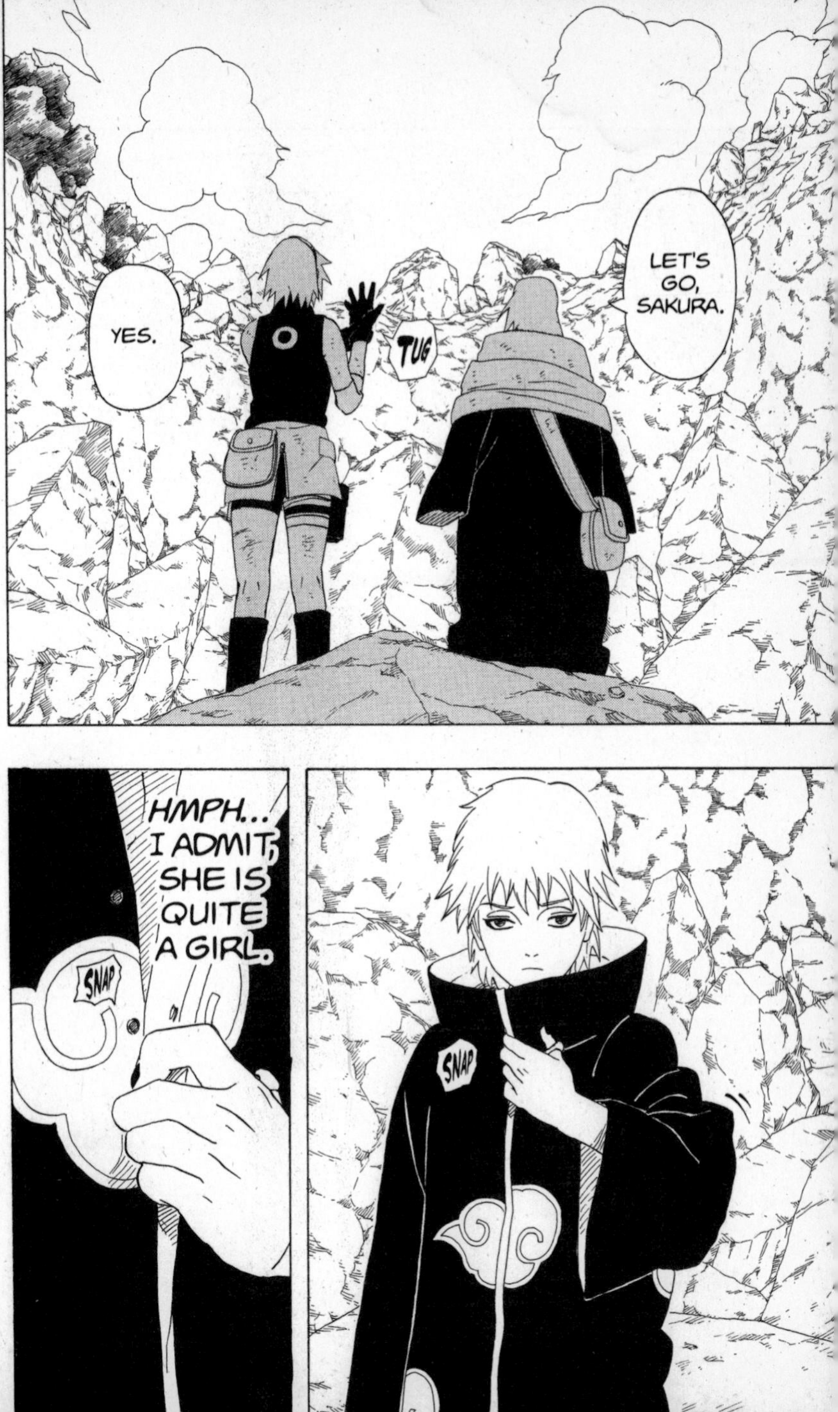
LET'S GO, SAKURA.
TUG
YES.
SNAP
HMPH... I ADMIT, SHE IS QUITE A GIRL.
SNAP

READ THIS WAY

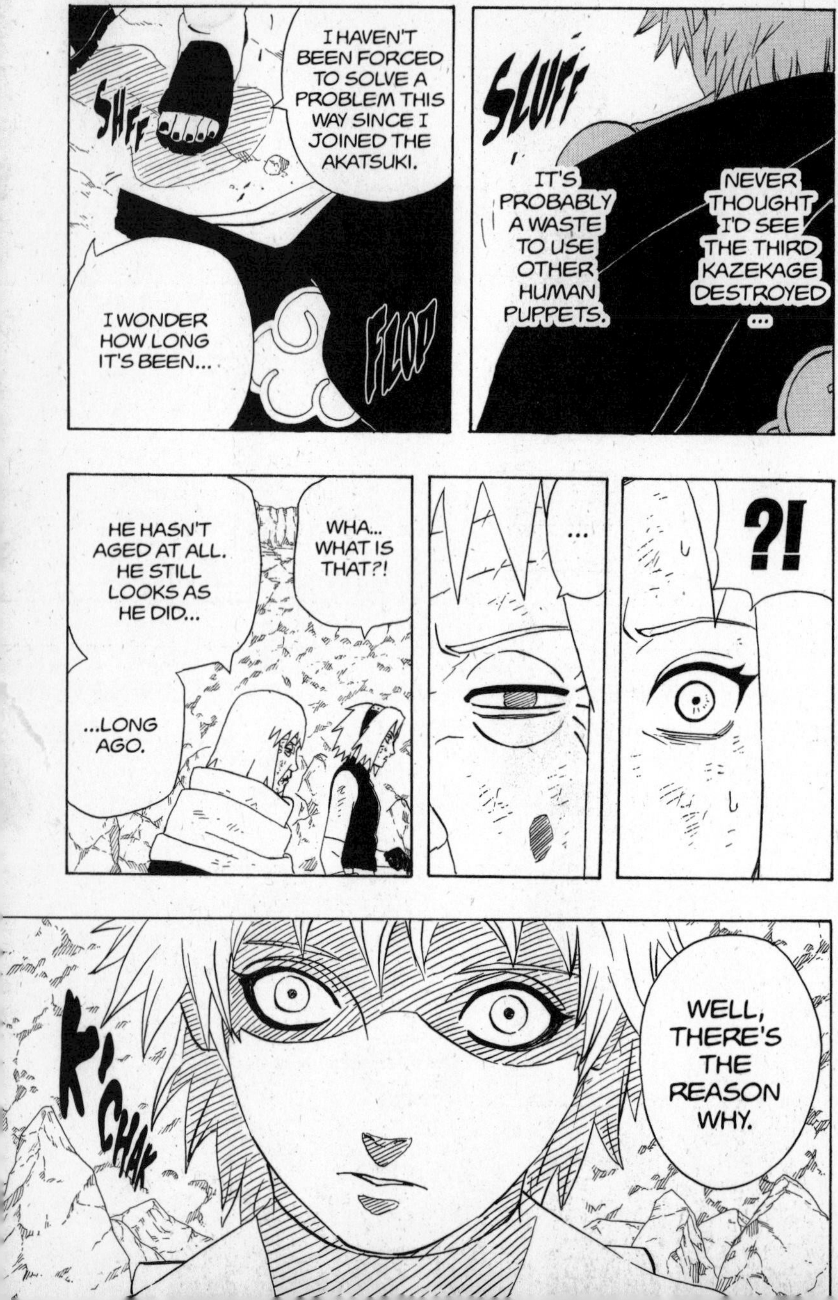
SLUFF
NEVER THOUGHT I'D SEE THE THIRD KAZEKAGE DESTROYED...
IT'S PROBABLY A WASTE TO USE OTHER HUMAN PUPPETS.
I HAVEN'T BEEN FORCED TO SOLVE A PROBLEM THIS WAY SINCE I JOINED THE AKATSUKI.
SHFF
I WONDER HOW LONG IT'S BEEN...
FLOP
?!
...
WHA... WHAT IS THAT?!
HE HASN'T AGED AT ALL. HE STILL LOOKS AS HE DID...
...LONG AGO.
WELL, THERE'S THE REASON WHY.
K'CHAK

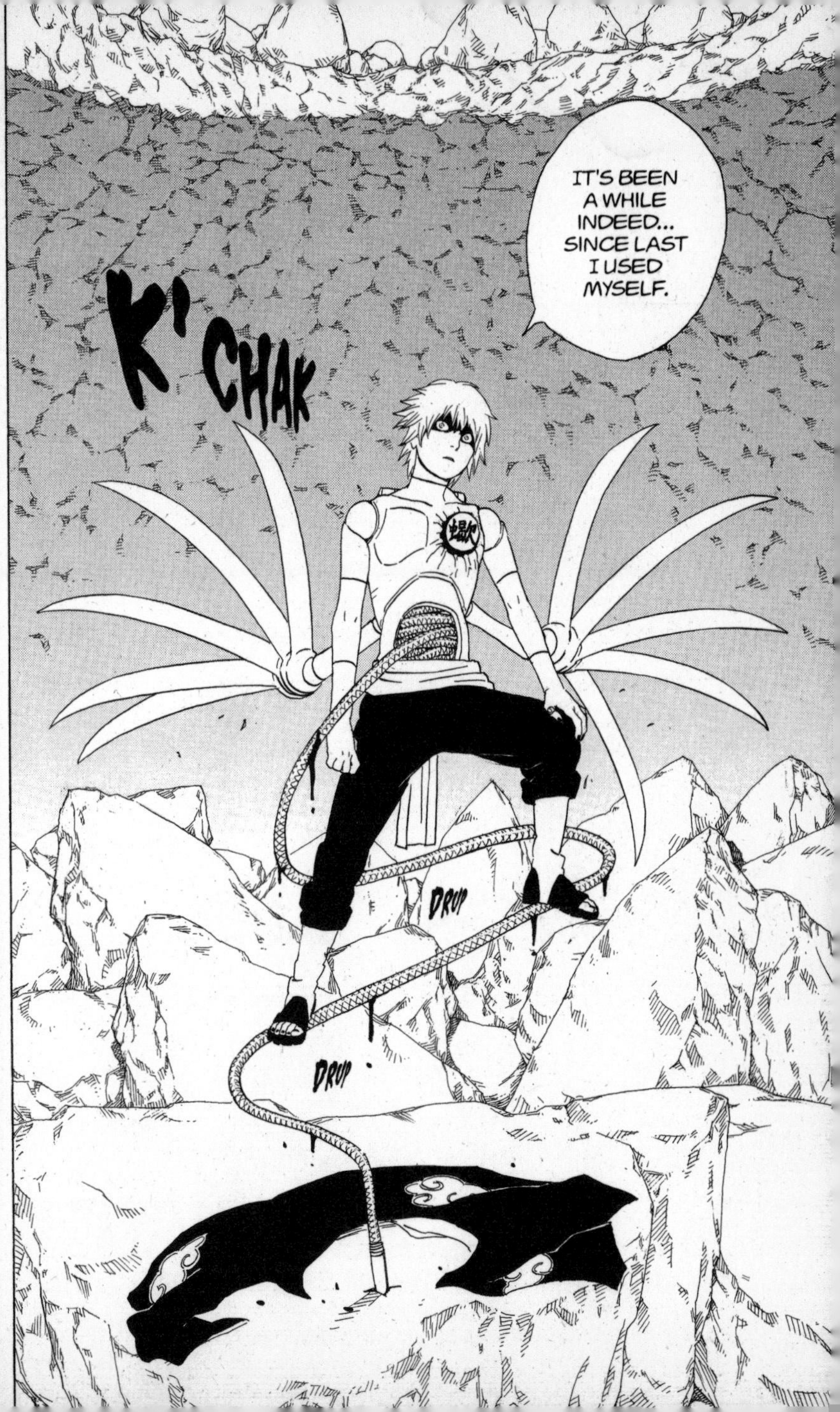

IT'S BEEN A WHILE INDEED... SINCE LAST I USED MYSELF.
K' CHAK
DRIP
DRIP

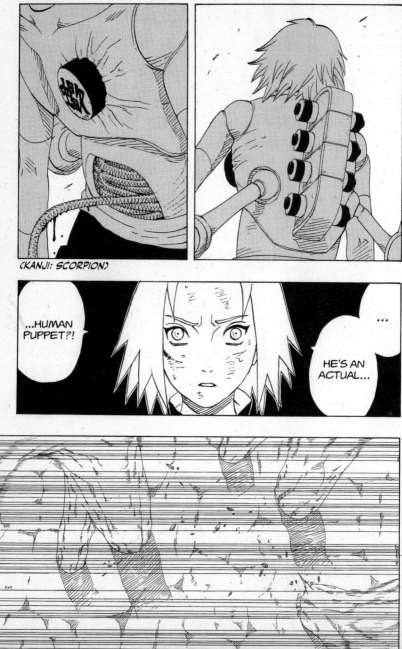

(KANJI: SCORPION)

...HUMAN PUPPET?!

HE'S AN ACTUAL...

...

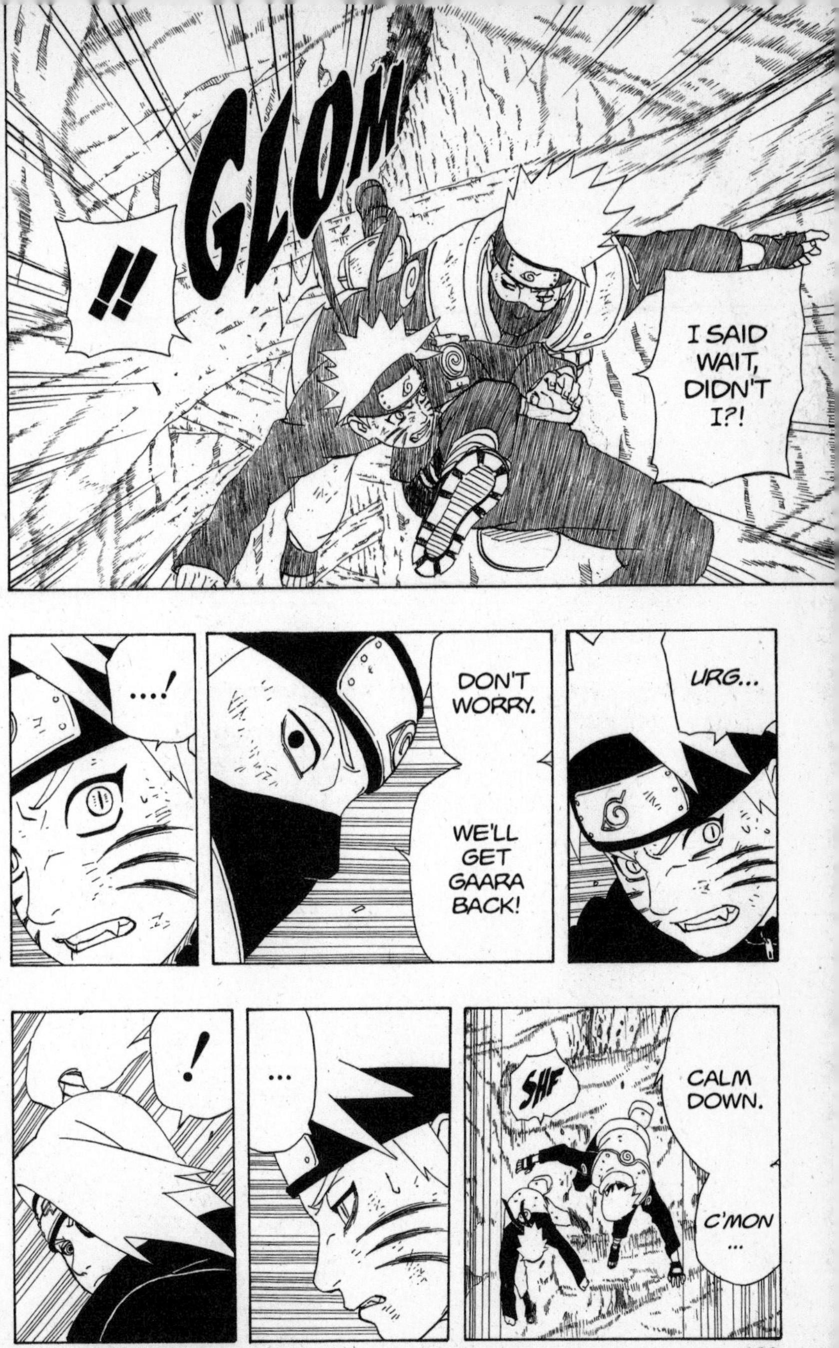
GLOM
I SAID WAIT, DIDN'T I?!
!!
URG...
DON'T WORRY.
WE'LL GET GAARA BACK!
....!
CALM DOWN.
SHF
C'MON ...
...
!

READ THIS WAY

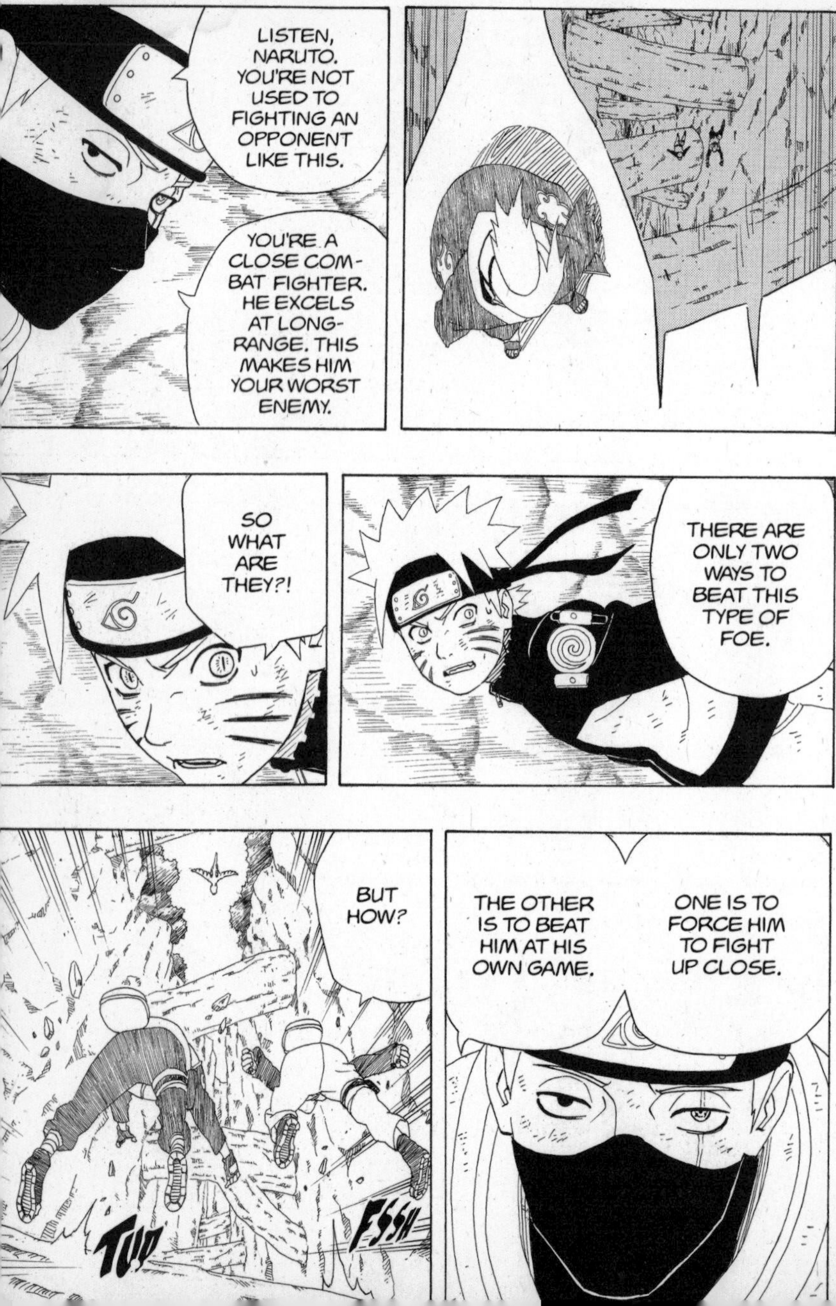
LISTEN, NARUTO. YOU'RE NOT USED TO FIGHTING AN OPPONENT LIKE THIS.
YOU'RE A CLOSE COM-BAT FIGHTER. HE EXCELS AT LONG-RANGE. THIS MAKES HIM YOUR WORST ENEMY.
THERE ARE ONLY TWO WAYS TO BEAT THIS TYPE OF FOE.
SO WHAT ARE THEY?!
ONE IS TO FORCE HIM TO FIGHT UP CLOSE.
THE OTHER IS TO BEAT HIM AT HIS OWN GAME.
BUT HOW?
FSSH
TUD

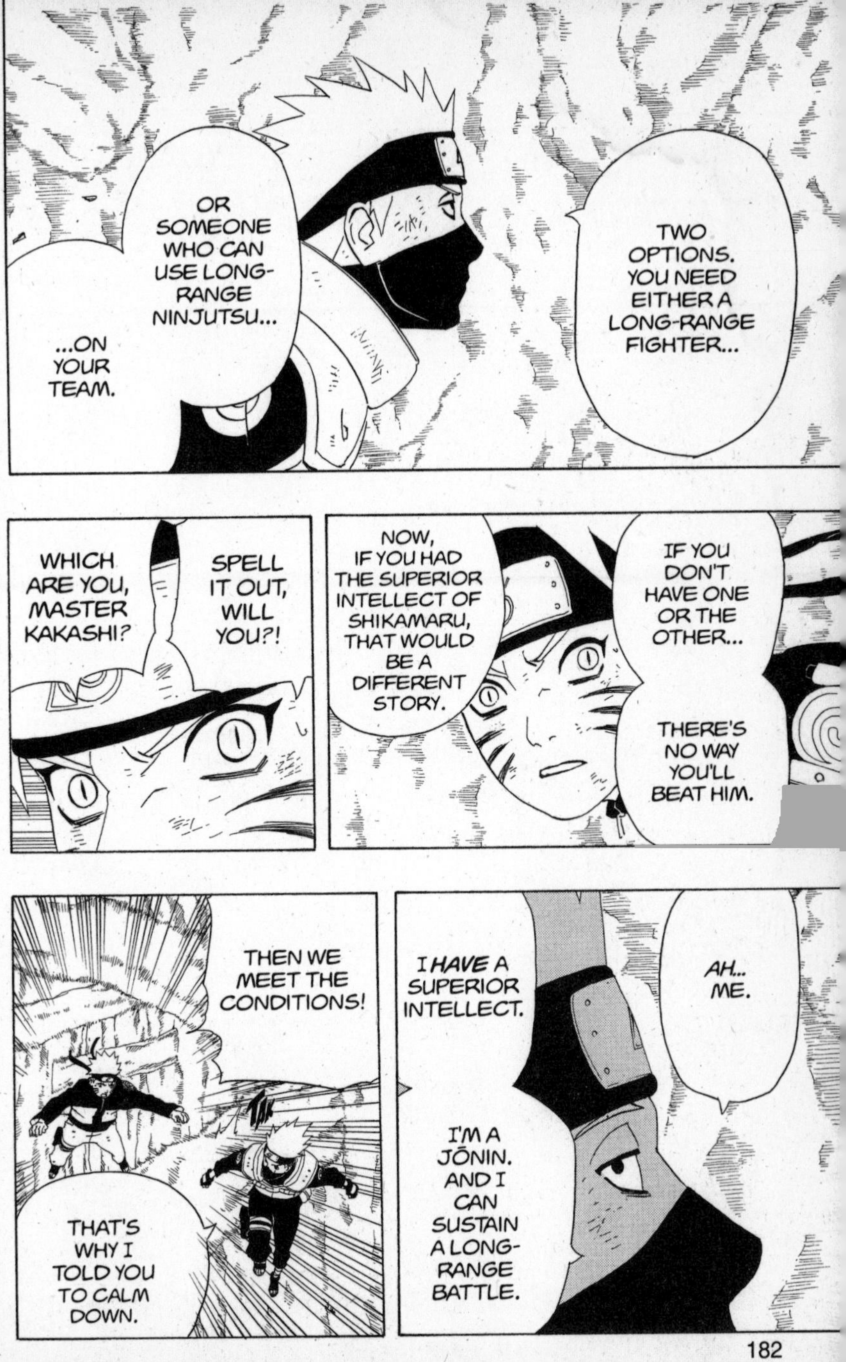
TWO OPTIONS. YOU NEED EITHER A LONG-RANGE FIGHTER...
OR SOMEONE WHO CAN USE LONG-RANGE NINJUTSU...
...ON YOUR TEAM.
IF YOU DON'T HAVE ONE OR THE OTHER...
THERE'S NO WAY YOU'LL BEAT HIM.
NOW, IF YOU HAD THE SUPERIOR INTELLECT OF SHIKAMARU, THAT WOULD BE A DIFFERENT STORY.
SPELL IT OUT, WILL YOU?!
WHICH ARE YOU, MASTER KAKASHI?
AH... ME.
I *HAVE* A SUPERIOR INTELLECT.
I'M A JŌNIN. AND I CAN SUSTAIN A LONG-RANGE BATTLE.
THEN WE MEET THE CONDITIONS!
THAT'S WHY I TOLD YOU TO CALM DOWN.

READ THIS WAY

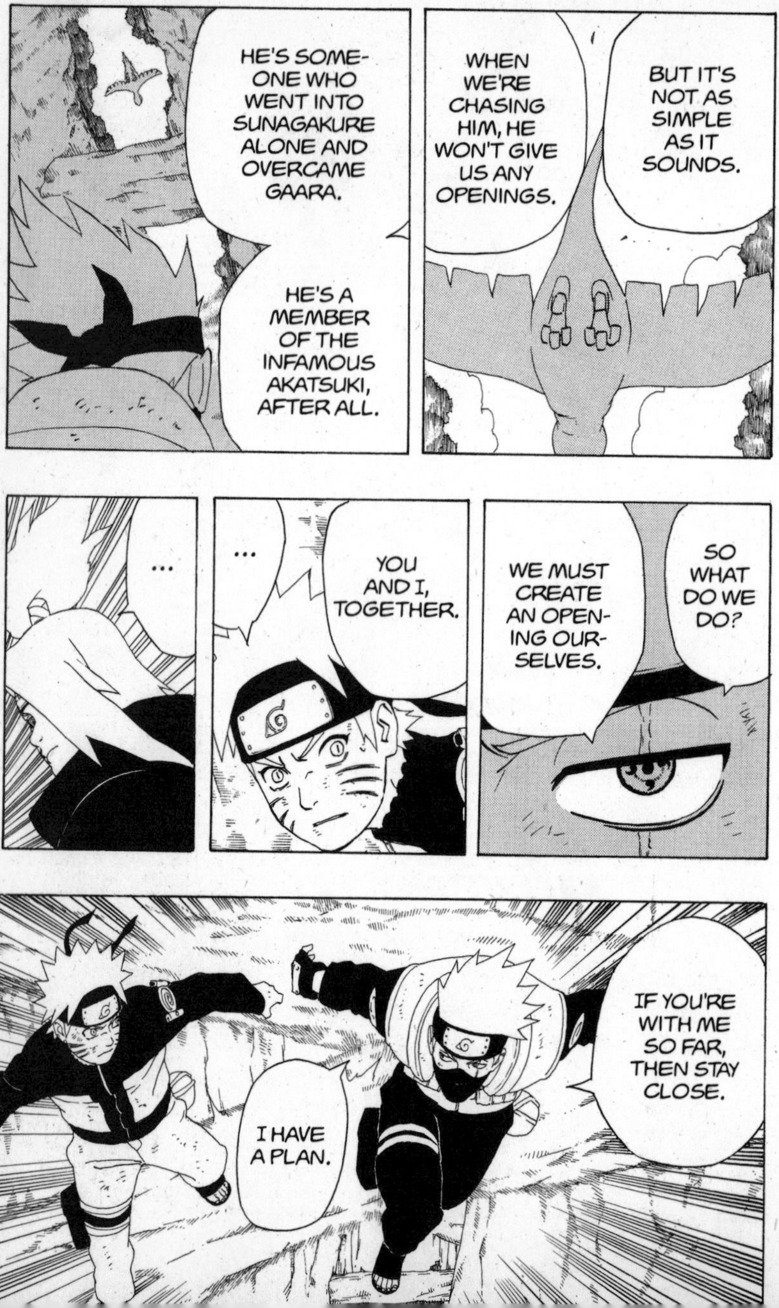
BUT IT'S NOT AS SIMPLE AS IT SOUNDS.
WHEN WE'RE CHASING HIM, HE WON'T GIVE US ANY OPENINGS.
HE'S SOME-ONE WHO WENT INTO SUNAGAKURE ALONE AND OVERCAME GAARA.
HE'S A MEMBER OF THE INFAMOUS AKATSUKI, AFTER ALL.
SO WHAT DO WE DO?
WE MUST CREATE AN OPEN-ING OUR-SELVES.
YOU AND I, TOGETHER.
...
...
IF YOU'RE WITH ME SO FAR, THEN STAY CLOSE.
I HAVE A PLAN.

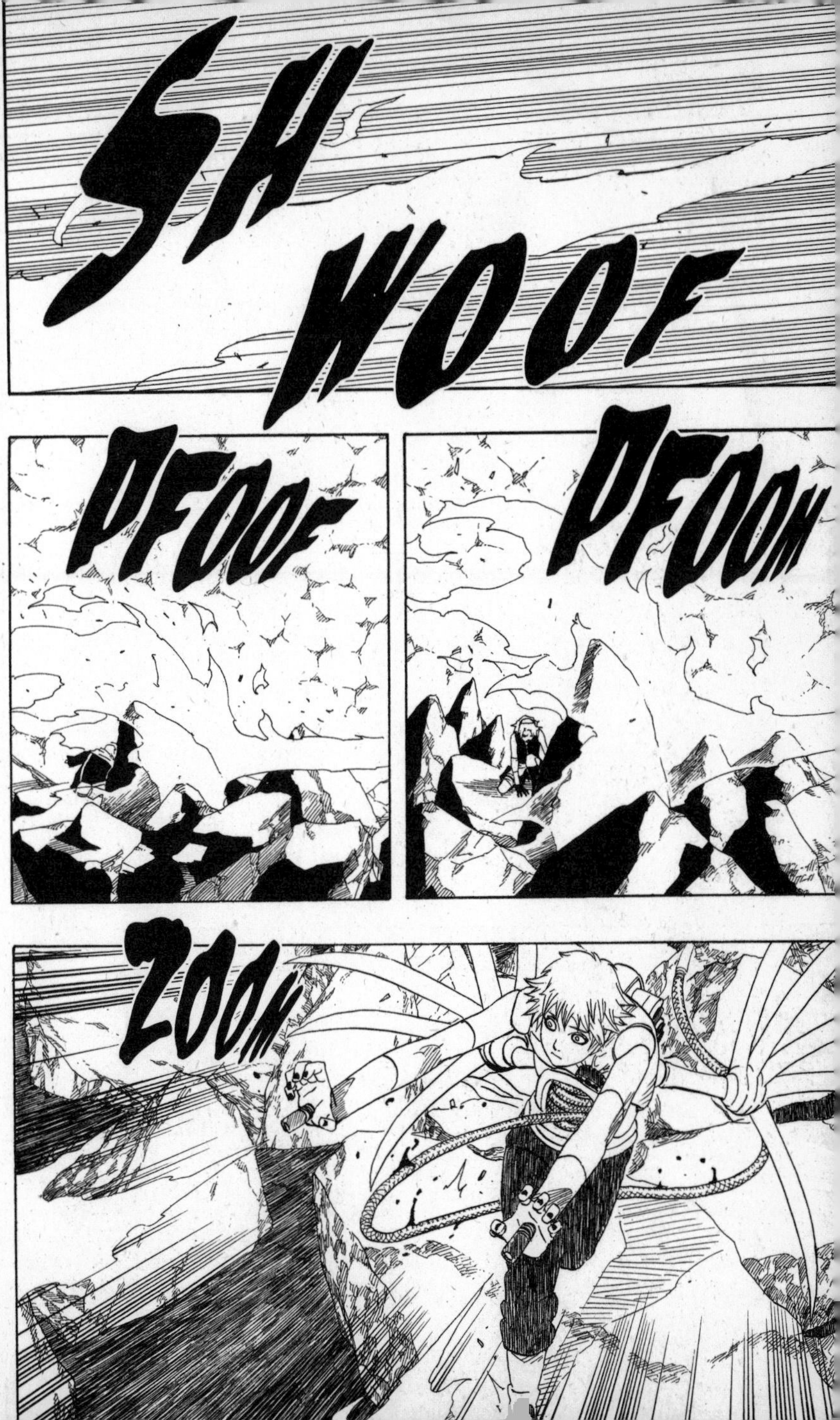
SHWOOF
PFOOM
PFOOF
ZOOM

READ THIS WAY

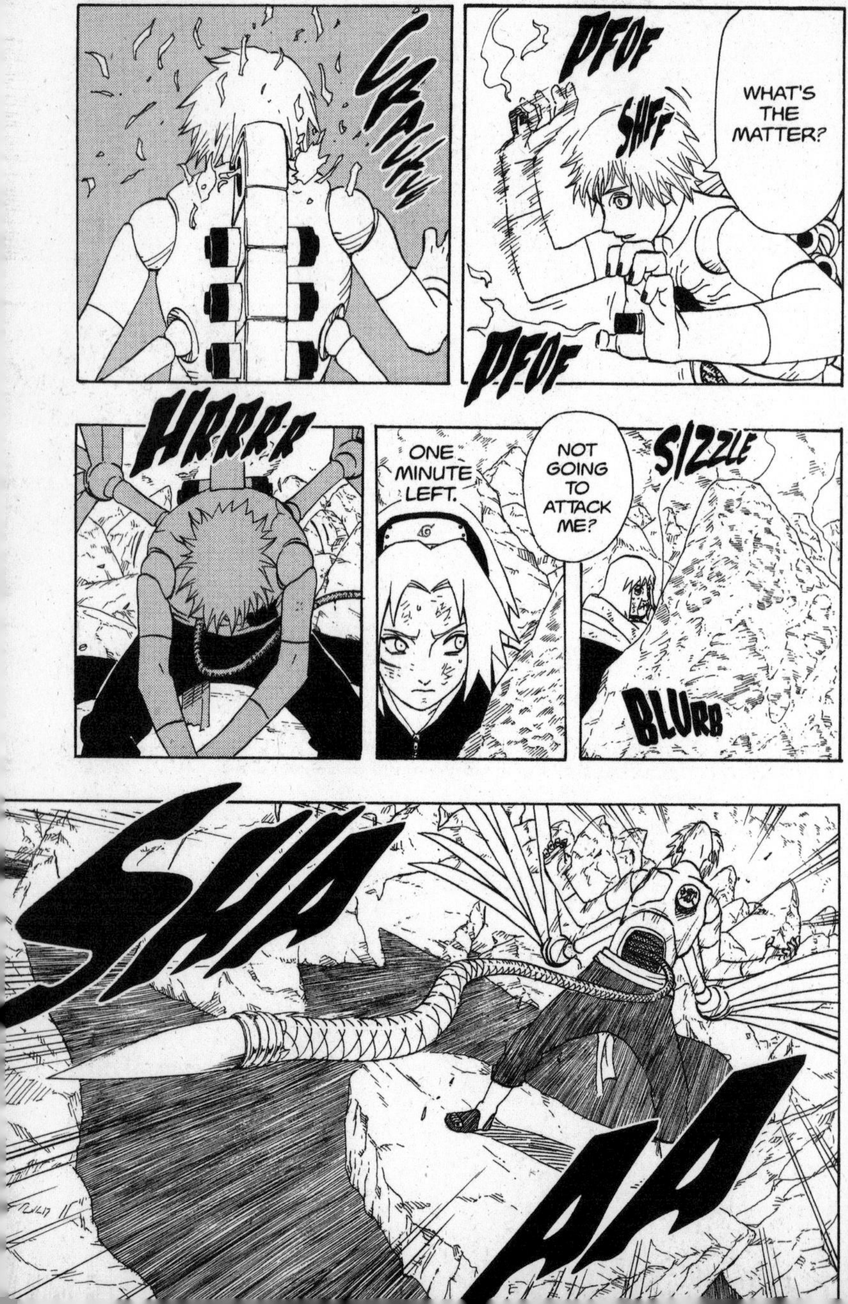
PFOF
SHFF
WHAT'S THE MATTER?
PFOF
SIZZLE
NOT GOING TO ATTACK ME?
BLURB
ONE MINUTE LEFT.
HRRRR
SHAAA

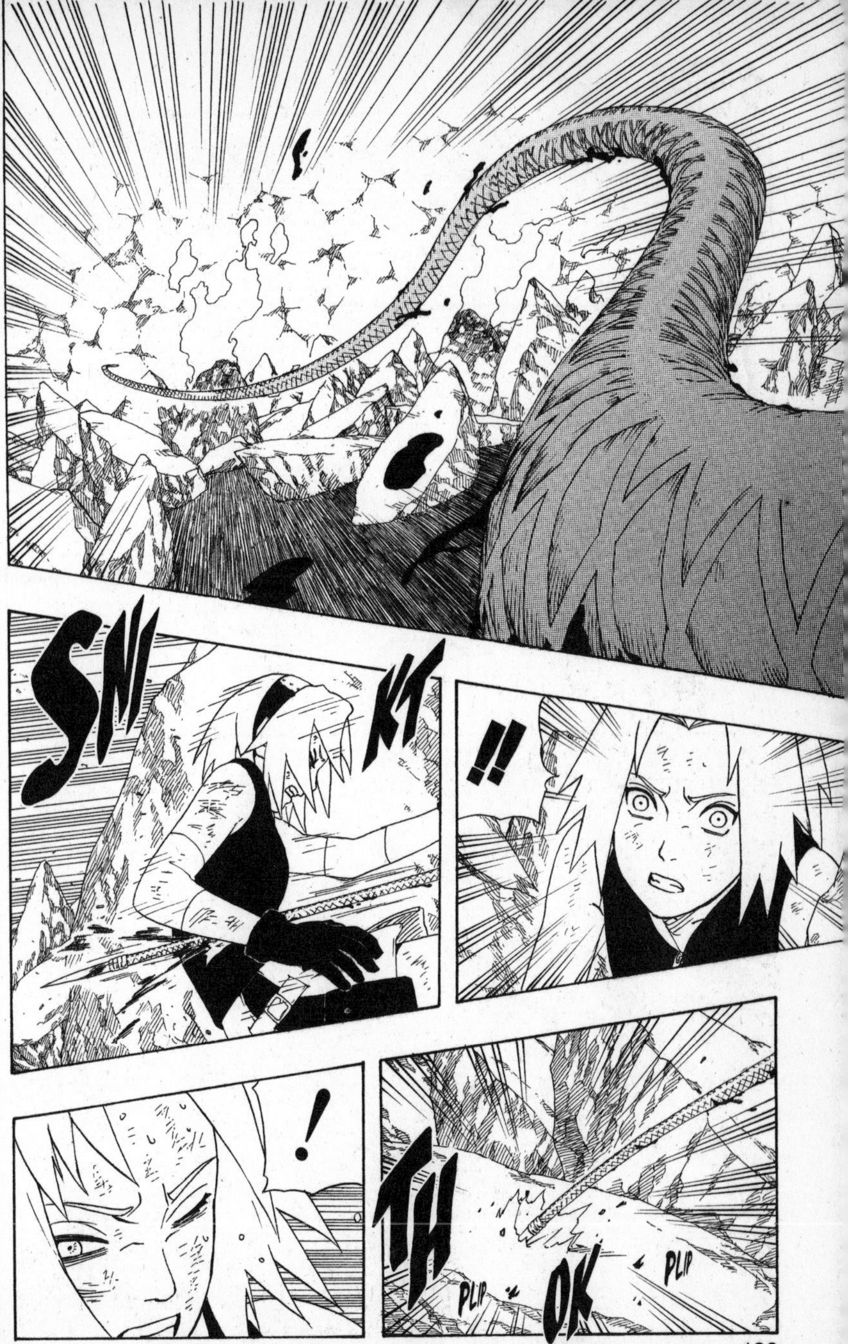
SNIKT
!!
!
THOK
PLIP
PLIP

READ THIS WAY

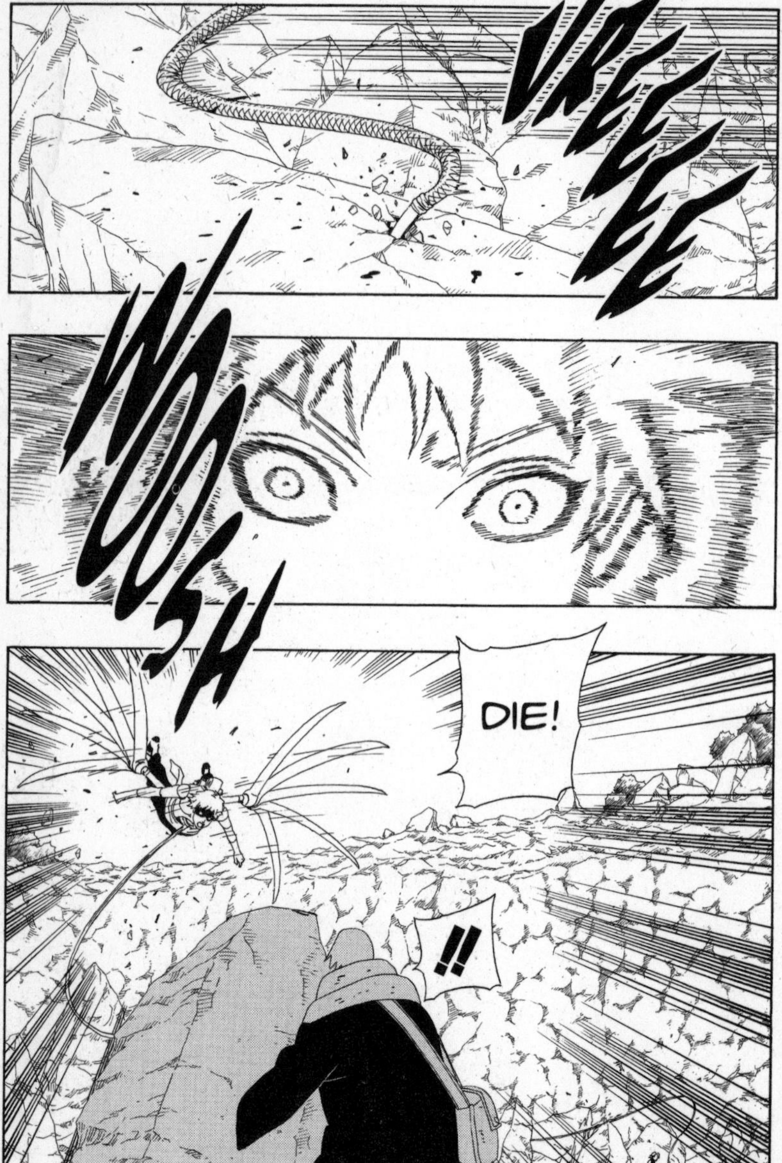
VREEEEE
WOOOSH
DIE!
!!

TO BE CONTINUED IN *NARUTO* VOL. 31!

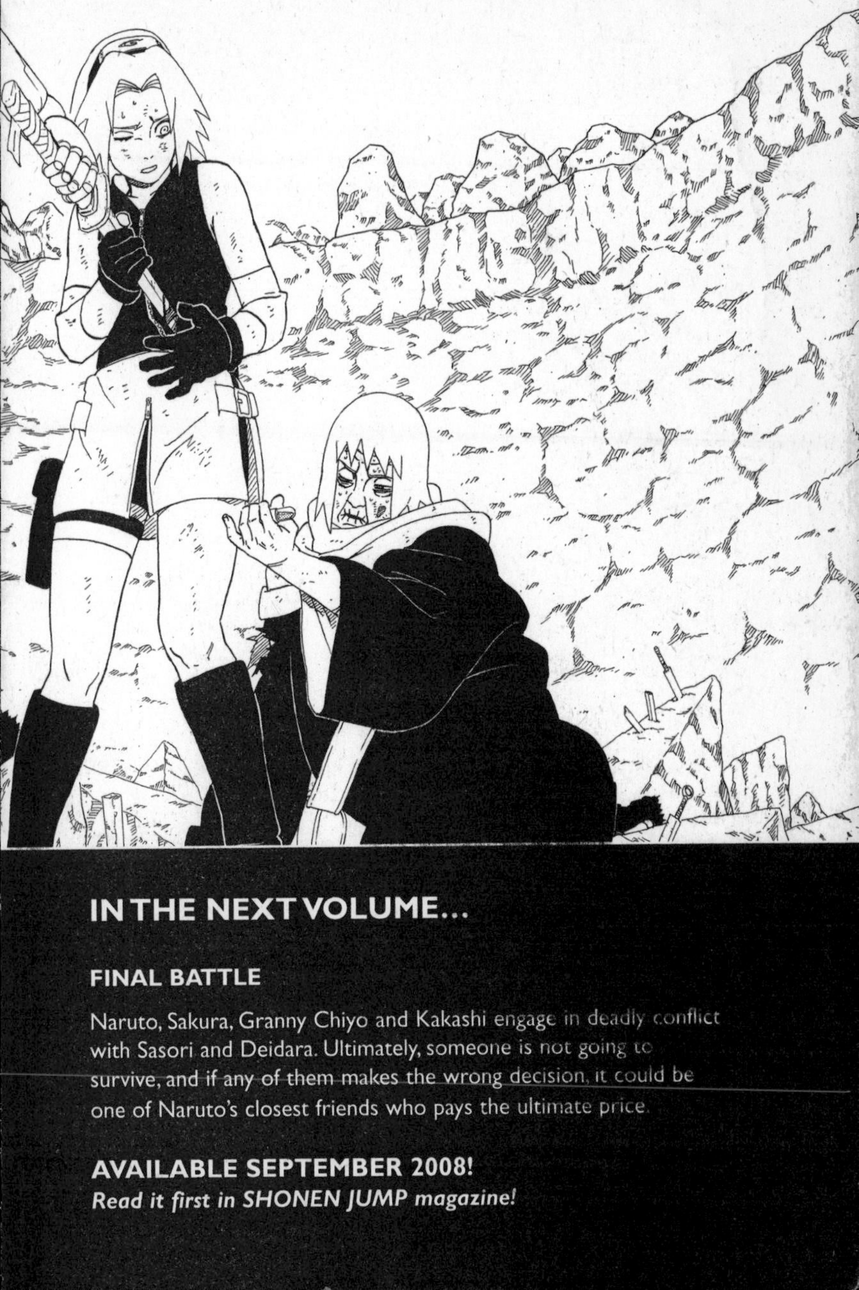

IN THE NEXT VOLUME...

FINAL BATTLE

Naruto, Sakura, Granny Chiyo and Kakashi engage in deadly conflict with Sasori and Deidara. Ultimately, someone is not going to survive, and if any of them makes the wrong decision, it could be one of Naruto's closest friends who pays the ultimate price.

AVAILABLE SEPTEMBER 2008!

Read it first in SHONEN JUMP magazine!

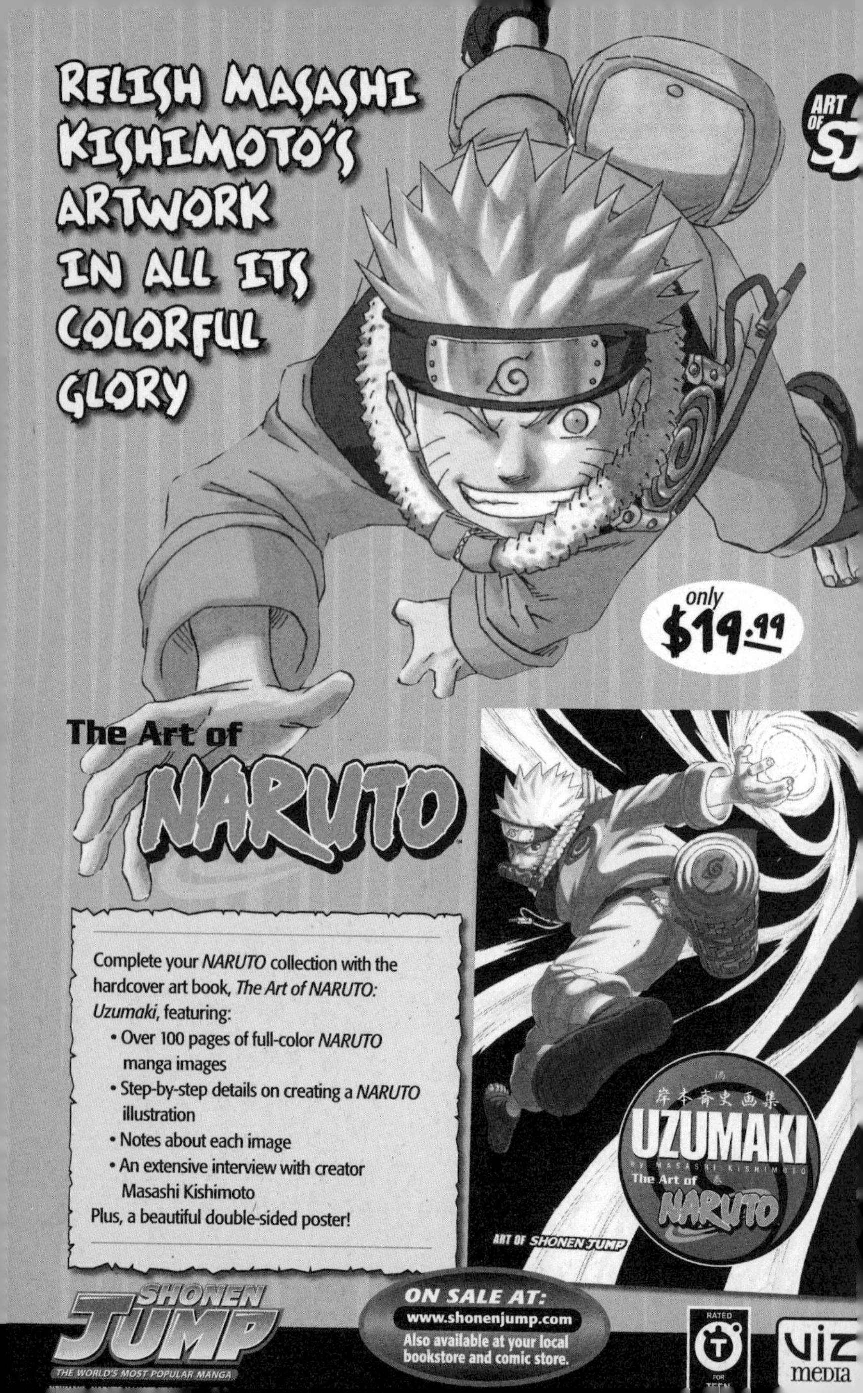
RELISH MASASHI KISHIMOTO'S ARTWORK IN ALL ITS COLORFUL GLORY
ART OF SJ
only $19.99
The Art of NARUTO
Complete your NARUTO collection with the hardcover art book, The Art of NARUTO: Uzumaki, featuring:
• Over 100 pages of full-color NARUTO manga images
• Step-by-step details on creating a NARUTO illustration
• Notes about each image
• An extensive interview with creator Masashi Kishimoto
Plus, a beautiful double-sided poster!
岸本斉史画集
UZUMAKI
BY MASASHI KISHIMOTO
The Art of NARUTO
ART OF SHONEN JUMP
SHONEN JUMP
THE WORLD'S MOST POPULAR MANGA
ON SALE AT:
www.shonenjump.com
Also available at your local bookstore and comic store.
RATED T FOR TEEN
viz media

Tell us what you think about SHONEN JUMP manga!

Our survey is now available online.
Go to: www.SHONENJUMP.com/mangasurvey

Help us make our product offering better!

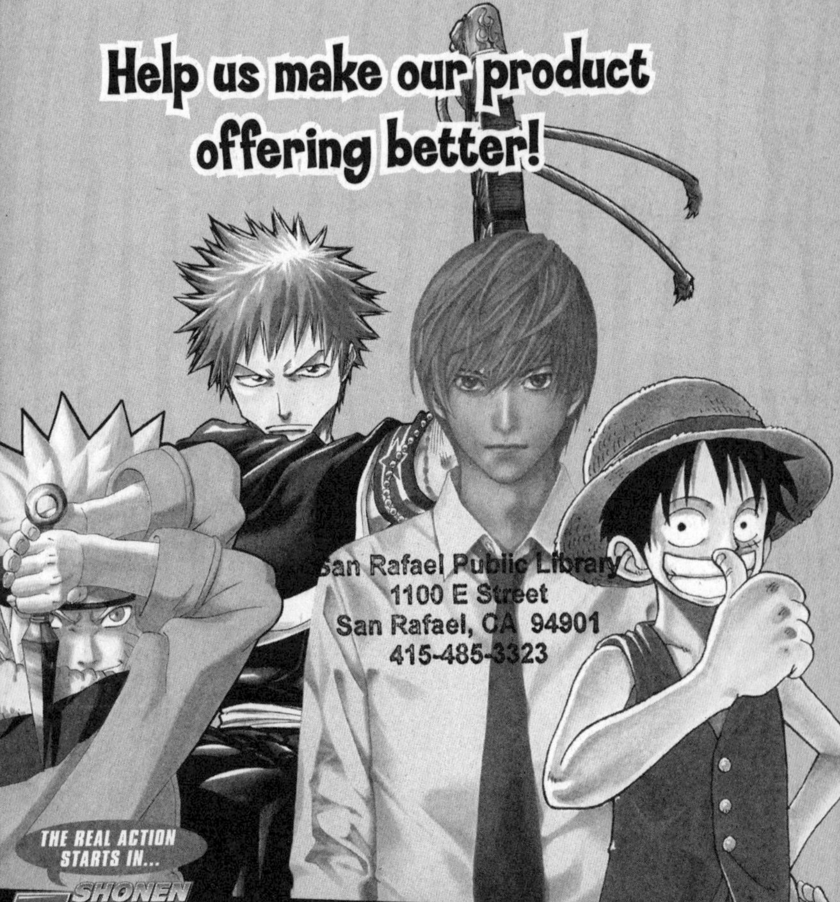

THE REAL ACTION
STARTS IN...

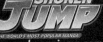

THE WORLD'S MOST POPULAR MANGA
www.shonenjump.com

ADVANCED

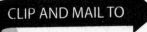

NARUTO VOL. 30
The SHONEN JUMP Manga Edition

This graphic novel contains material that was originally published in English in **SHONEN JUMP** #65-66. Artwork in the magazine may have been slightly altered from that presented here.

STORY AND ART BY MASASHI KISHIMOTO

Translation & English Adaptation/Naomi Kokubo & Eric-Jon Rössel Waugh
Touch-up Art & Lettering/Gia Cam Luc
Design/Sean Lee
Editor/Joel Enos

Editor in Chief, Books/Alvin Lu
Editor in Chief, Magazines/Marc Weidenbaum
VP of Publishing Licensing/Rika Inouye
VP of Sales/Gonzalo Ferreyra
Sr. VP of Marketing/Liza Coppola
Publisher/Hyoe Narita

Printed in the U.S.A.

Published by VIZ Media, LLC
P.O. Box 77010
San Francisco, CA 94107

SHONEN JUMP Manga Edition
10 9 8 7 6 5 4 3 2 1
First printing, July 2008

THE WORLD'S
MOST POPULAR MANGA

SHONEN JUMP

www.shonenjump.com

VIZ
media

www.viz.com

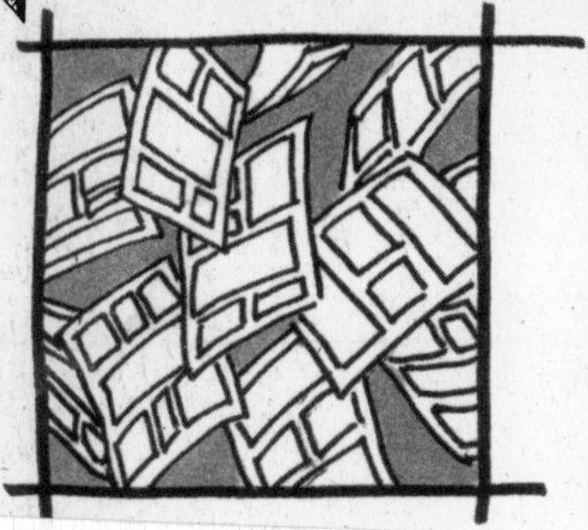

The movies and games coming out these days look so incredible it stuns me. I'm starting to suspect my readers are so used to rich imagery that manga must feel rather underwhelming by comparison. After all, it's still published in black and white... Remember, though, that manga's strength is in its rapid production. So please overlook its weaknesses.

—Masashi Kishimoto, 2005

Author/artist Masashi Kishimoto was born in 1974 in rural Okayama Prefecture, Japan. After spending time in art college, he won the Hop Step Award for new manga artists with his manga **Karakuri** (Mechanism). Kishimoto decided to base his next story on traditional Japanese culture. His first version of **Naruto**, drawn in 1997, was a one-shot story about fox spirits; his final version, which debuted in **Weekly Shonen Jump** in 1999, quickly became the most popular ninja manga in Japan.

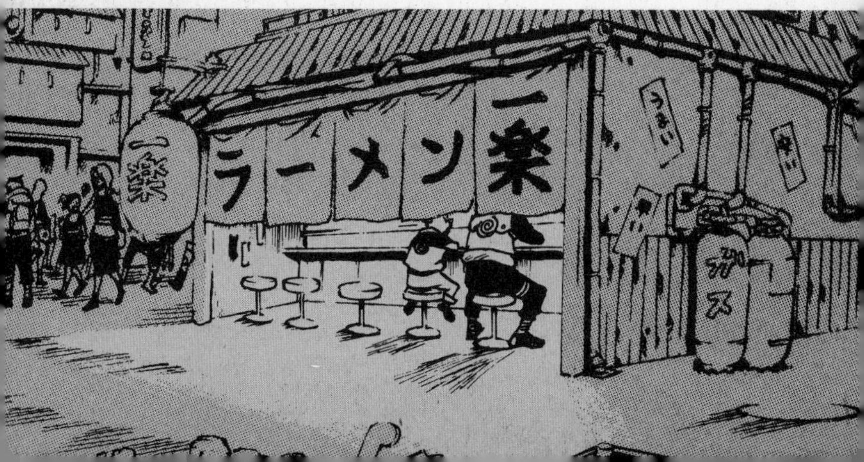
一楽
ラーメン
一楽